MICROAGGRESSIONS
IN EVERYDAY LIFE

MICROAGGRESSIONS
IN EVERYDAY LIFE

*Race, Gender, and
Sexual Orientation*

DERALD WING SUE

WILEY

John Wiley & Sons, Inc.

This publication is designed to provide accurate and authoritative information in regard to the subject matter covered. It is sold with the understanding that the publisher is not engaged in rendering professional services. If legal, accounting, medical, psychological, or any other expert assistance is required, the services of a competent professional person should be sought.

Library of Congress Cataloging-in-Publication Data:

Sue, Derald Wing.
    Microaggressions in everyday life : race, gender, and sexual orientation / Derald Wing Sue.
        p.   cm.
    Includes bibliographical references and index.
    ISBN 978-0-470-49140-9 (pbk.)
        1. Aggressiveness. 2. Offenses against the person. 3. Cross-cultural counseling. I. Title.
    BF575.A3S88 2010
    305—dc22

                                                                2009034007

Printed in the United States of America.

10 9 8 7 6 5 4 3 2 1

*I would like to dedicate this book to my wife Paulina Wee,
my son Derald Paul, my daughter Marissa Catherine,
my daughter-in-law Claire Iris,
and new granddaughter Caroline Riley.*

Contents

Foreword

I feel deeply honored to write this Foreword to Derald Wing Sue's *Microaggressions in Everyday Life: Race, Gender, and Sexual Orientation*. Before I comment on the book itself, I want to provide some context for absorbing the text by discussing your author, Dr. Derald Wing Sue.

Dr. Sue has been a role model and mentor to me and hundreds of mental health professionals engaged in multicultural counseling and research. For this reason, I was personally touched to receive his invitation to prepare this brief Foreword. It is fair to say that Dr. Sue is the most often cited and quoted scholar in the field of multicultural counseling. Moreover, his scholarly impact extends beyond the counseling field, as he has had a profound impact in clinical psychology, social work, psychiatry, social justice, political science, and education. Furthermore, Dr. Sue's impact has reached far beyond North American borders, particularly to Europe and Asia, and some of his classic works of scholarship (e.g., *Counseling the Culturally Diverse: Theory and Practice* [Sue & Sue, 2008]) have been translated into multiple languages.

A number of aspects of Dr. Sue's life and career have promoted his global status as a "legend in the field." Chief among these is that his own personal processing of life and career experiences have markedly informed his past and this current work, and have imbued his positions with logic, validity, and credibility. A few thoughts that I seem to always have in mind when I am reading and processing Dr. Sue's work (i.e., this new book, and recently, *Counseling the Culturally Diverse* [Sue & Sue, 2008] and *Overcoming Our Racism: The Journey to Liberation* [Sue, 2003]) are reflected in the following points:

1. There is a marked synergy between Dr. Sue as a scholar and author and as an individual, authentic person. For example, one definable characteristic of his

work and role modeling is his openness and courage. Dr. Sue has personally experienced countless microaggressions (as well as blatant macroaggressions) in his personal life and career, a number of which he candidly, vividly, and poignantly describes in his published life story (Sue, 2001), as well as in the current text. Dr. Sue discusses the impact of these racist incidents on himself and his family, and he describes the actions he took and the resources he drew on to cope with these experiences. Thus, what you are about to read in this destined-to-be-classic text has deep roots and anchors in Dr. Sue's personal life experiences. The result is a textural work of scholarship that is fluid, riveting to read, replete with real life day-to-day examples, at times alarming and upsetting to process, and in the end, hopeful in contemplating "the way forward."

2. Though as a reader and practicing clinician I am drawn to the unfolding interplay of Dr. Sue's life experiences and integrative, interdisciplinary writing, as a researcher I am impressed with the depth and breadth of his scholarship, his research vision, and his pure scientific skill. Dr. Sue is one of the few mixed methods researchers in multicultural psychology, and his mastery of both qualitative approaches (e.g., long interviews, discourse analysis, case studies, participant observation) and quantitative designs (e.g., large sample survey research and experimental designs) inform his writing and help him creatively investigate his personal perceptions garnered as a Chinese American living in the United States and a psychologist and educator who has worked directly on the topic of racism through decades of teaching, consultation, clinical service, and national leadership. In *Microaggressions in Everyday Life*, Dr. Sue masterfully pulls all of his life and work experiences together to frame a new theory and vision for the study of racism, sexism, and homophobia. What Dr. Sue has created in his "Taxonomy of Microaggressions" will ignite research in the field of racism and multiple oppressions that will ultimately lead to marked change in the way we all deal with and respect one another. This book is that good. It will change the way you think, it will move you to act and not just witness and observe, and it will even influence how you feel toward, communicate with, and care for your own loved ones, students, and clients.

Having provided a glimpse into Dr. Sue as a person, role model, and scholar, I now turn to my reactions to reading this new book. I have organized my impressions of *Microaggressions in Everyday Life* along six major areas:

1. *A Window of Clarity*. Most of us know blatant racism, sexism, and homophobia when we see it. Sexual harassment and domestic violence toward women, and hate crimes directed toward racial minorities and gays

and lesbians are definable, always illegal, and often open to redress through prosecution. However, as logically argued by Dr. Sue, overt hate crimes, though still all too common in society, represent only a small portion of the hurricane-wind of oppression faced minute to minute, hour to hour, and day to day by racial and sexual-orientation minorities and women. The majority of oppression faced by these group members is "micro" (not immediately visible to the eye), insidious, psychologically and physically draining, and often not definable, illegal, or open to redress.

Social science researchers have coined such terms as "modern racism," "aversive racism," and "subtle racism" in an attempt to capture and understand the essence of the many forms of non-blatant racism. However, heretofore, models for understanding non-blatant forms of racism and oppression have been difficult to fully visualize and comprehend, almost as if looking through a foggy window. Now, with *Microaggressions in Everyday Life*, we have a clear window through which to see the manifestations, process, and impact of everyday oppression. Through his decade-long research program, Dr. Sue has provided us with a vivid model and clear vocabulary to understand, empirically research, and hopefully reduce the day-to-day oppression faced by so many persons in America and beyond.

2. *Something About His Writing*! Whenever I sit down to read Dr. Sue's work, I cannot help but be riveted. This first happened for me in 1981, when as a graduate student I began reading his inaugural edition of *Counseling the Culturally Different* (now *Counseling the Culturally Diverse*; Sue, 1981). At the time there were few books on multicultural counseling, and Dr. Sue's was by far the most engaging, direct, and impactful. I felt the same way when reading his *Overcoming Our Racism* (Sue, 2003) and, just recently, in finishing this current work. In reading *Microaggressions in Everyday Life*, I felt as if I was in a small group talking with and interacting with Dr. Sue. His personhood, authenticity, and passion for justice shine through in every chapter. He uses everyday language that is understandable and impactful, and he does not tip-toe around issues of microaggressions and racism. He is direct in presenting his positions, clear and logical in reviewing and integrating a wide body of research, and hopeful in pointing a way forward for all of us in terms of working to understand microaggressions in ourselves, and to stop microaggressions against our fellow citizens.

Another reaction I had while reading Dr. Sue's newest work was more visceral in nature. Generally, when reading books about racism and prejudice I process them "in my head," intellectually. However, throughout reading *Microaggressions in Everyday Life*, my sensations and feelings were in my stomach—I could feel anger and frustration at the myriad injustices being unveiled by Dr. Sue's careful dialogic deconstruction; I felt guilt as I realized how I have and continue to microaggress against others. When reading the many real-life vignettes and scenarios throughout each chapter, I had a sense of verisimilitude; that is, I felt as if I were in the vignette seeing what was happening, while also now understanding what was happening and knowing what the destructive impact would be.

3. *Validity and Credibility*. These terms are used in quantitative and qualitative research, respectively, to describe the accuracy, interpretability, and substantive nature of empirical inquiry. Impressively, each chapter in this new text is marked by high levels of validity and credibility as Dr. Sue integrates a varied interdisciplinary body of research with the results of his own mixed methods research program to arrive at a model for understanding and intervening in daily microaggressions. A particular strength of this new book is the inclusion of direct quotes, dialogues, and mini–case studies in each chapter that serve to give voice to those regularly subjected to microaggressions and shed light on the thinking and behavior of the majority of us who perpetuate daily microaggressions.

Dr. Sue does a clear and crisp job in first presenting the dialogue, quotes, or case study, and then logically deconstructing and analyzing the material so that readers can vividly see what microaggressions are, how they operate, the prejudicial thinking that powers them, and the spoken words and subtle behaviors that operationalize the aggressions.

4. *Conceptual and Theoretical Understanding*. Dr. Sue's mastery of a wide and interdisciplinary body of theoretical writing and empirical research on racism and oppression is almost impossible to comprehend. He has been able to integrate and subsume multiple theoretical models and bodies of research into his overarching theory of microaggressions. Rather than add his own piece to the puzzle of understanding oppression, he has completed the puzzle through his comprehensive outline of microaggressions in everyday life.

Groundbreaking and integrative theoretical advances in this new work include Dr. Sue's Taxonomy for Understanding Microaggressions—microassaults (conscious), microinsults (unconscious), and microinvalidations (unconscious)—as well as his five-phase model for deconstructing the microaggression process: experiencing the incident → attributing the aggressor's intent → immediate cognitive, behavioral, and emotive reaction to the incident → interpreting and processing the incident and reaction → consequences of and consideration in coping with the microaggression. Through his systematically charted and long-standing qualitative research program, Dr. Sue clearly outlines these theoretical models and provides explicit examples and interpretations of their manifestation in individuals.

Clearly, Dr. Sue has provided a robust theoretical model and specific research tools (e.g., discourse analysis) that will guide ongoing and future research in the study of microaggression impact, coping, and intervention. I would not be surprised to see in the next decade that *Microaggressions in Everyday Life* serves as the theoretical model and conceptual rationale for 25 doctoral dissertations and 100 journal articles.

5. *Depth and Breadth of Coverage. Microaggressions in Everyday Life* builds off of Dr. Sue's decade-long systematic research program on microaggressions. As a result, Dr. Sue and his esteemed culture- and gender-diverse research team (inclusive of emerging international scholars such as J. M. Bucceri, C. M. Capodilupo, M. Esquilin, A. M. B. Holder, A. I. Lin, K. L. Nadal, D. P. Rivera, and G. C. Torino) have been able to extend the initial work on racial microaggressions to issues of gender and sexual orientation. What Dr. Sue's research team has found is that some aspects of microaggressions transcend targeted minority groups, while other aspects are rather unique to specific groups. As such, clinicians, educators, managers, employers, and politicians need to understand *both* transcendent and culturally specific manifestations of microaggression if they are to contribute to Dr. Sue's vision for the "way forward."

This text devotes substantive discussion to various racial/ethnic microaggressions (i.e., African Americans, Asian Americans, Latino/Hispanic Americans, and Native Americans), gender microaggressions, and sexual-orientation microaggressions. Furthermore, it specifically addresses microaggressions in critical spheres of life, such as employment, education, and the mental health therapy process itself. Dr. Sue addresses specifically and candidly the significant toll that microaggressions take on people's physical and mental health, quality of life, and sense of humanity.

Unique to this visionary text is a detailed discussion of the psycho-logical costs of microaggressions to the perpetrators, an often neglected topic in the social and behavioral sciences literature. These consuming and destructive costs include cognitive impairment (operating in a false and distorted reality), affective consequences (feelings of fear, anxiety, apprehension, guilt, and lowered empathy), behavioral manifestations (inhibited social interaction experiences), and spiritual/moral failings (losing spiritual interconnectedness with humanity).

6. *The Way Forward*. Though at times daunting and upsetting to now understand the prevalence, nature, and destructive force of microaggressions to *all* involved, Dr. Sue gives us hope in that every chapter presents an integrated "way forward" section that provides practical steps that we ourselves can take in order to better understand and control our own tendency to microaggress, as well as to help others who perpetuate or suffer from the wide array of microaggressions. To be sure, envisioning a society completely devoid of microaggressions is likely impossible, yet we must draw on Dr. Sue's wisdom and scholarship and begin to implement his "way forward" suggestions. As noted by Dr. Sue, simultaneous to understanding and limiting our own microaggressive behavior, we must continue to develop coping skills to help reduce the long-term impact of destructive microaggressions.

I am certain you will be both riveted and also personally and professionally impacted as soon as you start reading Dr. Sue's latest integrative and groundbreaking text. As a student, this book will enhance your personal and professional development and will provide you a path for an important research and/or dissertation program. As an educator and clinician, this book will increase your awareness and self-knowledge and make you more effective and impactful as an educator, healer, and role model.

Wishing you a good read!

Joseph G. Ponterotto, PhD
Professor, Fordham University
Private Practice, New York City

REFERENCES

Sue, D. W. (1981). *Counseling the culturally different: Theory and practice*. New York: Wiley.

Sue, D. W. (2001). Surviving monoculturalism and racism: A personal and professional journey. In J. G. Ponterotto, J. M. Casas, L. A. Suzuki, & C. M. Alexander (Eds.), *Handbook of multicultural counseling* (2nd ed., pp. 45–54). Thousand Oaks, CA: Sage.

Sue, D. W. (2003). *Overcoming our racism: The journey to liberation*. San Francisco: Jossey-Bass.

Sue, D. W., & Sue, D. (2008). *Counseling the culturally diverse: Theory and practice* (5th ed.). Hoboken, NJ: Wiley.

Preface

Microaggressions in Everyday Life: Race, Gender, and Sexual Orientation is about the damaging consequences of everyday prejudice, bias, and discrimination upon marginalized groups in our society. The experience of racial, gender, and sexual-orientation microaggressions is not new to people of color, women, and LGBTs. It is the constant and continuing everyday reality of slights, insults, invalidations, and indignities visited upon marginalized groups by well-intentioned, moral, and decent family members, friends, neighbors, coworkers, students, teachers, clerks, waiters and waitresses, employers, health care professionals, and educators. The power of microaggressions lies in their invisibility to the perpetrator, who is unaware that he or she has engaged in a behavior that threatens and demeans the recipient of such a communication.

While hate crimes and racial, gender, and sexual-orientation harassment continue to be committed by overt racists, sexists, and homophobes, the thesis of this book is that the greatest harm to persons of color, women, and LGBTs does not come from these conscious perpetrators. It is not the White supremacists, Ku Klux Klan members, or Skinheads, for example, who pose the greatest threat to people of color, but instead well-intentioned people, who are strongly motivated by egalitarian values, believe in their own morality, and experience themselves as fair-minded and decent people who would never consciously discriminate. Because no one is immune from inheriting the biases of the society, all citizens are exposed to a social conditioning process that imbues within them prejudices, stereotypes, and beliefs that lie outside their level of awareness. On a conscious level they may endorse egalitarian values, but on an unconscious level, they harbor antiminority feelings.

Bias, prejudice, and discrimination in North America has undergone a transformation, especially in the post–civil rights era when the democratic belief in equality of marginalized groups (racial minorities, women, and gays/lesbians) directly clashes with their long history of oppression in society. In the case of racism and sexism, its manifestation has been found to be more disguised and covert, rather than overtly expressed in the form of racial hatred and bigotry. Research also indicates that sexism and heterosexism have not decreased, but instead become more ambiguous and nebulous, making them more difficult to identify and acknowledge.

Although much has been written about contemporary forms of racism, sexism, and homophobia, many studies in health care, education, law, employment, mental health, and social settings indicate the difficulty of describing and defining racial, gender, and sexual-orientation discrimination that occurs via "implicit bias"; these are difficult to identify, quantify, and rectify because of their subtle, nebulous, and unnamed nature. Subtle racism, sexism, and heterosexism remain relatively invisible and potentially harmful to the well-being, self-esteem, and standard of living of many marginalized groups in society. These daily common experiences of aggression may have significantly more and stronger effects on anger, frustration, and self-esteem than traditional, overt forms of racism, sexism, and heterosexism. Furthermore, their invisible nature prevents perpetrators from realizing and confronting their own complicity in creating psychological dilemmas for minorities and their role in creating disparities in employment, health care, and education.

In reviewing the literature on subtle and contemporary forms of bias, the term "microaggressions" seems to best describe the phenomenon in its everyday occurrence. Simply stated, microaggressions are brief, everyday exchanges that send denigrating messages to certain individuals because of their group membership. The term was first coined by Pierce in 1970 in his work with Black Americans, in which he defined it as "subtle, stunning, often automatic, and nonverbal exchanges which are 'put downs'" (Pierce, Carew, Pierce-Gonzalez, & Willis, 1978, p. 66). They have also been described as "subtle insults (verbal, nonverbal, and/or visual) directed toward people of color, often automatically or unconsciously" (Solorzano, Ceja, & Yosso, 2000). In the world of business, the term "microinequities" is used to describe the pattern of being overlooked, underrespected, and devalued because of one's race or gender. They are often unconsciously delivered as subtle snubs or dismissive looks, gestures, and tones. These exchanges are so pervasive and automatic in daily conversations and interactions that they are often dismissed and glossed over as being innocent and innocuous. Yet, as indicated previously, microaggressions are detrimental to persons of color because they impair performance in a multitude of settings by sapping the psychic and spiritual energy of recipients and by creating inequities.

Microaggressions in Everyday Life is divided into four major sections:

Section One: Psychological Manifestation and Dynamics of Microaggressions is composed of three chapters.

Chapter 1: The Manifestation of Racial, Gender, and Sexual-Orientation Microaggressions introduces the reader to the overall definition of microaggressions, their everyday manifestations, hidden demeaning messages, and their detrimental impact upon recipients. It reveals how marginality is similarly expressed by well-intentioned individuals toward people of color, women, and LGBTs. It does this by providing numerous examples of the everyday indignities visited upon these groups. More disturbing is the conclusion that everyone has engaged in harmful conduct toward other socially devalued groups.

Chapter 2: Taxonomy of Microaggressions provides readers with a way to classify microaggressions, the three forms they take (microassault, microinsult, and microinvalidation), their hidden insulting and hostile messages, and their harmful impact upon recipients. Microaggressions appear to be classifiable under different racial, gender, and sexual-orientation themes. These themes appear to be a reflection of stereotypes and worldviews of inclusion–exclusion and superiority–inferiority.

Chapter 3: The Psychological Dilemmas and Dynamics of Microaggressions is an attempt to analyze how microaggressions create dilemmas and distress to people of color, women, and LGBTs. Four major psychological dilemmas confront targets when microaggressions make their appearance. First, there is a clash of racial, gender, and sexual-orientation realities, in which both perpetrator and target interpret the situation differently. Second, because the bias is invisible, perpetrators are unaware that they have insulted or demeaned the target and are allowed to continue in the belief of their innocence. Third, even when microaggressions become visible, they are seen as trivial or small slights that produce only minimal harm. Fourth, targets are placed in an unenviable catch-22 position where they are "damned if they do" (choose to confront the perpetrator) and "damned if they don't" (choose to do nothing).

Section Two: Microaggressive Impact on Targets and Perpetrators is composed of three chapters.

Chapter 4: The Microaggression Process Model: Microaggressions from Beginning to End describes our most recent findings on what triggers microaggressions (incidents), how they are perceived by the recipient, the numerous reactions that can occur, how events are interpreted, and their impact or consequences. I propose a process model to understand the various dimensional components of micro-aggressive dynamic flow.

Chapter 5: Microaggressive Stress: Impact on Physical and Mental Health summarizes the theory and research literature on the psychological and physical detrimental consequences that accrue to marginalized groups through microaggressions. Far from being benign, microaggressions have major mental and physical health consequences to the targets. The chapter discusses stress-coping models and makes a strong case that microaggressions are not only qualitatively different from the hassles of everyday life, but that they have even stronger effects.

Chapter 6: Microaggressive Perpetrators and Oppression: The Nature of the Beast is perhaps quite unique because it explores the consequences of oppression and racial, gender, and sexual-orientation microaggressions on perpetrators. In other words, research is beginning to reveal that microaggressions not only have detrimental impact on targets, but the perpetrators as well. Some of these findings suggest that perpetrators are likely to develop a warped sense of reality, callousness, anxiety, guilt, and other damaging effects.

Section Three: Group-Specific Microaggressions: Race, Gender, and Sexual Orientation is composed of three chapters.

Chapter 7: Racial/Ethnic Microaggressions and Racism discusses racial/ethnic minority groups (African American, Asian

American, Latino(a)/Hispanic American, and Native American) with respect to racial issues under the microaggression rubric.

Chapter 8: Gender Microaggressions and Sexism discusses the impact of bias on women with respect to gender issues under the microaggression rubric.

Chapter 9: Sexual-Orientation Microaggressions and Heterosexism discusses biases against LGBTs with respect to sexual-orientation issues under the microaggression rubric.

Section Four: Microaggressions in Employment, Education, and Mental Health Practice is composed of three chapters.

Chapter 10: Microaggressive Impact in the Workplace and Employment describes and analyzes the operation of racial, gender, and sexual orientation in the workplace. It reveals how microaggressions operate in the recruitment, retention, and promotion of marginalized groups in the world of work, how it disadvantages them, interferes with work performance, and leads to detrimental consequences. It broadens the analysis of microaggressions to how it creates a hostile and invalidating work environment.

Chapter 11: Microaggressive Impact on Education and Teaching: Facilitating Difficult Dialogues on Race in the Classroom explores how microaggressions are manifested in the curriculum, knowledge base, campus climates, and most importantly in the classroom. I present a series of studies specifically on how microaggressions are triggers to difficult dialogues on race, gender, and sexual orientation in the classroom and reasons why educators fail miserably in their ability to facilitate these dialogues.

Chapter 12: Microaggressive Impact on Mental Health Practice makes a strong case that underutilization of mental health facilities and premature termination may be due to microaggressions unknowingly delivered by well-intentioned therapists. Issues of trust–mistrust and counselor credibility are analyzed as they impact the credibility of the helping professional.

It is important to note that a major goal of the text is to present research data, theories, and practical suggestions as to how to overcome microaggressions directed at all marginalized groups, and to make specific suggestions related to how they can be ameliorated at individual, institutional, and societal levels. For that reason, not only are these remedial and preventive interventions discussed throughout each chapter, but a special concluding section, *The Way Forward*, ends each chapter with an outline of guidelines, strategies, and interventions that can be taken to free our society of microaggressions.

Acknowledgments

I would like to personally acknowledge research team members at Teachers College, Columbia University, for their valuable work with me on microaggressions: Christina Capodilupo, Peter Donnelly, Aisha Holder, Annie Lin, Kevin Nadal, David Rivera, and Gina Torino. Our five-year study of microaggressive phenomena would not have been possible without their dedicated work on the team. Some have already received their doctorates and I know they will join the ranks of major scholars in the field.

I would also like to express my appreciation to Rachel Livsey (Senior Editor), Peggy Alexander (Publisher), and the staff at John Wiley & Sons for their interest, encouragement, support, and help in this project.

As always, special thanks goes to my wife, Paulina, for constantly putting up with the long hours at my office and away from home spent in completing this book.

Derald Wing Sue
Teachers College, Columbia University

About the Author

Derald Wing Sue is Professor of Psychology and Education in the Department of Counseling and Clinical Psychology at Teachers College, Columbia University. He served as presidents of the Society for the Psychological Study of Ethnic Minority Issues, the Society of Counseling Psychology, and the Asian American Psychological Association. Dr. Sue is an Associate Editor of the *American Psychologist* and continues to be a consulting editor for numerous publications. He is author of over 150 publications, including 15 books, and is well known for his work on racism/antiracism, cultural competence, multicultural counseling and therapy, and social justice advocacy. Two of his books, *Counseling the Culturally Diverse: Theory and Practice* and *Overcoming Our Racism: The Journey to Liberation* (John Wiley & Sons), are considered classics in the field. Dr. Sue's most recent research on racial, gender, and sexual-orientation microaggressions has provided a major breakthrough in understanding how everyday slights, insults, and invalidations toward marginalized groups create psychological harm to their mental and physical health, and create disparities for them in education, employment, and health care. A national survey has identified Derald Wing Sue as "the most influential multicultural scholar in the United States" and his works are among the most frequently cited.

Psychological Manifestation and Dynamics of Microaggressions

CHAPTER ONE

The Manifestation of Racial, Gender, and Sexual-Orientation Microaggressions

Standing before his classroom, Charles Richardson, a White professor, asked for questions from the class. He had just finished a lecture on Greco-Roman contributions to the history of psychology. An African American male student raised his hand.

When called upon, the student spoke in a frustrated manner, noting that the history of psychology was "ethnocentric and Eurocentric" and that it left out the contributions of other societies and cultures. The student seemed to challenge the professor by noting that the contributions of African, Latin American, and Asian psychologies were never covered.

The professor responded, "Robert, I want you to calm down. We are studying American psychology in this course and we will eventually address how it has influenced and been adapted to Asian and other societies. I plan to also talk about how systems and theories of psychology contain universal applications."

Rather than defusing the situation, however, Professor Richardson sensed that his response had raised the level of tension among several students of color. Another Black male student then stated, "Perhaps we are looking at this issue from different perspectives or worldviews. Just as language affects how we define problems, maybe we all need to evaluate our assumptions and beliefs. Maybe we are ethnocentric. Maybe there are aspects of psychology that apply across all populations. Maybe we need to dialogue more and be open to alternative interpretations."

Throughout the semester, the professor had sensed increasing resentment among his students of color over the course content (he could not understand the reasons) and he welcomed the opportunity to say something positive about their classroom contributions. He responded, "Justin [who is a Black student], I appreciate your exceptionally thoughtful and intelligent observation. You are a most articulate young man with good conceptual and analytical skills. This is the type of nonjudgmental analysis and objectivity needed for good dialogues. We need to address these issues in a calm, unemotional, and reasoned manner."

To the professor's surprise, Justin and several other students of color seemed offended and insulted by the praise.

Kathleen, a graduating MBA business major, was conservatively dressed in her black blazer and matching skirt as she rode the number 1 subway train from Columbia University to downtown Manhattan. This would be her second job interview with a major brokerage firm and she was excited, sensing that her first interview with a midlevel manager had gone very well. She had been asked to return to be interviewed by the department vice president. Kathleen knew she was one of three finalists, but also sensed her advantage in having specialized and unique training that was of interest to the company.

During the train ride, Kathleen endured the usual smattering of admiring glances, as well as a few more lecherous stares. As she exited a very crowded subway train at Times Square, she attempted to squeeze out between the streams of commuters entering the train car. One man, seeing her dilemma, firmly placed his hand on her lower back to escort her out onto the platform. With his left arm, he steered her toward the exit and they walked briskly toward the stairs, where the crowd thinned. Upon separating, the man smiled and nodded, obviously believing he had acted in a chivalrous manner. Kathleen didn't appreciate being touched without her permission, but thanked him anyway.

During the interview, the vice president seemed very casual and relaxed. She noted, however, that he referred to male employees as "Mr. X" and to female employees by their first names. Several times he called her "Kathy." She thought about telling him that she preferred "Kathleen," but didn't want to alienate her potential employer. She very much wanted the job. When she inquired about the criteria the company would use to hire for the position, the vice president joked, "What do you need a job for, anyway? You can always find a good man."

When Kathleen did not laugh and remained serious, the vice president quickly said, "I believe the most qualified person should be offered the position. We treat all men *and women equally. In fact, I don't even think about employees as men or women. People are people and everyone has an equal opportunity to be hired and succeed."*

Kathleen felt very uncomfortable with the response. She left the interview knowing she would not be offered the position.

What do these incidents have in common?

In both case vignettes, racial and gender microaggressions were being unconsciously delivered—in the classroom by a well-intentioned professor, in the subway station by a fellow commuter, and in the job interview by a vice president. The term "racial microaggressions" was first coined by Chester Pierce in the 1970s to refer to the everyday subtle and often automatic "put-downs" and insults directed toward Black Americans (Pierce, Carew, Pierce-Gonzalez, & Willis, 1978). While his theorizing focused solely on racial microaggressions, it is clear that microaggressions can be expressed toward any marginalized group in our society; they can be gender-based, sexual orientation–based, class-based, or disability-based (Sue & Capodilupo, 2008). In this book I have decided to concentrate on three forms of microaggressions—race, gender, and sexual orientation—to illustrate the hidden and damaging consequences of the more subtle forms of bias and discrimination that harm persons of color, women, and lesbian, gay, bisexual, and transgendered persons (LGBTs).

Microaggressions are the brief and commonplace daily verbal, behavioral, and environmental indignities, whether intentional or unintentional, that communicate hostile, derogatory, or negative racial, gender, sexual-orientation, and religious slights and insults to the target person or group (Sue, Capodilupo, et al., 2007). Perpetrators are usually unaware that they have engaged in an exchange that demeans the recipient of the communication. During the 2008 presidential campaign, for example, Republican Senator John McCain appeared at a political rally taking questions from his supporters. One elderly White woman, speaking into a handheld microphone, haltingly stated, "I don't trust Obama. He's an Arab."

McCain shook his head, quickly took the microphone, and said, "No ma'am. He's a decent family man, a citizen that I just happen to have disagreements with. He's not!"

At first glance, John McCain's defense of then-candidate Barak Obama appeared admirable. After all, he was correcting misinformation and defending a political rival. Upon reflection, however, his response, while well-intentioned, represented a major microaggression. Let us briefly analyze the interaction, the words used, and their hidden meanings.

First, it was obvious that the elderly woman believed that there was something bad or wrong with being an Arab. Equating mistrust with a person's nationality or religion, especially being Muslim or of Middle Eastern heritage, has resurged since the 9/11 terrorist attacks. Similarly, during World War II Japanese Americans were interned because they were suspected as being more loyal to Japan, a threat to national security, and potential spies. Throughout history and to the present time, people of color continue to evoke fears and biases in White people who view them as potential criminals, less trustworthy, and undesirable (Feagin, 2001; Jones, 1997; Sue, 2003).

Second, McCain's denial that Obama was an Arab, and rather that he was a "decent family man," seems to indicate that, at some level, he too has bought into the perception that Middle Easterners and Muslims were somewhat less than decent human beings.

Third, the hidden message of this microaggression (communicated by the woman and probably shared at an unconscious level by McCain) was that Arabs cannot be trusted because they are potential terrorists. Being a Middle Easterner was akin to being a potential threat to national security, and to the safety of "true Americans."

Last, the question we ask is this: "Can't Middle Eastern men be good, moral, and decent family men as well?" According to former Secretary of Defense Collin Powell, who appeared on a Sunday news program following the televised exchange, the more appropriate response would have been: "No ma'am, he's not an Arab. But what would be wrong if he were?"

Critics have accused researchers of exaggerating the detrimental impact of microaggressions by making a "mountain out of a molehill" (Schacht, 2008; Thomas, 2008). After all, the example given above may seem minor and trivial. What great harm was done? This is certainly a worthwhile question to ask. As we will shortly see, microaggressions are constant and continuing experiences of marginalized groups in our society; they assail the self-esteem of recipients, produce anger and frustration, deplete psychic energy, lower feelings of subjective well-being and worthiness, produce physical health problems, shorten life expectancy, and deny minority populations equal access and opportunity in education, employment, and health care (Brondolo et al., 2008; Clark, Anderson, Clark, & Williams, 1999; Franklin, 1999; King, 2005; Noh & Kaspar, 2003; Smedley & Smedley, 2005; Solórzano, Ceja, & Yosso, 2000; Sue, Capodilupo, & Holder, 2008; Wei, Ku, Russell, Mallinckrodt, & Liao, 2008; Williams, Neighbors, & Jackson, 2003; Yoo & Lee, 2008).

Any one microaggression alone may be minimally impactful, but when they occur continuously throughout a lifespan, their cumulative nature can have major detrimental consequences (Holmes & Holmes, 1970; Holmes & Rahe, 1967; Meyer, 1995, 2003; Utsey, Giesbrecht, Hook, & Stanard, 2008; Utsey & Ponterotto, 1999). Many Whites, for example, fail to realize that people of color from the moment of birth are subjected to multiple racial microaggressions from the media, peers, neighbors, friends, teachers, and even in the educational process and/or curriculum itself. These insults and indignities are so pervasive that they are often unrecognized. Let's discuss the two case vignettes that open this chapter in terms of the origin, manifestation, and impact of microaggressions on two sociodemographic dimensions: race and gender.

RACIAL MICROAGGRESSIONS

Racism may be defined as any attitude, action, institutional structure, or social policy that subordinates persons or groups because of their color (Jones, 1997; Ponterotto, Utsey, & Pederson, 2006). The subordination of people of color is manifested in inferior housing, education, employment, and health services (Sue, 2003). The complex manifestation of racism can occur at three different levels: individual, institutional, and cultural (Jones, 1997).

Individual racism is best known to the American public as overt, conscious, and deliberate individual acts intended to harm, place at a disadvantage, or discriminate against racial minorities. Serving Black patrons last, using racial epithets, preventing a White son or daughter from dating or marrying a person of color, or not showing clients of color housing in affluent White neighborhoods are all examples. At the other end of the spectrum, hate crimes against people of color and other marginalized groups represent extreme forms of overt individual racism. In two incidents occurring in 1998, Matthew Shepard, a student at the University of Wyoming, was tortured and murdered because he was a homosexual, and James Byrd was killed by being beaten, chained, and dragged naked behind a pick-up truck until beheaded, solely because he was Black.

Institutional racism is any policy, practice, procedure, or structure in business, industry, government, courts, churches, municipalities, schools, and so forth, by which decisions and actions are made that unfairly subordinate persons of color while allowing other groups to profit from the outcomes. Examples of these include racial profiling, segregated churches and neighborhoods, discriminatory hiring and promotion practices, and educational curricula that ignore and distort the history of minorities. Institutional bias is often masked in the policies of standard operating procedures (SOPs) that are applied equally to everyone, but which have outcomes that disadvantage certain groups while advantaging others.

Cultural racism is perhaps the most insidious and damaging form of racism because it serves as an overarching umbrella under which individual and institutional racism thrives. It is defined as the individual and institutional expression of the superiority of one group's cultural heritage (arts/crafts, history, traditions, language, and values) over another group's, and the power to impose those standards upon other groups (Sue, 2004). For example, Native Americans have at times been forbidden to practice their religions ("We are a Christian people") or to speak in their native tongues ("English is superior"), and in contemporary textbooks the histories or contributions of people of color have been neglected or distorted ("Western history and civilization are superior"). These are all examples of cultural racism.

As awareness of overt racism has increased, however, people have become more sophisticated in recognizing the overt expressions of individual, institutional, and cultural bigotry and discrimination. Because of our belief in equality and democracy, and because of the Civil Rights movement, we as a nation now strongly condemn racist, sexist, and heterosexist acts because they are antithetical to our stated values of fairness, justice, and nondiscrimination (Dovidio, Gaertner, Kawakami, & Hodson, 2002; Sears, 1988). Unfortunately, this statement may apply only at the conscious level.

The Changing Face of Racism

Although overt expressions of racism (hate crimes, physical assaults, use of racial epithets, and blatant discriminatory acts) may have declined, some argue that its expression has morphed into a more contemporary and insidious form that hides in our cultural assumptions/beliefs/values, in our institutional policies and practices, and in the deeper psychological recesses of our individual psyches (DeVos & Banaji, 2005; Dovidio, Gaertner, Kawakami, & Hodson 2002; Nelson, 2006; Sue, Capodilupo, Nadal, & Torino, 2008). In other words, race experts believe that racism has become invisible, subtle, and more indirect, operating below the level of conscious awareness, and continuing to oppress in unseen ways. This contemporary manifestation has various names: symbolic racism (Sears, 1988), modern racism (McConahay, 1986), implicit racism (Banaji, Hardin, & Rothman, 1993), and aversive racism (Dovidio & Gaertner, 1996).

Aversive racism is closely related to the concept of racial microaggressions. Dovidio and Gaertner (1996) believe that most White people experience themselves as good, moral, and decent human beings who would never intentionally discriminate against others on the basis of race. Their studies reveal, however, that it is difficult for anyone born and raised in the United States to be immune from inheriting racial biases. In fact, many Whites who may be classified as well-educated liberals appear to be aversive racists. Aversive racists truly believe they are nonprejudiced, espouse egalitarian values, and would never consciously discriminate, but they, nevertheless, harbor unconscious biased attitudes that may result in discriminatory actions. Dovidio & Gaertner (1991, 1993, 1996, 2000) have produced many studies in support of this conclusion

Racial microaggressions are most similar to aversive racism in that they generally occur below the level of awareness of well-intentioned people (Sue, Capodilupo, et al., 2007; Sue & Capodilupo, 2008), but researchers of microaggressions focus primarily on describing the dynamic interplay between perpetrator and recipient, classifying everyday manifestations, deconstructing hidden messages, and exploring internal (psychological) and external (disparities in education, employment, and health care) consequences. Let us return to our opening chapter example to illustrate the dynamic interplay of racial microaggressions between the professor and the Black students.

The Black students in the class suffered a series of racial microaggressions that were unconsciously and unintentionally delivered by Professor Richardson. Rather than thinking he was insulting or invalidating students of color, the professor believed he was teaching the "real" history of psychology, teaching students to think and communicate in an objective fashion, and giving praise to a Black student. While that might have been his conscious intent, the hidden messages being received by students of color via racial microaggressions were perceived as invalidating and demeaning.

First, the professor seems to not even entertain the notion that the history of psychology and the curriculum comes from a primarily White Eurocentric perspective that alienates and/or fails to capture the experiential reality of students of color (cultural racism). Racial microaggressions, in this case, can be environmental in that the readings, lectures, and content of the course come from only one perspective and do not present the historical totality of all groups in our society or global community. Robert Guthrie (1998), an

African American psychologist, in the late 1970s produced the first edition of his now classic book *Even the Rat Was White*, which took psychology to task for being primarily a White Eurocentric field, neglecting the contributions of people of color in historical storytelling, and for unintentionally elevating the contributions of one group (primarily White males), while denigrating Asian, African, and Latin American contributors through "benign neglect." The hidden message to students of color was that American psychology is supe-rior (other psychologies are inferior), that it is universal, and that students of color should accept this "reality." White students are affirmed in this curricu-lum, but students of color feel that their identities are constantly assailed in the classroom. Black students are likely to expend considerable emotional energy protecting their own integrity while at the same time being distracted from fully engaging in the learning process (Sue, Lin, Torino, Capodilupo, & Rivera, 2009).

Second, Professor Richardson seems to equate rational discourse with approaching topics in a calm and objective manner. When he tells the Black student to "calm down" or implies that they are "too emotional," the Professor may unintentionally be delivering another racial microaggression with mul-tiple hidden fears, assumptions, and biased values: (a) Blacks are prone to emotional outbursts, can get out of control, and may become violent; (b) emo-tion is antagonistic to reason and conversations should be unemotional and objective in the classroom; and (c) the communication style of many Blacks is dysfunctional and should be discouraged (Sue & Sue, 2008). Pathologizing Black communication and learning styles has been identified as a common microaggression directed toward African Americans (Constantine & Sue, 2007; Sue, Capodilupo, Nadal, et al., 2008). Studies suggest that communica-tion and learning styles of Black Americans may differ from those of Whites (DePaulo, 1992; Kochman, 1981); for example, affect, emotion, and passion are considered positive attributes of the communication process because they indicate sincere interest and seriousness toward the material or subject matter, while objectivity and unemotional responses indicate insincerity and lack of connection.

Third, Professor Richardson's compliment toward Justin's intelligent analysis of both perspectives and his ability to articulate the issues well was found to be offensive by some of the Black students. Why? To answer this question requires an understanding of historical racial stereotypes and their interactional dynamics. This situation is very similar to what occurred in the 2007 to 2008 democratic presidential primaries when both Senators Joe

Biden (White) and Barak Obama (Black) announced their candidacies. After announcing his presidential run, Mr. Biden was asked by a reporter about the public's wild enthusiasm for a Black candidate, Barak Obama. Joe Biden responded, "I mean, you got the first mainstream African-American who is articulate and bright and clean and a nice-looking guy. I mean, that's a story-book, man."

There was an immediate uproar from many in the Black community who considered the statement insulting and offensive. To them, it represented a racial microaggression. Senator Biden, for his part, could not understand why a positive comment toward a fellow Democrat would evoke anger from Black Americans. It is important for us to understand that messages oftentimes contain multiple meanings. While on the surface the comment by Biden can be interpreted as praise, the metacommunication (hidden message) communicated to Blacks is "Obama is an exception. Most Blacks are unintelligent, inarticulate, dirty, and unattractive." Such a racial microaggression allows the perpetrator to acknowledge and praise a person of color, but also allows him or her to express group stereotypes. In other words, while praising the Black student might have come from the professor's best intentions, the comment was experienced as a microaggression because it seemed to indicate that the professor was surprised that a Black student could be capable of such insightful and intelligent observations.

GENDER MICROAGGRESSIONS

Like racism, sexism can operate at an overt conscious level or at a covert and less conscious one (Swim & Cohen, 1997). Blatant, unfair, and unequal treatment toward women can be manifested in sexual harassment, physical abuse, discriminatory hiring practices, or in women being subjected to a hostile, predominantly male work environment. Like overt racism and hate crimes, such sexist acts are strongly condemned by our society and many men have become increasingly sensitive to their sexist actions (Sue & Sue, 2008). As our society has become more aware of what constitutes sexism and its harmful impact on women, the conscious, intentional, and deliberate forms of gender bias have seemingly decreased, but also continue in the form of subtle and unintentional expressions (Butler & Geis, 1990; Fiske, 1993; Swim & Cohen, 1997). These subtle forms of sexism are similar to aversive racism in that they come from well-intentioned men who believe in gender equality and would never deliberately discriminate against women. Yet, they unknowingly engage in behaviors that place women at a disadvantage, infantilize or stereotype them, and treat them in such a manner as to deny them equal access and opportunity (Benokraitis, 1997; Fiske & Stevens, 1993; Swim, Aiken, Hall, & Hunter, 1995).

According to women, gender microaggressions occur frequently and they devalue their contributions, objectify them as sex objects, dismiss their accomplishments, and limit their effectiveness in social, educational, employment, and professional settings (Banaji & Greenwald, 1995; Benokraitis, 1997; Morrison & Morrison, 2002). In the world of work, for example, many women describe a pattern of being overlooked, disrespected, and dismissed by their male colleagues. During team meetings in which a female employee may contribute an idea, the male CEO may not respond to it or seemingly not hear the idea. However, when a male coworker makes the identical statement, he may be recognized and praised by the executive and fellow colleagues. It has been observed that in classrooms, male students are more frequently called upon to speak or answer questions by their teachers than are female students. The hidden messages in these microaggressions are that women's ideas and contributions are less worthy than their male counterparts.

In the second vignette involving Kathleen's job interview, several common gender microaggressions were delivered to her by well-intentioned fellow male commuters and the interviewer.

First, it is not unusual for attractive young women to get admiring glances from men. Upon entering the subway train, Kathleen noted the looks that she received from male passengers, seemed to enjoy being noticed, but also experienced a few stares as "lecherous." This is a double-edged sword that some women seem to face: wanting to be attractive and desired, but also feeling objectified and treated as sex objects. The overt expression of sexual objectification is often communicated in forms ranging from whistles and catcalls to more subtle ones such as "stares" that make a woman feel as if she were being undressed in public.

Second, while one of the male commuters meant well and saw a "damsel in distress," the liberty he took in placing his hand on Kathleen's back to guide her to the exit is an intrusion of personal space. For a stranger to place one's hand on the small of a woman's back or more boldly on her hips while passing and without her permission may be seen as a violation of her body. The messages in sexual objectification microaggressions are many: (a) a woman's appearance is for the pleasure of a man; (b) women are weak, dependent, and need help; and (c) a woman's body is not her own. Some women are offended by these actions, as they appear demeaning. Yet, the man who tried to help Kathleen probably acted with the best of intentions.

Third, calling female employees by their first names and even calling Kathleen "Kathy" would not seem "disrespectful" if the interviewer did likewise with male employees. Yet, he consistently referred to men more formally by adding "Mr." to their last names. And by implying that she did not need a job but rather a "good man" to take care of her (even jokingly), the vice president sends a microaggressive message that women should be married, their place is in the home, they should be taken care of by a man, and that Kathleen was potentially taking a job away from a man who has a family to support. This sequence of spontaneous and quick exchanges between the vice president and Kathleen trivializes her desire to find a job, treats her as a child, and does not take her seriously as a candidate.

Fourth, when the vice president is asked how candidates will be evaluated for the position, he responds by saying that the "most qualified person would be offered the job," that everyone is treated the same, that he did not see gender differences, that all have an equal chance to be hired, and that "people are people." Interestingly enough, from that interaction alone, Kathleen concluded she would not be offered the job. While it is entirely possible that it was an erroneous conclusion, we should inquire as to how Kathleen arrived at such a firm belief. As we discuss in Chapter 2, the response of the vice president reflects a worldview regarding the place of women in our society. Many women who hear the phrase "I believe the most qualified person should get the job" in the context of a job interview recognize this as a gender microaggression that communicates "women are not as qualified as men, so when a male candidate is selected, it has nothing to do with bias but concerns his qualifications." Implicit in the interviewer's statements is that he is incapable of gender prejudice, because he is gender-blind. The same phenomenon is reported by people of color regarding the myth of color-blindness. The vice president is unaware that denial of gender differences is a microaggression that denies the experiential reality of women, and allows men to deny their own privileged positions.

MICROAGGRESSIONS, MARGINALITY, AND HARMFUL IMPACT

Earlier it was stated that microaggressions can be directed at any marginalized group. Groups that are marginalized by our society exist on the margins (lower or outer limits) of social desirability and consciousness. We may view them in negative ways (undesirable) and/or be oblivious to their existence and their life experiences. Many sociodemographic groups in the United States are defined by sexual orientation (gay/lesbian/bisexual), disability, class (poverty), and religion (Islam and Judaism); are confined to the edge of a system (cultural, social, political, and economic); and may experience exclusion, inequality, and social injustice. When microaggressions make their appearance in interpersonal encounters or environmental symbols, they are reflections of marginality and/or a worldview of inclusion/exclusion, superiority/inferiority, desirability/undesirability, or normality/abnormality (Sue, 2003).

Like racial and gender microaggressions, for these groups microaggressions are a common and continuing experience in their lives. Microaggressions against these groups are plentiful as indicated by the examples below.

- A lesbian client in therapy reluctantly disclosed her sexual orientation to a straight male therapist by stating that she was "into women." The therapist indicated he was not shocked by this disclosure because he once had a client who was "into dogs." (Hidden message: Homosexuality is abnormal and akin to bestiality.)
- A gay adolescent was frequently made to feel uncomfortable when fellow classmates would describe silly or stupid behavior by saying "that's gay." (Hidden message: Homosexuality is deviant.)
- A blind man reports that, when people speak to him, they often raise their voices. A well-meaning nurse was actually "yelling at him" when giving him directions on taking his medication. He replied to her: "Please don't raise your voice, I can hear you perfectly well." (Hidden message: A person with a disability is defined as lesser in all aspects of functioning.)
- During a parent-teacher conference, a teacher suggested to a mother that her son, 16-year-old Jesus Fernandez, had learning problems. He was inattentive in class, unmotivated, late with homework, and frequently napped at his desk. The teacher was unaware that Jesus worked 4 to 5 hours after school to help support the family. (Hidden message: Lack of consciousness about how dealing with poverty can sap the energies of people.)
- In referring to an outfit worn by a woman on TV, the viewer described it as "trashy" and "classless." (Hidden message: Lower class is associated with being lesser and undesirable.)

- A friendly neighbor wished a Jewish mother "Merry Christmas." (Hidden message: Everyone is Christian.)
- While a customer was bargaining over the price of an item, the store owner commented "Don't try to Jew me down." (Hidden message: Jews are stingy.)

Countless examples of microaggressions are delivered daily without the awareness of perpetrators. And while these actions may appear harmless or innocent in nature, they are nevertheless detrimental to recipients because they result in harmful psychological consequences and create disparities. Microaggressions sap the spiritual energies of recipients (Pierce, 1995), lead to low self-esteem (Franklin, 2004), and deplete or divert energy for adaptive functioning and problem solving (Dovidio & Gaertner, 2000). The following adapted passage, for example, indicates how microaggressions affect Don Locke, an African American.

I am tired of —

Watching mediocre White people continue to rise to positions of authority and responsibility.

Wondering if the White woman who quickly exited the elevator when I got on was really at her destination.

Being told I do not sound Black.

Being told by White people that they "don't see color" when they interact with me.

The deadening silence that occurs when the conversation turns to race.

Having to explain why I wish to be called "African American."

Wondering if things will get better.

Wondering if the taxi driver really did not see me trying to hail a ride.

Being told that I should not criticize racially segregated country clubs because I wouldn't enjoy associating with people who belong to them anyway.

Being followed in department stores by the security force and pestered by sales clerks who refuse to allow me to browse because they suspect I am a shoplifter.

Never being able to let my racial guard down.

Listening to reports about people of color who failed as justification for the absence of other people of color in positions of authority.

Being told that "we are just not ready for a Black person in that position."

Having to explain that my sexual fantasies do not center on White women.

Feeling racially threatened when approached by a White law enforcement officer.

Explaining that not all African Americans are employed to meet some quota.

Being told that I need to openly distance myself from another African American whose words have offended someone.

Having people tell me that I have it made and then telling me that I have "sold out" in order to have what I have.

Explaining why I am tired.

Being tired. (Adapted from Locke, 1994, p. 30)

But it is important to note that microaggressions are not only confined to their individual psychological effects. They affect the quality of life and standard of living for marginalized groups in our society. Microaggressions have the secondary but devastating effect of denying equal access and opportunity in education, employment, and health care. While seemingly minimal in nature, the harm they produce operates on a systemic and macro level.

If we return to our earlier case vignettes, we can conclude that the students of color in Professor Richardson's class are being subjected to a hostile and invalidating educational climate. They expend energy in defending an assault on their racial/cultural identity and integrity (Solorzano, Ceja, & Yosso, 2000). They are placed in a situation of learning material from an ethnocentric perspective when they know a different history. They must comply and accept what they perceive as partial truths (and oftentimes mistruths) or fight to see themselves and their groups represented realistically in the curriculum. If they fight, they are likely to be labeled troublemakers and to be given lower grades. Even if they are exposed to relevant materials, they may lack the energy to be fully engaged in the learning process (Salvatore & Shelton, 2007; Steele, 1997). If, however, they decide to accept the reality espoused by the professor, they may feel that they have "sold out." Regardless of the actions they take, the students of color will be placed at an educational disadvantage that is often reflected in lower grades, lowered chances to be admitted to institutions of higher education, less education, and years spent in lower levels of employment.

Even when educational achievements are outstanding, as in the case of Kathleen, gender microaggressions may severely limit her ability to be hired, retained, or promoted in the company (Hinton, 2004; Pierce, 1988). While the brokerage firm interviewer might on a conscious level believe that the company would offer the job to the most qualified applicant, his micro-aggressive behaviors reflect strong unconscious gender biases. Thus, he can in good conscience offer the position to a man and at the same time maintain his innocence or the belief that he chose a candidate without bias. Few employers realize that the high unemployment rates, and the "glass ceiling" encountered by women and employees of color, are reflected in the many microaggressions delivered by well-intentioned coworkers and upper managers (Sue, Lin, & Rivera, 2009). The inequities in employment and education are not so much the result of overt racism, sexism, or bigotry, but the unintentional, subtle, and invisible microaggressions that place marginalized groups at a disadvantage. Ironically, hate crimes are illegal, but microaggressions are not (Sue, 2008)!

The Way Forward

Making the "Invisible" Visible

On July 16, 2009, a renowned African American scholar and professor at Harvard University, Henry Louis Gates, Jr., was arrested for disorderly conduct by a White Boston police officer, Sergeant James M. Crowley, because Gates "exhibited loud and tumultuous behavior." What was said between the two is in dispute, but what we do know are the following facts. Gates had just returned from China where he was filming a PBS documentary, *Faces of America*, and was being driven back to his Cambridge home. For some reason the door to his home was jammed, and he asked the driver, a dark-skinned Moroccan, to help force it open. A 911 caller reported two men suspiciously forcing open the door to a house. Sergeant Crowley was the first to arrive and saw Gates in the foyer of his home. He asked Gates for identification; that is when the encounter seems to have escalated. Both give different versions of the event. Gates reports that he asked Crowley several times for his name and badge number and Crowley reports that it took some time before Gates complied with his request to show identification. Within a short period of time, the street was clogged by six other

(Continued)

officers who arrived at the scene. When he was asked to step out of the house, Gates is reported to not have initially complied. When he finally did, Gates was arrested, handcuffed, and taken to jail. The charges, however, were subsequently dropped.

Within a short period of time, the incident made national headlines as an example of police profiling of Black men, and news programs and talk shows debated whether race had anything to do with the outcome. During a news conference held by President Obama, he described the arrest of Gates as "stupid," and his remark brought on a huge outcry from primarily White citizens who came to the defense of the police. The outcry resulted in the President expressing regret at not "calibrating" his words more carefully. He subsequently called both Gates and Crowley to invite them to the White House to bridge misunderstandings over a glass of beer.

The Henry Louis Gates, Jr., incident is a prime example of the central thesis of this book, microaggressions (racial, in this case).

- First, reports that Sergeant Crowley was a sensitive White officer, level-headed, a role model to younger officers, and a man who devoted time to training others on diversity and how not to racially profile are documented by fellow officers. Gates is well known at Harvard and nationally as someone who has worked for improved race relations, is good at putting people at ease, cool and calm under fire, and devoted to social justice. In other words, both men could be described as good, moral, and decent human beings who believed in equality between the races. Yet, as our future chapters indicate, no one is immune from inheriting the racial biases of their forebears. While I cannot definitively conclude that Crowley engaged in a series of microaggressions outside his level of awareness, the arrest of Gates clearly reveals insensitivity to what it must be like for a Black man (the resident of the home he was suspected of breaking into) to be confronted with police officers. Even when he showed pieces of identification that confirmed he was the legal resident of the home, Crowley persisted in asking him to step out of the house and onto the porch.
- This brings us to the second point. Both men are operating from different racial realities. For Gates, his life has probably been filled with many incidents of racial microaggressions (suspected of being a criminal, less trustworthy, likely to be dangerous, etc.) that have been continuous and cumulative. To be considered a criminal in his own home was the

(Continued)

ultimate indignity and insult. Showing reluctance at stepping out of his home as requested by Crowley may have evoked images of the shooting of Amadou Diallo, a Black man. In that event, police officers rushed toward an entryway to question a man whom they believed to be acting suspiciously. When Diallo reached into his pocket and pulled out his wallet, he was shot and killed because the officers thought he was reaching for a weapon. Even if unstated, Gates's belief that he was viewed more suspiciously than a White resident would not be unfounded or without merit. Yet Sergeant Crowley probably believed that he acted within legal guidelines, that his actions were free of racial bias, and that he was not racially profiling. His racial reality and the inability to understand that of people of color are major barriers to racial harmony.

- The Henry Louis Gates, Jr., incident does represent an opportunity to open a dialogue about race in the United States. As some have said, it represents a teachable moment. How do we begin to understand the racial realities of one another? The fact that many White Americans are unable to bridge their worldviews with those of people of color represents a major challenge to our society. The subtext to this incident involves the observation that a national dialogue on race is much needed, but it brings on so many fears, defenses, and antagonisms that even President Obama retreated from taking it on.

As long as microaggressions remain hidden, invisible, unspoken, and excused as innocent slights with minimal harm, we will continue to insult, demean, alienate, and oppress marginalized groups. In the realm of racial microaggressions, for example, studies indicate that

- Racial microaggressions are oftentimes triggers to difficult dialogues on race in the classroom (Sue, Lin, Torino, et al., 2009).
- White students and professors are confused and uncertain about what is transpiring (Sue, Torino, Capodilupo, Rivera, & Lin, 2009).
- White students and professors are very "hung up" about clarifying these racial interactions for fear of appearing racist (Apfelbaum, Sommers, & Norton, 2008).

When critical consciousness and awareness is lacking, when one is fearful about clarifying the meaning of tension-filled interactions, and when one actively avoids pursuing an understanding of these dynamics, the offenses remain invisible (Goodman, 1995; Henry, Cobbs-Roberts, Dorn,

(Continued)

Exum, Keller, & Shircliffe, 2007). Indeed, avoidance of race topics has been likened to "a conspiracy of silence" (Sue, 2005).

Making the "invisible" visible is the first step toward combating unconscious and unintentional racism, sexism, heterosexism, and other forms of bigotry. That is the primary purpose and goal of this book:

- to describe and make visible microaggressions
- to describe the dynamic psychological interplay between perpetrator and recipient
- to describe the individual and societal consequences of microaggressions
- to reveal how microaggressions create maximal harm
- to recommend individual, institutional, and societal strategies that will ameliorate the harms aimed toward marginalized groups in this nation

CHAPTER TWO

Taxonomy of Microaggressions

Michael Richards (aka Kramer) of Seinfeld *fame went on an insane racial tirade after being heckled by Black patrons while performing at a comedy club. During the interaction, Richards shouted, "Shut up! Fifty years ago we'd have you upside-down with a fucking fork up your ass [reference to lynching]! He's a nigger! He's a nigger! He's a nigger! A nigger! Look, there's a nigger!" The following night, Richards appeared with Jerry Seinfeld on an evening program to apologize.*

On the set of the popular program Grey's Anatomy *it was reported that African American actor Isaiah Washington used gay epithets toward fellow actors while arguing over a difference of opinion. There were reports that Washington taunted fellow actor Patrick Dempsey (Dr. Derek Shepherd or "Dr. McDreamy") by saying, "I'm not your little faggot like [name redacted]," referring to a fellow cast member. Washington later apologized stating he was not homophobic, but unfortunately several other similar incidents seemed to contradict his claim. He was subsequently fired from the show.*

When arrested while driving under the influence, Mel Gibson made highly anti-Semitic statements toward a Jewish officer: "Fucking Jews are responsible for all the wars in the world." At the police station, he is alleged to have used the term "sugar tits" to refer to female officers. Several days later, Gibson apologized and issued several statements. He claimed that he was neither anti-Semitic nor sexist and that "it was the alcohol talking."

Do these three examples indicate that Richards is a racist, Isaiah Washington is heterosexist (anti-gay), and that Mel Gibson is both anti-Semitic and sexist? Prior to these incidents, all three were seen as respected actors and well liked by the American public. Few would have suggested that they were bigots and/or that they would use or make such blatantly inflammatory language. These outbursts were roundly condemned by the public and a debate ensued over whether the language they used was a true reflection of personal bigotry; Richards blamed it on the hecklers, Washington blamed it on the "heat of the moment," and Gibson blamed it on the alcohol.

Were these three individuals bigots, skilled in disguising their biases (Apfelbaum, Sommers, & Norton, 2008), or were they generally decent people unaware of the racism, sexism, and heterosexism they harbored until they lost control (Conley, Calhoun, Evett, & Devine, 2001; Sue, Lin, Torino, Capodilupo, & Rivera, 2009)? More importantly, are we capable of such outbursts? Have we, ourselves, ever lost control and used racial epithets? What about telling or laughing at racist jokes? If so, does it make us bigots?

Scholars suggest that it is nearly impossible for any of us not to inherit the racial, gender, and sexual-orientation biases of our forebears (Baker & Fishbein, 1998; Banaji & Greenwald, 1995; Barrett & Logan, 2002; Dovidio, Gaertner, Kawakami, & Hodson, 2002; Fiske & Stevens, 1993; Sue, 2003). Such prejudices, however, may exist consciously, unconsciously, or on the margins of consciousness (Ponterotto, Utsey, & Pedersen, 2006; Nelson, 2006; Sue, 2003). One could make a strong argument, for example, that Richards, Washington, and Gibson (1) were aware of their biases but were generally successful in concealing them, (2) were only minimally (marginally) aware, or (3) were completely unaware until their outbursts. To understand racism means to realize that our prejudices, stereotypes, and biases exist on a continuum of conscious awareness. The avowed racist, for example, will use racial epithets freely, consciously believes in the inferiority of persons of color, and will deliberately discriminate. Those who are less aware, however, are likely to unintentionally behave in subtle discriminatory patterns against people of color, women, and LGBTs outside their level of conscious awareness.

Conscious and Deliberate Bigotry versus Unconscious and Unintentional Bias

People who are aware of their racial, gender, and sexual-orientation biases, believe in the inferiority of these groups, and will discriminate when the opportunity arises have been labeled conscious-deliberate bigots (Sue, 2003). In the area of racism, for example, they vary from people who privately harbor racial animosity but do a good job of concealing it, to those who are more overt and publicly demonstrable, and finally to those who might be labeled White supremacists. In most cases, these individuals are held in check from overt discrimination by legal, moral, and social constraints. These individuals form probably a small number, although they have great public impact. It is believed, for example, that fewer than 15% of White Americans can be classified as overtly racist (Pettigrew, 1981). Many multicultural scholars believe it is easier for people of color and women to deal with the overt and deliberate forms of bigotry than the subtle and unintentional forms, because no guesswork is involved (Dovidio & Gaertner, 2000; Salvatore & Shelton, 2007; Sue, 2003; Swim & Cohen, 1997). It is the unconscious and unintentional forms of bias that create the overwhelming problems for marginalized groups in our society (Sue, 2003; 2005).

The Changing Face of Racism, Sexism, and Heterosexism

Bias, prejudice, and discrimination in North America have undergone a transformation, especially in the post–civil rights era when the democratic belief in the equality of marginalized groups (racial minorities, women, and gays/lesbians) directly clashes with their long history of oppression in society (Dovidio & Gaertner, 2000; Hylton, 2005; Satcher & Leggett, 2007; Swim, Mallett, & Stangor, 2004). In the case of racism, its manifestation has been found to be more disguised and covert rather than overtly expressed in the form of racial hatred and bigotry (Sue, 2003). Research also indicates that sexism and heterosexism have not decreased, but instead have become more ambiguous and nebulous, making them more difficult to identify and acknowledge (Hylton, 2005; Morrison & Morrison, 2002; Swim & Cohen, 1997).

While hate crimes and racial, gender, and sexual-orientation harassment continue to be committed by overt racists, sexists, and heterosexists/homophobes, the greatest harm to persons of color, women, and homosexuals does not come from these conscious perpetrators. It is not the White supremacists, Klansmen or Skinheads, for example, who pose the greatest threat to people of color, but rather well-intentioned people, who are strongly motivated by egalitarian values, who believe in their own morality, and who experience themselves as fair-minded and decent people who would never consciously discriminate (Sue, 2005). These individuals have been labeled unconscious-unintentional oppressors or bigots (Sue, 2003). Because no one is immune from inheriting the biases of the society, all citizens are exposed to a social conditioning process that imbues within them prejudices, stereotypes, and beliefs that lie outside their level of awareness. On a conscious level they may endorse egalitarian values, but on an unconscious level, they harbor either promajority feelings (Dovidio et al., 2002) or antiminority feelings (Sue, 2003).

Although much has been written about contemporary forms of racism, sexism, and heterosexism, many studies in health care, education, law, employment, mental health, and social settings indicate the difficulty of describing and defining racial, gender, and sexual-orientation discrimination that occurs via "implicit bias"; they are difficult to identify, quantify, and rectify because of their subtle, nebulous, and unnamed nature (Johnson, 1988; Nadal, Rivera, & Corpus, in press; Rowe, 1990; Sue, Nadal, et al., 2008). Subtle racism, sexism, and heterosexism remain relatively invisible and potentially harmful to the well-being, self-esteem, and standard of living of many marginalized groups in society. These daily common experiences of aggression may have significantly more influence on anger, frustration, and self-esteem than traditional overt forms of racism, sexism, and heterosexism (Sue, Capodilupo, et al., 2007). Furthermore, their invisible nature prevents perpetrators from realizing and confronting their own complicity in creating psychological dilemmas for minorities and their role in creating disparities in employment, health care, and education (Coleman, 2004; Dovidio et al., 2002; Rowe, 1990).

Racial, Gender, and Sexual-Orientation Microaggressions

In reviewing the literature on subtle and contemporary forms of bias, the term "microaggressions" seems to best describe the phenomenon in its everyday occurrence. Simply stated, microaggressions are brief, everyday exchanges that send denigrating messages to certain individuals because of their group membership (people of color, women, or LGBTs). The term was first coined by Pierce in 1970 in his work with Black Americans where he defined it as "subtle, stunning, often automatic, and nonverbal exchanges which are 'put-downs'" (Pierce, Carew, Pierce-Gonzalez, & Willis, 1978, p. 66). They have also been described as "subtle insults (verbal, nonverbal, and/or visual) directed toward people of color, often automatically or unconsciously" (Solorzano, Ceja, & Yosso, 2000).

In the world of business, the term "microinequities" is used to describe the pattern of being overlooked, underrespected, and devalued because of one's race or gender (Hinton, 2004). They are often unconsciously delivered as subtle snubs or dismissive looks, gestures, and tones (Rowe, 1990). These exchanges are so pervasive and automatic in daily conversations and interactions that they are often dismissed and glossed over as being innocent and innocuous. Yet, as indicated previously, microaggressions are detrimental to persons of color because they impair performance in a multitude of settings by sapping the psychic and spiritual energy of recipients and by creating inequities (Sue, Capodilupo, et al., 2007).

ENVIRONMENTAL MICROAGGRESSIONS

The mechanisms by which microaggressions can be delivered may be verbal, nonverbal, or environmental. Because we will spend most of our time dealing with verbal and nonverbal manifestations, it seems important to indicate that microaggressions may be equally disturbing and may be even more harmful when they intentionally or unintentionally make their appearance environmentally. The term "environmental microaggression" refers to the numerous demeaning and threatening social, educational, political, or economic cues that are communicated individually, institutionally, or societally to marginalized groups. Environmental microaggressions may be delivered visually (Pierce, Carew, Pierce-Gonzalez, & Willis, 1978) or from a stated philosophy such as "color blindness" (Purdie-Vaughns, Davies, Steele, & Ditlmann, 2008; Stevens, Plaut, & Sanches-Burks, 2008). When people refer to the "campus climate" as hostile and invalidating, or when workers of color refer to a threatening work environment, they are probably alluding to the existence of environmental microaggressions (Solorzano, Ceja, & Yosso, 2000). It is important to note that these cues do not necessarily involve interpersonal interactions.

Several years ago I was asked by an Ivy League institution to conduct diversity training related to making the university a more welcoming place for students, staff, and faculty of color. Apparently, many students of color had complained over the years that the campus climate was alienating, hostile, and invalidating to students of color. As a means to address this observation, the university held a one-week event with many diversity activities. My part was to conduct a half-day training session with all the deans of the respective colleges.

As I was being introduced by the coordinator, I looked around the audience and was struck by the fact that not a single dean or representative of the office was a person of color. I also noted that most were men and that women were also underrepresented. As I stood before the group, I made the following observation: "As I look around the room and at the sea of faces before me, I am struck by the fact that not a single one of you seems to be a visible racial ethnic minority. Do you know the message you are sending to me and people of color on this campus?" Several participants shifted in their seats, looked at one another, but remained silent.

Microaggressions hold their power because they often send hidden, invalidating, demeaning, or insulting messages (Sue, Capodilupo, et al., 2007). From the perspective of students and faculty of color, the absence of administrators of color sent a series of loud and clear messages:

1. "You and your kind are not welcome here."
2. "If you choose to come to our campus, you will not feel comfortable here."
3. "If you choose to stay, there is only so far you can advance. You may not graduate (students of color) or get tenured/promoted (faculty of color)."

When people of color see an institution or organization that is primarily White or when they see that people at the upper levels of the administration or management team are primarily White and male, the message taken away by people of color and women is quite unmistakable and profound; the chances of doing well at this institution are stacked against them (Bonilla-Silva, 2006; Inzlicht & Good, 2006). When women in the workplace enter a conference room where portraits of all the past male CEOs or directors are displayed, the microaggressive message is that women are not capable of doing well in leadership positions and the "glass ceiling" is powerful. When a male colleague's office wall is filled with nude pictures of women or when *Playboy* magazines are present on desks at a place of employment, women employees may feel demeaned, insulted, and unwelcomed.

Environmental microaggressions often are packaged in symbols and even mascots. From 1926 to February 21, 2007, Chief Illiniwek was the mascot and official symbol of the University of Illinois at Urbana-Champaign sports teams. During university sporting events, Chief Illiniwek would perform a dancing routine before fans during games, at halftimes, and after victories. For two decades, Native American groups and allies deplored the choice of mascot as being demeaning, hostile, and abusive toward them, their culture, and their lifestyle. They claimed that the symbol/mascot of Chief Illiniwek misappropriated their indigenous figures and rituals and that it perpetuated harmful racial and ethnic stereotypes (Wikipedia, 2009).

In general, Chief Illiniwek, portrayed by a White student in Sioux regalia, was said to create a hostile environment toward diversity, hinder development of a positive learning community, promote an inaccurate image of Native Americans, and assail the integrity of indigenous peoples. Numerous organizations such as the National Association for the Advancement of Colored People, the National Education Association, Amnesty International, and National Congress of American Indians Society Americas supported the retirement of Chief Illiniwek (Wikipedia, 2009).

For years the university, the majority of the student body, and even the Illinois state legislature supported the mascot because it was meant to honor Native Americans and was a beloved symbol of the spirit of a great university. Native Americans, however, often asked, "Why don't we feel honored?" In February 2007, after decades of controversy, Chief Illiniwek was retired. This example not only points to how microaggressions may be delivered environmentally, but it points out a strong dilemma that Chapter 3 covers: the clash of realities between Whites and people of color, men and women, and straights and gays. As an epilogue, it is sad to note that, although not in the role of an official mascot, Chief Illiniwek has nevertheless reappeared on the University of Illinois campus in 2008 under the banner of "free speech."

Environmental microaggressions are powerful and can be transmitted through numerical imbalance of one's own group (Purdie-Vaughns et al., 2008), mascots or symbols, and inaccurate media portrayals of marginalized groups in films, television, radio, print media, and educational curriculum (books, course content, films, etc.). The sheer exclusion of decorations, literature, and ethnic aesthetic-cultural forms like music, art, language, and food can also assail the racial, gender, or sexual identity of various groups.

In a revealing study, researchers found that "diversity cues" (number of minority members at a worksite, diversity philosophy communicated through company brochures, etc.) in corporate America directly affected the perception of threat or safety experienced by Black American job applicants (Purdie-Vaughns et al., 2008). The researchers explored the institutional cues rather than interpersonal ones that signaled either safety or threat to African Americans. Environmental conditions directly impacted how marginalized groups perceive whether they will be valued or demeaned in mainstream settings. The term "social identity contingencies" refers to how individuals from stigmatized groups anticipate whether their group membership will be threatened (devalued or perceived negatively) or valued in corporate America. When the cues signal threat, lack of trust ensues, feelings of safety diminish, and vulnerability increases. This in turn has a major detrimental impact on the group identity of the worker and potentially lowered productivity.

FORMS OF MICROAGGRESSIONS

D. W. Sue and colleagues (Sue, Capodilupo, et al., 2007; Sue & Capodilupo, 2008) have proposed a taxonomy of racial, gender, and sexual-orientation microaggressions that fall into three major categories: microassaults, microinsults, and microinvalidations. All three forms may vary on the dimension of awareness and intentionality by the perpetrator, but they all communicate either an overt, covert, or hidden offensive message or meaning to recipients. Figure 2.1 presents the categorization and relationship of microaggressions to one another, using race as the example. Chapters 8 and 9 discuss specific microaggressions and their taxonomy related to gender and sexual orientation.

Microassaults

Microassaults are conscious, deliberate, and either subtle or explicit racial, gender, or sexual-orientation biased attitudes, beliefs, or behaviors that are communicated to marginalized groups through environmental cues, verbalizations, or behaviors. They are meant to attack the group identity of the person or to hurt/harm the intended victim through name-calling, avoidant behavior, or purposeful discriminatory actions (Miller & Garran, 2008; Nelson, 2006). Displaying a Klan hood, Nazi swastika, noose, or Confederate flag; burning a cross; and hanging Playboy bunny pictures in a male manager's office may all constitute environmental microassaults. The intent of these messages is to threaten, intimidate, and make the individuals or groups feel unwanted and unsafe because they are inferior, subhuman, and lesser beings that do not belong on the same levels as others in this society.

Verbal microassaults include the use of racial epithets: referring to African Americans as "niggers," Chinese Americans as "chinks," Japanese Americans as "Japs," women as "bitches" or "cunts," and gays as "fags." Again, the intent is to assail one's racial, gender, or sexual identity and to communicate to the recipient that they are "lesser human beings." Telling ethnic, racial, gender, or sexual-orientation jokes and laughing at them also fall into this category. With respect to behavior, forbidding a son or daughter from marrying outside of one's race, ignoring a group of women who are requesting a table at a restaurant, and promoting a less-qualified heterosexual employee over a gay one are a few examples. Again, such actions communicate to the recipient that

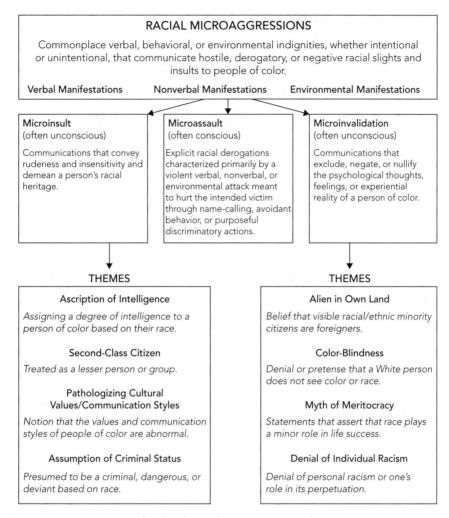

Figure 2.1   Categories of and Relationships among Racial Microaggressions

they are unworthy to be served and/or that they are not the "right kind of people" and do not belong.

Microassaults are most similar to what has been called "old fashioned" racism, sexism, or heterosexism conducted on an individual level. They are likely to be conscious and deliberate acts. However, because of strong public condemnation of such behaviors, microassaults are most likely to be expressed under three conditions that afford the perpetrator some form of protection (Sue & Capodilupo, 2008).

First, when perpetrators feel some degree of anonymity and are assured that their roles or actions can be concealed they may feel freer to engage in microassaults (scrawling anti-Semitic graffiti in public restrooms or hanging a noose surreptitiously on the door of a Black colleague).

Second, perpetrators may engage in a microassault when they feel relatively safe, such as being in the presence of people who share their beliefs and attitudes or knowing that they can get away with their offensive words and deeds. Safety often relies on the inaction of others in the face of biased actions. In fact, studies reveal that people often overpredict whether they would take action against a biased action (hearing a racist comment). While they may condemn and say they would take appropriate action, when faced with the real situation they remain silent or inactive (Kawakami, Dunn, Karmali, & Dovidio, 2009). The following example is representative of this condition.

> At a fraternity sports party, a group of White males were sitting around their living room during a late Sunday afternoon, chugging down beer after beer tapped from a keg. They had just finished watching the first half of a football game and were obviously quite inebriated. Excitedly talking about the last play from scrimmage that resulted in an incomplete pass, one of the boys exclaimed, "them niggers can't play quarterback!" This brought out a howl of laughter, and another member said, "That's because they're just jungle bunnies!" More laughter erupted in the room and others produced a flurry of racial slurs: "monkey," "coon," "burr head," "oreo," and "Uncle Tom"! Each slur brought on laughter and renewed attempts to outdo one another in finding the most degrading reference to Blacks. As they exhausted their list, the game became a form of free association with blackness. "Black pussy, black sheep, criminal, rapist, castration, welfare family, cattle prod," and so on, they shouted. It was clear that some of those in the group were quite uncomfortable with the game, but said nothing and chuckled at the responses anyway. (Sue, 2003, p. 88)

Third, many people who privately hold notions of minority inferiority will only display their biased attitudes when they lose control. Our opening examples of actors Michael Richards and Mel Gibson represent this condition. Neither had publicly displayed any attitudes/behaviors of racism, anti-Semitism, or sexism until they were caught in situations where conscious concealment and judgment broke down. In the case of Richards, the heckling by Black patrons so infuriated him that he simply "lost it" and exploded with anger expressed through racial epithets. In the case of Gibson, alcoholic intoxication so lowered his inhibitions and defenses that he made statements that have haunted him since.

Microassaults are most similar to "old-fashioned" racism: they are the type the public generally associates with "true racism": direct, deliberate, obvious, and explicit. There is no guesswork involved in their intent, which is to harm, humiliate, or degrade people of color, women, and GLBTs.

In many respects, microassaults or blatant racism are easier to deal with by marginalized groups because their intent is clear and the psychological energies of people of color, for example, are not diluted by ambiguity. In fact, there are indications that people of color are better prepared to deal with overt microassaults (Salvatore & Shelton, 2007) than unintentional biased behavior that reside outside the level of awareness of perpetrators—microinsults and microinvalidations. It is these invisible and unintentional forms of microaggressions that are the main subject of this book. Table 2.1 provides examples of common microaggression themes with examples and their hidden demeaning messages directed toward people of color, women, and LGBTs.

Please note that a more thorough coverage of group specific themes is presented in separate chapters for people of color (Chapter 7), women (Chapter 8), and LGBTs (Chapter 9). Many microaggressions are common and universal to the three groups, but there are differences in types, hidden messages, and impact. For example, it appears that LGBTs may experience more overt forms of microaggressions (microassaults) than the other two groups; that even with the category of racial microaggressions, Asian Americans and Latinos are more likely to experience "alien in one's own land" messages more than African Americans who are more likely to be seen as "criminals"; and women may experience a unique microaggression such as "sexual objectification" that is not present for racial minorities. Research and work in the area of similarities and differences in microaggressive manifestation and impact is in an infancy stage (Sue, Capodilupo, et al., 2007).

Microinsults

Microinsults are characterized by interpersonal or environmental communications that convey stereotypes, rudeness, and insensitivity and that demean a person's racial, gender, or sexual orientation, heritage, or identity. Microinsults represent subtle snubs, frequently outside the conscious awareness of the perpetrator, but they convey an oftentimes hidden insulting message to the recipient of these three groups.

MICROAGGRESSIVE THEMES

In the original racial microaggression taxonomy proposed by Sue & colleagues (2007) and later refined to include gender and sexual-orientation themes

Table 2.1 Examples of Racial, Gender, and Sexual-Orientation Microaggressions

THEMES	MICROAGGRESSION	MESSAGE
Alien in One's Own Land When Asian Americans and Latino Americans are assumed to be foreign-born.	"Where are you from?" "Where were you born?" "You speak English very well."	You are not American.
	A person asking an Asian American to teach them words in their native language.	You are a foreigner.
Ascription of Intelligence Assigning intelligence to a person of color or woman based on their race/gender.	"You are a credit to your race."	People of color are generally not as intelligent as Whites.
	"Wow! How did you become so good in math?"	It is unusual for a woman to be smart in math.
	Asking an Asian person to help with a math or science problem.	All Asians are intelligent and good in math/sciences.
Color Blindness Statements that indicate that a White person does not want to acknowledge race.	"When I look at you, I don't see color."	Denying a person of color's racial/ethnic experiences.
	"America is a melting pot."	Assimilate/acculturate to dominant culture.
	"There is only one race, the human race."	Denying the individual as a racial/cultural being.
Criminality/Assumption of Criminal Status A person of color is presumed to be dangerous, criminal, or deviant based on their race.	A White man or woman clutches their purse or checks their wallet as a Black or Latino approaches or passes.	You are a criminal.
	A store owner following a customer of color around the store.	You are going to steal/ You are poor/You do not belong.
	A White person waits to ride the next elevator when a person of color is on it.	You are dangerous.
Use of Sexist/ Heterosexist Language Terms that exclude or degrade women and LGBT persons.	Use of the pronoun "he" to refer to all people.	Male experience is universal. Female experience is meaningless.

(Continued)

Table 2.1   *(Continued)*

THEMES	MICROAGGRESSION	MESSAGE
	Two options for relationship status: married or single.	LGB partnerships do not matter/are meaningless.
	An assertive woman is labeled a "bitch."	Women should be passive.
	A heterosexual man who often hangs out with his female friends more than his male friends is labeled a "faggot."	Men who act like women are inferior (women are inferior)/gay men are inferior.
Denial of Individual Racism/Sexism/ Heterosexism A statement made when bias is denied.	"I'm not racist. I have several Black friends."	I am immune to racism because I have friends of color.
	"As an employer, I always treat men and women equally."	I am incapable of sexism.
Myth of Meritocracy Statements which assert that race or gender does not play a role in life successes.	"I believe the most qualified person should get the job."	People of color are given extra unfair benefits because of their race.
	"Men and women have equal opportunities for achievement."	The playing field is even so if women cannot make it, the problem is with them.
Pathologizing Cultural Values/Communication Styles The notion that the values and communication styles of the dominant/White culture are ideal.	Asking a Black person: "Why do you have to be so loud/animated?" "Just calm down."	Assimilate to dominant culture.
	To an Asian or Latino person: "Why are you so quiet? We want to know what you think. Be more verbal." "Speak up more."	
	Dismissing an individual who brings up race/culture in work/school setting.	Leave your cultural baggage outside.
Second-Class Citizen Occurs when a target group member receives differential treatment from the power group.	Person of color mistaken for a service worker.	People of color are servants to Whites. They couldn't possibly occupy high status positions.
	Female doctor mistaken for a nurse.	Women occupy nurturing roles.

(Continued)

Table 2.1 *(Continued)*

THEMES	MICROAGGRESSION	MESSAGE
	Having a taxi cab pass a person of color and pick up a White passenger.	You are likely to cause trouble and/or travel to a dangerous neighborhood.
	Being ignored at a store counter as attention is given to the White customer behind a person of color.	Whites are more valued customers than people of color.
	A lesbian woman is not invited out with a group of girlfriends because they thought she would be bored if they were talking to men.	You don't belong.
Traditional Gender Role Prejudicing and Stereotyping Occurs when expectations of traditional roles or stereotypes are conveyed.	When a female student asked a male professor for extra help on a chemistry assignment, he asks "What do you need to work on this for anyway?"	Women are less capable in math and science.
	A person asks a woman her age and, upon hearing she is 31, looks quickly at her ring finger.	Women should be married during child-bearing ages because that is their primary purpose.
	A woman is assumed to be a lesbian because she does not put a lot of effort into her appearance.	Lesbians do not care about being attractive to others.
Sexual Objectification Occurs when women are treated as though they were objects at men's disposal.	A male stranger puts his hands on a woman's hips or on the swell of her back to pass by her.	Your body is not yours.
	Whistles and catcalls as a woman walks down the street.	Your body/appearance is for men's enjoyment and pleasure.
Assumption of Abnormality Occurs when it is implied that there is something wrong with being LGB.	Two men holding hands in public are stared at by strangers.	You should keep your displays of affection private because they are offensive.
	Students use the term "gay" to describe a fellow student who is socially ostracized at school.	People who are weird and different are "gay."

Source: Taken from Sue & Capodilupo, 2008, p. 114–117.

(Sue & Capodilupo, 2008), some of the more common themes with their hidden messages are described below.

- *Ascription of Intelligence*—This microinsult is usually related to aspects of intellect, competence, and capabilities. Saying "You are a credit to your race" contains an insulting metacommunication ("People of color are generally not as intelligent as Whites."). The example in Chapter 1 in which Senator Joe Biden's compliment of Barack Obama was found offensive by some African Americans represents such an insult. The belief that African Americans are intellectually inferior is quite a common microaggression (Jones, 1997; Smedley & Smedley, 2005). When a male teacher expresses surprise at the math skills of a female student ("Wow, how did you get so good in math?") or when White students ask Asian Americans for help on their math/science problems (Asians are naturally good at math.), ascription of intelligence may be in operation.

- *Second-Class Citizen*—This microinsult contains an unconscious message that certain groups are less worthy, less important, and less deserving, and are inferior beings that deserve discriminatory treatment. While they may be conscious, most are delivered by well-intentioned people who would never knowingly discriminate (Bonilla-Silva, 2006). As a result, people of color, women, and LGBTs are accorded lesser treatment than Whites, men, and straights. A lesbian woman is ignored, left out, and not invited with a group of female coworkers because she "is not like one of us." Black patrons at a restaurant are seated at a smaller table near the kitchen door where waiters and waitresses constantly walk in and out. A female physician at an emergency room is mistaken by male patients as a nurse.

- *Pathologizing Cultural Values/Communication Styles*—The theme of this microinsult has two components: a belief that the cultural values/communication styles of White, male, and straight groups are normative and that those of people of color, females, and LGBTs are somehow abnormal. Telling Latino students to "leave your cultural baggage outside the classroom," and asking a Black person "Why do you have to be so loud, emotional, and animated?" are two examples. In the first case, the Latino students are being asked to assimilate and acculturate and are being told that their cultural values are dysfunctional and should be given up because they will interfere with their learning. In the latter case, the style of communication by many Blacks is being pathologized because appropriate communication is dispassionate and objective (Kochman, 1981).

But there is something more sinister and insidious in the reaction that fosters fear that Blacks will become violent and out of control. This is related to the next microinsult.

- *Criminality/Assumption of Criminal Status*—The theme of this micro-insult appears to be very race specific and relates to beliefs that a person of color is presumed to be dangerous, potentially a criminal, likely to break the law, or antisocial. Women and LGBTs are unlikely to encounter this form of microinsult. Numerous examples of this apply to African Americans and Latinos. A White woman who clutches her purse more tightly in the presence of Latinos, a White man checking for his wallet while passing a group of African Americans on the sidewalk, and a sales clerk requesting more pieces of identification to cash a check from a Black than from a White customer are examples. Interestingly, our studies suggest that assumption of criminal status is seldom attributed to Asian Americans. Indeed, they are often viewed as law abiding, conforming, unlikely to rock the boat, and less prone to violence (Sue, Bucceri, Lin, Nadal, & Torino, 2007; Sue, Capodilupo, & Holder, 2008).

- *Sexual Objectification*—Sexual objectification is the process by which women are transformed into "objects" or property at the sexual disposal or benefit of men. There is a dehumanizing quality in this process because women are stripped of their humanity and the totality of their human essence (personal attributes, intelligence, emotions, hopes, etc.). *Playboy* and *Hustler* magazine pictures of nude women, topless and bottomless entertainment clubs, using scantily clad attractive female models in commercials to sell goods or services, and countless other examples communicate that women's bodies are not their own, and that they exist to service the sexual fantasies and desires of men (Fredrickson & Roberts, 1997). The interaction of race and gender and sexual objectification can be quite complex (Lott, Aquith, & Doyon, 2001). In one study it was found, for example, that Asian American females often experienced microinsults related to exoticization (Sue, Bucceri, Lin, Nadal, & Torino, 2007). Participants complained of continual subjugation to the roles of sexual objects, domestic servants, and exotic images such as Geishas. They felt their identities were equated to that of passive companions to White men. Interestingly, some speculated that White men are often attracted to Asian American women, who are perceived as feminine and submissive, primarily as a backlash to feminist values and the feminist movement.

- *Assumption of Abnormality*—This theme is related to the perception that something about the person's race, gender, or sexual orientation is abnormal, deviant, and pathological. LGBT groups experience these microinsults frequently, especially in the area of sexual behavior that is equated with abnormality (Herek, 1998; Satcher & Leggett, 2007). When a gay man during a physical exam is suspected by a physician to have HIV/AIDS on the first visit, when students use the term "gay" to describe the odd or nonconformist behavior of a fellow classmate, and when someone expresses surprise that a Lesbian is in a monogamous relationship, an assumption of abnormality is present. Examples of assumptions could be *"LBGT people are promiscuous and engage in deviant sexual behavior"* or *"People who are weird and different are gay."*

Microinvalidation

Microinvalidations are characterized by communications or environmental cues that exclude, negate, or nullify the psychological thoughts, feelings, or experiential reality of certain groups, such as people of color, women, and LGBTs. In many ways, microinvalidations may potentially represent the most damaging form of the three microaggressions because they directly and insidiously deny the racial, gender, or sexual-orientation reality of these groups. As we shall see in the next chapter, the power to impose reality upon marginalized groups represents the ultimate form of oppression. Several examples of microinvalidation themes are given below.

- *Alien in One's Own Land*—This theme involves being perceived as a perpetual foreigner or being an alien in one's own country. Of all the groups toward which such microinvalidations are directed, Asian Americans and Latino Americans are most likely to experience them. When Asian Americans are complimented for speaking "good English," and persistently asked where they were born, the meta-communication is that *"You are not American"* or *"You are a foreigner."* When Latino Americans are told, *"If you don't like it here, go back to Mexico,"* there is an implied assumption that one's allegiance resides in another country. Interestingly, studies reveal that African Americans are perceived by the public as "more American" than either Asian or Latino Americans (Devos & Banaji, 2005). While highly speculative, it may be that the enslavement of Blacks in the United States is so tightly bound up in American history that such an association is partially reflected in the consciousness of White America.

- *Color, Gender, and Sexual-Orientation Blindness*—Being color, gender, or sexual-orientation blind, simply stated, is the unwillingness to acknowledge or admit to seeing race, gender, or sexual orientation. Color blindness is one of the most frequently delivered microinvalidations toward people of color. Statements such as *"When I look at you I don't see color," "There is only one race, the human race," "We are all Americans,"* or *"We are a melting pot,"* contain multiple and complex hidden messages. At one level they are messages asking the receiver not to bring the topic of race into the discussion or interaction. They are also messages that indicate people of color should assimilate and acculturate. But they are also on one hand intended as defensive maneuvers not to appear racist (Apfelbaum, Sommers, & Norton, 2008), and on the other hand as a denial of the racial experiences of people of color (Bonilla-Silva, 2005). Sue (2005) posits that denial of color is really a denial of differences. The denial of differences is really a denial of power and privilege. The denial of power and privilege is really a denial of personal benefits that accrue to certain privileged groups by virtue of inequities. The denial that we profit from racism is really a denial of responsibility for our racism. Lastly, the denial of our racism is really a denial of the necessity to take action against racism.
- *Denial of Individual Racism/Sexism/Heterosexism*—Related to the theme above is another form of denial. This involves an individual denial of personal racism, personal sexism, or personal heterosexism. Statements such as *"I'm not homophobic, I have a gay friend," "I have nothing against interracial marriages, but I worry about the children,"* and *"As an employer I treat all men and women equally"* may possess the following hidden messages: *"I am immune to heterosexism," "The only reason I have hesitations about interracial relationships is concern about the offspring and it has nothing to do with personal bias,"* and *"I never discriminate against women."* When such statements are made to a person of color, for example, they deny the racial reality of the individual (an experience that personal racial bias resides in everyone).
- *Myth of Meritocracy*—The myth of meritocracy is a theme that asserts that race, gender, and sexual orientation do not play a role in life successes. It assumes that all groups have an equal opportunity to succeed, and that we operate on a level playing field. Thus, success and failure are attributed to individual attributes like intelligence, hard work, motivation,

and family values. When people do well, they are considered to have achieved their success through individual effort. The flip side of the coin is those who do not succeed are also seen as possessing deficiencies (lazy, low intellect, etc.) (Jones, 1997). In the case of persons of color, there is little recognition that higher unemployment rates, lower educational achievement, and poverty may be the result of systemic forces (individual, institutional, and societal racism). Blaming the victim is the outcome of the myth of meritocracy. Statements made to marginalized groups may be reflected in these comments: *"Everyone has an equal chance in this society," "The cream of the crop rises to the top," "Everyone can succeed if they work hard enough,"* and *"Affirmative action is reverse racism."* All these statements potentially imply that racism, sexism, and heterosexism is of little importance in a group's or individual's success.

Microaggressions, whether they fall into the category of microassaults, microinsults, or microinvalidations are detrimental to the well-being and standard of living for marginalized groups in our society. In the next chapter, we turn to a discussion and analysis of the psychological dilemmas created by microaggressions and attempt to describe the psychological and internal processes of both recipients and unintentional perpetrators.

The Way Forward

Defining, Recognizing, and Deconstructing Hidden Messages in Microaggressions

Microaggressions are a constant and continuing reality for people of color, women, and LGBTs in our society. They hold their power over both perpetrators and targets because of their everyday invisible nature. In many respects, all of us have been both perpetrators and targets. With respect to the former, we have been guilty of having delivered microaggressions, whether they are racial, gender, sexual-orientation, ability, religious, or class based. Microaggressions are harmful to marginalized groups because they cause psychological distress and create disparities in health care, employment, and education. The first steps in overcoming racial, gender, and sexual microaggressions involve the following.

(Continued)

1. *Defining microaggressions.* Microaggressions can be overt or covert but they are most damaging when they occur outside the level of the conscious awareness of well-intentioned perpetrators. Most of us can recognize and define overt forms of bias and discrimination and will actively condemn such actions. However, the "invisible" manifestations are not under conscious awareness and control, so they occur spontaneously without any checks and balances in personal, social, and work-related interactions. They can occur among and between family members, neighbors, and coworkers, and in teacher–student, healthcare provider–patient, therapist–client, and employer–employee relationships. They are numerous, continuous, and have a detrimental impact upon targets. Being able to define microaggressions and to know the various forms they take must begin with a cognitive and intellectual understanding of their manifestations and impact. The taxonomy described in this chapter will, hopefully, provide readers with a template that will facilitate understanding of their concrete characteristics and qualities.

2. *Recognizing microaggressions.* Being able to define racial, gender, and sexual-orientation microaggressions is not enough. Recognizing microaggressions when they make their appearance is more than an intellectual exercise in definitions. Their manifestations are dynamic, with very real personal consequences that can only be ameliorated when recognized in their interactional or environmental forms. Appropriate intervention can only occur when microaggressions are recognized in the here and now. Recognition may involve two different situations: (1) when they are observed as occurring between external parties (delivered by others), and (2) when you are one of the actors involved (perpetrator or recipient). When you observe a microaggression being delivered by someone else, the possibility of intervention may present a personal or professional dilemma: *"Should I or shouldn't I intervene? If I do, what is the most appropriate way to do so? What are the consequences if I choose to take action?"* The second situation involves you as either the target or perpetrator. We will spend considerable time in future chapters analyzing target impact and response issues. More importantly, however, is your recognition that perhaps you have or are personally engaging in the delivery of microaggressions. Self-monitoring, being open to exploring the possibility that you have acted in a biased fashion, and controlling defensiveness are crucial to recognizing when you have been guilty of a microaggression.

(Continued)

3. *Deconstructing the hidden meaning of microaggressions.* Microaggressions are reflections of worldviews that are filled with ethnocentric values, biases, assumptions, and stereotypes that have been strongly culturally inculcated into our beliefs, attitudes, and behaviors. Microaggressions usually send double messages that are often contradictory to one another. A common microaggression directed toward people of color and women is symbolized in this statement: *"I believe the most qualified person should be offered the job."* While few of us would disagree with this statement, in certain contexts, when made to a devalued group member by a majority person, there may be a hidden message: *"Minorities and women are generally not qualified, so don't blame me of bias when it is offered to a White male."*

Being able to define and recognize microaggressions and being able to deconstruct the metacommunications are very challenging goals. They are the necessary preconditions to effective interventions, whether in personal or professional settings. Only when awareness is present can action be taken in education, training, or remediation to overcome racial, gender, and sexual-orientation microaggressions.

CHAPTER THREE

The Psychological Dilemmas and Dynamics of Microaggressions

Our taxonomy of microaggressions provides us with a clear understanding of the medium by which they are delivered (verbal, behavioral, and environmental), the forms they take (microassault, microinsult, and microinvalidation), the overt or hidden messages they deliver (offensive themes), and specific examples of their manifestations. Yet, how they impact people of color, women, and LGBTs, the psychological dilemmas they present for both recipients and perpetrators, and the internal (intrapsychic) and interpersonal dynamics have been an understudied phenomena (Inzlicht & Good, 2006; Solórzano, Ceja, & Yosso, 2000; Sue, Capodilupo, et al., 2007). While the example below is used to illustrate the dilemmas and dynamics posed by racial microaggressions, it is important to note that the principles and processes uncovered appear similar to subtle gender and sexual-orientation offenses as well.

> I [Derald Wing Sue, the author, an Asian American] recently traveled with an African American colleague on a plane flying from New York to Boston. The plane was a small "hopper" with a single row of seats on one side of the aisle and a double row on the other. Because there were only a few passengers, we were told by the flight attendant (White) that we could sit anywhere, so we sat close to the front, across the aisle from one another. This made it easy for us to converse and provided a large, comfortable space for both of us. As the attendant was about

to close the hatch, three White men in suits entered the plane, were informed they could sit anywhere, and promptly seated themselves in the row in front of us. Just before take-off, the attendant began to close the overhead compartments and seemed to scan the plane with her eyes. At that point she approached us, leaned over, interrupted our conversation, and asked if we would mind moving to the back of the plane. She indicated that she needed to distribute the weight on the plane evenly.

Both of us (passengers of color) had similar negative reactions. First, balancing the weight on the plane seemed reasonable, but why were we being singled out? After all, we had boarded first and the three White men were the last passengers to arrive. Why weren't they being asked to move? Were we being singled out because of our race? Was this just a random event with no racial overtones? Were we being oversensitive and petty?

Although we complied by moving to the back of the plane, both of us felt resentment, irritation, and anger. In light of our everyday racial experiences, we both came to the same conclusion: the flight attendant had treated us like second-class citizens because of our race. But this incident did not end there. While I kept telling myself to drop the matter, I could feel my blood pressure rising, my heart beating faster, and my face flushing with anger. When the attendant walked back to make sure our seat belts were fastened, I could not contain my anger any longer. Struggling to control myself, I said to her in a forced calm voice: "Did you know that you asked two passengers of color to step to the rear of the 'bus'?" For a few seconds she said nothing, but looked at me with a horrified expression. Then she said in a righteously indignant tone, "Well, I have never been accused of that! How dare you? I don't see color! I only asked you to move to balance the plane. Anyway, I was only trying to give you more space and greater privacy."

Attempts to explain my perceptions and feelings only generated greater defensiveness from her. For every allegation I made, she seemed to have a rational reason for her actions. Finally, she broke off the conversation and refused to talk about the incident any longer. Were it not for my colleague, who validated my experiential reality, I would have left that encounter wondering whether I was incorrect in my perceptions. Nevertheless, for the rest of the flight, I stewed over the incident and it left a sour taste in my mouth. (Sue, Capodilupo, et al., 2007, p. 275)

The example above fully illustrates several of the psychological dilemmas posed to both the passengers of color and the White flight attendant. Both parties in the interaction experienced and interpreted the situation in different ways. Both were attributing meaning to the event through their life experiences and racial realities. For the White flight attendant, racism does not represent a continuing force that impacts her life. For the Asian American passenger, however, the incident represents one of many similar situations. The clash of worldviews presents a psychological dilemma that relates to the accuracy of perceptions, and begs the question "Whose reality is the correct reality?"

Furthermore, if a microaggression has occurred, how does one prove it when the perpetrator is unaware of his/her hidden motives? Studies support the conclusion that racial interactions are often tinged with racial overtones that are outside the level of awareness of well-intentioned individuals (Banaji & Greenwald, 1995; Bonilla-Silva, 2006; Dovidio, Gaertner, Kawakami, & Hodson, 2002). Four major psychological dilemmas seem to be in operation in this incident: clash of racial realities, invisibility of unintentional bias, perceived minimal harm, and the catch-22 of responding (Sue, Capodilupo, et al., 2007).

CLASH OF RACIAL REALITIES

Studies reveal that the racial reality of White Americans is very different from that of people of color. It has been found, for example, that Black Americans believe racism is a constant and continuing reality in their lives, while most Whites seem to minimize it (Astor, 1997; Babbington, 2008; Harris Poll, 1994; Pew Research Center, 2007). This perception is especially true today with the historic election of our current president, Barack Obama. Recent polls point out the stark perceptual differences between these groups.

- When asked how much discrimination still exists against Blacks, only 10% of Whites said "a lot," while 57% of Blacks said "a lot." Even more disturbing was a question that asked how much the existing racial tensions are created by Blacks. Over one-third of Whites attributed it to Black Americans, while only 3% of Blacks found their group at fault (Babbington, 2008).
- Sixty-seven percent of Blacks described encountering discrimination and prejudice when applying for jobs, 50% reported incidents during shopping or dining out, and many stated that it was a common occurrence to hear derogatory racial comments (Pew Research Center, 2007).
- In general, over 50% of Whites believe that people of color have achieved equality and that most are doing better than they really are, in contradiction to standard-of-living data (Harris Poll, 1994). On specific measures of employment, education, and housing opportunities, the gap between Black and White perceptions are startling. Seventy-six percent of Whites

believe that Blacks receive equal treatment, while less than 50% of Blacks believe so (Astor, 1997).

- There is tremendous resentment of Whites by all minority groups (African Americans, Asian Americans, and Latino/Hispanic Americans). Two-thirds of people of color say that White Americans believe they are superior, entitled to control others, insensitive to race issues, and reluctant to share power and wealth with minorities (Harris Poll, 1994).

How one views the world, especially when it comes to race relations and racial interactions, serves as a prism from which data and information are filtered. Black pedestrians in New York City attempting to hail a taxi are constantly wondering whether the cab that passed them did so because of discrimination. Studies in Manhattan reveal that Blacks attempting to flag down a cab are 25% less likely to be picked up when compared to White pedestrians (Sue, 2003). Whites, however, never entertain the possibility that they will be passed over because of the color of their skin. Nor when waiting on the street with arms outstretched do they ever think about being passed over because of the color of their skins. Yet, most Black Americans in a similar situation are very aware of that possibility. These represent two different consciousnesses and/or realities.

Another example of how racial realities are shaped can be given in the following incident. In 1999, Amadou Diallo, an innocent and unarmed 23-year-old Black immigrant, was shot and killed in a hail of 41 rounds by four New York City Police Department plain-clothed officers. At their request for identification, Diallo was holding out his wallet when shot and killed. Officers stated they thought he was pulling out a weapon. A firestorm of controversy erupted subsequent to the event as the circumstances of the shooting prompted outrage both within and outside New York City. Issues such as police brutality, racial profiling, and contagious shooting were central to the ensuing controversy (Fritsch, 2000). It is not my intent to relive the controversies and outcome of the decisions, but to describe how it differentially impacts disenfranchised groups in our society. The following narrative illustrates the psychological impact and the differences in racial realities between Blacks and Whites.

Directly after that incident, I [Derald Wing Sue] recalled a professional forum on "Racial Realities and Worldviews" during which a Black female psychologist started off her address to a primarily White audience by asking the following question: "Do any of you know what every Black mother with a teenage son experienced right after the shooting of Amadou Diallo? Do you know that every morning I rehearse with my teenage son possible scenarios of the day? Do you know I frequently ask him, when (not 'if') you are stopped by the police when driving, what will you do? Do you know that I tell him he must be polite, say 'yes sir, no sir' when responding to questions, not make any sudden moves, and to keep his hands in clear sight? Do you know that on weekends, when he is going to hang out with friends at the shopping mall, I grill and drill him with the same questions and advice about mall security guards? Do you know that as a Black mother, I live in constant fear for the safety of my own son? Can you truly understand what it is like to be Black in this society?" As White parents, this is not your reality, but it is mine!

These two examples suggest how the experiences of Whites and Blacks differ from one another and how the experiences of discrimination are invisible to White Americans. The possibility that race may affect interpersonal interactions, for example, may be far removed from the consciousness of the flight attendant. However, for the two passengers of color, race is a constant factor in their experience and touches upon nearly all aspects of their lives. Thus the issue is not whether the flight attendant was deliberately discriminating, but that her "unawareness" and "obliviousness" to race issues may allow her to impose her worldview upon marginalized groups by denying another group's experiential reality. The ability to impose a worldview upon other groups who differ in their perspectives is based upon power.

In Chapter 1, I refer to the fact that power is often correlated with economic and military might, but that "true" power resides in the ability to define reality (Guthrie, 1998; Hanna, Talley, & Guindon, 2000; Keltner & Robinson, 1996). When a clash of racial realities occurs, it is highly likely that it is mainstream groups that possess the tools (education, mass media, peers, and social groups and institutions) to define and impose realities (racial as well) upon other groups (Sue, 2004). When those in a majority culture believe that racism is no longer a problem, when difficulties in race relations are due primarily to people of color (blaming the victim), when people assume that all groups play on a level field, when everyone is perceived to have an equal chance to succeed, and when people of color are seen as being overly sensitive to slights, then it makes sense that our well-intentioned flight attendant might not recognize her potentially biased actions and the detrimental consequences they might have on passengers of color.

We return to our earlier question about whose racial reality is the most accurate: the flight attendant who truly believes in her innocence and feels betrayed because of her concern for the safety of fellow fliers, or the two passengers of color who believe the actions were tinged with racial overtones? This is not an easy question to answer and represents a true psychological dilemma. There are, however, some studies and anecdotal observations that may shed light on this question. It has been found, for example, that (1) unconscious racial, gender, and sexual-orientation biases exist in many mainstream individuals (Bonilla-Silva, 2006; Burn, Kadlac, & Rexer, 2005; Dovidio et al., 2002; Fukuyama, Miville, & Funderburk, 2005; Swim, Hyers, Cohen, & Ferguson, 2001), (2) they often appear in the form of unintentional discrimination (Dovidio & Gaertner, 2000; Rowe, 1990; Sue, Lin, Torino, Capodilupo, & Rivera, 2009), and (3) the most disempowered groups have a more accurate assessment of reality, especially relating to whether discriminatory behavior is bias-motivated (Hanna et al., 2000; Keltner & Robinson, 1996).

This last finding seems to make sense because it is consistent with the life experience of marginalized groups. Women, for example, who work for a primarily male-dominated company often say they must understand the thinking and mind-set of their male colleagues in order to do well in the company (earn retention and promotion). They often complain that no such reciprocity exists with male colleagues; for them to do well, they need not understand the worldview of female coworkers! People of color and many LGBTs also say that their individual and group survival is based on the ability to read the minds of persons of other groups. To survive in a highly racist or homophobic society, people of color and LGBTs must understand the thinking of the dominant group. Forced to operate in a predominately White, Eurocentric, male, and straight society, survival for people of color, women, and LGBTs depends on their ability to accurately discern "the truth," the potential biases they are likely to encounter, and the thoughts and actions of those who hold power over them. Some have suggested that people of color, for example, have developed a heightened perceptual awareness that is derived from adversity (Hanna et al., 2000; Sue, 2003). Thus, the hypervigilance in discerning the motives, attitudes, and the often unintentional biased contradictions of White Americans is perceived by marginalized groups not as "paranoia," but rather as functional survival skills.

Thus, in answering the question as to understanding racial realities, I pose the following questions: If you want to understand sexism, do you ask men or women? If you want to understand homophobia or heterosexism, do you ask straights or gays? If you want to understand racism, do you ask Whites or people of color? In general, if you want to understand oppression, do you ask the oppressor or the oppressed? The answers seem obvious.

INVISIBILITY OF UNINTENTIONAL BIASES

There were few doubts in the minds of the passengers of color that the flight attendant did not act from conscious bias, and that she was sincere in her belief that she acted in good faith. Her actions and their meaning were invisible to her, and she was truly stunned and dismayed that anyone could suggest that she carried out racist actions. From her racial reality, race had nothing to do with her actions; it was her role to ensure that weight was distributed in a balanced way for the safety of all occupants. She probably felt betrayed that anyone could attribute such horrendous motives to her actions, which were motivated by good intentions.

Yet, the body of research on aversive racism (Dovidio et al., 2002; Gaertner & Dovidio, 2005; Ridley, 2005), subtle sexism (Swim et al., 2001), and heterosexism (Herek, 1998; Morrison & Morrison, 2002) strongly suggest that socialization and cultural conditioning imbues within people unconscious and biased attitudes and beliefs that are directed toward specific groups; they make their appearance in unintentional biased behaviors. Interestingly, some evidence suggests that racial microaggressions—for example, through cultural conditioning—can become connected neurologically to the processing of emotions that surround prejudice (Abelson, Dasgupta, Park, & Banaji, 1998).

Let us return to the example of Amadou Diallo to illustrate the powerful conditioning that may have affected police reactions. As you recall, police officers who killed Diallo claimed that they believed he was pulling out a weapon. They believed their lives were in danger and that they had only a split second to respond (Fritsch, 2000). Many African Americans asked, however, Would police have been so quick in their actions were the suspect White? Of course, all the officers denied that they harbored racial animosity and the defense portrayed the officers as decent human beings. Yet, it is undeniable that Black men in this society have been stereotyped as hostile and angry, prone to violence, out of control, more likely to be criminals, and extremely dangerous (Jones, 1997; Plant & Peruche, 2005). The fear of Black men is likely to reside deep in the psyche of White Americans and will make its appearance unintentionally when certain specific situations trigger it (Ridley, 2005; Sue, 2003). Two important studies seem to support this conclusion.

In a study of 50 certified sworn law-enforcement officers in the state of Florida, investigators examined decisions to shoot or not to shoot Black and White criminal suspects in a computer simulation (Plant & Peruche, 2005). Participants were instructed that they would see pictures of suspects holding either a gun or a neutral object like a wallet or cell phone. In essence, the findings revealed that officers were more likely to shoot unarmed Black suspects than unarmed White ones. In another study on hidden biases, investigators examined the influence of Afrocentric facial features in criminal sentencing (Blair, Judd, & Chapleau, 2004). A random sampling of inmate records indicated that (a) Black and White inmates with similar criminal records were given roughly equivalent sentences, but (b) within each group, those with more Afrocentric features received harsher sentences than those with lesser Afrocentric features. In both studies, it appears that neither officers nor juries/judges were consciously aware that they responded differently to race.

Invisible or hidden biases from the standpoint of well-intentioned White subjects were also demonstrated in a study of "failure to help" (Dovidio et al., 2002). The investigators reasoned that unintentional racists are less likely to discriminate against people of color when appropriate behavior (nonracist) is clearly defined. However, when situations are ambiguous, and other reasons can be given for discriminatory actions, biases will be more likely to appear. To test their theory of aversive racism, two experimental conditions were created: (1) one in which subjects believed they were the only witnesses to an emergency situation and (2) one in which witnesses believed others also witnessed the situation. The emergency situation varied with the race of the injured motorist: Black or White in a disabled car. Results revealed that White bystanders offered help equally (over 80% of the time) whether the motorist was White or Black when they believed they were the only ones who witnessed the incident. However, in the second condition (believing others also saw the motorist) the Black victim was helped half as often as the White victim (38% versus 75%)!

How do we make sense of these findings? The researchers speculate that people with unconscious biases are less likely to respond in a discriminatory fashion in situations where right and wrong, and appropriate or inappropriate behaviors are clear and unambiguous. As the only person witnessing the distress, failing to help would constitute racial bias that challenges the self-image of the White bystander as a nonracist. This is far different from our earlier findings that overt and conscious racists are more likely to discriminate when anonymity exists (Sue & Capodilupo, 2008). However, in a situation that is filled with other onlookers, the appropriate behaviors become less clearly defined because other reasons (excuses) can be given for lack of involvement. For example, when asked why the White bystanders did not help, reasons such as "I thought someone else had already called," or "I planned to call when I got to the office," and so on. But, if those reasons were valid, why did the White bystanders continue to help White victims at such a high rate (75% of the time)? Dovidio and colleagues (Dovidio & Gaertner, 1996, 2000; Dovidio et al., 2002; Gaertner & Dovidio, 2005; Kawakami, Dunn, Karmali, & Dovidio, 2009) have also concluded the following:

- Modern forms of bias, especially the unconscious kind, are most likely to be manifested in a failure to help rather than in a desire to hurt. This is especially true when "inaction" is the center of bias expression. Many believe that Hurricane Katrina was the prime example of inaction and a failure to help because those left behind were people of color, the poor, and those with disabilities (Office of Ethnic Minority Affairs, 2006).
- Modern forms of bias are most likely to emerge in ambiguous situations where right or wrong behavior is not clear or when other reasons may be given for biased actions. Being able to give legitimate-sounding reasons for actions taken protects the individual from realizing their unintentional discrimination; it allows people to maintain the illusion that they acted properly and without bias.
- All these examples reveal that unintentional and unconscious bias, while seemingly trivial, can cause significant and major harm to the recipients. If indeed the injury to the Black motorist was life threatening, one can only conclude that the Black motorist is twice as likely to die as the White one. As we will shortly discuss, unintentional bias may seem small, but the consequences can be devastating.

Thus, we return to the actions of the flight attendant. Like White bystander reasons for not helping the Black motorists in distress, the flight attendant can provide many reasons for her actions: balancing weight for safety reasons, giving the passengers of color greater privacy and space, or that it was a random act, and so on. It is truly difficult for her to even entertain the notion that her actions might have been tinged with racial overtones. Because her biases may be invisible and outside her consciousness, no amount of convincing arguments by the passengers of color will allow her to see her actions in a contextual manner. Given this psychological dilemma, how do we make the "invisible" visible for well-intentioned people who harbor unconscious racist, sexist, or heterosexist attitudes and beliefs? That is not only a psychological dilemma for Whites and people of color, but it is a major challenge that is addressed in later chapters.

PERCEIVED MINIMAL HARM OF MICROAGGRESSIONS

When discussing the plane incident with White colleagues, some have encouraged me to "let go of the incident," "forgive the flight attendant," "don't make a big deal out of it," "it's not worth the time or effort to ruminate about it," "it was an innocent act," and "it's such a small thing, why are you so bothered?" The flight attendant, they contend, may indeed have engaged in a racial microaggression, but it was a "harmless and innocent" act. Even several brothers and sisters of color have encouraged me to "drop the matter." Yet I can recall sitting on the plane, deeply disturbed and bothered, ruminating about my actions, about what I should or should not have done, and feeling my blood pressure rise. Yes, the incident alone might appear to be a "small thing," harmless and trivial, but it had a major psychological impact upon me. Why should this one incident, however, have such a strong effect on my emotional state? Are people of color, women, and LGBTs "oversensitive" to small slights? I am sure that the flight attendant probably drew such a conclusion about my colleague and me.

While most of us are willing to acknowledge the harmful impact of overt racism and hate crimes on the psychological and physical well-being of persons of color (Jones, 1997), racial microaggressions are usually considered banal or small offenses (Pierce, 1978, 1988). Trivializing and minimizing racial microaggressions by some Whites often appear to be a defensive reaction to feeling blamed and guilty (Sue, Capodilupo, Nadal, & Torino, 2008). Studies reveal that racial microaggressions, while seemingly trivial in nature, have major consequences for persons of color and women. They have been found to (1) assail the mental health of recipients, causing anger, frustration, low self-esteem, and emotional turmoil (Brondolo et al., 2008; Crocker & Major, 1989; Sue, Capodilupo, & Holder, 2008; Swim et al., 2001), (2) create a hostile and invalidating campus or work climate (Rowe, 1990; Solórzano et al., 2000), (3) perpetuate stereotype threat (Cadinu, Maass, Rosabianca, & Kiesner, 2005; Steele, Spencer, & Aronson, 2002), (4) create physical health problems (Brondolo, Rieppi, Kelly, & Gerin, 2003; Clark, Anderson, Clark, & Williams, 1999; Sinclair, 2006), (5) saturate the broader society with cues that signal devaluation of social group identities (Purdie-Vaughns, Steele, Davies, & Ditlmann, 2008), and (6) lower work productivity and problem-solving abilities (Cadinu et al., 2005; Dovidio, 2001; Salvatore & Shelton, 2007).

Far from having minimal impact, microaggressions have major harmful psychological consequences to marginalized groups in this society. Even in the face of powerful evidence, some well-intentioned professionals have argued, however, that microaggressive researchers are "building a mountain out of a molehill," portraying minorities as weak and overly sensitive (Thomas, 2008), or that the analysis is one-sided by placing the blame on "perpetrators" when an interactional analysis should consider "interpersonal complementarity" (both parties contribute to the outcome) (Schacht, 2008). Let us look at these arguments in a systematic manner and see how they are flawed because they trivialize and minimize the impact of microaggressions.

First, are we building a mountain out of a molehill? Thomas (2008) characterizes racial microaggressions as "pure nonsense" and concludes that racial microaggressions "hardly necessitate the hand-wringing reactions" of people of color. He dilutes the impact of racial microaggressions by asserting that "everyone, regardless of race, occasionally experiences verbal, behavioral, or environmental indignities," and uses an example of how political conservatives might be offended by seeing yet-to-be removed "Kerry/Edwards bumper stickers." In one respect Thomas is correct: all groups and nearly everyone have experienced insults and slights in their lives. The important point missed by Thomas, however, is equating the experience of a political conservative with the experience of racism. These differ not only in quantity but in the quality of the offense.

First, many White brothers and sisters fail to understand how European Americans have historically had the power to impose and define the reality of those with lesser power. People of color must live through the indignities and oppression that have been omnipresent throughout the history of our country and continue to the present day. It has been reflected in our governmental leadership, educational systems, places of employment, and the media. People of color do not just occasionally experience racial microaggressions. Rather it is a constant, continuing, and cumulative experience. Thus, racial microaggressions remind them that they live in a country where persons of color are not frequently represented in Fortune 500 companies, that they continue to occupy the lower rungs of employment, that segregation continues in many facets of their lives, that they continue to receive inferior education and health care, and that they continue to fill the ranks of the unemployed. They may be reminded that history books never taught them about the contributions of their groups and when they are presented, it is often a dysfunctional or pathological portrayal. They may be reminded of the lack of positive images of people of color on television or in the media, or that they were once enslaved, placed in internment camps, and had their land taken from them. Again, one can hardly compare being "offended" by political bumper stickers to such experiences.

Second, Schacht (2008) claims that our analysis is one-sided, dubbing Whites as perpetrators. He likens microaggressions to an "interpersonal and psychodynamic dance" and states that whenever two people engage in such an unconscious interaction "neither party is merely a perpetrator and . . . . in meaningful ways both are victims." Thomas (2008) also harps on this theme as he asserts that contrary to our negative views of racism, which he labels "victim philosophy," we should instead focus on positive human nature, client assets, and potential solutions. These are ludicrous statements because they divert and dilute responsibility for racism. An interpersonal "dance" analysis fails to consider that a dance between two people is often characterized by an unequal status relationship; someone leads. His thinking would lead us to conclude that people of color contribute equally to their oppression. Taken to its logical consequence, for example, the interpersonal dance advocated by Schacht would actually suggest that a 7-year-old daughter who is sexually molested by her father actually contributes to her own victimization. In other words, this interpretation not only has the perpetrator "blaming the victim," but it also has the perpetrator "playing the victim"!

The perception of minimal harm from microaggressions is a psychological dilemma frequently encountered by people of color, women, and LGBTs when they try to discuss the harmful impact of a microaggressive encounter. On the surface, at times, such singular incidents of microaggressions can appear quite innocuous and innocent, but they nevertheless contribute to major harm for the recipients.

THE CATCH-22 OF RESPONDING TO MICROAGGRESSIONS

When a potential microaggression occurs, the recipient is placed in a very unenviable position, or a catch-22. In the case of the flight attendant's request to move to the rear of the plane, many possible questions flood the targeted passenger:

> "Did what I think happened really happen? Was this a deliberate act or an unintentional slight? How should I respond? Sit and stew over it or confront the person? If I bring the topic up, how do I prove it? Is it really worth the effort? Should I just drop the matter?" (Sue, Capodilupo, et al., 2007, p. 279).

First, a potential microaggression induces attributional ambiguity:*"What was behind the flight attendant's request?"* (Crocker & Major, 1989). It depletes psychological energy by diverting attention away from the surrounding environment in an attempt to interpret the motive and meaning of the person's actions. A female middle manager who is never invited by male colleagues to lunch may wonder about the motives of her male coworkers. A gay man who is passed over for a promotion and told the company offered it to the "most qualified" applicant may spend considerable time and energy trying to discern whether the action was biased. A student of color who is presented with readings that seem to portray his group stereotypically may feel demeaned and alienated. In all three examples, psychological energy must be expended to (1) discern the truth, (2) protect oneself from insults and invalidations, and (3) try to ascertain what actions should be taken. In all three cases, these individuals may be disadvantaged in fully engaging in the worksite or classroom. Their work productivity, problem-solving abilities, and learning capabilities can suffer immensely (Cadinu et al., 2005; Salvatore & Shelton, 2007; Steele et al., 2002).

Attributional ambiguity causes major energy-depleting problems for marginalized populations when "double messages" are sent. On one hand, the actions from the perspective of the sender can be seen as rational and bias-free. But, on the other hand, the actions may become suspect because they seem to happen with consistency only to people of color, women, and LGBTs. Returning to our flight attendant example, being asked to move was not the first time that similar requests have occurred to both passengers. Most marginalized groups use contextual interpretations to add meaning to interpersonal encounters: that is, they evaluate similar experiences they have encountered over time and in different places (Dovidio & Gaertner, 2000). When done, they may conclude that the only thing that ties together the multiple experiences they have in similar situations is "the color of their skin," "their gender," or "their sexual orientation." The flight attendant, however (like many White brothers and sisters), does not share these experiences; she is likely to evaluate the plane encounter as a singular or isolated event. She finds it difficult to see a pattern of bias and is defended by a belief in her own morality.

Second, a decision to respond or not to respond to a potential microaggression may have complex effects on the recipient (Sue, Capodilupo, Nadal, et al., 2008; Sue, Lin, Torino, et al., 2009). One of the greatest concerns of people of color, women, or LGBTs is the consequences of confronting perpetrators with their actions or statements. Should a female employee who is constantly complimented by her male boss for "classy and sexy attire," but never once acknowledged for her work contributions, confront him? Should a Latino student who experiences a microaggression from his or her professor raise the matter in class? How does a gay male adolescent, who hears a fellow classmate describing another's behavior as "gay," deal with the remark, especially if he has not "come out of the closet"? (Sue & Capodilupo, 2008). Work on racial microaggression seems to suggest several possible reactions (Sue, Capodilupo, et al., 2007; Sue, Nadal, et al., 2008; Sue, Capodilupo, Nadal, et al., 2008). The most frequent reaction to microaggressions seems to be doing nothing. This happens for several reasons.

1. *Attributional ambiguity—inability to determine whether a microaggression has occurred.* When a potential racial, gender, or sexual-orientation offense occurs, heightened vigilance and attempts to make sense of the encounter is likely to occur. Attributional ambiguity may make it very difficult to conclude that an offense was committed. While a woman may suspect that a remark or behavior constituted a gender microaggression, she remains uncertain even though skeptical. In these cases, the recipient may simply drop the matter or choose to do nothing. Certainly, the two passengers on the plane may have chosen to do nothing because the reasons given by the flight attendant, on the surface, appeared reasonable and rational.

2. *Response indecision—not knowing the best way or how to respond.* Even when the microaggression is obvious, the individual may experience confusion and uncertainty about how best to respond. How does one, for example, respond to the flight attendant's request to move? Should the passengers of color simply refuse? Should they make a fuss and ask why the three White men were not requested to move? Should the passengers simply comply and not make a big issue out of it? If a choice is made to respond, should the passengers express their outrage, or try to do so in an educative and objective manner?

3. *Time-limited responding—the incident is over before a response can be made.* Most microaggressive messages are embedded in a wider array of communications in which multiple messages and meanings are delivered during an interaction and encounter. They are also likely to occur rapidly and are usually over in a very short period of time (usually seconds). The passing innocent remark (a damning compliment), ignoring a colleague of color (you are not worth my attention), describing a female employee as "bitchy" (sexist remark), refusing to shake the hand of a gay male (may catch AIDS), and many other incidents occur so quickly that the moment for possible intervention has come and gone.

4. *Denying experiential reality—engaging in self-deception by believing it did not happen.* Occasionally, people of color, in the face of a microaggression, may deny the hidden and demeaning intent, meaning, and impact. Statements such as "They didn't mean anything by that," "It's just an innocent remark," or "I've known John for years and he doesn't have a racist bone in his body" are used to excuse the offender, to minimize the offense, and to interpret the situation in a nonbiased manner. In most of these cases, it appears that the denial of experiential reality is due to two factors: (1) a close and interdependent relationship with the offender, and/or (2) fear of acknowledging what the microaggression may say about the recipient. In the first instance, entertaining the notion that a favorite uncle or relative, close neighbor, or colleague, classmates, or a friend might be unconsciously biased toward you and members of your group may be quite devastating to a valued relationship. In the latter instance, it might be equally difficult for marginalized group members to accept the fact that they are perceived negatively. An adolescent of color who yearns to be accepted by peers would be devastated to entertain the possibility that he/she is perceived negatively because of his/ her race. To counter these two dynamics, self-deception may occur.

5. *Impotency of actions—"It won't do any good, anyway."* Believing that one's actions will have minimal positive impact on the situation is another reason for inaction. People of color, women, and LGBTs have often been in situations in which they have raised objections and acted to educate others with the end result of only a minimal difference. Indeed, sometimes the situation is made worse, as when a student of color constantly raises multicultural and diversity issues in class, only to be seen as a "troublemaker" and as having an "axe to grind" about race issues. The individual may develop a sense of helplessness, powerlessness,

or hopelessness of having any impact upon the situation. Another reason may be a conscious desire to conserve one's energies, rather than to expend oneself in situations that have minimal chances for success.

6. **Fearing the consequences—interpersonal power differentials determine degree of threat.** A lack of response is often the result of an assessment between action benefits versus threat (negative personal consequences). When people of color, women, and LGBTs hold greater power or occupy an equal status relationship with people in the majority society, they are more likely to respond directly to a microaggression. Those who are least empowered are more likely to raise issues in organizations or with colleagues when they reach a critical numerical mass, generally considered to be 20% to 25% of the population. Even if a critical mass is reached, power still resides with those most representative of the dominant group. By definition, then, marginalized groups in our society generally do not hold greater interpersonal, institutional, or social influence and power. In most group relationships, men–women, gays–straights, and Whites–people of color are inherently unequal. In the work setting, for example, how do female employees confront their male colleagues when microinequities occur? What happens to them when they do? How do Black students in class respond to White professors who commit racial microaggressions? What happens to them when they do? Threat of retaliation in various forms is always on the minds of those who are disempowered systemically. Social isolation, being perceived as a troublemaker, not getting a promotion or being fired at work, and receiving a lower grade in class are possible consequences. In such an environment, people of color, women, and LGBTs are likely to think twice about taking action.

While all of these reasons hold some validity for nonresponse on the part of marginalized individuals, they potentially possess major psychological and physical harm. It may mean the loss of integrity, lowered self-esteem, experiencing pent-up anger and frustration, somaticizing problems, and so forth. However, choosing to take action in the face of microaggressions may also hold dangers that lead directly to the catch-22.

Returning to the plane incident, I [Derald Wing Sue] would also like to share additional details of my encounter with the flight attendant. During my heated conversation, I had expected my African American colleague to come to my aid or to at least support me. Yet she said nothing throughout the interaction and only smiled and laughed so loudly that many passengers kept looking back. When the flight attendant left, I turned to her and angrily asked, "Why didn't you say anything?" She responded by saying "Derald, it just feels so good to not always be the angry Black woman."

My colleague's response is representative of what many Black women often share with me. When they decide to confront the microaggressor, they may trigger stereotypes that label them as "angry Black women" who are overly sensitive and paranoid. Thus, responding in an emotional or angry manner may be pathologized by the transgressor. Jones (1997) has revealed how stereotypes are often triggered when protestations by Blacks are made to unfair and discriminatory treatment: an emotional outburst often lends credence to the belief that African Americans are hostile, angry, impulsive, and prone to violence.

R. D. Laing, an existential psychiatrist, once asked the following question concerning schizophrenia: Is schizophrenia a *sick response to a healthy society* or is it a *healthy response to a sick society*? What he was trying to say was that the symptoms or reactions of individuals must be evaluated or judged from some standard or context. If microaggressions are acknowledged as pathological and defined as the problem, then reactions like anger and a desire to strike back become more understandable and normative. However, if the context and actions (microaggressions) are unseen and considered normative, then the reactions of those oppressed take on a pathological meaning. As long as microaggressions remain invisible to the aggressor, reactions to them by marginalized groups place them in an unenviable position: they are damned if they don't (not take action) and damned if they do (take action)! This is the catch-22 posed by microaggressions.

The Way Forward

Dealing with Psychological Dilemmas

One of the most important questions addressed in future chapters is "What types of responses would be functional and adaptive for marginalized groups, and what type of responses would be most beneficial and educational for microaggressors?" On the awareness and knowledge level, however, the following may prove helpful to readers.

1. As Chapter 2 indicates, all of us are both perpetrators and targets of racial, gender, and sexual-orientation microaggressions. We have served

(Continued)

in both roles. As such, it should be easier to understand how damaging microaggressions are to marginalized groups in our society. A gay man who has experienced heterosexist microaggressions can use that experience to more honestly appraise his own attitudes and behaviors toward African Americans. When Black Americans speak about racial microaggressions they have experienced from others or even from you personally, it is important to attempt to understand. I am often amazed about how similar experiences of discrimination (racial, gender, or sexual orientation) do not necessarily make it easier to relate to other oppressed groups. One would think that having experienced oppression, an oppressed group member would find it easier to relate to other devalued groups. None of us are free from inheriting the racial, gender, and sexual-orientation biases of our ancestors and society. We are all victims in one way or another by a social conditioning process that has imbued within us biases, fears, and stereotypes about others. We must be honest with ourselves and be willing to own up to our shortcomings. Becoming defensive or using our own oppression to invalidate other socially devalued groups (e.g., "I have it worse than you") is a form of microaggression itself.

2. Contrary to what many well-intentioned people believe, it is important for the general public and especially those in employment, health care, and education to realize the detrimental consequences of racial, gender, and sexual-orientation microaggressions. As indicated in the chapter, many psychologists are unsympathetic with those who conduct research on microaggressions and claim that they are detrimental to the well-being of marginalized groups. They assert that these claims are "building a mountain out of a molehill," "exaggerating their effects," and "inaccurately painting targets as weak and unable to deal with small slights." In essence, they express minimal sympathy for the plight of people of color, women, or LGBTs who complain about the everyday slights and indignities visited upon them. As long as people perceive microaggressions as innocent and "small hurts" delivered by good, moral, and decent people, inaction in practice and policy will allow the continuance of injustice and unfairness to flourish without conscious awareness. It is important for people to realize that contrary to a belief that microaggressions do minimal harm, research reveals that they oppress, create disparities in our society toward marginalized groups, and contribute to psychological stress and distress for these groups.

(Continued)

3. Do not invalidate the experiential realities of diverse groups in our society. Be aware that privilege and power oftentimes makes it difficult to see the perspectives of those who experience discrimination and prejudice in their day-to-day lives. Don't be quick to dismiss and negate challenges. Entertain the notion that disempowered groups in our society often have a more accurate perception of reality that deals with their day-to-day experiences of insults and invalidations due to their racial, gender, or sexual identities. If indeed microaggressions are indicative of worldviews of inclusion–exclusion, normality–abnormality, and superiority–inferiority, then it is important to become aware that your view of the world may be culture-bound and prevent you from seeing the world through the eyes of other groups. Instead of denying their racial, gender, or sexual-orientation realities, try to understand their frame of reference. Don't become defensive and impose your interpretation of situations or actions upon those who challenge your views. This recommendation dictates that (1) you become aware of your values, biases, and assumptions about human behavior—your worldview—and (2) the experiential realities of other groups—their worldviews.

4. Related to all the points above has been our constant emphasis on not becoming defensive when people of color, women, or LGBTs imply that you have personally engaged in a microaggressive remark or behavior. Being open to discussing, exploring, and clarifying the matter will do much to engender trust and to positively seal a relationship. Not only will you grow from the experience, but it will have a healing and liberating effect on marginalized group members that will counteract the years of pain and humiliation they have been forced to endure. I would surmise that all of us have committed microaggressions or racial, gender, and sexual-orientation blunders. The issue should not be "to cover up" but how to recover. In many cases a simple "I'm sorry" is all that may be called for.

5. Finally, it is important to view microaggressions as reactions to unjust exposure to hostile and invalidating societal climates that insult, demean, and invalidate marginalized groups. Reactions of anger, impatience, and frustration communicated to perpetrators should be seen in an empathic manner and not pathologized. To do so blames the victim by focusing on their responses, rather than on the unhealthy environments that create such responses. I am not arguing that there

(Continued)

may be different, more productive ways for those victimized by microaggressions to respond, but that understanding that the cause resides in the systems of unfairness and in the unconscious acts of well-intentioned people allows us to address wrongs at the core of the true problem.

Microaggressive Impact on Targets and Perpetrators

CHAPTER FOUR

The Microaggression Process Model: From Beginning to End

In many respects, I was naive, but now I'm cynical . . . . When I took my science courses, I had to fight every day through all the racism I felt . . . . Each time I took a new class, the same thing happened over and over and over and over again. Many times I was the only African American in the class. [The White students and professor] were like, "You know what, I don't think she knows what she's talking about," or . . . "Well, you got here because of affirmative action, not your grades or your merit." And when you try and voice something to somebody, they don't want to hear it. They're not about to hear it! And they're like, "Well, you need to be alone with your other peers." I'm upset. I'm tired of it. That's why I changed my major to English." (Solórzano, Ceja, & Yosso, 2000, p. 64)

I [White woman] was at my desk and I saw the boss [male] going around our cubicle introducing a new male coworker to each member of the team. He would spend a few minutes with each worker. When he got to me, the boss introduced me as "Jenny" and I'm "Jeannie." Worse yet, he said I had been there about a year, and I've been with the firm for nearly three years! Come on, what does it take to be noticed. The new worker shook my hand, but instead of looking at me, kept looking at my breasts and I thought "Jeez, another one. I'm only a boob to them."

Hiding was so exhausting. I always had to watch myself. I always had to make sure that I was not acting too butch or dressing too much like a dyke. I always felt like I was trying to be someone who I wasn't, always trying to fit in where I knew I didn't fit. It was really hard. I really felt all alone, I thought I was the only person in the world who felt this way . . . . I was tired of hiding it and I got to a point where I didn't care who knew. (Mallon, 1998, p. 119)

In Chapter 3 we speak about how microaggressions are a constant and continuing reality for people of color, women, and LGBTs. They often appear to be small slights that in isolation produce minimal harm to recipients. However, being exposed to a lifetime of daily assaults, insults, disregard, and disrespect has been shown to be extremely harmful unless mitigated in some fashion. The effects of microaggressions may be compared to the perennial "slow death by a thousand cuts."

It is reported that Maya Angelou has likened racial microaggressions or petty humiliations to "small murders," in contrast to the blatant forms of oppressions called "grand executions," in which the lethal nature of biased acts is obvious (Greene, 2000). Microaggressions have the lifelong insidious effects of silencing, invalidating, and humiliating the identity and/or voices of those who are oppressed. Although their lethality is less obvious, they nevertheless grind down and wear out the victims.

Studies reveal that a lifetime of microaggressions takes a major toll on the psychological functioning of marginalized groups in our society (Constantine & Sue, 2007; Crocker & Major, 1989; Herek, Gillis, & Cogan, 2009; Lyness & Thompson, 2000; National Academies, 2006; Pierce, 1978, 1988, 1995; Salvatore & Shelton, 2007; Solórzano et al., 2000; Steele, Spencer, & Aronson, 2002; Symanski, 2009). When speaking about the Black experience, for example, microaggressions have been described as "offensive mechanisms used against blacks"; they are "often innocuous," but the "cumulative weight of their never-ending burden" may result in "diminished mortality, augmented morbidity, and flattened confidence" (Pierce, Carew, Pierce-Gonzalez, & Willis, 1978).

In the three examples above, racial, gender, and LGBT microaggressions have exacted a tremendous and terrible psychological toll on the targets and have potentially altered their life course. In the case of the African American student, racial microaggressions (environmental isolation, ascription of lower intelligence, and denial of racial reality) have led to fatigue, cynicism, anger, and even actions to change from a science to an English major. This is a sad state of affairs when we realize that these incidents have irreparably altered the career path and possible quality of life for this young African American woman.

Likewise, in the second example, the female worker at her place of employment is also asked to endure constant sexual objectification, belittlement, and disregard. Her lack of recognition by a superior and male coworker who seems only to notice her body demean and diminish whatever contributions and accomplishments she achieves in the workplace. The boss does not even remember her name. In this case, the lack of recognition, through no fault of her own, may result in missed opportunities for a promotion (Sue, Lin, & Rivera, 2009).

Finally, in an environment that sends messages of heterosexism such as "Don't ask, don't tell," and that directly and indirectly punishes gays, lesbians, and transgendered people for "coming out," invisibility, isolation, and silencing are a way of life for LGBTs (Hunter & Mallon, 2000). In order to "get along with others" or to even have any relationship with significant others (parents, siblings, and relatives), for example, a gay man may feel compelled to maintain silence because his sexual orientation is a taboo topic. Sexual orientation, silence, and shame become equated with one another (O'Brien, 2005).

THE MICROAGGRESSION PROCESS MODEL

Few studies have actually traced the impact of microaggressions from beginning to end. From the moment a microaggression presents itself, what internal psychological mechanisms are activated? How does a woman, for example, process an incident of subtle sexism from a cognitive, emotional, and behavior standpoint? What goes into the process of deciding how one should act in the face of a microaggression? What short-term and long-term consequences do microaggressions have on recipients? How do marginalized groups cope in the face of these assaults and are some coping mechanisms more adaptive than others?

To address these questions, my research team conducted two separate studies, one on a group of African American participants (Sue, Capodilupo, & Holder, 2008), and another on a mixed group of informants of color (Sue, Lin, Torino, Capodilupo, & Rivera, 2009). While the findings reported below apply mainly to racial microaggressions, I believe the process described may also be applicable to how women and LGBTs process and deal with subtle sexism and heterosexism as well. Nevertheless, research on these two populations and other marginalized groups would be invaluable in identifying similar and dissimilar variants of microaggressive processes. Table 4.1 identifies and summarizes the five domains (phases) that seem likely to occur

Table 4.1   The Microaggression Process Model

DOMAIN	DOMAIN EXAMPLES
Phase One—Incident: An event or situation experienced by the participant.	"[The hostess] says, 'Your table's ready.' And [my friend asks] 'Is it in the main dining room?' and the lady says 'No.' 'Well, we want to sit in the main dining room.' She's like, 'I wasn't aware that you wanted the main dining room.' My friend asks, 'Is it because we're Black and we're young? You can't seat us in the main dining room because we can't afford the main dining room?'"
	"Sometimes they follow you. I mean, you go to Macy's or Bloomingdale's, I mean, especially as a black man, I mean every time I go in that place, somebody's watching me, somebody's walking behind me, trying to monitor me. They don't want me out of their sight until I leave."
Phase Two—Perception: Participant's belief about whether or not the incident was racially motivated. Responses reflect: Yes/No/ Unsure, Questioning.	"Well, to me it's almost one of those things where you actually have to admit to a level of paranoia. I mean, you are constantly asking 'was that racist?' Am I wrong? Times are I can tell one way or another. Other times it's being constantly on guard. I have to now look at the state of my mental health."
	"I don't know, for me it's hard because you're taught to not try to attribute everything, everything that happens to racism. I mean, there's still that kind of, well, is there a reason why it happened? Is it just me?"
Phase Three—Reaction: Participant's immediate response to the incident.	
1. Cognitive: A reaction that involves thought processes, whether spoken or internal.	"Or like—and I'm thinking, 'What do you mean why do I work so hard? Am I not supposed to work hard?' You know, I guess I had never been looked at negatively for working hard. Usually, it's like, oh, you know, 'Thanks for staying.' But you know, like there was no praise for being a good worker.
2. Behavioral: A reaction that involves an action.	"I'm determined that I'm not going to allow racism to take my voice—which is how I see it, as opposed to being paranoid—is that I have people in my sphere of influence that I can call up and share my authentic feelings with."
3. Emotional: A reaction that involves an emotion.	"I get so angry. What a racist! There it goes again. It's this whole damn thing, and I'm thinking, 'Oh my God! Over and over. I'm so tired and exhausted.'"

(Continued)

Table 4.1   *(Continued)*

DOMAIN	DOMAIN EXAMPLES
	"My date is looking for me to get a cab. But they keep passing. So it's just constant humiliation. It's just humiliation."
Phase Four—Interpretation: The meaning the participant makes of the incident, answering such questions as: Why did the event occur? What were the person's intentions?	"They treated me like the angry black woman and like afraid how I'm going to come back." "But subtle, it's more like they want to find out what I know and who I am before they trust me with it."
Phase Five—Consequence for Individual: Behavioral, emotive, or thought processes which develop over time as a result of said incident.	"And I think I've learned in a lot of ways to sort of shield myself from any kind of, like, personal hurt that would come out of it. Like I don't blame it on myself, it's not like 'What's wrong with me?' It's like, "Oh, that's that White unconsciousness that they're so well-trained in.'"

when a potential racial microaggression presents itself: Incident, Perception, Reaction, Interpretation, and Consequence.

Phase One—The Potential Microaggressive Incident or Event

Potential microaggressive incidents set in motion a chain of psychological events within recipients that may directly or indirectly effect their interpersonal interactions. Incidents may be the result of (a) ongoing interactions between perpetrators and recipients (discussions of topics between individuals or groups of people during social events), (b) more distant and passive relationships (overhearing comments made by a stranger in a subway), or (c) those in which environmental cues signal a devaluation of group identities (all male pictures of past CEOs in a board room). For African Americans, communications regarding the following themes have been found to be especially offensive, but very common (Sue, Nadal, et al., 2008):

- Ascription of intellectual inferiority
- Second-class citizenship
- Assumption of criminality
- Assumption of inferior status
- Assumed universality of the Black experience
- Assumed superiority of White cultural values/communication styles

While there is considerable overlap and commonality, Asian American microaggressions with the following themes have been found to be directed toward them (Sue, Bucceri, Lin, Nadal, & Torino, 2007):

- Alien in one's own land
- Ascription of intelligence
- Denial of racial reality
- Exoticization of Asian American women
- Invalidation of interethnic differences
- Pathologizing cultural values/communication styles
- Second-class citizenship
- Invisibility

For women, it has been proposed that the following microaggressive themes are quite common (Nadal, in press; Sue & Capodilupo, 2008):

- Sexual objectification
- Second-class citizenship
- Use of sexist language
- Assumption of inferiority
- Restrictive gender roles
- Denial of the reality of sexism
- Denial of individual sexism
- Invisibility
- Sexist humor jokes

For LGBT people, it has been proposed that the following microaggressive themes are common (Nadal, Rivera, & Corpus, in press; Sue & Capodilupo, 2008):

- Oversexualization
- Homophobia
- Heterosexist language/terminology
- Sinfulness
- Assumption of abnormality
- Denial of individual heterosexism
- Endorsement of heteronormative culture and behaviors

Incidents possessing these themes may be interpreted as microaggressions as they contain derogatory racial, gender, or LGBT overtones. The medium of their delivery may be through verbal, behavioral, and environmental channels.

Verbal

Verbal incidents are direct or indirect comments to targets. For example, during a racially mixed social gathering for students at the university, a White male faculty member was engaged in a conversation with a Black male student. The faculty member lamented how many well-qualified and quite brilliant students were being rejected by the university because of enrollment limits. The Black student agreed and stated that he felt quite fortunate to have been admitted to Columbia. The faculty member then stated: *"Yes, you certainly are, young man. I pity White males now because they are the ones being discriminated against."*

Hidden Messages: *"You did not make it into an Ivy League school on your own merit but through some affirmative action program. White males are the ones now being discriminated against."*

Nonverbal/Behavioral

Nonverbal incidents are experiences that include the use of body language or more direct physical actions. For example, in class, openly gay/lesbian students often report that fellow straight classmates often choose not to sit near them. One Black male information technology employee/troubleshooter describes how he oftentimes gets "double takes" when he enters a company and announces that he has been sent to fix their malfunctioning informational system. Another Black informant describes how clerks often treat her: *"The way that my money is given back to me when I go shopping . . . . I put money in someone's hand and they won't put the money back in my hand. They'll make sure that they put the money on the counter"* (Sue, Capodilupo, & Holder, 2008). She goes on to describe how offensive these incidents are, especially when the clerk freely places change back into the hands of White customers.

Hidden Messages: *"Blacks are not supposed to be intelligent." "I don't want to risk catching anything from Gays/Lesbians or Blacks."*

Environmental

In many situations, the physical surroundings represent the microaggressive event (Purdie-Vaughns, Davis, Steele, & Ditlmann, 2008; Solórzano et al., 2000).

We have already described how symbols and mascots may convey insulting and demeaning messages. Educational curriculum that comes only from a White, European American, and male perspective represents invalidating micro-aggressions. Others are more commonly observed in everyday interactions. For example, a Black participant reports a frequent workplace experience, "*And you notice that, all right, yeah . . . there's a lot of minorities. But what positions are they in? Entry-level. Maybe middle management. And then they thin out, you know, if you're talking about execs and you know, managing directors*" (Sue, Capodilupo, & Holder, 2008).

Hidden Messages: "*People of color do not belong in the higher echelons of the work force. They are not leadership material.*"

Phase Two—Perception and Questioning of the Incident

This phase pertains to the recipient's attempt to determine whether an event was racially motivated or not. Was the incident racist, sexist, or heterosexist? Perception refers to the participants' belief about whether an incident was bias-motivated. It is a more complex and dynamic phenomenon than simply ascertaining whether the target arrives at a "yes, bias motivated" or a "no, not bias motivated" conclusion. There is an internal struggle that is often-times energy depleting. In our studies (Sue, Capodilupo, & Holder, 2008; Sue, Nadal, et al., 2008), one of the important core ideas of the perception phase is the process of "Questioning."

As mentioned in other chapters, microaggressions are often ambiguous, filled with double messages, and subtle in their manifestations. The overt message is often at odds with the hidden one. Questioning refers to participants who question whether or not an incident was racially motivated. Many factors often go into the assessment process: relationship to the perpetrator (relative, friend, coworker, or stranger), the racial/cultural identity development of the recipient, the thematic content of the microaggression, and personal experiences of the target. All are factors in construing meaning to the event. For example, a Black participant may wrestle with an incident in which a White instructor told her an answer was "very smart:" "*Like it feels like a compliment but not really. It leaves you feeling like, did you just compliment me or what?*" Another participant has a similar struggle when a White woman changed seats on the subway train from sitting next to her: "*Maybe it just so happened that the person that she decided to sit next to wasn't Black, and she wasn't Black. I can't say that's why she moved, but maybe she wanted to be close to the window. I don't know*" (Sue, Capodilupo, & Holder, 2008).

Phase Three—Reaction Processes

In the reaction phase, a more integrated response of the person becomes central in dealing with the offending event, the emotional turmoil, and the need for self-care. This process refers to the target's immediate response that is more than a simple "yes," "no," or "ambiguous" perception of the event. It represents an inner struggle that evokes strong cognitive, behavioral, and emotional reactions. Several common reactions are described here (Sue, Capodilupo, & Holder, 2008; Sue, Capodilupo, et al., 2007).

Healthy Paranoia

A very common response from many marginalized group members is called "healthy paranoia or cultural mistrust," which seems to operate before, during, and after a microaggressive incident. Because experiences of prejudice and discrimination are a social reality for many marginalized groups, they have developed a healthy suspicion of the motives and behaviors of members of the dominant culture (Croteau, Lark, et al., 2005; Ponterotto, Utsey, Lance, & Pedersen, 2006; Ridley, 2005; Sue & Sue, 2008). As indicated by racial minorities, for example, survival is dependent on the ability to discern the true motives of their oppressors (Sue, 2003). Healthy paranoia calls for the recipient of microaggressions to give equal or even greater weight to viewing incidents from past experiences of prejudice and discrimination, and not simply by what the offending person says: *"I'm not against interracial relationships, but I worry about the children."* This statement contains an overt and explicit statement ("I'm not racist") followed by a more ambiguous one ("I am ambivalent about interracial relationships only because I worry about the children"). From past experiences of people of color, the coded message of the last statement is really an unconscious statement of one's own racial bias.

Many people of color, women, and LGBTs will thus determine their reality by viewing events through the prism of their experiences with racism, sexism, and homophobia. People of color often state that they encounter numerous White colleagues, neighbors, and friends who often deny their racial biases, but that their behaviors belie such denials. To live in a constant state of "questioning" is emotionally draining because of the overwhelming number of microaggressive incidents that take place in the course of any given day. The following conversation from a Black informant typifies this dilemma:

> "Well, to me it's almost one of those things where you actually have to admit to a level of paranoia. I mean you have to sort of somehow—to begin to examine,

well, was that racist? That's sort of the fine line you have to walk around letting things go by and then also taking them on, 'cause I'm telling you, you could find a thousand offenses in any moment of the day." (Sue, Capodilupo, & Holder, 2008)

Healthy paranoia serves several functions: (1) it warns against simply accepting offender definitions of whether racial, gender, or sexual-orientation microaggressions were delivered; (2) it allows targets to use lived experiences as a counterbalance in determining racial, gender, and sexual-orientation realities; (3) it reduces energy depletion by terminating constant internal questioning and rumination; and (4) it may lead to functional and adaptive mechanisms to deal with the slights, invalidations, and insults that are delivered.

Sanity Check

One of the greatest oppressive elements of microaggressions is in the form of microinvalidations where the experiential reality and racial, gender, or sexual-orientation reality of targets are challenged (Sue, Capodilupo, Nadal, & Torino, 2008). As we have stressed, power is in a group's ability to define reality. When a microaggression occurs, for example, the perpetrator may deny the hidden message and challenge the experiential reality of the target. People of color, for example, are often caught in a double bind because of double messages being sent by perpetrators. Most microaggressions, especially those that arise from aversive racism, contain an overt message and a metamessage. In many cases, the targets are often told they have misinterpreted the incident, are overly sensitive, and should accept the perpetrator's statements: *"Race had nothing to do with it." "I believe you are misreading the situation." "Why does everything have to do with race?" "Just let go of it, I didn't mean to offend you."*

When a microaggression occurs in the context of other majority group members, they most likely share the beliefs of the perpetrator. Can you imagine what it is like to be, for example, the only student of color in a predominantly White institution where everyone and everything conveys that your reality is wrong or inaccurate? One Black participant put it succinctly: *"At times, you begin to question your own sanity. Like, am I going insane?"*

The sanity check is often used by people of color in such situations. In our study, we found that Black targets reported using one another (other Black/African American friends, family members, and coworkers) as a way to check the accuracy of their perceptions. One participant stated that *"As opposed to being paranoid—I have people in my sphere of influence that I can call up and share my authentic feelings with, so that there's sort of this healing, there's just this healing circle that I have around myself, and these are people who I don't have to be rational with if I'm battling racism."* One Black coworker described how he checks things out with other Blacks in the worksite nonverbally, *"I mean, you see it in their eyes, like a connection across the room . . . and they tell you all the things that have been going on in their office that's been driving them crazy."* The sanity check serves multiple purposes: (1) it reaffirms one's experiential reality, (2) it communicates that the target is not alone and that others experience similar things, and (3) it creates a validating group experience that immunizes targets against future subtle expressions of racism, sexism, or heterosexism.

Empowering and Validating Self

Victim blaming is a common process often facilitated because of attributional ambiguity (Crocker & Major, 1989). Is the plight of people of color (high unemployment rates, low educational attainment, poverty, etc.), for example, due to internal weaknesses and undesirable attributes (less intelligence, weak motivation, poor family values), or does the blame reside in the larger external environment (prejudice and discrimination, structural inequities, etc.)? Are targets of a microaggression simply misreading the situation due to oversensitivity or a defect in reality testing, or have they accurately assessed the hostile and invalidating external situation?

One of the adaptive mechanisms used by our participants against microaggressive incidents is the shifting of "fault" to the aggressor rather than the target. People of color in our study reported this type of reaction as "empowering" and "shielding" because it locates blame and fault in the perpetrator rather than themselves. One participant stated, *"I don't blame it on myself; it's not like, what's wrong with me? It's like, oh, that's that White unconsciousness that they're so well trained in."* This sentiment is also shared by others in our study:

> African American male: *"I feel good in that, you know, 'cause I won't want to go home anymore trying to figure out what happened, and it does take a certain amount of courage for me to say, you know, I'm going to stop asking myself this question, I'm going to ask it to you."*
>
> African American female: *"I find that is keeping your voice . . . . If I decide I want to do an intervention, I'm not necessarily doing it for them. I'm doing it for me."*

In many respects empowering and validating the self seems to be highly correlated with people of color, women, and LGBTs who are firmly rooted in their own racial, gender, and sexual-orientation identities. They trust their intuitive thoughts, beliefs, and feelings, evaluate events and experiences from an internal locus of control, are less externally oriented, and are active in using contextual cues to evaluate situations. While they may engage in sanity checks with others, their interpretations and actions are less determined by how others respond.

Rescuing Offenders

Among the most surprising of the findings related to reactions of targets to microaggressions was the theme of "rescuing offenders," or at least of excusing them for their actions. Several of our Black participants reported feeling a pull to take care of White people who committed a microaggressive offense. Their stories seemed to indicate a tendency to consider offenders' feelings in the situation before their own. One informant described a very typical microaggression experienced by Black Americans. *"I got on the elevator of a hotel, from their parking garage, and it was really late at night, really early morning . . . around 2 A.M., I think. Anyway, I had just come back with friends from a baseball game . . . . the elevator stopped at the lobby level and a White woman, really dressed up, got on. She didn't see me at first and pushed the button to go to her room, I think. When the elevator started, she turned and saw me. She immediately gripped her purse, and her hand covered her necklace . . . . I felt sorry for her. She doesn't have to be afraid . . . . I wasn't going to rob her. So, I took off my baseball cap, and moved back. I said good evening and smiled. Poor woman, she still didn't relax."*

Despite the microaggressive message (Assumption of Criminality) that many African Americans interpret as offensive and insulting, this young Black man seemed more concerned with the welfare of the woman than himself. His intent and actions seemed to be aimed at putting the woman at ease, communicating that she had nothing to fear, and portraying himself as law abiding. Not only was he cognizant of the fears of the woman, but he did not seem overly offended, if any, with her behavior. Several other examples given by our participants also revealed similar and varying degrees of this "other directed" response. Explaining this reaction appears complex. Most of our work generally reveals people of color to become incensed and/or very bothered by microaggressions.

In speaking with these individuals, it appears that several factors may account for this "rescuing the offender" reaction. First, some people of color have stated that White people "just can't help it." The recognition is that Whites have inherited the racial biases of their ancestors and are culturally conditioned to fear Black men. Behind this reasoning lies an implicit assumption or belief that not only are people of color victims, but that Whites are also victimized. In other words, no one at birth was born with the conscious intention of becoming racist, sexist, or homophobic. These attributes were not chosen through free choice but instead culturally conditioned upon Whites.

Second, it appears that some people of color make an attempt to distinguish between whom and what is the "true enemy." In the film *The Color of Fear* (Stir-Fry Productions, 1994), a group of White men and men of color engage in an intense and difficult dialogue on race. At one point, one of the Black participants refers to White people as "the enemy." He is immediately corrected by Victor, another Black man, who states "White people are not the enemy. White supremacy is!" The observation below by a White woman may typify an equivalent recognition that motivates "rescuing the offender."

> In this sense we Whites are the victims of racism. Our victimization is different from that of minorities, but it is real. We have been programmed into the oppressor roles we play, without our informed consent in the process. Our unawareness is part of the programming: None of us could tolerate the oppressor position, if we lived with a day-to-day emotional awareness of the pain inflicted on other humans through the instrument of our behavior. (Winter, 1977, p. 25)

Phase Four—Interpretation and Meaning

Interpretation refers to what meaning is construed to a microaggressive incident; its significance, intention of the aggressor, and any social patterns related to it. In the Sue, Capodilupo, and Holder (2008) study, several meanings emerged that are consistent with the microaggressive themes identified earlier. The themes or meanings are not exhaustive, but should give readers an idea of their dynamics and significance to the targets.

You Do Not Belong

This message conveys that targets are undesirables who do not belong in a particular environment, neighborhood, school, worksite, store, or society in general. Black motorists who drive through a primarily White neighborhood may be stopped by police because "they do not belong." A Black customer in a convenient store states *"They just don't want to deal with me, or don't want me in there, I don't belong in there or whatever, just want me out of there as fast as possible."* Another described walking into an office building and being directed toward the entrance for messengers, instead of the general entrance for people using the building. He shared, *"I took it as I was Black, he saw me,*

I didn't really belong going where the rest of the people were going, you know, so I was sent that way."

You Are Abnormal

Abnormality in this case is defined from a White Western-European male perspective. Normality can be defined in terms of (1) a statistical average (whatever occurs most frequently in the population), (2) deviations from accepted standards of behavior, or (3) some idealized notion of desirability endorsed by the dominant society (D. Sue, D. W. Sue, & Sue, 2010). These standards of normality and abnormality may apply to cultural values, personality traits and attributes, behaviors, and even dress and appearance. LGBTs are believed to be abnormal in their sexual orientation and behaviors (Douce, 2005; Herek, 1998). Asian American students may be labeled shy, inhibited, and repressed because their cultural dictates emphasize subtlety and indirectness in approaching tasks. Communication styles of African Americans, because they emphasize passion, may be viewed as "out of control and too emotional." African Americans have a sarcastic saying: "The White way is the right way."

The abnormality theme can also affect appearance and dress. A Black woman describes conversations that get generated among her White coworkers about Black hairstyles: *"You're being made to feel like a novelty, and it's insulting to you because you're like, well where do you come from that there's no one else like me? Because what I look like is normal, you know?"* A male participant referred to his traditional African dress: *"I mean, that's my traditional way of dressing, you know, why should I have to explain it? It makes me feel like I am being questioned. Something is wrong with me, or what?"*

You Are Intellectually Inferior

Attributions of general intellectual inferiority and specific intellectual deficits are often correlated with skin color and gender. Women are seen to be deficient in rational thinking (math and sciences) (Banaji & Greenwald, 1995), Asian Americans are poor in people relations and make weak leaders (S. Sue, Sue, Zane, & Wong, 1985; Wong & Halgin, 2006), and African Americans lack abstract conceptual reasoning (Jones, 1997). These messages are conveyed in a variety of ways. One participant reports, *"Their face drops, like, surely you couldn't be the manager. But you're a young Black female! Why would you be the manager?"* Another participant shares a similar experience, *"So when I walk into a hospital and say I'm here to fix your machine, I either get a double-take initially . . . . They're not too sure of the skills level. They ask me a lot of questions . . . it's subtle, it's more like they want to find out what I know and who I am before they trust me with it."* Several other participants describe interview incidents: *"You know, 'you articulate so well.' Shouldn't that be something you expect all your applicants to do? I have a Bachelor's degree. Do you think I didn't pass seventh-grade English?"*

You Are Not Trustworthy

"I go to [department stores], especially as a Black man, I mean every time I go into that place, somebody's watching me, somebody's walking behind me, trying to monitor me or whatever. I'm there to steal, or I'm there to rob someone, right?" According to many Black Americans, the distrust issue can be environmentally communicated: *"[In the music store], the hip hop and rap section has the protective case over it, but the rest of the music didn't. Why does it have this huge white frame around it . . . you can't look at the songs on the back, and the rest don't have that, so it kind of speaks to the idea that the owners are afraid these CDs will get stolen."* Some of the most frequently reported microaggressive incidents were being closely monitored in stores, constant questions regarding their identities, and being asked about their motives and intentions in a multitude of settings. The association of criminality was strong in all of these reported incidents.

You Are All the Same

On a symbolic physical level, the statement "You people all look alike," captures the essence of this microaggression. There are several offensive assumptions made in this statement: (1) individual differences do not exist, and (2) the Asian or Black experience is universal. As a result, members of marginalized groups are expected to represent or speak for all their members. One Black informant expressed irritation at his boss who constantly came to him to check on the pronunciation of names he deduced were Black ones. For example, *"I can pronounce 'Darrell,' but am I pronouncing 'Malachi' and 'Aiysha' correctly?"* Another made a similar observation: *"The same manager in the same job, he came to me, and he was like, 'Do I say African American or Black?' . . . Don't assume that because I'm Black I know how everyone in my race wants to be called."* Another participant stated *"[White people] are asking this information not so much to learn about you, but because they're trying to obtain some information about Black people . . . . Maybe I don't know what other Black people do fifty percent or more of the time. It just puts you in an awkward situation where you have to feel like you have to define yourself to them because they decide you're Black so you're going to have a lot more information."*

Phase Five—Consequences and Impact

What consequences do microaggressions have on recipients? It is difficult to clearly separate out this phase from the others in answering this question, because the "impact" on the psyche of marginalized groups makes itself felt throughout the entire appraisal and reaction process. Indeed, one could make a strong case that the microaggressive process from beginning to end (Incident, Perception, Immediate Response, and Interpretation) is interwoven with short- and long-term consequences. However, the focus of the consequence phase attempts to specifically describe the psychological effects of microaggressions on the recipient. It covers more thoroughly how the microaggression impacted the individual's behavioral patterns, coping strategies, cognitive reasoning, psychological well-being, and worldview over time. There are four consequences that seem especially relevant for us to understand.

Powerlessness

Again, the sense of powerlessness is the result of an inability to control the definition of reality (racial, gender, or sexual orientation) and the catch-22 dilemma that is evoked when attempts are made. When a microaggression occurs, the response—be it confronting the person, getting upset, or questioning/challenging the motives—leads perpetrators or others to label the target as hypersensitive or angry. The belief that one has little effect or control over a situation leads to feelings of impotence. Through repeated experiences of being made to feel helpless and ineffective in determining one's own fate, the locus of control becomes externalized (Sue & Sue, 2008). Common comments are *"It's no use trying," "There's nothing I can do about it,"* and *"You don't want to rock the boat."* One Black participant stated the dilemma quite succinctly: *"If you were to address every microaggression, it's like all, 'Oh, there you go again, you people' . . . so it's like, you sort of are conditioned to not say anything, thereby becoming oblivious to it. Not oblivious but, you know—if you're hypersensitive about it then they're like, 'See, we told you.'"* Another stated, *"It is how your context gets translated through someone else's lens. I think that's another way that the very essence of your life is up for definition, based on any particular lens that a White person is wearing on any particular day in any particular moment."*

Invisibility

Invisibility takes many forms. Our opening chapter vignette indicates how women are frequently objectified and their accomplishments and other attributes are overlooked and ignored, making them feel invisible. When female students in class are called upon less frequently than their male counterparts, their contributions and presence are deemed less valuable and visible. People of color are often well aware of the invisibility syndrome (Franklin, 1999, 2004) and will take countermeasures to combat this phenomenon. To gain recognition and be noticed, one informant stated: *"You deal with that as a Black person, there's a certain real invisibility, or where White people just can't recognize your face, your distinction, something like that, unless you really impress upon them in a relationship."* One Black woman recalls an incident of invisibility in which White women in her office were being "ranked." During this conversation, she stood next to them: *"It's more like, wow, I'm not even seen as, you know, not as a person, but just like not even seen, invisible. So it made me feel like, okay, you have to do something above and beyond in order to be noticed."*

Forced Compliance/Loss of Integrity

Being forced to think and behave in a manner antagonistic to your true beliefs and desires makes people feel inauthentic and disingenuous. These feelings were commonly reported by our participants of color and were described as navigating two different worlds on a daily basis: the White world and their own world. The dual navigation allowed them to survive, function, and even occasionally prosper in the White world, but the cost was reported to be high. Feelings of "selling out," projecting a false self, and not being true to one's self created feelings of uneasiness and superficiality. Nearly all participants in our study spoke about their behaviors in terms of "forced compliance" and the potential loss of integrity. *"I was angry at myself for not speaking out. What a coward I must be."*

Conforming to White standards in the classroom, on the job, and in social gatherings, and being concerned or fearful of potential consequences of breaking social norms and/or letting one's true beliefs and feelings be known often resulted in extreme emotional turmoil (feelings of cowardice, having sold out, self-flagellation, etc.). These feelings seemed directly related to one's loss of integrity. A Black woman describes the feelings of forced compliance and loss of integrity that occurred around an incident of "wrapping her hair" and the resulting comments from her boss: *"I can't remember exactly what he said, but it was kind of like, 'you're wearing a turban' or something regarding it. He didn't—not like he was saying it in a negative way, but you could still feel that hint of, like, there's some kind of negative connotation, so you just feel like, well, can I not be myself here? And you feel like, why do you have to conform, but then it's like, this is the way society is and you're forced to conform in a certain way, but you kind of hate to do it."* Another described it in the following way: *"there's a part of me that always feels like I'm pretending at my job . . . . I always feel like it's a mask . . . you can't really say what's on your mind, or you have to filter it through so many lenses till it comes out sounding acceptable to whoever's listening."*

Pressure to Represent One's Group

A very common experience reported by people of color is a powerful pressure to represent their groups well. They had a heightened awareness that every mistake, every failing, and every deficiency exhibited by them would be attributed to their respective minority groups. For example, one participant relayed her feeling that any mistakes she makes will affect Black women who come after her in the job: *"If I screw up, every Black woman after me, or every Black person after me is going to have to take it, because I screwed up . . . so I carry that pressure with me."* Some participants felt an increased pressure to act or perform in a certain way so as not to confirm particular stereotypes about their group. For example, "as a Black woman, you have to put in that extra because maybe their expectations of you are going to be lower." As will be reported shortly, this latter phenomenon has been labeled "stereotype threat" and its effects can have devastating consequences for people of color and women (Cardinu, Maass, Rosabianca, & Kiesner, 2005; Steele, 2003; Steele et al., 2002).

In conclusion, our studies (Sue, Capodilupo, & Holder, 2008; Sue, Lin, Torino, et al., 2009; Sue, Nadal, et al., 2008) identified five general phases which could be logically ordered from inception to consequence in a sequential fashion: Incident → Perception → Reaction → Interpretation → Consequence. It is important to note, however, that these phases did not arise sequentially. In other words, responses from people of color might begin with a discussion of their reactions before addressing their perceptions and interpretations of the incidents. We must entertain the possibility that these phases may occur in a different order, overlap with one another, be cyclical, and/or interact in a more complex manner.

Nevertheless, it is safe to say that potential microaggressive incidents set in motion a chain of events that may be energy-depleting and/or disruptive to cognitive, emotional, and behavioral domains (Purdie-Vaughns et al., 2008; Salvatore & Shelton, 2007; Sue, Lin, Torino, et al., 2009). Perceptual questioning

("*Was it racially motivated?*") aimed at trying to determine whether an action or statement was racially motivated can be a short- or long-term process ("yes," "no," "maybe," or "don't know"). Regardless, considerable psychic energy is expended during this process, which is dependent on a number of factors: ambiguity of the incident, personal attributes of the recipient, form of the microaggression, perpetrator's relationship to the recipient, power differential between the players, and so on. If the event is deemed to be a microaggression, it appears to impact three domains: cognitive, emotional, and behavioral (Sue, Lin, Torino, et al., 2009).

1. On the cognitive level, an internal dialogue seems to take place: "*Was it a microaggression? How should I respond? What will be the consequences if I do? Will I be supported by others or attacked/invalidated?*"

2. On the behavioral level, most people of color chose to do nothing for a number of different reasons (fear of retaliation, fleeting nature of the microaggression, unable to determine appropriate response, paralyzed by emotional turmoil, etc.). Of those who responded to the perpetrator, behaviors took many forms (confrontation and attack, attempt to educate the perpetrator while maintaining a relationship, forced compliance, rescuing the offender, etc.).

3. Microaggressions appear to take the greatest toll on the emotional functioning of our participants and might also have long-term implications on their mental health and subjective feelings of well-being (Sue, Lin, Torino, et al., 2009). When racial microaggressions occur in the classroom, for example, students of color commonly reported becoming (1) "incensed" when their integrity was assailed, (2) "anxious" when they feared consequences, and (3) "exhausted" in having to deal with a never-ending string of microaggressions. Participants frequently described "being sucked dry" and "constantly being the one to keep on stepping up to the plate to educate people."

The microaggressive process model proposed here is a descriptive one and attempts to identify the internal psychological dynamics that occur within targeted individuals and groups. It is certainly not exhaustive and future research would be helpful in clarifying possible other processes and themes involved in each phase. Such knowledge may prove valuable in developing possible adaptive strategies that help shield marginalized groups from the harm inflicted by microaggressions.

The Way Forward

Strength through Adversity

Our analysis of microaggressions from inception to end and the recognition that there are cognitive, emotional, and behavioral costs to targets suggest it would not be far-fetched to assume that microaggressions represent psychological and social stressors likely to have an impact on the psychological well-being and mental health status of targets. One of the most important areas for future research deals with the need to identify and proactively devise functional survival or adaptive mechanisms that can be used to immunize people of color, women, and LGBTs against the stress and distress of microaggressions (Utsey, Giesbrecht, Hook, & Stanard, 2008; Wei, Ku, Russell, Mallinckrodt, & Liao, 2008; Yoo & Lee, 2008).

Two possible avenues of focus seem to exist: (1) we can remove or mitigate the causes of microaggressions that reside in individuals, institutions, and our society, and/or (2) at the same time, we can teach targeted groups and individuals about how to effectively take care of themselves. The former focus requires massive changes in our cultural and social systems and represents a major challenge that involves much time and effort. Meanwhile, marginalized groups continue to be targets and to be potentially harmed. Chapter 5 addresses how marginalized groups may have developed specific strategies to deal with these insults.

Nevertheless, it is important to address one of the problematic perceptions that often arises when acknowledging the harmful impact of microaggressions: the perception that people of color, women, and LGBTs are weak, helpless, overly sensitive, and powerless victims (Thomas, 2008). Nothing could be further from the truth. Throughout the first four chapters we allude to strengths and resources developed by oppressed groups to survive and, indeed, thrive under adverse conditions (Hanna, Talley, & Guindon, 2000; Sue, 2003; Utsey et al., 2008; Yoo & Lee, 2008). A few identified attributes taken from Sue (2003) are:

1. *Heightened perceptual wisdom*—There is considerable evidence to suggest that oppressed groups have developed an ability to discern the truth and to determine reality better than those who occupy positions of power and privilege. Forced to operate within a predominantly White, male, and straight culture, marginalized groups have been immersed

(Continued)

in the prejudices and biases of the society. Accurate perception means the ability to read between the lines, to see beyond the obvious, and to become aware of inconsistencies between verbal and nonverbal behaviors of oppressors. For people of color, for example, it has meant vigilance in discerning the motives, attitudes, and the unintentional biased contradictions of White people. In many cases, Whites sense this ability on the part of people of color and become uncomfortable in their presence because they fear having their biases and prejudices unmasked. Heightened perception and wisdom are functions of optimal human functioning among oppressed groups who rely heavily on their intuitive and perceptual wisdom. It protects them from having their experiential realities invalidated.

2. *Nonverbal and contextualized accuracy*—There is a saying among African Americans that goes like this: "To truly understand White people, don't listen to what they say, but how they say it." This saying refers to recognition that nonverbal behaviors are more accurate barometers of biased attitudes and actions. It has been suggested that women are better at reading nonverbal behaviors than men and that people of color are also better at reading nonverbal communication than Whites. Communication theory reveals that only 30–40% of communication occurs verbally, while the remainder depends on nonverbal/contextual cues; then, nonverbal behaviors are least under conscious control; and nonverbal messages are more accurate than verbal ones. As healthy functioning is correlated with the ability to accurately read nonverbal communication and discern "the truth," this suggests that oppressed groups may possess strengths unmatched by oppressors.

3. *Bicultural flexibility*—Because people of color, women, and LGBTs are always exposed to the cultural values, beliefs, and standards of the dominant society, they must deal with pressures to conform to the larger standards of those in power. In dealing with forced compliance and pressures to assimilate and acculturate, marginalized groups have developed a bicultural flexibility that allows them to maintain their own sense of integrity. They may be said to be multicultural rather than monocultural. One of the major advantages of being bicultural or multicultural is the ability to see multiple worldviews and more readily understand the other's point of view. In contrast, those in power are seldom called upon to learn and experience minority cultures; in essence they are monocultural and disadvantaged.

(Continued)

4. *Collectivistic sense of group identity and peoplehood*—Our studies on microaggressions suggest that oppressed groups rely heavily on one another for a collective sense of identity, for validation and confirmation of their experiences, and for sharing with one another healthy coping mechanisms to overcome invalidation. Reliance on one's group, family/community, and other social networks provide strengths to overcome oppressive environments. In many respects, marginalized groups use the term "peoplehood" (sociopolitical) to refer to a sense of group identity forged through common experiences of oppressions and lessons learned that survival depends on one another. Cultural values from collectivistic cultures, too, seem invaluable in overcoming prejudice and discrimination and enhancing the ability of marginalized groups to flourish in a toxic environment. Racial and ethnic pride also seems to immunize minority groups against forces like racism.

Developing healthy cultural identities and self-esteem is challenging for people of color, women, and LGBTs as they continuously combat an oppressive society that equates differences with deviance and pathology. Social support, as we will shortly see, is a powerful means of combating and ameliorating stressful racism, sexism, and heterosexism. It appears that social support through a sense of belonging, ethnic collectivistic cultural values, extended family systems, communities, and group resources buffer oppressed groups against a hostile society and provide cultural nutrients that validate their worldviews and lifestyles.

CHAPTER FIVE

Microaggressive Stress: Impact on Physical and Mental Health

"It gets so tiring, you know. It sucks you dry. People don't trust you. From the moment I wake up, I know stepping out the door, that it will be the same, day after day. The bus can be packed, but no one will sit next to you . . . . I guess it may be a good thing because you always get more room, no one crowds you. You get served last . . . when they serve you, they have this phony smile and just want to get rid of you . . . . You have to show more ID to cash a check, you turn on the TV and there you always see someone like you, being handcuffed and jailed. They look like you and sometimes you begin to think it is you! You are a plague! You try to hold it in, but sometimes you lose it. Explaining doesn't help. They don't want to hear. Even when they ask, 'Why do you have a chip on your shoulder?' Shit . . . I just walk away now. It doesn't do any good explaining." (African American male)

It is well documented that overt and obvious forms of discrimination (racism, sexism, and homophobia) detrimentally impact the mental and physical health, quality of life, self-esteem, and identity of nearly all marginalized groups in our society (Baker & Fishbein, 1998; Barrett & Logan, 2002; Barry & Grilo, 2003; Brondolo, Rieppi, Kelly, & Gerin, 2003; Cardinu, Maass, Rosabianca, & Kiesner, 2005; Frederickson & Roberts, 1997; Hamelsky & Lipton, 2006; Herek, Gillis, & Cogan, 2009; Utsey, Chae, Brown, & Kelly, 2002). The type of stresses ʝgh microaggressions, however, are less obvious and visible. ᴗn of a hate crime or overt deliberate racism, for example, leaves little doubt that harm was inflicted on the target (racial taunts, refusing service, physical assaults, and murders). The impact is immediate and visible. Yet, the impact of microaggressions is generally subtle, not immediately visible, and the effects are often delayed or not noticeable (internal struggle).

Microinsults and microinvalidations often come from a catch-22 created by double messages (Sue, Capodilupo, et al., 2007). The type of conflict and stress occurs outside the view of well-intentioned perpetrators and observers. The internal conflict between explicit and implicit messages (meanings) creates an exceptionally stressful situation because it (1) fosters confusion between the overt message and one's experiential reality, (2) implies perpetrators are not true friends or allies, (3) alters an important personal, social, or professional relationship with perpetrators, and (4) places targets in an unenviable position of ascertaining when, where, and how to resist oppression versus when to accommodate it (Pierce, 1988; Sue, Lin, Torno, et al., 2009).

In the psychological literature, microaggressions fulfill the criteria of being stressors; they represent external events or situations that place a psychological or physical demand on targets (King, 2005; Lazarus & Folkman, 1984; Utsey, Giesbrecht, Hook, & Stanard, 2008). In addition to the normal life stressors experienced by everyone, people of color, women, and LGBTs experience race-related, gender-related, or sexual-orientation-related stress. Further, while hate crimes or deliberate sexual harassment may threaten physical safety, microinsults and microinvalidations attack the self-esteem, belief systems, and racial, gender, or sexual-orientation identity of targets (Sue & Capodilupo, 2008). Few would question that the young African American male above is under severe and continuing stress. He is exposed to constant microaggressions, feels powerless to do anything about them, suppresses internal racial rage, and is tired and exhausted from the constant racial bombardment directed toward him.

BIOLOGICAL STRESSORS AND CONSEQUENCES

In many respects, the early general adaptation syndrome (GAS) model developed by Selye (1956, 1982) to explain the body's reaction to biological stressors (invasion by viruses, bacteria, or toxins) appears to be a good psychological analogy for understanding the effects of microaggressions, as well. Selye identified three stages that he labeled alarm, resistance, and exhaustion.

1. The *alarm stage* represents a "call to arms" of the body's defenses when invaded or assaulted biologically. The response is one of heightened physiological reactivity that involves rapid heartbeat, loss of muscle tone, and decreased temperature and blood pressure. Increased secretion of corticoid hormones from the adrenal glands occurs quickly to help ward off the invader. All of these bodily responses are attempts to warn the body of an invader presence (Underwood, 2005). Like the alarm stage, when a microaggression occurs, the person becomes vigilant and attempts to determine whether his/her integrity or identity is being attacked. There may be initial confusion with the ambiguity of the incident or event, but warning signs about the offensive race-related, gender-related, or sexual-orientation-related communication are deciphered.

2. If exposure to the biological stressor continues, the *adaptation or resistance stage* follows. The body mobilizes resources to defend against, destroy, or coexist with the disease or injury. Symptoms such as fever, sore throat, swelling of infected tissues, and other biological reactions occur. Unless the disease is destroyed, prolonged resistance may weaken the immune system so that susceptibility to other infections or illnesses is possible (Ho et al., 1995). It is important to note that symptoms of a disease may disappear or not be noticed initially; regardless, the underlying biological battle can rage on silently for many years. The parallel psychological process involves feelings of anger, anxiety, guilt, depression, and other reactions. The marginalized group member can also coexist with the microaggression by accepting it as a reality of life. The psychological toll may not be immediately visible, as in the development of low self-esteem. The internal struggle with microaggressions can fester and eat away at the integrity of the person for long periods of time. For many, it is a lifelong struggle.

3. Because the body's defenses are finite, continued stress will lead to the *stage of exhaustion* with the ultimate symptom being death of the biological organism. The symptoms may change or become worse as the body weakens and begins to shut down (Segerstrom & Miller, 2004). Physical activity decreases and the effects are also manifested psychologically in depression, lowered desire for life, narrowing and decrease in cognitive functioning/alertness, and withdrawal from social situations. Likewise, chronic microaggressive stressors have often been found to "wear down" the target and they often describe feelings of exhaustion or a depletion of energy. Ability to learn in classrooms, to produce at work, and to be functional in personal/social/familial responsibilities may suffer.

Although the GAS model was developed to account for how the body deals with biological stressors, research now suggests that psychological and social stressors have comparable effects. Stress has been found to make a person more susceptible to illness and may affect the course of a disease (Keltner & Dowben, 2007; Underwood, 2005). For example, recently bereaved widows are 3 to 12 times more likely to die than married women; tax accountants are more susceptible to heart attacks around April 15; people residing in high-noise airport areas have more medical complaints and hypertension; and air traffic controllers suffer from hypertension at a rate that is four times higher than the general population (Luoma, Pearson, & Pearson, 2002; Wilding, 1984).

PSYCHOLOGICAL/SOCIAL STRESSORS AND CONSEQUENCES

Taking into account the GAS model of physical response to biological stressors, De La Fuente (1990) proposed that psychological and social stressors activate a similar internal process within the cognitive, emotional, and behavioral make-up of the person. The model was developed from his intensive work with earthquake victims, but De La Fuente felt it was applicable in explaining psychological responses across a wide range of stressful events. Briefly, his Crisis Decompensation Model (CDM) also contains three stages: impact, attempted resolution, and decompensated adjustment.

In the first stage, the *impact* of a crisis or other stressors induces confusion and disorientation. In interviewing earthquake victims, he found that many expressed bewilderment and had a hard time understanding what had or was happening, and why it was happening. Anxiety, guilt, anger, dissociation, and depression were common emotional reactions. If we compare our process model of microaggressions to the CDM, the impact of microaggressions appears to have a comparable effect on targets (initial confusion and disorientation). The disequilibrium of the first stage is generally followed by *attempted resolution* in which all the resources of the person are mobilized to deal with the situation. The coping strategies and available resources often determine the outcome of this stage. For example, it was found that social support from significant others was crucial to a successful resolution. Indeed, De La Fuente found that successful coping led to a precrisis level of functioning and, at times, a growth adjustment phase. Similarly, in Chapter 4 we described many attempts by marginalized groups to *resolve their internal conflicts* using specific strategies and/or inner resources. If coping, however, is ineffective, the person enters into the *decompensated adjustment* phase, which is marked by withdrawal, depression, guilt, apathy, anxiety, anger, and any number of physical illnesses. Likewise, unsuccessful or ineffective means of coping with microaggressions may lead to a lowered sense of well-being, heightened physiological reactivity with biological consequences, and psychological problems.

While these two models of stress and coping (GAS and CDM) appear similar to the five-phase process model of microaggressions described in the last chapter, the stressors studied by researchers such as Selye and De La Fuente have generally concentrated on extreme psychological or physical trauma (natural disasters, robberies, murders, automobile accidents, terrorist attacks, airplane crashes, etc.) outside ordinary human experience. Indeed, acute stress disorders (ASD) and posttraumatic stress disorders (PTSD) are described in DSM-IV-TR as having to meet certain criteria: threat of possible death or injury, and likely to induce intense fear or horror (American Psychiatric Association, 2000). Racism, sexism, and homophobia in the form of violence, hate crimes, and rape clearly fulfill these criteria. Women are more likely than men to suffer from a stress disorder because of their greater exposure to violent interpersonal situations (Cortina & Kubiak, 2006; National Institute of Mental Health, 2007) and rape is clearly associated with extreme trauma. Immediately following a sexual assault, for example, one study found that 74% of the victims met criteria for ASD; and after three months, 35% met the criteria for PTSD (Valentiner, Foa, Riggs, & Gershuny, 1996).

Yet, the question remains as to whether microaggressions in the form of insults and invalidations are sufficiently stressful to produce psychological and physical harm to targets. Are critics correct when they claim people of color are making a mountain out of a molehill and that these small, petty humiliations indicate that minorities should simply "suck it up" and not make a big deal of them (Schacht, 2008; Thomas, 2008)? The impact of rape, they may contend, is not comparable to that of sexual objectification. Or is it?

MICROAGGRESSIONS AND DAILY HASSLES

In the last chapter, we outlined a five-phase process dealing with how marginalized groups perceive, interpret, and respond to microaggressions: incident → perception → reaction → interpretation → consequence. The microaggression process model assumes that microaggressions are stressful, that the stress-coping dynamics described in the GAS and CDM models are similar, and that significant harm can result unless mitigated through effective coping or external intervention. While there are many similarities among these models, a strong case is often made that microaggressions are simply not comparable to traumatic events such as rape, overt assaults, and experiencing a natural disaster (e.g., earthquake, volcanic eruption, and floods/ hurricanes). Applying these models to microaggressions, they contend, represents a false analogy. Two lines of research on the impact of daily hassles and race-related stress challenge this conclusion.

Challenge One—Everyday Hassles and Stress

While it is true that microaggressions, when placed side-by-side with hate crimes and rapes, may appear minimally harmful and even benign, it is now known that for harmful effects to occur, the stressors need not be of crisis proportion (Astin, Ogland-Hand, Foy, & Coleman, 1995; Holmes & Holmes, 1970; Rahe, 1994; Scott & Stradling, 1994). Subtraumatic stressors such as employment problems, marital distress, and immigration adjustment have all been shown to be stressful. In fact, seemingly small, everyday events such as moving to a new neighborhood, driving to work in heavy traffic, breaking up with a significant other, and changing jobs can create stress and impact health and personal adjustment. Even a change in a small routine such as sleeping in another bed, dietary restrictions, or having a houseguest can create stress (Crandall, Preisler, & Aussprung, 1992). Table 5.1 outlines sample stressors ranked by college undergraduates for stress. Note that even taking exams, trying to decide on a major, and sitting through boring classes generate stress. The point being made by analyzing these studies is that even small demands on people in the form of "daily life hassles" produce stress; thus, entertaining the notion that microaggressions can be stressful is certainly not far-fetched (Spangenberg & Pieterse, 1995).

Life Change and Stress

Some 40 years ago, researchers found other interesting correlations with stress. Not only could small hassles create stress, but two other factors were important to consider: life change and cumulative impact (Holmes & Rahe, 1967; Holmes & Holmes, 1970). Their pioneering work led to the formulation of the *life-change model* which assumes that all changes, large or small, desirable or

Table 5.1   Sample Stressors and Their Rankings by Undergraduate College Students

SITUATION	SEVERITY	FREQUENCY
Death of family member or friend	3.97	1.89
Had lots of tests	3.62	4.39
Finals week	3.62	3.64
Breaking up a relationship	3.45	2.21
Property stolen	3.41	1.96
Roommate conflicts	3.10	2.68
Lack of money	3.07	3.36
Arguments with friends	2.97	2.43
Trying to decide on a major	2.79	3.25
Attending a boring class	1.66	4.07

Source: Crandall, Preisler, & Aussprung (1992).

Note: Event *severity* was measured on a 4-point scale from "none" to "a lot" and *frequency* was measured on a 5-point scale from "never" to "always."

undesirable, can act as stressors. Further, the accumulation of small changes could summate into a powerful and potent form of stress equal in force to one extremely traumatic event (deJong, Timmerman, & Emmelkamp, 1996; Holmes & Holmes, 1970; Rahe, 1994).

The researchers created an instrument, the Social Readjustment Rating Scale (SRRS), which ranked events as to their potential stress value. The total *life change units* (LCUs) could be calculated for individuals based upon the number and ranking of the daily hassles they encountered over a given period of time. For example, they found that 93% of health problems such as infections, allergies, bone/muscle injuries, and psychosomatic illnesses occurred in patients who in the previous year obtained LCU values of 150 or more (mild crisis or stress). Higher accumulated LCUs were correlated with the number of people who displayed illnesses, and greater severity of illnesses, as well. The findings from their studies led to one major conclusion that has since altered our conception of stress severity: Although minor life changes and daily hassles were not sufficient alone to constitute a serious stressor, the cumulative impact of many events could be considered a crisis. As race-related, gender-related, and sexual-orientation-related microaggressions have been shown to be a lifelong and continuing experience of marginalized groups, a strong case can be made that microaggressions are anything but insignificant: they are extremely harmful and detrimental to people of color, women, and LGBTs.

Stressor–Person Transactions

The *general adaptation syndrome, crisis decompensation,* and *life change* models of stress place minimal emphasis on the person's subjective definition or interpretation of stressful events or life changes. As we have seen in earlier chapters, microaggressions almost inevitably evoke a strong assessment and appraisal process that moderates the reactions or outcomes. The thoughts and interpretations we make about the stressor, the emotions we attach to them, and the actions taken to avoid them can either increase or decrease the impact of stressors (Levenstein et al., 1993). In his classic book, *Psychological Stress and the Coping Process* (1966), Richard Lazarus proposed a *transaction model of stress* based on the notion that stress resides neither in the person alone nor in the situation, but rather is a transaction between the two.

How a person of color, for example, perceives a racial microaggression, the adaptive resources he or she possesses, his or her racial identity development, the presence of familial/social support, what he or she decides to do, and so forth may moderate or mediate the meaning and impact of the incident (King, 2005; Liang, Alvarez, Juang, & Liang, 2007; Yoo & Lee, 2008; Utsey et al., 2008). Recall in Chapter 4 that one of the responses made by people of color to a microaggression is "rescuing the offender." Most African Americans would be strongly offended and angered by the White woman in the elevator who showed fear toward them. While the Black male passenger accurately saw the nonverbals as a microaggression (clutching the purse more tightly in his company—assumption of criminality), he reacted by attempting to put the woman at ease because "She can't help it. It's that White cultural conditioning that is the problem." Thus, while some Black Americans might interpret this incident as stressful, this young Black man seemingly did not. Something within his worldview, experience, and inner resources allowed him not to be upset or offended, but instead to interpret and cope with the situation in such a manner as to minimize its harmful impact upon him (Sellers & Sheldon, 2003; Wei, Ku, Russell, Mallinckrodt, & Liao, 2008).

Challenge Two—Racial, Gender, and Sexual-Orientation Microaggressions: Quantitative and Qualitative Differences

While the transaction model of stress added considerably to recognizing that people are not passive organisms who simply respond to stressors without internal appraisal (Lazarus, 1966; Lazarus & Folkman, 1984), the formulation has been criticized for lacking cultural sensitivity and relevance (Carter, 2007;

Slavin, Rainer, McCreary, & Gowda, 1991). In many respects the transaction model may accurately describe the process of stress-coping, but fails in addressing racial/cultural, gender, and sexual-orientation factors that involve group-specific race-related, gender-related, and sexual-orientation-related stress. It also neglects the sociopolitical context under which marginalized groups exist in the society and overlooks group-specific traumatic stress. Because these conceptions are based primarily on a European American perspective, it fails to understand or sympathize with the life experience of marginality, the oppression that many experience, and how "small slights" symbolize strong memories of historical and continuing injustice (Duran, 2006; Feagin, 2006; Feagin & McKinney, 2003). The following quote captures the essence of this lack of appreciation and understanding of race-related traumatic stress in stress-coping models and perspectives:

> I don't think white people, generally, understand the full meaning of racist discriminatory behaviors directed toward Americans of African descent. They seem to see each act of discrimination or any act of violence as an "isolated" event. As a result, most white Americans cannot understand the strong reaction manifested by blacks when such events occur . . . . They forget that in most cases, we live lives of quiet desperation generated by a litany of daily large and small events that, whether or not by design, remind us of our "place" in American society. [Whites] ignore the personal context of the stimulus. That is, they deny the historical impact that a negative act may have on an individual. "Nigger" to a white may simply be an epithet that should be ignored. To most blacks, the term brings into sharp and current focus all kinds of acts of racism—murder, rape, torture, denial of constitutional rights, insults, limited opportunity structure, economic problems, unequal justice under the law and a myriad of . . . other racist and discriminatory acts that occur daily in the lives of most Americans of African descent. (Feagin & Sikes, 1994, pp. 23–24)

The above quote is consistent with what may be referred to as "historical trauma," or the "soul wound" by American Indians (Duran, 2006). Microaggressions are linked to a wider sociopolitical context of oppression and injustice (historical trauma) that results in a soul wound passed on from generation to generation of those who understand their own histories of discrimination and prejudice (Sue, 2003). Each small race-related slight, hurt, invalidation, insult, and indignity rubs salt into the wounds of marginalized groups in our society. For American Indians, their everyday lives are filled with reminders that their lands were unfairly seized from them, that they were forced onto reservations, and that physical and cultural genocide were visited upon them. Just like Jews who also suffer from a historical trauma (the Holocaust), Japanese Americans remember their internment experience during World War II, and African Americans remember their enslavement. Thus to equate microaggressions with only everyday hassles may be an inaccurate comparison.

In a revealing study exploring stressful life events and race-related stress, the researchers found that the latter was a more powerful predictor of psychological distress than everyday hassles (Utsey et al., 2008). In other words, racial microaggressions were more impactful, harmful, and distressing to African Americans than ordinary stressful life events. This may be true for several reasons: (1) microaggressions are symbols and reminders of racism, sexism, and heterosexism; (2) microaggressions are continual and perpetual while stressful life events are time-limited; (3) microaggressions impact nearly all aspects of the target's life—education, employment, social interactions, and so forth; and (4) stressful life events have a recognizable cause while microaggressions are often ambiguous and invisible. If this finding and assumptions hold true for other marginalized groups, it means that qualitatively, microaggressions occupy a class by themselves; they are more detrimental for disempowered groups than ordinary life stressors. Further, it has been found that people of color report experiencing discriminatory incidents at a very high rate (being ignored, overlooked, not given service, treated rudely, reacted to in a fearful manner, made fun of, taunted, called names, and harassed) (Klonoff & Landrine, 1995; Landrine & Klonoff, 1996; Sellers & Shelton, 2003). In other words, marginalized groups are not only exposed to greater number of stressors, but also a more potent and powerful form than those experienced by majority individuals. When one realizes that devalued groups in our society not only contend with ordinary stressful life events but must also cope with additional stressors associated with race, gender, and sexual orientation, one can only conclude that they are being asked to endure an inhuman amount of stress.

THE EFFECTS OF MICROAGGRESSIVE STRESS

Microaggressive stressors can be defined as race-related, gender-related, or sexual-orientation-related events or situations that are experienced as a perceived threat to one's biological, cognitive, emotional, psychological, and social well-being, or position in life. The effects and severity of microaggressive stressors depend very much on the nature of the challenge posed by the threat and the perceived available resources of the person. When a marginalized group member encounters microaggressive stressors, four pathways may show their negative impact: (1) biological: there may be direct physiological reactions (blood pressure, heart rate, etc.) or changes in the immune system; (2) cognitive: it may place in motion a cognitive appraisal involving thoughts and beliefs about the meaning of the stressor; (3) emotional: anger, rage, anxiety, depression, or hopelessness may dominate the person's immediate life circumstance; and (4) behavioral: the coping strategies or behavioral reactions utilized by the individual may either enhance adjustment or make the situation worse.

Biological Health Effects of Microaggressive Stressors

Chronic microaggressive stress is the reality of women, LGBTs, and people of color (Barrett & Logan, 2002; Feagin, 2006; Fiske, 1993; Glick & Fiske, 1996; Greene, 2000; Hamilton & Mahalik, 2009; Harrell, 2000; Harrell, Hall, & Taliaferro, 2003; Stambor, 2006). Marginalized groups must deal with monocultural standards that equate differences with deficiency or deviance; forced compliance to contradictory cultural role expectations; and pervasive and chronic prejudice and discrimination have a significant impact upon health (Brondolo et al., 2009; Clark, Anderson, Clark, & Williams, 1999; Fang & Myers, 2001; Worthington & Reynolds, 2009). Women who perceived greater job stress or reported conflicting and contradictory role relationships with their bosses have been found to have higher fibrinogen levels. Fibrinogen, a blood-clotting compound, is believed to contribute to coronary heart disease (Davis, Mathews, Meilahn, & Kiss, 1995). LGBTs who reported experiencing greater levels of indirect microaggressions (assumption of heterosexuality) reported more health-related problems (Smith & Ingram, 2004). Studies on African Americans, Asian Americans, and Latino/Hispanic Americans all report that race-related stress negatively impacts the biological health of these groups (Brondolo et al., 2008; Brondolo et al., 2005; Clark et al., 1999; Liang & Fassinger, 2008; Moradi & Risco, 2006).

These findings are not surprising in light of what we know about social and psychological stress as it relates to physiological reactivity and detrimental consequences to the immune system. In a series of studies on subtle racism, African American men showed increases in heart rate, blood pressure, and other cardiovascular responding associated with hypertension (Clark, 2006; Merritt, Bennett, Williams, Edwards, & Sollers, 2006; Utsey & Hook, 2007).

In one study, when African American men watched videos of social situations depicting biased interactions, heart rate and blood pressure rose significantly (Fang & Myers, 2001). The impact of race-related stress is demonstrated in a plethora of studies suggesting that the physical well-being of people of color is constantly threatened in this society. Thus, people of color may be at increased risk for certain illnesses such as coronary heart disease, diabetes, hypertension, allergies, asthma, and so forth due to the body's heightened physiological reactivity to chronic stressors.

Further, while a strong relationship between microaggressive stressors and illnesses seems to exist, it appears that the former also affects the biological disease process as well. Stress itself does not appear to cause infections, but it seems to decrease the immune system's efficiency and increases susceptibility to a disease. White blood cells in the immune system help to maintain health by recognizing and destroying bacterial or viral invasions of the body. The two classes of blood cells, lymphocytes and phagocytes, are responsible for detecting and destroying invaders, producing antibodies, preventing the growth of tumors, and so forth (Cohen & Herbert, 1996). When under stress, the body responds by releasing neurohormones such as corticosteroids that impair immune functioning.

Exposure to chronic stress like microaggressions may make the person more susceptible to diseases and also affects the speed of their progression (Miller, Chen, & Zhou, 2007). Vulnerability to upper respiratory infections such as colds and other illnesses seems to be affected by the severity, duration, and type of stressor (Cohen et al., 1998). Lower immune system functioning has been correlated with abrasive marital interactions, spouses living with dementia victims, separated men, acculturative stress, and so on (Kiecolt-Glaser et al., 1987; Kiecolt-Glazer, Glaser, Cacioppo, & MacCallum, 1997; Pike, Smith, Hauger, et al., 1997; Steele & McGarvey, 1997). Clearly, microaggressive stress may affect the physical health of targets.

Emotional Effects of Microaggressive Stressors

Many scholars have noted that racism, sexism, and heterosexism affect the psychological adjustment, subjective well-being, self-esteem, and mental health of people of color, women, and LGBTs (Buser, 2009; Cortina & Kubiak, 2006; Utsey & Hook, 2007; Moradi, van den Berg, & Epting, 2009; Hwang & Goto, 2008). These studies, however, do not necessarily separate out the overt forms of biases from more subtle manifestations, but it appears that microaggressions in the form of insults and invalidations have strong detrimental effects (Sue, Capodilupo, & Holder, 2008). Evidence suggests that microaggressive stressors can be implicated in the manifestation of mental disorders such as depression and anxiety.

Most microaggressions involve interpersonal interactions between perpetrator and target. It has been demonstrated that stressors, especially interpersonal ones, are strongly related to various forms of depression (Hammen, 2006). Four characteristics of stressors are especially important in facilitating depression. The disorder is more likely to occur when stressors (1) are severe in nature (*severity*), (2) are chronic rather than acute (*chronicity*), (3) where the onset is early (*onset*), and (4) when they involve loss or humiliation as opposed to dangerous events or threat (*type of stressor*) (Brown & Harris, 1989; Lara, Klein, & Kasch, 2000; McGonagle & Kessler, 1990). Microaggressions fit these criteria in that they are continuing and cumulative, begin from the moment of birth, and assail a person's integrity, producing humiliation. While any one act may not be severe in nature, we have already seen how historical trauma and multiple microaggressions can summate into a powerful force.

Homophobia for LGBTs, for example, is a lifelong reality that interferes with identity development and healthy self-concept (Frost & Meyer, 2009; Herek, 2004). A heterosexist social environment produces an intrapsychic conflict between attractions to same-sex persons and being forced to alter one's desires for heterosexual partners. An inhospitable environment or climate to LGBTs produces "minority stress," a term used to describe specific sexual-orientation stressors that involve antigay stereotypes, prejudice, and discrimination (Meyer, Schwartz, & Frost, 2008). It has been proposed that internalized homophobia is the most insidious and damaging form of minority stressors that are the result of a heterosexist climate for LGBTs. The relationship between increased depression and low feelings of subjective well-being is well documented in the literature (Croteau, Lark, & Lance, 2005; Igartua, Gill, & Montoro, 2003; Meyer, 1995; Szymanski, 2009).

Much has also been written about the relationship of gender to depression. Depression is far more common among women than men regardless of race, social class, and region in the world (Strickland, 1992); major depressions (not bipolar) are twice as high as those for men in the United States (Kessler, 2003). Some believe these findings are artificially inflated due to the greater likelihood of women seeking treatment, their greater willingness to report depression to other people, hormonal differences, and gender bias in the diagnostic system (Ricker & Bird, 2005; Goldberg, 2006). While these explanations hold some validity, evidence now points to social and psychological factors as important contributors as well: gender-role conflicts; sexism in overt, covert, and subtle forms; subservience to men; lack of educational opportunities; lower sense of self-control; and sexual and child abuse (Capodilupo et al., in press; Hill & Fisher, 2008; D. Sue, Sue, & Sue, 2010).

A significant relationship between depression and subjective well-being also seems to exist between perceived discrimination and that of depression among African Americans, Asian Americans, and Latino/a Americans (Hwang & Goto, 2008; Utsey et al., 2008; Williams, Neighbors, & Jackson, 2003). Indeed, rates of depression have been found to be higher for Native Americans and Southeast Asians (Vega & Rumbaut, 1991; Chung & Okazaki, 1991). Recall that researchers believe that stressors that humiliate tended to be correlated with depressive disorders, while stressors that produce fear are associated with anxiety disorders. As microaggressions have been described as demeaning, insulting, and humiliating, one can understand how these race-related stressors may produce depression and lead to negative subjective feelings in people of color.

Cognitive Effects of Microaggressive Stressors

Racism, sexism, and heterosexism affect many more aspects of mental health functioning than just depression and feelings of subjective well-being. The cumulative impact of chronic stressors diminishes the quality of life; lowers life satisfaction, happiness, and self-esteem; increases cultural mistrust, feelings of alienation, anxiety, and feelings of loss, helplessness, and racial rage; and may result in fatigue and exhaustion (Clark et al., 1999; Harrell, 2000; Jackson et al., 1992; Jackson et al., 1995; Jones, 1997; Sue, 2003; Ponterotto, Utsey, & Pedersen, 2006). We have already seen how stress affects the biological and physical well-being of marginalized groups. On a biological level, stress depresses the immune system and makes people more susceptible to catching colds and other illnesses. We briefly turn our attention now to how stress impacts the cognitive functioning of marginalized groups.

In Chapter 4, we describe how a microaggression often sets off a chain of cognitive processes aimed at attempting to understand and make sense of the incident. The greater the ambiguity of microaggressions, the more difficult it is for the target to determine the meaning of the conflicting messages. Thus, a request from a White teacher to an Asian American student to move to the blackboard and show other students how to solve a math problem, because "You people are good at that," may provoke an internal thought process aimed at determining the meaning of the statement (*"Was it a compliment or stereotype?"*). Considerable energy may be expended in cognitively appraising the situation. Besides the ambiguity, the target may expend more energy deliberating whether or not to respond or evaluating the consequences of making a response, especially when the power differential is so great. The fact that an internal cognitive process is stimulated may divert the student's attention and energies away from the task and/or affect his or her problem-solving and learning ability.

Cognitive Disruption

In a study dealing with the cognitive costs of exposure to racism, investigators used a laboratory experiment to directly test the impact of overt racism versus the more ambiguous messages from racial microaggressions (Salvatore & Shelton, 2007). Volunteers witnessed a company's hiring decisions from the inside (competing resumes of candidates and the interviewer's comments and recommendations) believing it was a real company. They created a situation in which little doubt was present which candidate was best qualified. Sometimes these candidates were fairly chosen and at other times they were not. Experimenters varied the reasons (blatantly racist versus ambiguous racial reasons) in all combinations to Black and White volunteers. They would see Black candidates reviewed by Whites and Blacks, and the same for White candidates.

Following the simulation, volunteers were then given the "Stroop test," a measure of cognitive and mental effort functioning. Blacks who witnessed the unfair decisions showed pronounced impairment of problem solving; but those who witnessed subtle racism showed more impairment than those confronting overt racist conditions. The investigators believe that Blacks have developed coping strategies to deal with overt racism, in which no "guess-work" is involved. But the constant, vague, just-below-the-surface acts of covert racism impair performance by draining psychological energy or detracting from the task at hand. Interestingly, the findings were reversed for the White volunteers; they were more impaired by overt rather than subtle racism. We will elaborate more thoroughly the meaning of this finding later.

Stereotype Threat

Cognitive disruption and diminished functioning are also supported by studies on stereotype threat (Cadinu et al., 2005; Steele, 1997; 2003; Steele, Spencer, & Aronson, 2002). A very common microaggressive theme is "ascription of intelligence," in which certain racial groups are presumed to be intellectually inferior. For example, a common stereotype for African Americans is that they lack global abstract/conceptual reasoning, have lower intellectual skills, and are not capable of higher-level thinking (Jones, 1997). While women are seen as having higher verbal skills, they lack mathematical and scientific type reasoning that is required in objective linear thinking (Cadinu et al., 2005). Asian Americans are perceived as having high mathematical/science skills, but weaker verbal and people skills (Sue & Sue, 2008).

The concept of stereotype threat was first proposed by Steele (Steele, 1997; 2003; Steele et al., 2002) to describe a process by which many bright Black students underperform on intellectual tests not because of biology, lack of preparation, or poor motivation, but due to the chance that they will confirm a stereotype. The threat instigates two psychological processes: (1) apprehension that one will be evaluated by the stereotype and confirm it, and (2) protective disidentification or a tendency to reject the situation, deeming it irrelevant or unimportant. In other words, at the cognitive level the person tells himself or herself that the situation doesn't mean much, thereby separating self-esteem from outcome. Steele tested this hypothesis by selecting outstanding Black and White math students and giving them a difficult math test. In one condition (stereotype threat), students were told the test was a problem-solving exam, and in the other condition (nonthreat), the students were assured the test was not a measure of problem solving or abilities. Blacks under the stereotype threat condition performed worse than their White counterparts, but performed equally well under the nonthreat test conditions.

Stereotype threat has also been demonstrated in women who underperform in math tests. Using a similar strategy as Steele, investigators also explored the internal thought processes of the women exposed to stereotype threat (Cadinu et al., 2005). Not only did they underperform in the stereotype threat condition, but they recorded a higher number of negative intrusive thoughts that interfered with their performance. These included negative math-related thoughts, such as *"I am not good at math. I hate math"* and distress reactions, such as *"I am so tired."* Cognitive energy expenditure, disruption, deflection, and fatigue may all result from microaggressions.

Behavioral Effects of Microaggressive Stressors

Throughout all our chapters, we have identified a number of behaviors and coping responses used by people of color, women, and LGBTs to deal with microaggressions that are environmentally, verbally, and behaviorally directed at them. The range of responding is immense and depends on many factors. Some of the coping responses seem functional and adaptive (taking care of the self and educating the perpetrator), while others may prove dysfunctional and maladaptive (becoming depressed, overconsumption of alcohol, engaging in risky sexual behavior, striking back in anger). Even when a behavior appears functional in the moment—deciding to do nothing for fear of retaliation—we have seen how long-term consequences can be detrimental to both the biological and psychological well-being of the person.

Microaggressions can signal a hostile and invalidating climate, threaten the physical safety, self-esteem, and racial/gender/sexual identity of the target, and be oppressive. Forced compliance (either accept White, straight, and male definitions of the situation or suffer the consequences) is a chronic demand placed on marginalized groups in this society. We outline below five observed reactions that have either adaptive or maladaptive implications: (1) hypervigilance and skepticism, (2) forced compliance (surviving or being coopted), (3) rage and anger, (4) fatigue and hopelessness, and (5) strength through adversity.

Hypervigilance and Skepticism

Microaggressive stressors may partially explain the "cultural mistrust" or "healthy paranoia" in the form of suspiciousness, skepticism, and hypervigilance directed toward majority group members (Ridley, 2005; Sue & Sue, 2008). Some have referred to this form of behavior as "anticipatory racism reaction" developed because of multiple experiences of stereotyping, prejudice, and discrimination (Ponterotto et al., 2006). In the area of race relations, for example, people of color have experienced historical racism through governmental actions that include forced enslavement, taking of lands from indigenous groups, and the incarceration of Japanese Americans.

This historical racist legacy is compounded by the everyday subtle forms of racism that may deprive people of color equal access and opportunity. Thus the lack of trust or skepticism exhibited by many marginalized groups toward those in the majority society has become a healthy functional survival mechanism as well as a sanity check. On the functional end, it is an adaptive mechanism used to survive and even thrive, but on the other side, it may result in an inability to form close relations with members of the majority culture. In the extreme case, marginalized group members may begin to see racism, sexism, and heterosexism everywhere; they may be prone to externalizing all their failings and avoiding responsibility for their own actions.

Forced Compliance: Surviving or Being Coopted

Among African Americans, the "Uncle Tom" label is often used to describe members of their group who sell out or are subservient to the dominant White culture. For LGBTs it may refer to "staying in the closet" and not revealing their sexual orientation or dealing with internalized homophobia. In general, these behaviors need to be viewed from the perspective of a racist, sexist, and heterosexist environment that is responsible for the various behaviors used by marginalized groups. Concealing true feelings, conforming to the norms of the larger group, and behaving and expressing feelings in such a way as to prevent offending or threatening Whites enhances the chances of survival (Boyd-Franklin, 2003; Sue & Sue, 2008). Thus African Americans may use defense mechanisms such as the Uncle Tom syndrome, "playing it cool" for the purpose of protecting themselves from harm and exploitation. In the days of slavery, many Blacks acted in a subservient manner, appeared docile, and behaved passively for the sake of their own survival and loved ones. The downside of the forced compliance demand may be internalized racism, internalized sexism, and internalized heterosexism, or "selling out" to advance in society. These behaviors reveal an underlying attempt to please oppressors in order be avoid punishments and attain rewards (being coopted), at the cost of one's identity or sense of integrity.

Rage and Anger

Behaviorally, a person may act out their rage, frustration, and hostility to others, generally toward members of the dominant group (Grier & Cobbs, 1971). Years of forced compliance, assaults, and insults may lead some to decide "not to take it any more." They are often described as being constantly angry, overly sensitive, and unpleasant to be around. They are likely to avoid the oppressor, and not to form close interpersonal relationships. The opening chapter monologue by an African American male reveals the intense irritability and aggravation that sets off others, who see him as "always having a chip on his shoulder." In some respects, the intense rage may prove dysfunctional because it leaves the person in a constant state of agitation, pushes people away, and diminishes the joys of deep relationships with others. This is especially true when the anger becomes bitterness (Sue, 2003).

Fatigue and Hopelessness

Microaggressive stressors are taxing to a person both physically and psychologically. Many people of color, women, and LGBTs report exhaustion and fatigue from the constant petty humiliations, insults, and demeaning situations they must face in their lives. Physically, they find little energy to deal with microaggressions, but they also have less energy to devote to things that bring them joy. They may withdraw from social interactions, isolate themselves, and evidence poor or little social behavior. Energy levels are severely diminished to deal with everyday life events, and they may appear to have "given up." Hopelessness and helplessness may mean making little effort to take control of one's life because "it won't do any good." The behavioral signs of hopelessness have been found to be correlated with depression and suicide.

Strength through Adversity

The "strength through adversity" concept was developed primarily through observing how people of color, despite inhuman racial stressors in their lives (poverty, lower standards of living, conflicting value systems, racial microaggressions, etc.), seemed to continue functioning adaptively and even thriving in a less than accepting society (Sue, 2003). In Chapter 4, we describe the positive strengths and resources available to marginalized groups: heightened sense of perceptual awareness, ability to accurately read nonverbal and contextual cues, bicultural flexibility, and sense of group identity. These attributes have allowed people of color, women, and LGBTs to cope in a positive way with racism, sexism, and heterosexism.

The Way Forward

Coping with Microaggressions

It is clear that racial, gender, and sexual-orientation microaggressions, far from being benign forms of small, trivial, and innocent slights and insults, represent major stressors for marginalized groups. Their chronicity and cumulative lifelong nature make microaggressions extremely powerful stressors. They have been found to cause physiological distress, depress the immune system, increase susceptibility to infections and diseases, decrease subjective well-being and life satisfaction, and increase anxiety,

(Continued)

depression, and all forms of mental disorders. Microaggressions have been found to affect the biological, emotional, cognitive, and behavioral well-being of marginalized groups. Our chapter review, however, seems to reveal characteristics of microaggressive stress and how marginalized groups cope that provide insight into some basic survival and coping principles that are helpful toward reducing microaggressive stress.

1. Aversive events that are ambiguous, nebulous, and uncertain are more likely to be stressful than those which have a discrete and clearly defined and obvious cause. Life events such as preparing to take a final exam, losing a job, not getting a raise, going through a divorce, or becoming ill are all stressful, but the causes are clear and obvious to the individual and others. Microaggressions, however, are oftentimes invisible, diffuse, and intangible to both the perpetrator and potential target. As indicated earlier, people of color are less disturbed by overt and blatant forms of racism than microaggressions that are less obvious and difficult to determine. Reducing ambiguity and uncertainty and making the invisible visible would do much to lower the stress levels among marginalized groups. Indeed, one of the major contributions of microaggression research has been giving oppressed groups the language and concepts to speak about their experiences, to be able to name the offenses, to be liberated, and to feel empowered by the understanding of their experiences. The microaggression taxonomy has allowed many people of color, women, and LGBTs to define their experiences in concrete terms, to lower uncertainty, and to increase predictability of aversive events.

2. For the benefit of marginalized groups, education, training, and research aimed at identifying practical coping strategies in dealing with microaggressions may prove beneficial. How to confront microaggressors, take care of one's psychological health, and promote the education of oppressors are all very important. We know, for example, that psychological withdrawal, escapism, disengagement, resignation, internalizing racist, sexist, and heterosexist attributions, and denial of group identities are unhealthy coping behaviors. Yet little is known about healthy and effective ways that people of color, women, and LGBTs use to survive microaggressions. Most of the research on coping with perceived discrimination has defined it as an inner resource or "protective factors" (resistance to stress, high self-esteem, group identity, optimism, etc.) (Meyer, 2003; Utsey et al., 2008; Wei et al., 2008; Yoo & Lee, 2008). Few studies have actually

(Continued)

been conducted on specific behavioral or cognitive strategies employed by marginalized groups to cope with microaggressive events. Are active coping strategies better than passive ones (Liang et al., 2007)? What about early distinctions made between emotion-focused (reducing the impact of emotions) versus problem-focused (direct action) approaches to dealing with racism (Lazarus & Folkman, 1984)? Some promising work has been done in identifying styles of coping skills—problem-solving, reactive, suppressive, and reflective—in an attempt to answer this question (Heppner, Cook, Wright, & Johnson, 1995; Yoo & Lee, 2008).

3. Social reassurance and support are powerful forces that act as either a resource or buffer against microaggressive stress. We have already indicated how microaggressions are different from stressful life events: in the latter case, the cause is clear, problem solving and coping can be goal directed, others will not deny the difficulties and will be empathetic and generally offer emotional support, if not direct help. This is not necessarily true for microaggressive stress. Oftentimes, when a person points out a microaggression, the perpetrators deny it, are unsympathetic, and do not offer emotional support. In fact, they will frequently and actively attribute it to the target's oversensitivity. Our studies, for example, show that seeking social support and social validation from one's group is a powerful means of maintaining one's sanity and integrity (Sue, Capodilupo, & Holder, 2008; Sue, Lin, Torino, et al., 2009). Whether the cultural nutrients come from one's group members, family, friends, or allies is unimportant. Social support and reassurance allows one to not feel isolated and alone, supports and validates a person's worldview, and offers possible responses to the invalidating and insulting events.

4. Preparation and practice in dealing with microaggressions are important for people of color, women, and LGBTs. It seems incumbent upon parents to teach their sons and daughters about microaggressions, what they mean, and how to deal with them. It may be a sad statement, but it is important for people of color, women, and LGBTs in our current culture to experience racism, sexism, and heterosexism (Sue, 2003). Racism, sexism, and heterosexism are realities in the everyday life of these three marginalized groups. If a member of one of these groups is to survive, he or she must learn to develop the ability to deal effectively with "put downs" and insults. Protecting people of color, women, or LGBTs or attempting to

(Continued)

insulate them from such forms of prejudice and discrimination will lead to a false sense of security and consequently not allow them to develop the necessary survival tools. Teaching them how to recognize micro-aggressions reduces confusion and uncertainty, allows them to practice coping skills, and helps to maintain self-esteem.

5. As mentioned previously, considerable research has been directed at identifying inner resources or protective factors that make some people stronger and more immunized against microaggressions. High self-esteem, optimism, resilience, collectivism, and racial, gender, and sexual-orientation group identities (social identities) have all been posited as possible internal resources that (1) deter the onset of stress by functioning as an immunizing psychosocial resource (stress inoculation), (2) suppress the stressful experience, and (3) increase the availability of resources to combat a stressor (Ensel & Lin, 1991; Utsey et al., 2008). Studies do support the notion that high self-esteem and collectivism may suppress the negative impact of stress. However, the role of social group identity (for example, racial identity) has revealed mixed results (Sellers & Shelton, 2003; Utsey et al., 2008; Yoo & Lee, 2008). Some have speculated that ethnic identity would serve as a protective factor against experiences of racism (Lee, 2003; Liang & Fassinger, 2008), but some research suggests otherwise. In fact, some findings indicate that those with higher racial identity may experience greater distress than those with low racial identity (Yoo & Lee, 2008). It has been hypothesized that highly group-identified individuals may be more sensitive and willing to label negative incidents as prejudice. Thus, they may experience greater stress than those with lower group identities, who may not label a negative incident as race-related.

6. It is clear that not all forms of racial, gender, and sexual-orientation microaggressions have the same impact. Research has only just begun to scratch the surface in understanding the impact of microaggressions. Some future research areas involve:

   • First and foremost, in what ways are racial, gender, and sexual-orientation microaggressions the same or different from one another? Do they operate under similar or different processes? There are clearly defi-nite thematic differences between the three groups. Likewise, anec-dotal reports seem to suggest that microassaults are more common for LGBTs than for people of color and women. How does being an

(Continued)

invisible minority (LGBT) differ from being a visible minority group member with respect to the experience of microaggressions?

- Within racial groups, what similar and different racial microaggressions do African Americans, Asian Americans, Latino(a) Americans, and Native Americans experience? What are the specific racial or ethnic microaggressions associated with each group? Our studies suggest, for example, that Asian Americans and Latino(a)s are more likely to experience microaggressive themes associated with being "an alien in one's own land" while African Americans are more likely to experience themes of "criminality." In fact, Asian Americans seldom experienced criminality themes.

- In the taxonomy of microaggressions, are there differences in how microassaults, microinsults, and microinvalidations impact marginalized groups. Which are more harmful? Sue (2003) has asserted that he believes microinvalidations are the most harmful because they deny the racial, gender, and sexual-orientation realities of these three groups, while the other two forms represent a more direct attack.

- What are other factors that mediate or moderate the impact of microaggressions? Do microaggressions from strangers have less impact than those delivered by family, friends, or colleagues? Is the experience of a microaggression more severe when an unequal status relationship exists between perpetrator and target?

These are important areas of research that hopefully will lead us to shed light on microaggressive stresses and coping with them.

CHAPTER SIX

Microaggressive Perpetrators and Oppression: The Nature of the Beast

All the white people I know deplore racism. We feel helpless about racial injustice in society, and we don't know what to do about the racism we sense in our own groups and lives. Persons of other races avoid our groups when they accurately sense the racism we don't see (just as gays spot heterosexism in straight groups, and women see chauvinism among men). Few white people socialize or work politically with people of other races, even when our goals are the same. We don't want to be racist—so much of the time we go around trying not to be, by pretending we're not. Yet, white supremacy is basic in American social and economic history, and this racist heritage has been internalized by American white people of all classes. We have all absorbed white racism; pretence and mystification only compound the problem. (Winter, 1977, p. 2)

Spoken by Sara Winter, a White woman, nothing could be a more straight-forward statement about the internal struggle that she and many other well-intentioned people experience as they confront racism, sexism, and heterosexism: (1) a realization of the pervasiveness of oppression and injustice toward marginalized groups; (2) burgeoning recognition of their own role and complicity in the oppression of others; (3) pretending that they are free of biases and prejudices; (4) avoiding marginalized groups so they are not reminded about the racism, sexism, and heterosexism that lies inside and outside of them; (5) feeling impotent about changing social injustices in our society; (6) a realization that White, male, and heterosexual "supremacy" is a basic and integral part of U.S. society; and (7) an awareness that no one is free from inheriting the racial, gender, and sexual-orientation biases of this society.

Winter's quote, while addressing mainly racism, is directed toward well-intentioned Whites who are only marginally aware of their biases and their roles in the oppression of others. The internal struggle she describes is manifested cognitively (awareness vs. denial, mystification, and pretense) and behaviorally (isolation and avoidance of marginalized groups). The internal struggle, however, brings about strong, intense, and powerful emotional feelings as well:

> When someone pushes racism into my awareness, I feel guilty (that I could be doing so much more); angry (I don't like to feel like I'm wrong); defensive (I already have two Black friends. . . . I worry more about racism than most whites do—isn't that enough?); turned off (I have other priorities in my life than guilt about that thought); helpless (the problem is so big—what can I do?). I HATE TO FEEL THIS WAY. That is why I minimize race issues and let them fade from my awareness whenever possible. (Winter, 1977, p. 2)

On cognitive, behavioral, and emotional levels, little doubt exists that when microaggressive perpetrators become increasingly aware of their biases, they often experience debilitating emotional turmoil (guilt, fear, defensiveness) (Bowser & Hunt, 1981; Sue, 2003), cognitive distortion and constriction (false sense of reality) (Goodman, 2001; Spanierman & Heppner, 2004), and behavioral avoidance or inauthentic actions that impair relationships with marginalized individuals and/or groups (Hanna, Talley, & Guindon, 2000). So far, we have concentrated our discussion and analysis of racial, gender, and sexual-orientation microaggressions on the recipients, especially with respect to their harmful impact upon people of color, women, and LGBTs.

In this chapter, however, we turn our attention to describing the social and psychological dimensions of oppression as it relates to microaggressive perpetrators. Specifically, we are interested in addressing several questions. First, how and why do people become microaggressive perpetrators with oppressive attitudes, beliefs, and behaviors? Second, what makes it so difficult for those most empowered to become aware of their biased attitudes and behaviors? What mechanisms prevent them from realizing how they hurt and oppress others? Third, what are the psychosocial costs to perpetrators of racism, sexism, and heterosexism? This last question may seem contradictory as most discussions of oppression seem to focus on the benefits of racism for Whites, sexism for men, and heterosexism for straights (Pinterits, Poteat, & Spanierman, 2009; Spanierman, Todd, & Anderson, 2009; Sue, 2003, 2005). But increasing interest and scholarly works on the psychosocial costs of racism, for example, have spawned renewed interest in looking at the detrimental impact on those who oppress (Goodman, 2001; Hanna, Talley, & Guindon, 2000; Spanierman, Oh, et al., 2008) and even the development of a White Privilege Attitudes Scale (Pinterits et al., 2009).

OPPRESSION, OPPRESSORS, AND MICROAGGRESSIVE PERPETRATORS

Racism, sexism, and heterosexism are forms of oppression that unjustly persecute, subjugate, and denigrate others through the cruel exercise of power over individuals or groups (Hanna et al., 2000; Sue, 2003, 2004). When biases and prejudices become institutionalized and systemized into the norms, values, and beliefs of a society, they are passed on to generations of its citizens via socialization and cultural conditioning. These normative standards and beliefs are enforced by society through education, mass media, significant others, and institutions (Banks, 2004; Cortes, 2004). The effects of oppression may move through a progression of denigration, dehumanization, and demonization that adversely affect marginalized groups in our society.

None of us, however, would consciously and willingly consent to such heinous actions. In order to assure the continuance of the oppressor–oppressed relationship, and to keep such injustices hidden, therefore, it is desirable to perpetuate a "culture of silence" among oppressed groups (Freire, 1970) as well as perpetrators (Sue, 2004). When the oppressed are not allowed to express their thoughts and outrage, when their concerns are minimized, and when they are punished for expressing ideas at odds with the dominant group, their voices are effectively silenced. This allows perpetrators to hold on to a belief that they are good, moral, and decent human beings. In other words, pretense and mystification that racism, sexism, and heterosexism have been minimized or that they no longer pose a problem is reinforced by a "code of silence" that leaves perpetrators guilt-free and inequities unchallenged.

The nature of oppression can take many forms, as described by Hanna and colleagues (2000). The first form is oppression by force, coercion, or duress.

> It is the act of imposing on another or others an object, label, role experience, or set of living conditions that is unwanted, needlessly painful, and detracts from physical or psychological well-being. An imposed object, in this context, can be anything from a bullet, a bludgeon, shackles, or fists, to a penis, unhealthy food, or abusive messages designed to cause or sustain pain, low self-efficacy, reduced self-determination, and so forth. Other examples of oppression by force can be demeaning hard labor, degrading job roles, ridicule, and negative media images and messages that foster and maintain distorted beliefs. (p. 431)

With respect to microaggressions, labels or messages of inferiority, criminality, sexual objectification, and foreigner status may be imposed upon marginalized groups. Eroticization of Asian American women and using symbols and mascots that coopt and diminish the importance of American Indian cultures are a few of the examples.

The second form identified by Hanna et al. (2000) involves oppression by deprivation. It is the converse of imposition and involves depriving others of an object, label, role experience, or living conditions that are desirable for physical and mental well-being. A person can be deprived of psychological and social needs such as respect, love, social support, and dignity, or material needs such as clothing, food, shelter, and so forth. For example, in the early history of the Sioux nation, the U.S. Government banned certain spiritual and religious practices they considered subversive: American Indians were deprived of the rights to practice their religions.

"Elderspeak" is a microaggressive example of oppression by deprivation; it deprives the elder person the role of being a competent and capable adult by infantilizing him or her. It has been found that using the terms "Sweetie" and "Dear" are forms of belittlement directed toward the elderly. The doctor who talks to an elderly man's children about his health problems, a store clerk who assumes the older customer doesn't know how to work a computer, and a new acquaintance who speaks loudly to an elderly woman, send clear messages that assume less competence and capability (Leland, 2008). In other words, they are "being spoken down to." These negative messages of feebleness and forgetfulness deny the dignity of the elderly. It has been found that "elderspeak" may cause a downward spiral for older persons, result in physical health problems, and create low self-esteem, depression, and withdrawal (Leland, 2008).

The manifestations of oppression come in many forms. From the examples given throughout these chapters, it is inescapable that microaggressions are forms of oppression. Oppression can be overt or covert, subtle or obvious, intentional or unintentional, conscious or unconscious. In light of our democratic ideals and beliefs about egalitarianism, however, how do well-intentioned people fall into occupying roles that oppress and engage in prejudicial actions that harm others? The answer seems to reside in a dominant culture that values ways of being, thinking, and acting that reflects the reality of a primarily Eurocentric, masculine, and heterosexual worldview that is imposed upon racial, ethnic, gender, and sexual minorities (Hanna et al., 2000; Sue, 2004).

To illustrate the conversion process, I will use the concept of "whiteness" and White racial conditioning as it applies to racism and racial microaggressions. It would be an oversimplification and disservice to attempt equating the development of sexism and heterosexism to that of racism. Nevertheless, many of the sociopolitical and sociocultural dynamics describing the transformation of Whiteness to that of White supremacy and finally White racism may share similarities with the development of group-specific biases and prejudices experienced by other marginalized groups. We now turn our attention to "the nature of the beast."

THE INVISIBLE WHITENESS OF BEING: THE NATURE OF THE BEAST

One of the major characteristics of both microinsults and microinvalidations is that perpetrators are often minimally aware that they have engaged in a demeaning or denigrating manner toward people of color. Because Whites are socialized into Eurocentric values, beliefs, standards, and norms, they become invisible to them, and represent a default standard by which all other group norms and behaviors are consciously and unconsciously compared, contrasted, and made visible (Sue, 2004; Wildman & Davis, 2002). Some have argued that Whiteness in our society is considered to be normative and ideal and, as a result, dominance is automatically conferred on fair-skinned people (McIntosh, 2002; Jensen, 2002). It could also be argued that masculine and heterosexual standards are likewise operative, which disadvantages women and LGBTs.

The term "visible racial/ethnic minorities" was coined by Helms (1992, 1995) to refer to sociodemographic groups such as people of color who possessed phenotypical characteristics (skin pigmentation, head form, hair texture, and facial features such as nasal index and lip form) that distinguished them from the idealized physical features of the dominant group (fair skin, blue-eyed, straight hair, etc.). Although there is a lack of scientific support for a clear biological definition of race (Helms, Jernigan, & Mascher, 2005; Wang & S. Sue, 2005; Rowe, 2005), people continue to differentiate between groups on the basis of phenotype. In general the term "White," as used in the United States, refers not only to White Anglo-Saxon Protestants, but other White ethnics as well (Ponterotto, Utsey, & Pedersen, 2006). As they point out, the defining Anglolike features, primarily white skin, allowed White ethnics to assimilate and acculturate into mainstream America.

The experience of people of color, however, has been qualitatively different; their physical characteristics were seen as unacceptable by White people who blocked them from fully participating in the "land of opportunity." Thus, a color line that separated visible racial/ethnic minority features from those in the majority (dominant) culture became institutionalized with resulting psychological, sociological, economical, political, and legal implications. Whiteness became associated with everything desirable, while other physical features became associated with undesirability. In a broad sense, physical differences like Whiteness would not be problematic if it were not predicated on White supremacy, imposed overtly or covertly on people of color, and made invisible to well-intentioned perpetrators (Sue, 2003, 2004).

The deleterious effects of racial microaggressions, for example, are cloaked within an invisible White veil. In this manner, perpetrators are allowed to enjoy the benefits that accrue to them by virtue of their skin color. They resist the realization that Whiteness, White supremacy, and White privilege are three interlocking forces that disguise covert forms of racism. It allows many Whites to continue their oppressive and harmful ways while maintaining their individual and collective advantage and innocence. Covert racism hides in the background of Whiteness: (1) it is an unacknowledged secret protected through silence, (2) it advantages many Whites who enjoy unearned advantages due to skin color, and (3) it allows many Whites to deny responsibility for how it disadvantages and harms other groups of color (Sleeter & Bernal, 2004; Tatum, 2002).

Four-Step Process Model of Whiteness-to-Racism Conversion

The symbolic manifestation of Whiteness is an everyday occurrence and its normative features are insidiously manifested in our institutions and culture.

It becomes invisible, transparent, and an inseparable part of the background when White people are taught to think of their lives as morally neutral, average, or ideal (Sleeter & Bernal, 2004). The result is that both White supremacy and overt/covert racism become culturally conditioned into the lives of White people, albeit without their informed consent, and institutionalized in the very organizations that control their lives (Jones, 1997; Ridley, 2005; Smedley & Smedley, 2005). This transformation is quite insidious and Sue (2006a) has proposed a four-step process model to explain how Whiteness becomes converted to racism (see Table 6.1). The majority of White Americans are unaware of how the process of social conditioning has affected their worldview; some may understand the process on an intellectual level, but still emotively and behaviorally lag far behind their cognitive insights. Nevertheless, liberation psychology speaks to making the "invisible" visible as the first step to combating oppression and its consequences (Freire, 1970; Sue, 2004).

Transformation One—Association of Whiteness with White Supremacy

White skin color is a given and by itself carries no positive or negative connotations. It is when Whiteness becomes inextricably linked with White supremacy that the foundations are set for the development of racism. White supremacy notions rest on an interlocking set of beliefs and principles that justify discrimination, segregation, and domination of people of color (Feagin & Feagin, 1996; Welsing, 1991): (1) fair skin color is elevated to superior status while darker colors symbolize inferiority (Sue, 2005); (2) strong in-group preferences develop that reject or view other customs as unacceptable, deviant, or primitive (Jones, 1997); and (3) a sense of entitlement or divine destiny associated with White superiority develops (Sue, 2006a). The doctrine of White supremacy can operate at both a conscious and unconscious level. As we have mentioned previously, the extreme conscious manifestation of White racial superiority and minority inferiority are most clearly associated with White supremacists such as Skinheads and Ku Klux Klan members. Most White Americans in our society, however, inherit and possess unconscious White supremacist notions that are revealed in aversive racism or forms of racial microaggressions.

Table 6.1   Four-Step Process Model of Whiteness-to-Racism Conversion

Whites vary in the level of awareness they possess regarding the transformation process and how they are situated in the process.

Completely Unaware ------------------→ Minimally Aware -------------→ Fully Aware

----

Whiteness

The constellation of physical features most characterized by fair or light skin color/tone. Other physical features may be considered ideal (associated with Western traits) such as blond hair, blue eyes, or elongated face. Whiteness alone conveys neither positive nor negative valence.

+

White Supremacy

A doctrine of White racial superiority and non-White inferiority that justifies domination and prejudicial treatment of minority groups. It strongly attributes positive qualities to Whiteness and negative qualities to non-White groups.

+

Power Imposition

The ability to define racial reality by imposing White supremacist ideology and beliefs on the general population (both Whites and people of color).

+

Tools of Imposition

Schooling and Education + Mass Media + Significant Others and Organizations

These three mechanisms are used to convey the superiority of Whiteness and its associated correlates through a process of social conditioning.

=

White Racism

The individual, institutional, and cultural expression of the superiority of one group's cultural heritage over another and the power to impose and enforce that worldview upon the general populace.

**1. White Privilege
(Advantage)**

Unearned advantages and benefits that accrue to Whites by virtue of a system normed on the experiences, values, and perceptions of the group.

**2. Non-White Inferiority
(Disadvantage)**

Unequal/unfair treatment that occurs to people of color, not from their own actions, but based solely on the color of their skin or visible physical features.

Source: Adapted from Sue (2006).

Transformation Two—Power to Impose a Biased Racial Reality

Elsewhere, we have indicated that true power lies in a group's ability to define reality. If one looks at the history of the United States, it is the history of racism: enslavement of Black Americans, taking land from Native Americans, the World War II internment of Japanese Americans, and many other racist actions (Jones, 1997; Ponterotto et al., 2006; Ridley, 2005). In each case, such actions were justified by a racialized worldview that was primarily Western European in origin and filled with racist beliefs, attitudes, and myths: (1) Blacks were intellectually inferior, not truly human, and freedom was an unnatural state for them; (2) Japanese Americans, despite "two-thirds" being citizens by virtue of birth, were still more loyal to Japan and potentially spies; and (3) "manifest destiny" decreed it a divine mandate for Whites to expand across the continent and take land away from Native Americans (Jones, 1997; Sue, 2003). These views, which have been challenged and subsequently found inaccurate and harmful, were shared by the general populace in recent history. In all three cases, beliefs that one's own group held the corner on "truth" and that imposed a view of White superiority and minority inferiority resulted in oppression toward groups of color.

To this very day, White supremacist notions, whether intentional or unintentional, conscious or unconscious, continue to be transmitted to its citizens via a racial curriculum that glorifies the history of certain groups (White Western Europeans) while denigrating others and portraying them as inferior, primitive, and undesirable (Hanna et al., 2000; Jones, 1997). People are conditioned and taught to believe that Asian Americans are sneaky, foreigners, disloyal, and lack leadership skills; African Americans are dangerous, criminals, drug addicts, and intellectually inferior; Latinos are illegal aliens, welfare recipients, poor, and lazy; and Native Americans are alcoholics, primitive, savages, superstitious, and uneducable. These images teach children that certain groups are to be feared and avoided and evoke feelings of revulsion, fear, disgust, and contamination.

Transformation Three—Using the Tools: Socialization Mechanisms to Enforce Social Conditioning

The actual imposition of power to create a false racial reality and to enforce mistruths occurs through social and cultural conditioning where schooling and education, the mass media, significant others, and institutions collude in perpetuating a racial curriculum that is equated with "truth" and "reality" (Jones, 1997; Ridley, 2005; D. W. Sue, 2003).

First, our schools and curriculum are monocultural in nature and come primarily from a White Western European perspective that omits, distorts, or demonizes the history of non-White groups in America. Many multicultural scholars argue that changing the racial reality of people necessitates incorporating the accurate histories and cultures of people of color not only into the study of Western civilization but also into the materials used for education, teaching and learning styles, the attitudes and behaviors of teachers and administrators, and the school campus culture (Banks, 2004; Sleeter & Bernal, 2004). We have already shown how falsehoods can have major negative consequences for groups of color when they are disguised as educational truths: when students are taught that Columbus discovered America, the internment of Japanese Americans was a national security issue (not racism), and the taking of land from Native Americans was manifest destiny, worldviews are shaped to reflect White racial superiority and non-White racial inferiority.

Second, the mass media that includes printed materials (newspapers, magazines, websites, etc.), television, film, and radio often dispense powerful images of race and racial beliefs to the general public. The continual repetition of themes and messages about race that involve criminality, poverty, intellectual deficiencies, foreignness, and so on provides an information base by which we learn about other groups in our society (Cortes, 2004). Interestingly, the portrayal of people of color in the media may also have devastating consequences for the oppressed as well as the oppressor. In a media study carried out by Children Now (1998), it was found that children representing all racial groups were most likely to associate positive qualities with White characters and negative ones with minority characters. Latino and Asian children were more likely to be omitted in media portrayals; Whites usually played high status roles such as doctors, police officers, and bosses; Blacks played the roles of criminals or domestic servants. The study concludes that media portrayals of persons of color showed them as less worthy of respect, less capable, dangerous, and to be feared.

Third, peers and social/organizational groups exert an equally powerful means of dispensing a racial curriculum to the general populace. The Boy Scouts of America propagates its attitudes toward gays by denying the existence of gay scouts and barring prospective gay scout leaders from admission or leadership positions, and the U.S. military conveys its beliefs about gays through its policy of "don't ask, don't tell." The exclusion and codified taboo against "coming out" silences those who are oppressed and demeans them as deviant and socially unacceptable. Messages received from schools, places of employment, churches, and one's own family perpetuate racism. The social conditioning of young children, for example, can occur nonverbally through parental actions as described below.

> It was a late summer afternoon. A group of white neighborhood mothers, obviously friends, had brought their 4- and 5-year-olds to the local McDonald's for a snack and to play on the swings and slides provided by the restaurant. They were all seated at a table watching their sons and daughters run about the play area. In one corner of the yard sat a small black child pushing a red truck along the grass. One of the white girls from the group approached the black boy and they started a conversation. During that instant, the mother of the girl exchanged quick glances with the other mothers who nodded knowingly. She quickly rose from the table, walked over to the two, spoke to her daughter, and gently pulled her away to join her previous playmates. Within minutes, however, the girl again approached the black boy and both began to play with the truck. At that point, all the mothers rose from the table and loudly exclaimed to their children, "It's time to go now!" (D. W. Sue, 2003, pp. 89–90)

Transformation Four—Racism through Whiteness

> Cultural racism comprises the cumulative effects of a racialized worldview, based on belief in essential racial differences that favor the dominant racial group over others. These effects are suffused throughout the culture via institutional structures, ideological beliefs, and personal everyday actions of people in the culture, and these effects are passed on from generation to generation. (Jones, 1997, p. 472)

The conditioning aspect of culture is well known as it guides us in how we think, feel, and act. The association of Whiteness with White supremacy through social conditioning and the imposition of racial realities that advantage one group but disadvantage another become transformed into White racism. In broad terms, racism is the individual, institutional, and cultural expression of the superiority of White Western cultural heritage over all non-White groups. Inherent in this definition is the power to impose and enforce that worldview on those in this society (Whites and non-Whites). There are three outcomes associated with White racism: (1) justification of unequal and unfair treatment to people of color based solely on the color of their skin or visible physical features, (2) unearned advantages and benefits that accrue to Whites by virtue of their skin color (White privilege), and (3) inherent disadvantages (inferior education, segregated housing, lower wages, and negative sociopsychological consequences) to people of color.

THE RELATIONSHIP OF IMPLICIT BIAS TO MICROAGGRESSIONS

The transformation of Whiteness to racism and the social/cultural condition-ing described above have broad scholarly support (Banks, 2004; Cortes, 2004; Jones, 1997; Ridley, 2005). One of the questions we posed at the beginning of this chapter was how and why people become unintentional oppressors. Why do they have biases and prejudices? If White Americans experience them-selves as good, moral, and decent human beings, why would they engage in racial microaggressions that harm others? It is clear from our analysis that Whites are unwitting victims in a social conditioning process that imbues within them biased racial attitudes; many biases exist outside the level of awareness because they are deeply embedded in the psyche and made invis-ible. As a society, we have come a long way in recognizing our racist heritage and have actively sought to deal with the overt and obvious manifestations of racism. While we have had success in reducing overt and explicit forms of bias and discrimination, we have been less successful in eradicating covert or implicit forms (Baron & Banaji, 2006; Boysen & Vogel, 2008).

Studies on racial microaggressions (microinsults and microinvalidations) suggest that they are implicit in nature and, therefore, less prone to change over time than explicit expressions (Sue, Capodilupo, et al., 2007; Sue, Capodilupo, Nadal, & Torino, 2008; Sue, Bucceri, Lin, Nadal, & Torino, 2007). There is some evidence supporting this conjecture in the "implicit attitudes" studies in social psychology (Baron & Banaji, 2006; Greenwald, McGhee, & Schwartz, 1998). The traditional measurement of biases, stereotypes, and prej-udices comes primarily from conscious self-reports in which participants are directly asked about their attitudes toward specific social groups. These meth-ods are prone to the influence of social desirability and political correctness, and they do not adequately tap the underlying implicit attitudes that are outside conscious awareness (Sue, 2003). In the field of social psychology, implicit measurement of bias relies on having people make decisions or judgments that avoid conscious introspection. One such instrument is the Implicit Attitudes Test (IAT) in which reaction time in associating a target group with positive and negative qualities is measured. It is possible to measure pro-White and anti-Black implicit attitudes, for example, using the IAT.

In viewing the conversion model outlined above, it is clear that explicit attitude (conscious) and implicit attitude (unconscious) are subject to the same socialization process, but there may not be a one-to-one correspondence with one another. In other words, it is possible for someone to consciously denounce racism, and believe they would never willingly discriminate against others, but still harbor unconscious racist beliefs and attitudes. In one of the first studies to measure the development and change of implicit and explicit racial attitudes over time, the investigators sampled three different age groups: 6-year-olds, 10-year-olds, and adults (Baron & Banaji, 2006). The 6-year-old age group was chosen because studies indicate that children between 3 and 6 years of age begin to form attitudes about specific social groups, and by age 5 usually have an adultlike concept of race (Aboud, 1988; Hirschfeld, 2001). The investigators created a children's version of the adult IAT and administered it to the children. They found the following: (1) at age 6, implicit and explicit race bias attitudes were relatively similar; (2) at age 10, a dissociation began to occur between implicit and explicit race bias—explicit bias tends to decrease, but implicit bias remains unchanged; and (3) at adulthood, explicit bias dropped even further, but implicit bias remained unchanged.

These findings are extremely meaningful because they suggest that implicit biases (pro-White and anti-Black attitudes) among all three age groups remained constant, but that explicit biases were significantly decreased. Implicit racial biases appear to be highly resistant to change, as indicated in another study that explored the relationship between level of training, implicit bias, and cultural competence (Boysen & Vogel, 2008). Boysen and Vogel studied the effects of multicultural training on implicit bias associated with African Americans, lesbians, and gay men. While multicultural competence increased with more training, implicit biases toward these groups remained untouched!

These findings are extremely disturbing and indicate the "nature of the beast." Microaggressions reflect a worldview of inclusion–exclusion, and superiority–inferiority at both the implicit and explicit levels. At the explicit and conscious levels, we have made great strides in combating racism, sexism, and heterosexism, but our task is daunting at the implicit level. To adequately address implicit racial, gender, and sexual-orientation attitudes, however, means to somehow understand the mindset of unintentional oppressors—their psychological defenses and resistances.

Confronting Implicit Biases and Microaggressions

I was deeply troubled as I witnessed on a daily basis the detrimental effects of institutional racism and oppression on ethnic-minority groups in this country.

The latter encounters forced me to recognize my privileged position in our society because of my status as a so-called Anglo. It was upsetting to know that I, a member of White society, benefited from the hardships of others that were caused by a racist system. I was also disturbed by the painful realization that I was, in some ways, a racist. I had to come to grips with the fact that I had told and laughed at racist jokes and, through such behavior, had supported White racist attitudes. If I really wanted to become an effective, multicultural psychologist, extended and profound self-reckoning was in order. At times, I wanted to flee from this unpleasant process by merely participating superficially with the remaining task . . . while avoiding any substantive self-examination. (Kiselica, 1998, p. 10–11)

We had posed earlier the question as to why it is so difficult for people to acknowledge their biases and preconceived notions about marginalized groups in our society. Why do they react so angrily or emotionally when it is suggested that they may have expressed a biased attitude or belief, or acted in a discriminatory manner (microaggression)? Mark Kiselica's (1998) quote of his own racial/cultural awakening, his realization of his own racism, the guilt experienced in benefiting from the hardship of others, and his desire to flee from further exploration or self-examination are typical of many Whites (Sue & Constantine, 2007). Herein lay clues as to why many Whites (1) pretend not to see race (color); (2) resist the notion that they may hold racist, sexist, or heterosexist attitudes; and/or (3) find it disconcerting to conclude that they may be racist, sexist, or homophobic. A review of the scholarly literature suggests four psychological fears or obstacles to honest self-examination: fear of appearing racist, realizing one's own racism, acknowledging White privilege, and accepting the consequences of action or inaction (Sue & Constantine, 2007). Each is layered one upon another and represents defensive barriers with deeper and deeper fears and meanings.

Layer One—Fear of Appearing Racist

One of the disconcerting microaggressions experienced by people of color from well-intentioned Whites is color-blindness; the avoidance by Whites of talking about race or even acknowledging that they notice a racial difference. A multitude of studies, however, indicate that race is among the most automatic and quickest ways to categorize people and that perceiving the race of the other person is more the norm than the exception (Apfelbaum, Sommers, & Norton, 2008; Ito & Urland, 2003). Yet, why do people continue to claim they do not see color or race in social situations? The use of "strategic color-blindness" is an attempt to appear unbiased in social interactions by pretending not to notice racial differences (Apfelbaum et al., 2008; Sue, 2004). Studies suggest that many Whites fear that whatever they say or do will appear racist; thus, avoidance, pretense, and mystification guide their behaviors (Dunton & Fazio, 1997; Gaertner & Dovidio, 2005; Plant & Devine, 1998). Denial is the major defense used in this stage of development.

The fear of appearing racist has both a positive and negative quality about it. On the one hand, and in an ironic way, it reaffirms a belief in equity and the intrinsic worth of everyone. It is heartening to know that many Whites consciously believe in equal opportunity, democracy, and social justice as taught to us in the U.S. Constitution, Bill of Rights, and Declaration of Independence. Thus, managing and/or preventing prejudice from occurring may be seen as a positive aspect of personal character. On the other hand, it indicates that many people may possess less than desirable attributes associated with race and gender. In some respects, it may indicate recognition that many possess hidden biases that are at odds with these cherished beliefs. Considerable evidence indicates, however, that in racially related situations, strategic color blindness and impression management are unsuccessful for Whites; their nonverbal behaviors give the opposite impression, and their verbalizations become hesitant, convoluted, and full of broken utterances, all of which are indicative of anxiety (Apfelbaum et al., 2008; Utsey, Gernat, & Hammar, 2005). In essence, many Whites desperately attempt to hide their prejudicial attitudes, beliefs, and behaviors not only to others, but to themselves as well.

Layer Two—Fear of Acknowledging One's Racism

Strategic color blindness has been postulated as an attempt to appear unbiased to others in interpersonal interactions that possess race-related implications. If we peel away that layer, however, there appears to be a deeper fear—a potential revelation that one possesses racial biases. More frightening may be what Mark Kiselica concludes in the extract from his book quoted previously: *"I was also disturbed by the painful realization that I was, in some ways, a racist."* He continues his racial awakening by indicating that he has been complicit in benefiting from the oppression of others, although unknowingly (Kiselica, 1998). The resistance to acknowledging racist attitudes, beliefs, and behaviors in oneself is linked to a major conflict dealing with self-image and identity. As mentioned previously, White Americans on a conscious level have been taught and genuinely believe in egalitarian values, that everyone should be treated equally, and that they would never intentionally discriminate against others (Dovidio & Gaertner, 1996; Watt, 2007). Their self-identity is encased in a strong belief in their own morality and decency as human beings.

For White Americans to acknowledge that they harbor antiminority feelings and have acted in ways that oppress others shatters their self-concept as good and moral human beings. To realize that one is racist or at least holds prejudicial attitudes is both frightening and unsettling because it strikes at the core of human decency. No wonder so many White Americans find even entertaining the notion of their own racism anxiety-provoking and painful. No wonder they react with defensiveness and anger when there is even a slight hint of possible racial bias.

Layer Three—Fear of Acknowledging White Privilege

When the first and second layers are unmasked, when Whites begin to acknowledge that they have been complicit in the oppression of others, and when they admit that they harbor racial biases, another deeper layer of realization presents itself: the possibility that they have benefited from racism and the present racist arrangements and practices of society that oppress one group, but advantage another (McIntosh, 2002; Jones, 1997; Sue, 2004). As the invisible White veil of self-deception begins to lift, they no longer can deny their complicity in the oppression of others and that they directly and indirectly benefit from the current state of affairs. While denial is most prevalent in level one and anger/defensiveness in level two, level three is marked by strong feelings of guilt.

White privilege is the term used to describe the unearned benefits and advantages that automatically accrue to Whites by virtue of their skin color (McIntosh, 2002; Watt, 2007). Many have broadened this concept to address "male privilege" and "heterosexual privilege" as well. While most Whites are seemingly willing to entertain the notion that people of color suffer from prejudice and discrimination and are thus "disadvantaged," they resist considering the possibility that they are automatically "advantaged" because of their skin color (Sue, 2003). Acknowledging White privilege is difficult for two reasons. First, as shown in our transformation process model, it is clear that White privilege could not exist outside the confines of White supremacy. Second, if Whites benefit from White privilege, then they must entertain the notion that they did not achieve their success in life through their own individual efforts, but through a system normed and standardized on the experiences of Whites. They are unfairly advantaged in nearly all aspects of employment and education. The following quote illustrates this realization and meaning:

> I know I did not get where I am by merit alone. I benefited from, among other things, white privilege. That doesn't mean that I don't deserve my job, or that if I weren't white I would never have gotten the job. It means simply that all through my life, I have soaked up benefits for being white. I grew up in fertile farm country taken by force from non-white indigenous people. I was educated in a well-funded, virtually all-white public school system in which I learned that white people like me made this country great. There I also was taught a variety of skills, including how to take standardized tests written by and for white people.
>
> There certainly is individual variation in experience. Some white people have had it easier than me, probably because they came from wealthy families that gave them even more privilege. Some white people have had it tougher than me because they came from poorer families. White women face discrimination I will never know. But, in the end, white people all have drawn on white privilege somewhere in their lives. (Jensen, 2002, 104–105)

Layer Four—Fear of Taking Personal Responsibility to End Racism

Once Whites achieve level-three awareness, they are confronted with another dilemma in level four: How do they deal with their own racism and the benefits and advantages that they have enjoyed individually and collectively? Does the realization of inequities built upon racism and how they personally profit from it motivate change and action? Or do Whites deny responsibility for it? The ultimate White privilege may be the ability to acknowledge one's privileged position in life, but do nothing about it! One would hope that awareness of racial injustice at this level would be powerful motivation to take action against these unfair personal and structural advantages for Whites and disadvantages for people of color.

It is therefore disheartening to realize that despite awareness of inequities and injustice (cognitive insight), many White Americans may not follow through affectively and behaviorally in taking responsibility to intervene when racial injustice occurs and/or proactively combat discrimination. In a study aimed at predicting affective and behavioral responses to racism, for example, investigators found that Whites mispredict their affective and behavioral responses to racism (Kawakami, Dunn, Karmali, & Dovidio, 2009). While they (1) clearly recognized racist actions, verbalizations, and events, and (2) indicated that they would find such situations distressing, and (3) predicted they would take responsible action against the person (rejecting the racist person), White participants in the study were not only less distressed about racist incidents, but also less likely to take any action at all!

What, therefore, keeps Whites from acting against racism when they no longer deny its existence within themselves and fellow Whites? Don't these insights demand action? Sue and Constantine (2007) summarize the overwhelming insights that may flood the person at this level and provide a clue of the forces that make change difficult. The magnitude of the change is so overpowering that helplessness and hopelessness may ensue.

> Most White Americans who come to this realization find the implications frightening. It means seeing some family and friends in a different light; for example, a favorite relative could engage in racist comments or jokes. It may mean realizing you may have been offered a job over a candidate of color because you had the "right" (White) skin color and not because of your qualifications. It means understanding how systemic societal forces produce segregation, allowing only certain groups to purchase homes in affluent neighborhoods. It means knowing that you participate in perpetuating segregated schools that dispense inferior education to one group, but advantaged education to another. It means seeing how your school uses biased curricula, textbooks, and materials that reaffirm the identity of one group while denigrating other groups. It means knowing that hiring policies and practices that utilize the "old boy's network" to recruit and hire prospective employees work to your advantage.

> To accept responsibility for combating racism and injustice means actions that would forever change their lives because it means constant vigilance and action against the forces of oppression. It means potentially alienating family, friends, or colleagues when you confront them about their biases. It means risking their position at work (not getting a promotion or being fired) by speaking up against unfair employment practices. It means making new friends that include people of color in an attempt to change their experiential reality. It means confronting forces in our society that constantly attempt to have them move back to a stance of denial, to once again enter into a conspiracy of silence and to maintain a naïve posture. (Sue, 2005, pp. 141–142)

Each of these layers of awareness has their own unique challenges, but all represent the herculean task of getting White Americans to understand racism. When seen from this perspective, it becomes clear why denial, anger, defensiveness, guilt, and helplessness/hopelessness represent unpleasant emotional roadblocks that prevent Whites from recognizing racial microaggressions. To do so changes their self-concept and shatters the false racial reality that has been instrumental in shaping their identities and establishing their positions in life.

THE PSYCHOLOGICAL COSTS OF OPPRESSION (MICROAGGRESSIONS) TO PERPETRATORS

While most people describe racism, sexism, and heterosexism as unfairly benefiting oppressors, an increasing body of literature suggests they are not without costs for perpetrators. Some scholars have described the downside for perpetrators of oppression across various marginalized groups at both the national and international levels (Bowser & Hunt, 1981; Freire, 1970; Goodman, 2001; Hanna et al., 2000; Sue, 2003). Spanierman and colleagues (Spanierman & Heppner, 2004; Spanierman, Oh, et al., 2008; Spanierman, Poteat, Wang, & Oh, 2008; Spanierman et al., 2009) have been instrumental in researching and contributing to our understanding of the "psychosocial costs of racism to Whites." They developed a tripartite model of cognitive, affective, and behavioral costs to Whites of racism and an instrument to measure their effects (Spanierman & Heppner, 2004). More recently, the initial development of the White Privilege Attitudes Scale has indicated the tripartite division as very useful in understanding how oppression affects these dimensions (Pinterits et al., 2009). We will use their conceptual framework to organize our discussion around the psychosocial costs of oppression to oppressors, but add a spiritual/moral component as well (Goodman, 2001; Kivel, 1996).

Cognitive Costs of Oppression

Many have argued that being an aversive racist requires a dimming of perceptual awareness and accuracy that is associated with self-deception (Bowser & Hunt, 1981; Goodman, 2001; Hanna et al., 2000). The detrimental cognitive and perceptual consequence to White Americans comes from two psychological dynamics related to oppression. First, few oppressors are completely unaware of their roles in the oppression and degradation of others. To continue in their oppressive ways, however, they must engage in denial and live a false reality that allows them to function in good conscience. Second, the oppressors' empowered status over marginalized groups may have a corrupting influence in the ability to attune to the plight of marginalized groups. The oft-quoted saying that "Power tends to corrupt and absolute power corrupts absolutely" has been attributed to Lord Acton in 1887. In essence, an imbalance of power acutely affects perceptual accuracy and diminishes reality testing. In the corporate world, for example, women must attune to the feelings and actions of their male colleagues in order to survive in a male culture. People of color must be constantly vigilant to read the minds of their oppressors lest they incur their wrath. Oppressors, however, do not need to understand the thoughts, beliefs, or feelings of various marginalized groups to survive. Oppressors do not have to account for their actions to those without power, and they need not understand the marginalized groups to function effectively. Therefore, it is not surprising to find that those who are most empowered are least likely to have an accurate perception of reality (Keltner & Robinson, 1996). Thus, it is clear that racism serves as a clamp on the mind of many White Americans, distorting their perception of reality. Their obliviousness to racism, sexism, and heterosexism allows people to misperceive themselves as superior and other groups as inferior; it allows oppressors to live in a false reality.

Affective Costs of Oppression

As we have seen, when racism, sexism, or heterosexism is pushed into the consciousness of oppressors, they are likely to experience a mix of strong and powerful disruptive emotions. These intense feelings represent emotional roadblocks to self-exploration and must be deconstructed if oppressors are to continue in their journey to self-reckoning (Kiselica, 1998). Three especially disturbing emotional costs are outlined below.

1. *Fear, anxiety, and apprehension* are common and powerful feelings that arise when race, gender, or sexual-orientation related situations present themselves (Apfelbaum et al., 2008; Pinterits et al., 2009; Spanierman et al., 2009). The fear may be directed at members of marginalized groups—that they are dangerous, will do harm, are prone to violence, or contaminate the person (catching AIDS). Thus, avoidance of certain group members and restricting interactions with them may be chosen. Fear of people of color has been found to be related to lower racial awareness, fewer interracial friendships, less openness to diversity, and many other negative features (Spanierman & Heppner, 2004).

Fear of seeming racist (strategic color blindness) is another type of fear that takes a toll because it fosters pretense and inauthenticity (Apfelbaum et al., 2008; Spanierman, et al., 2009; Sue, 2003) in social interactions. In fact, there are indications that color blindness as a means to manage impression formation fails miserably and has the opposite effect; it makes people appear more biased through their nonverbal behaviors. Such constant vigilance related to color blindness has been found to result in cognitive depletion, less warmth, and the sending of mixed signals in social situations (Dovidio, Gaertner, Kawakami, & Hodson, 2002; Apfelbaum et al., 2008).

2. *Guilt* is another strong and powerful emotion that many Whites experience when racism is brought to their awareness. As we have indicated, an attempt to escape guilt and remorse means dulling and diminishing one's own perception. Knowledge about race-based advantages, the continued mistreatment of large groups of people, and the realization that people have personally been responsible for the pain and suffering of others elicits strong feelings of guilt (Spanierman & Heppner, 2004). Guilt creates defensiveness and outbursts of anger in an attempt to deny, diminish, and avoid such a disturbing self-revelation.

3. *Low empathy* and sensitivity toward the oppressed is another outcome of oppression for the perpetrator. The harm, damage, and acts of cruelty visited upon marginalized groups can only continue if the person's humanity is diminished; oppressors lose sensitivity to those that are hurt; they become hard, cold, and unfeeling to the plight of the oppressed; and they turn off their compassion and empathy for others. To continue being oblivious to one's own complicity in such acts means objectifying and dehumanizing people of color, women, and LGBTs. In many respects it means separating oneself from others, seeing them as lesser beings, and in many cases treating them like subhuman aliens (Sue, 2005).

Behavioral Costs of Oppression

Behaviorally, the psychosocial costs of racism include fearful avoidance of diverse groups and/or diversity activities/experiences in our society; impaired interpersonal relationships; pretense and inauthenticity in dealing with racial, gender, or sexual-orientation topics; and acting in a callous and cold manner toward fellow human beings (Freire, 1970; Hanna et al., 2000; Spanierman & Heppner, 2004; Spanierman, Poteat, Beer, & Armstrong, 2006; Spanierman et al., 2009; Sue, 2005).

Fearful avoidance deprives oppressors the richness of possible friendships and an expansion of educational experiences that open up life horizons and possibilities. If we use racism as an example, there is great loss in depriving oneself of interracial friendships, forming new alliances, and learning about differences related to diversity. Self-segregation because of fear of certain groups in our society and depriving oneself of multicultural/diversity experiences constricts one's life possibilities and results in a narrow view of the world.

We have already mentioned how interpersonal relationships are seriously undermined because of racist, sexist, or homophobic fears. The fear of appearing racist, for example, makes people avoid talking about the subject, even when it is central to the interaction or situation (Sue, Rivera, Capodilupo, Lin, & Torino, 2009; Young & Davis-Russell, 2002). When Whites do speak about race, however, they become convoluted in their communications and their utterances are marked by excessive hesitations, stammering, and pauses (Utsey et al., 2005). All of this conveys anxiety as they deny or pretend not to see race (inauthenticity). The internal dialogue and conflict of Whites regarding race is aptly captured in the following quote:

> We avoid people of color because their presence brings painful questions to mind. Is it OK to talk about watermelons or mention "black coffee"? Should we use Black slang and tell racial jokes? How about talking about our experiences in Harlem, or mentioning our Black lovers? Should we conceal the fact that our mother still employs a Mexican cleaning lady? . . . We're embarrassedly aware of trying to do our best but to "act natural" at the same time. No wonder we're more comfortable in all-White situations where these dilemmas don't arise. (Winter, 1977, p. 3)

Spiritual and Moral Cost of Oppression

During the so-called "war on terror," and as a direct result of fears associated with the terrorist attack of 9/11, the Abu Ghraib prison in Iraq was used to hold suspected terrorists who were captured or arrested. In 2004, reports of torture, sodomy, abuse, and homicide of prisoners were leaked to the press and public. A criminal investigation along with disturbing photos of torture and humiliation visited on prisoners by American sons and daughters of the military surfaced. Seven soldiers were convicted of dereliction of duty, maltreatment, and aggravated assaults. The pictures of our own soldiers taking such delight in torturing prisoners were shocking and prompted many to ask, "How could good and decent Americans, our sons and daughters, have engaged in such grotesque, humiliating, and perhaps murderous actions toward prisoners (fellow human beings)?" The answer seems to lie in the dehumanization process that portrayed the prisoners as subhuman aliens that were even lower than animals. This is certainly not a new phenomenon. During World War II and the Vietnam War, the Japanese and Viet Cong were referred to in demeaning racial epithets: "Japs," "gooks," and "slants." This allowed soldiers to kill their enemies without guilt or compassion, because they were lesser beings. To carry out the atrocities of the Holocaust, soldiers and German citizens needed to believe that the Jews were subhuman and unworthy of life.

In essence, oppression inevitably means losing one's humanity for the sake of the power, wealth, and status attained from the subjugation of others. It means losing a spiritual connection with fellow human beings. It means a refusal to recognize the polarities of the democratic principles of equality and the inhuman and unequal treatment of the oppressed. It means turning a blind eye to treating marginalized groups like second-class citizens, imprisoning groups on reservations or in concentration camps, inferior schools, or segregated neighborhoods, in prisons, or in lifelong poverty. To allow the continued degradation, harm, and cruelty to the oppressed means diminishing one's humanity, and lessening compassion toward others. People who oppress must, at some level, become callous, cold, hard, and unfeeling toward the plight of the oppressed.

The Way Forward

The Ethical Mandate

Racial, gender, and sexual-orientation microaggressions are manifestations of oppression. They reflect a worldview of superiority–inferiority, albeit in a much more subtle but equally harmful manner as overt forms of oppression. They remain invisible because of a cultural conditioning process that allows perpetrators to discriminate without knowledge of their complicity in the inequities visited upon people of color, women, LGBTs, and other marginalized groups.

Because bigotry is such a despised concept in our society, the actions of others are protected through a conspiracy of silence that allows perpetrators to benefit in good conscience and innocence. The herculean task of making the "invisible" visible is met with many psychosocial defenses that consistently prevent oppressors from realizing their biases and acting in ways to change themselves, others, and systemic injustices.

The costs of inaction for perpetrators can be calculated in the cognitive, emotional, behavioral, and spiritual toll to oppressors. As we have indicated, even when perpetrators recognize and acknowledge their responsibility in combating oppression, and even when they state they will take action, they tend not to do so.

(Continued)

The way forward is a difficult journey, but the moral and ethical mandate for social justice requires action, not passivity and inaction. Since publication in 1954 of his classic book, *The Nature of Prejudice*, Gordon Allport's work still serves as the foundations of revealing basic principles of prejudice reduction and lowering intergroup hostility. Since that time, continued work on antiracism has shown the importance of establishing the following conditions to combat racial bias and prejudice. Additionally, each is a necessary, but not a sufficient condition to combat racism. In other words, change is most likely to be positive when all seven conditions exist. Each would require considerable elaboration, but are only briefly listed here. A more thorough description can be found in D. W. Sue (2003).

1. Having intimate contact with people who differ from us in race, culture, ethnicity, gender, and sexual orientation.
2. Working together in a cooperative rather than a competitive environment.
3. Sharing mutual goals (superordinate goals) as opposed to individual ones.
4. Exchanging and learning accurate information rather than stereotypes or misinformation.
5. Sharing an equal status relationship with other groups instead of an unequal or imbalanced one.
6. Having leadership and authority as supportive of group harmony and welfare.
7. Feeling a sense of unity or spiritual interconnectedness with all humanity.

It is easy for me to outline these conditions, but the question is how to achieve them in this society. There are no simple answers, but I end this chapter with the following quote, attributed to Albert Einstein: "The world is too dangerous to live in—not because of the people who do evil, but because of the people who sit and let it happen."

Group-Specific Microaggressions: Race, Gender, and Sexual Orientation

CHAPTER SEVEN

Racial/Ethnic Microaggressions and Racism

Then, in his calm, baritone voice, Judge Parker spoke to me slowly and deliberately . . .

"I believe you were terribly wronged by being held in custody pretrial in the Santa Fe County Detention Center under demeaning, unnecessarily punitive conditions. I am truly sorry that I was led by our executive branch of government to order your detention last December.

"Dr. Lee, I tell you with great sadness that I feel I was led astray last December by the executive branch of our government through its Department of Justice, by its Federal Bureau of Investigation, and by its United States attorney for the district of New Mexico, who held the office at that time . . .

"I sincerely apologize to you, Dr. Lee, for the unfair manner you were held in custody by the executive branch."

The judge then adjourned the court: I was moments away from being freed.

I leaned over to [my lawyer] Mark Holscher and asked him, "Is it common for a judge to talk like this?"

Mark replied, "No, Wen Ho. This is very, very rare." (W. H. Lee, 2001, pp. 6–7)

In his book, *My Country versus Me* (2001), Wen Ho Lee, a patriotic American scientist who had devoted decades of his life to science and helping improve

137

U.S. defense capabilities, tells the riveting story of how he was arrested, shackled, and jailed in a tiny solitary-confinement cell for 9 months based upon suspicions that he was a spy. The case sparked controversy throughout the country and brought forth issues of national security, McCarthyism paranoia, and racism. Judge Parker's apology made on behalf of the American people spoke volumes about how the government profiled, mistreated, manufactured evidence, and deceived others based upon their belief that he was a disloyal American who had sold out his country.

While many of the acts were forms of blatant racism directed against Lee, reading the book gives a firsthand account of how racial microaggressions played a major role in his incarceration. As he states, the government's suspicions, and the bias and beliefs of the media (most prominently the *New York Times*), played on the fears of the American public that Asians are foreigners, spies, sneaky, and have greater allegiance to Asia. These beliefs, attitudes, and fears reflected both a conscious and unconscious worldview of Asians in America: they are more loyal to Asia, not true Americans, and are not to be trusted in international affairs (DeVos & Banaji, 2005; Lee, 2001). The many racial microaggressions directed toward Wen Ho Lee symbolized a White Western European worldview that has historically been held toward Asian Americans since immigration began.

In a study, for example, it was found that one of the most frequent racial microaggressions directed toward Asian Americans is being perceived as an alien or perpetual foreigner in one's own country (Sue, Bucceri, Lin, Nadal, & Torino, 2007). And, in a first of its kind survey conducted by the Committee of 100 about American attitudes toward Chinese Americans and Asian Americans (Hire Diversity, 2001), the following disturbing statistics were found:

- 46% say Chinese Americans passing secret information to the Chinese government is a problem.
- 32% believe Chinese Americans are more loyal to China than the United States.
- 34% believe they have too much influence in U.S. high technology.
- 25% indicated strong negative attitudes and stereotypes toward Chinese Americans.
- 23% are uncomfortable voting for an Asian American to be president of the United States. This is in marked contrast to 15% for African Americans, 14% for a woman candidate, and 11% for a Jewish candidate.

As we have repeatedly emphasized, racism in the form of racial microaggressions may seem trivial, harmless, and innocent enough (conscious and unconscious associations that Asians are not "real Americans" but aliens) (DeVos & Banaji, 2005), but their impact may create maximum harm to the individual. Wen Ho Lee's personal life was shattered, his family and friends suffered, and to this day, he may continue to live under a cloud of suspicion in spite of the outcome of his case. Since the terrorist attack of 9/11, many Muslim brothers and sisters have also experienced the sting of suspicion and the many detrimental consequences of mistrust.

Personal consequences, however, may pale in comparison to systemic actions that can be and were perpetrated against people of color under the umbrella of a racially biased worldview. The belief that Japanese Americans were more loyal to Japan and might aid "their country" by passing on state secrets during World War II resulted in the incarceration of 120,000 Japanese Americans, two-thirds of whom were citizens by virtue of birth in the United States. As in the case of Wen Ho Lee, the actions of the U.S. government were justified by the need for "national security," and racism was never acknowledged. Many well-intentioned White brothers and sisters went along with these actions because they also shared these beliefs and suspicions. There was a failure, however, to realize that not only were we at war with Japan, but also Italy and Germany; yet Italian Americans and German Americans were not incarcerated into camps! Asian Americans continue to ask: "How much did skin color have to do with the differential treatment?"

As we saw in the last chapter, White supremacy forms a worldview that justifies oppressive actions. This worldview and its detrimental impact upon many groups of color operated on a systemic governmental level for Native Americans and African Americans as well. The belief in "manifest destiny," a philosophy that the United States was destined (even divinely decreed) to acquire land, provided a rationale for the unchecked taking of land from indigenous peoples in this country. It justified expansion into the western and southern territories during the early 1800s and legitimized taking land from Native Americans and from Mexico. Acts of racism were also contained in belief systems that justified and maintained the system of slavery. For example, it was believed that Blacks living under "unnatural conditions of freedom" were prone to anxiety and that for their own mental health Blacks were better off in conditions of subservience (Jones, 1997; Thomas & Sillen, 1972). During the 1840s, for example, a psychiatric disorder called "drapetomania" (flight-from-home) was used to describe the abnormal desire for freedom and the subsequent behavior of enslaved persons who attempted to escape from their slave masters (Thomas & Sillen, 1972).

Racism was thus couched in a language of beliefs that justified discriminatory actions, but provided convenient nonracist rationalizations to oppress, take advantage of, and deny the humanity of people of color. As research on racial microaggressions indicates, such beliefs and attitudes continue to be manifested in the actions of well-intentioned White brothers and sisters (Sue, Capodilupo, & Holder, 2008; Sue, Bucceri, et al., 2007; Sue, Lin, Torino, Capodilupo, & Rivera, 2009). Thus, when well-intentioned Whites express annoyance with these facts by stating "Why blame me, my parents and grandparents didn't own slaves" or "Why blame me, I didn't take land away from American Indians" they do not realize that they are committing a gross racial microaggression by denying responsibility for these past and continuing injustices. Yes, it is true that Whites today did not take land from Native Americans, and yes, it is true that Whites today do not own slaves. They are not responsible for these past injustices. But they fail to realize one important fact: White Americans continue, to this present day, to benefit from these past actions and the current structural arrangements that arose from systems of unfairness!

FROM OLD-FASHIONED RACISM TO MODERN RACISM: THE MORPHING OF BIGOTRY

Most people recognize racism when it is manifested in overt, conscious, and deliberate acts of hatred and discrimination directed toward people of color. Racism has been defined as the individual and institutional expression of the superiority of one group's cultural heritage (Whites), its arts/crafts, traditions, language, religion, history, and values over all other groups (non-White) (Sue, 2003). Others have more specifically defined it as any attitude, action, institutional structure, or social policy that subordinates groups because of their color (Jones, 1997; Nelson, 2006).

Old-Fashioned Racism

The term "old-fashioned racism" has been used to define its blatant and visible forms (Dovidio & Gaertner, 2000) at three different levels: individual, institutional, and cultural (Jones, 1997).

1. *Individual racism* is associated with personal acts of racial prejudice and discrimination that may be manifest in violent hate crimes toward people

of color to less dramatic and more subtle forms such as refusing to rent an apartment or sell a house to a Black couple or discouraging sons or daughters from marrying outside of their race. Most Whites would actively condemn these acts as illegal, immoral, and contrary to the democratic ideals we hold in this society (Sue, 2003). Individual racism occurs between people and/ or between groups. However, open expressions of racism are not the only manifestations of racism. More broad definitions of racism include acknowledgment that it may be expressed unintentionally and unconsciously as well. Whether intentional or unintentional, and conscious or unconscious, it has the effect of subordinating or oppressing a person or group because of attributes such as color.

2. *Institutional racism* does not reside in individuals, but in the very institutional policies, practices, and structures of governments, businesses, courts, law enforcement agencies, schools, unions, churches, and other organizations. It unfairly subordinates groups of color while allowing White European American groups to profit or to be advantaged. There are many examples of such inequities created by unfair policies and practices: segregated neighborhoods and schools, discriminatory employment and promotion policies, racial profiling, inequities in health care, and an educational curriculum that ignores or distorts the history of people of color.

Ironically, institutional structures and practices are designed to regularize procedures, to increase efficiency, and to allow for application of fairness, but in reality they often contribute to oppression and discrimination: for example, (1) Blacks were once defined as three-fifths of a man, (2) laws forbade Native Americans to practice their religions, (3) Asians were not allowed to own land, and (4) the "separate but equal doctrine" justified educational segregation. These unfair policies continue in the forms of bank lending practices, environmental racism (allowing factories to set up shops that pollute minority neighborhoods, but preventing them from entering affluent and White neighborhoods), housing segregation, and so on.

3. *Cultural racism* is the overarching umbrella under which both individual and institutional racism flourish. It is composed of a worldview that contains a powerful belief: the superiority of one group's cultural heritage over another. There is a collective sense of superiority in a White Western European way of life that possesses elements of "chosenness" and "entitlement" (Eidelson & Eidelson, 2003; Sue, 2004): individualism is perceived as more desirable than collectivism, and the Protestant work ethic, capitalism, Christianity, use of English, written traditions, and European physical features (blond hair, blue

eyes, and fair skin) are seen as normal and ideal (Guthrie, 1998; Jones, 1997; Katz, 1985; Sue & Sue, 2008). Individuals or groups that adhere to these beliefs/values and/or possess such physical features are allowed easier access to the rewards of society.

Such a worldview has another equally damaging effect. For example, historical references to "rugged individualism," "taming the West," civilizing "heathens," "helping other groups adopt a single-god concept," and bringing a Western way of life to "less developed" and "primitive" cultures all speak to the converse of superiority—the inferiority of other groups, cultures, and societies (Hanna, Talley, & Guindon, 2000).

Physical characteristics such as dark complexion, black hair, and brown eyes; cultural characteristics such as belief in non-Christian religions (Islam, Confucianism, polytheism, etc.), collectivism, present-time orientation, and the importance of shared wealth; and linguistic characteristics such as bilingualism, nonstandard English, speaking with an accent, use of nonverbal and contextual communications, and reliance on the oral tradition are usually seen as less desirable by the society (Sue & Sue, 2003, p. 70).

Modern Racism

In his book, *The Psychology of Prejudice*, Nelson (2006) asks a sarcastic question: "Where have all the bigots gone?" He observes that it was once common for Whites to openly express racist attitudes and beliefs, advocate for segregation, and denigrate people of color—especially Black Americans—as morally and intellectually inferior. Over many decades, however, the old-fashioned forms of racism that characterized the segregated Southern States diminished greatly in importance and seemed to have disappeared (Dovidio, Gaertner, Kawakami, & Hodson, 2002; Jones, 1997; Miller & Garran, 2008; Nelson, 2006). Much of this change has been attributed to the landmark rulings of the Supreme Court, the Civil Rights Movement, and the Third World Movements (Sue & Sue, 2008). If one traces the stereotypes of Black Americans over time, for example, early characterizations of them as superstitious, lazy, and ignorant have declined dramatically (Dovidio & Gaertner, 1991, 1993).

Many race scholars, however, believe that racism has not disappeared, but (a) morphed into a highly disguised, invisible, and subtle form that lies outside the level of conscious awareness, (b) hides in the invisible assumptions and beliefs of individuals, and (c) is embedded in the policies and structures of our institutions (Dovidio et al., 2002; McConahay, 1986; Sears, 1988; Sue,

Bucceri, et al., 2007). These researchers and scholars do not deny that major advances in positive race-relations have occurred because of legal, political, and social forces against racism, but they cite an increasing body of evidence suggesting that prejudice is alive and well under the labels "modern racism," "symbolic racism," "aversive racism," and "racial microaggressions." These modern forms of racism have been described more thoroughly elsewhere, so we will only briefly mention them here.

In general, the body of literature on the morphing of racism suggests that while old-fashioned racism has declined significantly, it has manufactured a new face: it is more covert, has become implicit, and is not under conscious control (Dovidio, et al., 2002; Jones, 1997; Nelson, 2006). Central to our understanding of modern racism is the outstanding work of Dovidio and colleagues (Dovidio & Gaertner, 1991, 1993, 1996, 2000; Dovidio et al., 2002; Dovidio, Kawakami, Smoak, & Gaertner, 2009; Kawakami, Dunn, Karmali, & Dovidio, 2009) on aversive racism. According to the aversive racism theory, individuals who believe in equality and embrace democratic ideals may continue to harbor nonconscious racist attitudes and beliefs toward people of color.

In predicting what facilitates or impedes the expression of modern racism, they identified several guiding principles derived from their research. First, egalitarian beliefs of most Whites generally operate on a conscious level where deliberate and careful thought can be used to guide their actions related to race-related situations. Open displays of bias, prejudice, and racism are unlikely to occur when conscious cognitive processes and awareness can be brought to bear on actions or decisions. Second, if one does harbor unconscious negative attitudes toward people of color, they are most likely to occur when more spontaneous responses are called for and/or when careful cognitive deliberation is not possible. In other words, modern racists are most likely to express their implicit negative attitudes and behaviors in the form of microaggressions under the following conditions:

- *Situational ambiguity*—When the situation is ambiguous and unclear, right or wrong responding is not obvious. For example, when White participants witnessed Black or White motorists in distress alone, they would offer help to both at approximately the same rates. However, if Whites believed others also witnessed the emergency situations along with them, they were less likely to offer help to Black than White motorists. One of the reasons given for inaction was "I thought others would step in to help." We know, however, that this reason does not explain the fact that Whites offered help at a much higher rate to White motorists even when others witnessed the emergency along with them! In other words, a diffusion of responsibility offered cover for them to mask their racist behaviors to others, or to deceive themselves.

- *Ideological ambiguity*—When a philosophical ideology is used to justify discriminatory treatment. In many cases, racism can be masked or disguised when it is linked to symbols of conservative ideology and values. For example, during the 2008 presidential campaign, Barack Obama was severely criticized for not wearing an American flag on the lapel of his jacket. He was called unpatriotic and people questioned his devotion to the country. Philosophical ideology can even combine in complex ways to influence biased behaviors. When people express beliefs in meritocracy, that racism has been eradicated, that anyone can succeed if they work hard enough, and that we all operate on a level playing field, then it allows Whites in good conscience to vote against affirmative action, or to openly express opinions that people of color are lazy and simply need to work harder to succeed. The racial microaggressive statement "I believe the most qualified person should get the job" may reflect this constellation of worldview beliefs.

- *Failure to help instead of conscious desire to hurt*—The type of racism most likely to emerge is not a behavioral desire to hurt or injure, but is instead a failure to help. Most White Americans no longer harbor intense hatred and hostility toward people of color, but instead may express a more "benign" form of racism that involves feelings of discomfort, uneasiness, and anxiety that result in avoidance or inaction. No other incident better exemplifies this statement than the disastrous consequences of Hurricane Katrina. The long-delayed FEMA rescue of primarily African American residents left behind in New Orleans was scandalous, resulting in many lost lives. Questions were asked about whether governmental rescue attempts would have been quicker if the residents were primarily White. Accusations of racism abound and President Bush was accused of "not caring." In essence, aversive racism theory would probably not accuse Bush of not caring, but that White Americans "did not care enough." The failure to help in the case of Katrina is a ringing statement of racism.

- *Availability of other explanatory options*—In essence, discrimination is likely to emerge not when a behavior would look prejudicial, but when other rationales can be offered for prejudicial behavior, and when we attempt or pretend not to notice differences. In other words, racism is least likely to emerge in situations where behaviors would appear prejudicial to others. This statement is also related to situational ambiguity, but the dynamics are broader. One particular study presented participants with records of Black and White students and told White participants to rate them for admission. The two criteria they looked at were grade-point average (GPA) and SAT scores. When both criteria were equally high or equally low for Black and White participants, they were rated equally. However, when presented with candidates that had either high GPA/low SAT or high SAT/low GPA, Whites selected the White candidate more often. White participants would often favor the White candidate by shifting the importance of the criteria they used for their ratings. A Black person with high GPA and low SAT, for example, would be denied because SAT scores were more important. However, if Blacks had high SAT, but low GPA, the raters would also decide against the Black candidate, in this instance because "GPA was more important"! In other words, the definition of the "most qualified candidate" shifted depending on the race of the candidate.

In summary, it is clear that the modern forms of racism operate in such a manner as to preserve the nonprejudiced self-image of Whites by offering them convenient rationalizations for their actions; they are prevented from recognizing their own racial biases or the implicit prejudicial attitudes they harbor toward others. Such a form of self-deception is reinforced by several continuing and problematic beliefs: (a) racism is a sickness and does not exist in good and decent human beings, (b) racism is only associated with dramatic and overt hate crimes, and (c) good citizens do not engage in such heinous acts.

Racism as Only a Sickness

It goes without saying that many people perceive White supremacists, Ku Klux Klan members, or Skinheads as suffering from some defect of character, pathology, or even mental disorder. Who could argue, for example, that John William King and his two accomplices, who killed African American James Byrd in Jasper, Texas, were not depraved murderers? Recall that these men chained Byrd to the back of a pick-up truck and dragged him for miles until his body was shredded and he was decapitated. The actions of these men were certainly those of "sick minds." In fact, some have argued that racism should be classified in the American Psychiatric Association Diagnostic and Statistical Manual (American Psychological Association, 2000) as a mental disorder, and that "racists" should be considered mentally disturbed (Sue, 2005). Early theories on racism did attempt to explain "racists" and racism as internal attributes and forms of individual pathology, such as the "authoritarian personality theory," which assumes such individuals are predisposed to racism (Adorno, Frenkel-Brunswik, Levinson, & Sanford, 1950).

Further, a strong case can be made that hatred, bigotry, and stereotypes are delusional belief systems, and White supremacists are out of contact with reality. There are two potential downsides to equating racism to a manifestation of pathology. First, although many overt racists could be classified as suffering from some form of mental disorder, these individuals represent an extremely small part of the racism problem. The overwhelming number of people who harbor implicit biases are not "hate mongers," "racists," or likely to engage in hate crimes (Pettigrew, 1981). Thus, limiting our concepts of racism to only extreme acts of overt hatred is to deny its pervasiveness. Studies indicate that racism is far more common and that nearly everyone in our society has inherited the racial biases of their forebears (Dovidio & Gaertner, 2002; Jones, 1997; Pettigrew, 1981; Sue, 2003). Equating racism with pathology, unfortunately, diminishes its widespread nature by fostering an illusion that good, normal, moral, and decent human beings do not harbor racist attitudes and beliefs; thus, they do not discriminate or oppress. It allows many to personally condemn racism and racists, but still cling to a personal deception that they are free of bigotry.

In conclusion, it is not overt racists or White supremacists who create and control the tools that result in personal pain suffered by people of color or in the damaging disparities in education, health care, and employment. It is ordinary citizens we elect to office, teachers who educate our children, business leaders who carry out the policies and practices of their corporations, government leaders, law enforcement officers, physicians, dentists, construction workers, our family, friends, and neighbors. Let us briefly address how racial microaggressions not only reflect a worldview of White supremacy, but affect groups of color in the United States.

RACIAL MICROAGGRESSIONS AND AFRICAN AMERICANS

Race-related stress in the form of racism is a constant and continuing reality of African Americans (Carter, 2007; USDHHS, 2001; Utsey & Hook, 2007). As we have seen, racism may occur in any combination of these qualities: acute or chronic, overt or covert, deliberate or unintentional, and dramatic or subtle. All forms are oppressive and harmful, but what makes them especially damaging are their continuing and cumulative nature (e.g., daily experiences of racist hassles). In the previous section we indicated that modern racism in the form of racial microaggressions reflects a worldview that denigrates people of color through biased belief systems and attitudes. For African Americans, the worldview that they are lesser human beings with negative qualities can be seen in this quote from the early 1940s, contrasted with a quote from 2003:

White male, age 38, newspaperman in Newport News, Virginia:

Our colored people are hard-working, self-respecting, and do not attempt to mix anywhere with the whites. There are some who try to butt in with their rights. . . . The best evidence of the fair treatment they get are the public school facilities. They have very excellent nigger schools. . . . The Negro is a black and kinky-haired person from whose body comes a not entirely pleasant odor. He is always regarded as an inferior person and race, mentally and morally, destined by birth and circumstances to serve the white people. . . . I don't understand the northerners. How would they like a nigger to marry their daughter? (Jones, 1997, p. 46)

White male, age 25, student in New York City:

I have nothing against the Blacks, or should I say African Americans. I go to my classes with them and we work alongside one another at my office. Okay, I don't socialize with them much outside of class, but they keep to themselves anyway. There is nothing wrong with being with people who share your interests. Frankly, I don't like rap music and I'm not sure it's really music anyway. . . . Please don't misunderstand me, if they like it, that's fine. Interracial relationships are fine. I don't object. Inter-marriage is fine. I don't object. But, I do worry about the children, though. It's going to be hard on them . . . being mixed.

The first quote represents the belief systems of old-fashioned racism toward African Americans. The speaker is sincere in expressing his thoughts on Black inferiority, the necessity of keeping the races separate, and the many negative qualities possessed by Blacks that justify his beliefs and actions. He states these as absolute truths.

In the second quote, bias toward African Americans is expressed more subtly and is couched in vagueness and external reasons that do not reflect on potential racist attitudes and actions. In the first quote, for example, the speaker indicates that "good" Blacks who know their place do not attempt to mix with Whites. The second speaker couches his observations as "self-segregation" due to different interests (i.e., music). The first speaker addresses the issue of fair treatment toward the "Negro" as evidenced in the excellent facilities in their segregated public schools; the second speaker acknowledges that Blacks attend his classes (equal education), but they do little together on the outside. The first speaker is publicly and adamantly opposed to interracial marriages; the second speaker disguises his objections as being "worried about the children."

Despite the morphing of old-fashioned racism to modern racism illustrated in these two quotes, both are based upon a worldview of negative perceptions and biases toward African Americans. For those interested in tracing the historical evolution of Black racial stereotypes from the 1600s to the present, and how White supremacy has played a major role, please see the excellent analysis in Jones (1997).

When the general public thinks about Black Americans, certain historical and current images and stereotypes are often invoked: hostile, angry, impulsive, dangerous, drug dealers, criminals, pimps, prostitutes, addicts, unintelligent, mentally retarded, low skills, lack abstract thinking, concrete, inhuman, animalistic, undesirable, smelly, unkempt, dirty, mentally ill, abnormal, insatiable sexual appetite, large sex organs, musically inclined, natural athletes, superstitious, happy-go-lucky, and "all Blacks are the same." Imagine what it must be like to live your daily life, day in and day out, with these demeaning racial images, insults, and invalidations hurtled at you in the form of racial microaggressions. In fact, it is not surprising that studies on racial microaggressions directed toward African Americans have revealed themes or hidden messages that follow many of these beliefs: assumption of intellectual inferiority, second-class citizen, assumption of criminality, assumption of inferior status, assumed universality of the Black experience, and superiority of White cultural values/communications styles (Sue, Nadal, et al., 2008).

Harmful Effects of Racial Microaggression toward Black Americans

The physiological and psychological detrimental consequences of racism toward African Americans are well documented in the professional literature (Carter, 2007; USDHHS, 2001; Williams, Neighbors, & Jackson, 2003).

Physical Health Consequences

Racial microaggressive stress that is continuous and cumulative in nature has damaging physical health consequences for African Americans (Clark,

Anderson, Clark & Williams, 1999; Utsey & Hook, 2007; Williams et al., 2003). The reactions described in the *microaggression process model of stress* include constant vigilance, bodily arousal, and depletion of resources leading to medical conditions such as cardiovascular disease, hypertension, respiratory problems, cirrhosis of the liver, obesity, and diabetes (Brondolo et al., 2008; Karlsen & Nazroo, 2002; Kumanyika, 1993; McCord & Freeman, 1990; USDHHS, 2001; Utsey & Hook, 2007). Rates of hypertension are higher than that of the White population (National Center for Health Statistics, 1996). While hypertension is believed to have a strong biological component among African Americans, psychological stress has also been strongly implicated in the high rates. African Americans exposed to videotaped or imaginal depictions of racism showed increases in heart rate and digital blood flow (Jones, Harrell, Morris-Prather, Thomas, & Omowale, 1996). Other studies support these findings; encounters with race-related stress cause elevated heart rates and blood pressure in both Black men and women (Armstead, Lawler, Gordon, Cross, & Gibbons, 1989; Clark, 2000; National Center for Health Statistics, 1996).

Psychological Health Consequences

The experience of discrimination has been found to be related to lower levels of mastery and control, and to high levels of psychological distress (Broman, Mavaddat, & Hsu, 2000). Perceived racism is associated with depression, lowered life satisfaction, low self-esteem, and intense feelings of racial rage, anxiety, paranoia, and helplessness (Carter, 2007; Clark et al., 1999; Feagin & Sykes, 1994; Ridley, 2005; Solórzano, Ceja, & Yosso, 2000). In summarizing the scholarly works of Black psychologists on prolonged exposure to racism, Ponterotto, Utsey, and Pedersen (2006) outline several psychological consequences.

- *Alienation*—Adoption of the cultural and racial reality of White America can result in a profound sense of alienation. The alienation can be widespread, such as being (1) detached from one's personal identity (not knowing who one is as a racial/cultural being) and taking on the definition of yourself from the oppressor; (2) estranged from your own family, friends, and group; (3) isolated from other groups; (4) disaffected by one's own language, history, and culture; and (5) separated from one's humanity.
- *Internalized racism*—This process involves accepting the racial reality of the oppressor, accepting the standards, values, and beliefs of the larger system, and developing an aversion to one's own racial/ethnic heritage

and culture. It is similar to the alienation described above, but resides primarily in how the Black person views himself or herself from a White perspective. A Black person may come to see White ways as more desirable and develop a loathing for their own Blackness. Low self-esteem is masked through attempts to seek validation from the larger society. Oftentimes, the contempt for blackness is expressed toward other African Americans.

- *Race-related trauma*—As we have indicated in an earlier chapter, traumatic stress need not be a singular, overwhelming, and life-threatening event, but can be induced through many small daily assaults that become cumulative. Many racial microaggressions, for example, can have a similar effect as being exposed to a hate crime. The two, however, can be interrelated; hate crimes can be experienced vicariously and made even more traumatic because of hypervigilance and sensitivity to racism, and racial microaggressions can be felt more intensely because they symbolize hate crimes and their historical force. Trauma symptoms include heightened autonomic arousal, emotional fluctuations, nightmares, or intrusive thoughts.

- *Race-related fatigue*—At the end of Chapter 1, we cited the essay "Fatigue" by Don Locke, an African American psychologist. The essay speaks to the effect of constant insults, invalidations, and racial hassles. The efforts to be constantly vigilant, to hold on to one's racial/cultural identity, to defend against insults and invalidations, and to claim one's humanity in the face of chronic and never-ending White supremacy are truly exhausting. The toll on Black Americans is related to a depletion of psychological and spiritual energies that distract them from learning in the classroom, working at maximum efficiency in employment, and even dealing with the daily routines of life. Racial microaggressions deplete and sap the psychological, cognitive, and spiritual energies of African Americans.

- *Racial mistrust*—Past and present racial discrimination against African Americans has resulted in a defense against racism whereby Whites are perceived as potential enemies unless they prove otherwise. Elsewhere, we have indicated that racial or cultural mistrust may represent a healthy functional survival mechanism developed and used by Blacks to survive in a highly racist society (Sue & Sue, 2008). Rightly or wrongly, Whites may be perceived as symbols of racism. As a result, Blacks may approach interracial interactions with a great deal of suspicion and guardedness, may not readily disclose their true thoughts and feelings, and may engage in constant hypervigilance to discern the motives of others. In addition to depletion of energy, extreme forms of cultural mistrust may result in the inability to establish authentic cross-cultural relationships.

RACIAL MICROAGGRESSIONS AND ASIAN AMERICANS

The Asian American population constitutes approximately 4% of the population of the United States, but they do not represent a monolithic group (Sue & Sue, 2008). Between-group differences are great, as over 40 distinct subgroups differ in language, religion, and values (Sandhu, 1997). These include larger Asian groups (Chinese, Filipinos, Koreans, Asian Indians, and Japanese), refugees and immigrants from Southeast Asia (Vietnamese, Laotians, Cambodians, and Hmongs), and Pacific Islanders (Hawaiians, Guamanians, and Samoans). Despite this diversity, White Americans continue to have a difficult time distinguishing between Asian American groups and often respond as if no difference exists (Sue & Sue, 2008). As a result, there are common racial assumptions and beliefs in the White Western worldview of nearly all Asian Americans. Two are especially powerful in the manifestation of racial microaggressions toward Asian Americans: (1) negative stereotypes of Asian Americans as foreigners and (2) positive stereotypes of them as a successful minority group.

First, the persecution of Wen Ho Lee (2001) is an example of how the majority of citizens in the United States perceive Asian Americans; they are aliens in their own country, not to be trusted, and potentially disloyal. Many racial microaggressions directed at Asian Americans reflect this worldview (Sue, Bucceri, et al., 2007). For example, complimenting an Asian American for speaking English well when they were born and raised in the United States communicates a worldview that only Whites are true "Americans" (DeVos & Banaji, 2005).

Second, an equally strong but somewhat opposite belief about Asians in America is that they are a highly successful minority who has "made it" in society (Sue & Sue, 2008). Often referred to as a "model minority," Asian American/Pacific Islanders are often portrayed in popular press headlines as, "Asian Americans: The Model Minority" or "Asian Americans: Outwhiting Whites." Statistics give credence to this notion: When compared to their White counterparts, Asian Americans have higher educational attainment, higher median income, and lower official rates of divorce, delinquency, and mental disorders

(Sue & Sue, 2008). These facts seem to attest to the validity of their image of success, and many conclude that Asian Americans are somehow immune to racism. Words such as "hardworking," "disciplined," "intelligent," and "enterprising" are often used to describe Asian Americans (Morrissey, 1997).

However, a critical analysis of the Asian American success myth reveals truths that are at odds with these conclusions. The higher median income does not take into account (1) per family income in instances where Asian families have more than one wage-earner, (2) a higher incidence of poverty in many Asian American/Pacific Islander groups than among Whites, and (3) the huge discrepancy between education and income (e.g., Asian Americans must attain a higher education to earn the same amount as White coworkers). Further, statistics mask a bimodal distribution; many may have higher education, but there is a huge undereducated group. Measures of mental health, divorce, and delinquency fail to distinguish between "official" and "actual" rates, a discrepancy that may be due to cultural factors such as the disgrace or shame associated with admitting or seeking outside public service help (Sue & Sue, 2008).

The success myth also contributes to a belief that unlike other groups of color, Asian/Pacific Americans have not been exposed to racism, do not suffer from discrimination and, therefore, should not be considered an oppressed minority group (Sue & Sue, 2008). Such beliefs deny the historical and continuing racism visited upon Asians in America. Indeed, the history of Asian Americans is replete with racism and discrimination: denied ownership of land and citizenship, locked in internment camps, denied voting rights, subjected to widespread assaults that include hanging, torture, and even enslavement (Mio, Nagata, Tsai, & Tewari, 2007). The phrases "not a Chinamen's chance" and the "yellow peril" refer to perceptions of Asian Americans as unlikely to succeed and as a threat to Whites. The number of hate crimes against Asian Americans has risen dramatically (assaults by 11% and aggravated assaults by 14%), which attests to the continuing overt racism expressed toward them (Matthee, 1997).

When the general public thinks about Asian Americans, these are some of the images and stereotypes that come to mind: spies, sneaky, backstabbers, disloyal, slanted eyes, stingy, subhuman, model minority, bright, hardworking, obedient, studious, quiet, good in math and science, wealthy, passive, lack of leadership skills, poor interpersonally, unassertive, men are unmasculine/sexually unattractive, women are domestic, exotic, and sexually pleasing, and poor English skills (Sue, 2003). All of these images are reflected in racial microaggressive themes directed against Asian Americans: aliens in their own land, ascription of intelligence, denial of racial reality, eroticization of Asian American women, invalidation of interethnic differences, pathologizing of cultural values/communication styles, second-class citizens, and invisible (Sue, Bucceri, et al., 2007).

Psychological and Physical Health Consequences

Unlike the research on the effects of racism on African Americans, little exists with respect to the impact on Asian Americans (Hwang & Goto, 2008; Liang, Li, & Kim, 2002). Almost the entire research and scholarly literature on racism, aversive racism, perceived racism, racism-related stress, and psychological/physical health consequences are based upon the African American population. Anecdotal and clinical observations and a few studies indicate that Asian Americans do suffer enormously from the prejudice and discrimination they receive (Inman & Yeh, 2007; Liang, Alvarez, Juang, & Liang, 2007; Mio et al., 2007; Yoo & Lee, 2008).

In a study on the cost of racism to Asian American college students, it was found that racism-related stress is associated with low self-esteem and interpersonal and career problems (Liang & Fassinger, 2008; Zane & Song, 2007). They believe low self-esteem may result from the internalization of devaluing messages sent to Asian Americans, who thus feel more ashamed of themselves or inferior; poorer or fewer interpersonal relationships were due to an increased hypervigilance and suspicion of others; and the internalization of messages makes them question their worth or ability to pursue certain higher-level occupations. In addition to these life adjustment difficulties, racism-related stress is associated with psychological distress, anxiety, and depression (Barry & Grillo, 2003; Contrada et al., 2001; Hwang & Goto, 2008; Noh & Caspar, 2003), feelings of social competence (Zane & Song, 2007), psychological well-being (Kim, 2002), and feelings of belittlement, anger, rage, frustration, and alienation (Sue, Bucceri, et al., 2007). It is clear that more research on the harmful impact of racism on Asian Americans and how this group copes with race-related stressors is needed (Liang et al., 2007).

RACIAL MICROAGGRESSIONS AND LATINO/HISPANIC AMERICANS

Latinas/os comprise approximately 14% of the population, are among the fastest growing group in the United States, have surpassed Black Americans as the largest racial/ethnic group, and represent ancestries from Mexico, Puerto Rico, Cuba, El Salvador, the Dominican Republic, and other Latin American groups (Sue & Sue, 2008; U.S. Bureau of Census Statistics, 2007). It is important to note that "Latina/o" is not a racial designator, but an ethnic one. Thus, Latinas/os may come from any racial category. Like their Asian/Pacific American counterparts, they are varied and diverse in customs, traditions, cultures, and so forth. They are, however, held together by one powerful and common denominator: their primary language is Spanish. Compared to the general population, Latinas/os are relatively younger, have higher fertility rates, and continue to be among the least educated in the U.S. population (Casas, Vasquez, & de Esparza, 2002).

Little doubt exists that Latinas/os experience widespread prejudice and discrimination (National Survey of Latinos, 2002). They are over-represented among the poor, unemployment is high, most are in semiskilled or unskilled occupations, and they suffer many more health problems when compared to the general population (tuberculosis, AIDS, obesity, heart disease, etc.) (Sue & Sue, 2008). Many Latinas/os believe that their lower standard of living and personal well-being are affected by prejudice, stereotyping, and discrimination (Krupin, 2001; National Survey of Latinos, 2002). Latinas/os, for example, were often believed by others to be less warm and less competent, unwanted and unskilled newcomers, and having less social status (Jimeno-Ingrum, Berdahl, & Lucero-Wagoner, 2009). As a group, they reported levels of perceived discrimination equal to reports of Black Americans and much higher than reports of Whites (Moradi & Risco, 2006).

When the general public thinks about Latinas/os, these are some of the images and stereotypes that come to mind: illegal aliens, foreigners, drug dealers, farm workers, poor, welfare recipients, tax avoiders, domestic servants, unskilled, criminals, dangerous, untrustworthy, greasy, sloppy, irresponsible, lazy, never on time, carefree, uninhibited, poor English, uneducated, stupid, and religious (Sue, 2003). All of these images are consistent with findings on microaggressive themes for Latinas/os: Ascription of intelligence, second-class citizens, pathologizing of communication style/cultural values, speech characteristics, aliens in their own land, criminality, and invalidation of Latina/o experience (Rivera, Forquer, & Rangel, in press).

Psychological and Physical Health Consequences

Like their Asian American counterparts, less research on the psychological and physical health consequences has been done on Latinas/os (Moradi &

Risco, 2006). There is an abundance of health statistics, however, that address the physical and medical problems of this group. As mentioned previously, heart disease, tuberculosis, and obesity (48% of women and 40% of men are overweight) (Johnson et al., 1995) are much higher for Latinas/os, and death rates from heart disease, pneumonia, asthma, and liver disease are high among Puerto Ricans (Flack et al., 1995). While a strong case can be made that actual or perceived discrimination may be at the root of many of these health problems, a direct causal link is difficult to make. It has been shown that perceived discrimination is linked to many medical problems, such as higher blood pressure among Mexican Americans (James, Lovato, & Khoo, 1994).

Perceived discrimination does seem to be linked to psychological distress, depression, higher levels of stress, and anxiety (Finch, Kolody, & Vega, 2000; Lopez, 2005). The evidence regarding psychological well-being is more mixed, but low levels do seem to be a result of perceived discrimination (Hwang & Goto, 2008; Moradi & Risco, 2006). It has been hypothesized that a sense of well-being is most strongly reflected in self-esteem; high self-esteem indicates high sense of well-being, while low self-esteem reflects low well-being (Moradi & Risco, 2006). The mixed findings, they contend, fail to consider the "sense of self-control," which mediates the perceived discrimination and well-being link. When this link is considered as an intervening variable, then perceived discrimination indirectly influences not only a psychological sense of well-being, but also personal efficacy. Thus, like African Americans and Asian Americans, it appears that Latinas/os are psychologically impacted by overt and covert forms of prejudice and discrimination.

RACIAL MICROAGGRESSIONS AND NATIVE AMERICANS

Native Americans are a highly heterogeneous group, and represent less than 1% of the population of the United States, with over 500 distinct tribes (Trimble & Thurman, 2002). The population is relatively young, with fewer married-couple families, higher female householders without husbands, and a much lower number of high school graduates (U.S. Bureau of the Census, 2001). The Native American Indian experience is unique and not comparable to any other ethnic group. First, racial/ethnic groups who voluntarily came (as immigrants) or were forced to come (as refugees and enslaved persons) to the United States struggled to gain resources and equality. Native Americans had resources and were the original indigenous people of this country.

Second, they had land and status that were stolen and seized from them, and they were subjected to systematic extermination (Sue & Sue, 2008).

When the general public thinks about Native American Indians, these are some of the images and stereotypes that come to mind: alcoholics, drunkards, nonverbal, uneducable, retarded, savages, animalistic, uncivilized, blood-thirsty, primitive, subhuman, superstitious, poor, passive, and noncompetitive (Sue, 2003). To date, no studies have been conducted on racial microaggressive themes directed toward Native Americans. When one reviews the historical and continuing racist treatment of Native Americans, however, it does not take much to conclude that they have been subjected to an invalidation of their life style (religions, cultural values, and ways of being) and like all marginalized groups are subjected to microassaults, microinsults, and microinvalidations. As we have seen from the example in Chapter 2, the mascot Chief Illiniwek represents a major environmental microaggression toward Native Americans.

Psychological and Physical Health Consequences

Life expectancy among Native Americans is the lowest of any group of color, health problems plague the population, suicide rates are among the highest in the nation, and some describe substance abuse (alcohol and tobacco) as "dev-astating" (Alcantara & Gone, 2008; Duran, 2006; Frank et al., 2000; Trimble & Thurman, 2002). Duran (2006) has coined the term "soul wound" or histori-cal trauma (massacres, decimation of the population through diseases, forced relocation, trauma, unemployment, broken treaties, and racism) that is felt to this present day (Trimble & Thurman, 2002). Just like the lingering effects of the Holocaust for Jewish Americans, historical traumas have left a deep soul wound among Native Americans that continues to affect their psychologi-cal well-being. The invalidation of religion, beliefs, values, and their ways of life has caused an epidemic of alcohol abuse, poverty, family breakdown, and suicides. Suicide among Native Americans is the second-leading cause of death for ages 15–24 and the third leading cause of death for 5–14 and 25–44 years (Alcantara & Gone, 2008). These rates are astounding and speak to the hopelessness, alienation, depression, and widespread alcoholism among this population.

Historical traumas and the creation of the soul wound are best described in this passage taken from Napoleon (1996) as cited in Trimble & Thurman (2002):

> The Yup'ik world was turned upside down, literally overnight. Out of the suffer-ing, in confusion, desperation, heartbreak, and trauma was born a generation of

Yup'ik people. They were born into shock. They woke to a world in shambles, many of their people and their beliefs were strewn about them, dead. In their minds, they had been overcome by evil. Their medicines and the medicine men and women had proven useless. Everything they had believed in failed. They woke up in shock, listless, confused, bewildered, heartbroken, and afraid. (p. 65)

The Way Forward

Similarities and Differences between Racial Groups

Racial/ethnic microaggressions toward groups of color are a reality in their life experience. Research into thematic similarities, their manifestations, meaning, and impact is important. Thus far, studies and theorizing suggest that racial microaggressions against African Americans, Asian Americans, Latinas/os, and Native Americans share many similarities.

- First, microaggressions reflect a biased worldview of superiority–inferiority, and inclusion–exclusion in favor of Whites, and unfavorable attitudes and beliefs toward people of color.
- Second, every racial/ethnic minority group has been shown to be subjected to all three forms of microaggressions: microassaults, microinsults, and microinvalidations.
- Third, racial microaggressions are often outside the level of awareness of the well-intentioned White person, but they are nevertheless detrimental to the psychological and physical health of persons of color.
- Fourth, microaggressions seem to follow racial/ethnic stereotypes or images about the various groups of color.

However, research to discover unique stressors for different racial groups would do much to clarify similarities and differences among them. Such understanding might aid in developing more effective and specific racial/ethnic interventions that would benefit the four groups discussed in this chapter. Some areas to explore involve several avenues of research that may prove helpful in education, employment, and health care.

- Preliminary research already suggests that African Americans, Asian Americans, Latinas/os, and Native Americans may share both similar and dissimilar microaggressions. Being treated as a second-class citizen is common for all four groups. It also appears that microaggressive themes

(Continued)

of pathologizing communication styles and ascription of intelligence (Rivera, Forquer, & Rangel, in press) may be common experiences.

- However, noticeable thematic differences exist between the groups. It was found that themes of being an alien in one's own land and invisibility were shared most by Asian Americans and Latinas/os, but not necessarily with African Americans. However, Asian Americans were seldom victims of assumption of criminality, while both Blacks and Latinas/os experienced these themes consistently (Sue, Bucceri, et al., 2007). Our earlier analysis supports the fact that historical stereotypes of Black Americans as violent and dangerous and Asian Americans as law-abiding and quiet may be at play.

- Another area that requires further research involves determining the relative impact of different forms of microaggressions. Are certain themes more likely to evoke distress and/or physiological, cognitive, emotional, behavioral reactions? Is the impact of criminality greater for African Americans than being perceived as a foreigner in one's own country for Asian Americans? Are some racial groups more likely to experience microassaults (explicit) than microinvalidations (subtle)?

- There are also questions about the different impacts of microaggressions when they are delivered by strangers, casual acquaintances, personal friends, or family members. It would appear that the perpetrator's relationship to the target would influence greatly how racial microaggressions are perceived. Likewise, the status relationship between perpetrator and target (power differential) is likely to influence how they are received. In general, these are all researchable questions.

- Do different racial groups cope with microaggressive stressors differently? Considerable evidence exists that reveals that coping is often influenced by culture. It has been observed that African Americans are more likely to be action-oriented than their American Indian counterparts. Research to determine cultural coping strategies may allow us to build upon culture-specific strategies in dealing with race-related stress.

- No one is free of bias, prejudice, or discrimination. When we speak about racial microaggressions, one of the common questions is whether people of color can microaggress toward one another. The answer is "yes." It is clear that different racial/ethnic groups can hold biases and stereotypes toward one another. Some of the interracial and interethnic conflicts between Latinas/os and African Americans, for example, are filled with bias and discrimination. People of color, however, are wary

(Continued)

about discussing these matters for fear that those in power may use the issue to assuage their own feelings of guilt and racism, to serve as a "divide and conquer ploy," and to divert action away from the injustices of society. Yet, understanding and dealing with interethnic and inter-racial microaggressions is as necessary as acknowledging and dealing with the hidden prejudices of all groups.

- If research on racial microaggressions is to advance, there must be the development of measurement instruments that allow us to quantify their manifestations before we can begin to truly understand their detrimental impacts on people of color. Currently, instruments that measure race-related stress, perceived ethnic discrimination, and schedules of racist events/racial hassles exist. However, the items in these measures are generally confounded by a lack of distinction between overt old-fashioned racism, aversive racism, and their more subtle manifestations: no instrument currently distinguishes between the forms of microaggressions (assaults, insults, and invalidations), whether they are from perpetrator or target, and their degrees of conscious intentionality. Developing such instruments will allow us to quantify the microaggressions experienced by populations of color, to distinguish between ethnic-specific manifestations, and to allow research into their detrimental impact (physical, psychological, and standard-of-living factors).

In the study of racial microaggressions, there are many unanswered questions. It is incumbent upon our profession to begin systematically to acknowledge, understand, and unmask the dynamics, power, and impacts of these forms of oppression so that intervention strategies can be developed to aid in stopping the constant denigration of people of color.

CHAPTER EIGHT

Gender Microaggressions and Sexism

During the democratic presidential campaign, when candidates Hillary Clinton and Barack Obama ran against one another, the following op-ed piece appeared in the January 10, 2008, *New York Times*, contrasting how gender and race were influencing voter perceptions.

Women Are Never Front-Runners
by Gloria Steinem

The woman in question became a lawyer after some years as a community organizer, married a corporate lawyer and is the mother of two little girls, ages 9 and 6. Herself the daughter of a white American mother and a black African father—in this race-conscious country, she is considered black—she served as a state legislator for eight years, and became an inspirational voice for national unity.

Be honest: Do you think this is the biography of someone who could be elected to the United States Senate? After less than one term there, do you believe she could be a viable candidate to head the most powerful nation on earth?

If you answered no to either question, you're not alone. Gender is probably the most restricting force in American life, whether the question is who must be in the kitchen or who could be in the White House. This country is way down the list of countries electing women and, according to one study, it polarizes gender roles more than the average democracy.

That's why the Iowa primary was following our historical pattern of making change. Black men were given the vote a half-century before women of any race were allowed to mark a ballot, and generally have ascended to positions of power, from the military to the boardroom, before any women (with the possible exception of obedient family members in the latter).

If the lawyer described above had been just as charismatic but named, say, Achola Obama instead of Barack Obama, her goose would have been cooked long ago. Indeed, neither she nor Hillary Clinton could have used Mr. Obama's public style—or Bill Clinton's either—without being considered too emotional by Washington pundits.

So why is the sex barrier not taken as seriously as the racial one? The reasons are as pervasive as the air we breathe: because sexism is still confused with nature as racism once was; because anything that affects males is seen as more serious than anything that affects "only" the female half of the human race; because children are still raised mostly by women (to put it mildly) so men especially tend to feel they are regressing to childhood when dealing with a powerful woman; because racism stereotyped black men as more "masculine" for so long that some white men find their presence to be masculinity-affirming (as long as there aren't too many of them); and because there is still no "right" way to be a woman in public power without being considered a you-know-what.

I'm not advocating a competition for who has it toughest. The caste systems of sex and race are interdependent and can only be uprooted together. That's why Senators Clinton and Obama have to be careful not to let a healthy debate turn into the kind of hostility that the news media love. Both will need a coalition of outsiders to win a general election. The abolition and suffrage movements progressed when united and were damaged by division; we should remember that.

I'm supporting Senator Clinton because like Senator Obama she has community organizing experience, but she also has more years in the Senate, an unprecedented eight years of on-the-job training in the White House, no masculinity to prove, the potential to tap a huge reservoir of this country's talent by her example, and now even the courage to break the no-tears rule. I'm not opposing Mr. Obama; if he's the nominee, I'll volunteer. Indeed, if you look at votes during their two-year overlap in the Senate, they were the same more than 90 percent of the time. Besides, to clean up the mess left by President Bush, we may need two terms of President Clinton and two of President Obama.

But what worries me is that he is seen as unifying by his race while she is seen as divisive by her sex.

What worries me is that she is accused of "playing the gender card" when citing the old boys' club, while he is seen as unifying by citing civil rights confrontations.

What worries me is that male Iowa voters were seen as gender-free when supporting their own, while female voters were seen as biased if they did and disloyal if they didn't.

What worries me is that reporters ignore Mr. Obama's dependence on the old— for instance, the frequent campaign comparisons to John F. Kennedy—while not challenging the slander that her progressive policies are part of the Washington status quo.

What worries me is that some women, perhaps especially younger ones, hope to deny or escape the sexual caste system; thus Iowa women over 50 and 60, who disproportionately supported Senator Clinton, proved once again that women are the one group that grows more radical with age.

This country can no longer afford to choose our leaders from a talent pool limited by sex, race, money, powerful fathers, and paper degrees. It's time to take equal pride in breaking all the barriers. We have to be able to say: "I'm supporting her because she'll be a great president and because she's a woman."

The opinion editorial by Steinem (2008) generated heated discussion among many in the news media, and from the public at large. Despite disclaiming an attempt to "play the gender card" or the "who's more oppressed" game (women or Blacks) in her editorial, Steinem's comments did precisely what she did not want them to do. She provoked reactions that deviated from the points she was trying to make to questions that were debated in the press and among certain parties: Is sexism stronger than racism in our society? Do women suffer more than Blacks due to prejudice and discrimination? Is it more acceptable to be overtly sexist than overtly racist? These questions are important ones, but they (1) detract from the issues of prejudice and discrimination directed toward women, (2) act as a "divide and conquer" wedge between women and people of color, and (3) prevent an enlightened dialogue about sexism and its detrimental impact on women. As a result, let us try to look carefully and objectively at the points being made by Steinem regarding sexism.

First, the title of Steinem's editorial is a strong statement that women in the United States are never front-runners for leadership positions, whether they are vying for political offices, boardrooms, or at the executive levels in our places of employment. This is in marked contrast to many countries where women play a pronounced role in the highest echelons of government. For every Nancy Pelosi (2007: first female speaker of the U.S. House of Representatives) in leadership positions, she represents a statistical rarity when compared against men.

For every Carly Fiorina (former CEO of Hewlett-Packard) heading a Fortune 400 company, she represents a statistical rarity when compared against men. When gender is introduced into the leadership equation, women seem to always come out second, third, or fourth best.

Second, Steinem bemoans the double-standard used to judge women and to keep them in their place. While she never uses the word "sexism," she makes it clear that it is prejudicial attitudes, beliefs, and stereotypes that have created a sex barrier that have shackled women to inferior positions and roles. These double standards create no-win situations for women. While men are valued for their assertiveness, an attribute of leadership, women evidencing these traits are described as "bitchy." Ironically, women are also aware that they must conform to masculine roles or behavior standards in order to be perceived as credible leaders. They are told to be wary of showing emotions or social sensitivities to others or they will be perceived as being "weak" or "too emotional" to deal with the rough and tumble of logical decisions. Appearance, too, can be a double-edged sword for women. Rubin (2008) makes the following observation:

> Let's turn to the snapshot afforded us by a special section the *Wall Street Journal* publishes annually, the most recent titled "Fifty Women to Watch 2007." Its front page features a thumbnail-size photo of each woman. What some observers might be thinking, but no one actually says, is that a number of these women appear deliberately studiously unfeminine. Why might this be so?
>
> Well, maybe because, regardless of gender, holding a top job in today's marketplace means you have to court attention in the media. And for women, that attention inevitably focuses on how they look. . . .
>
> When Senator Clinton turned down *Vogue*'s request for a photo shoot, editor-in-chief Anna Wintour wrote, "Imagine my amazement, then, when I learned that Hillary Clinton, our only female presidential hopeful, had decided to steer clear of [being photographed for] our pages at this point in her campaign for fear of looking too feminine. The notion that a contemporary woman must look mannish in order to be taken seriously as a seeker of power is frankly dismaying." She went on to ask, "How has our culture come to this" and state, "This is America, not Saudi Arabia."

In many respects, the concerns expressed by Steinem (2008) point to the operation of gender microaggressions as reflected in the hidden themes of individuals, institutions, and our society directed toward women. "A women's place is in the home," "You've come a long way baby!" "Don't worry your pretty little head." These statements are filled with hidden messages: "Housework, care of children, and attractiveness are the domain of women." "Don't push so hard, and be content with the progress you have made." "Problem solving and rational thinking are the domain of men." Thus, it is not surprising that Judge Sonia Sotomayor, during her confirmation hearing in July 2009, in answering questions from primarily male Senators responded in what others described as "steady," "unemotional," "flat and detached," and even "boring" tones. In fact, one headline in the *New York Times* proclaimed "Sotomayor Leaves Passion Behind" (Stolberg, 2009). For a woman who has been described by others as a woman of passion who feels strongly about issues, this aspect of her character did not come across in the hearings. Perhaps she knew that her strong feelings, humor, and passion would be interpreted by men as out-of-control and irrational; they may think that as a Supreme Court justice she could not be objective.

Similar to racial microaggressions, gender microaggressions are brief and commonplace daily verbal or behavioral indignities, whether intentional or unintentional, that communicate hostile, derogatory, or negative gender slights and insults that potentially have a harmful impact on women. They too can vary on a continuum from being intentional and conscious to being unintentional and unconscious. Gender microaggressions are often visited upon women by well-intentioned men who themselves may be unaware of the role they play in inflicting psychological harm on their female counterparts, in restricting career and job choices, in creating a lower standard of living for them, and in perpetuating inequities in employment and health care (Rubin, 2008; Sue & Sue, 2008; U.S. Census Bureau, 2002). Likewise, gender microaggressions are often delivered through educational texts, mass media, institutional norms, and cultural scripts that are not necessarily overtly sexist, but communicate hidden messages that may be internalized by both perpetrator and victim. In keeping with our contention that it is not overt bigotry that is most damaging to the life of women but instead its contemporary invisible forms, I describe how sexism has evolved into its everyday manifestations.

From Old-Fashioned Sexism to Modern Sexism: The Morphing of Bigotry

Negative attitudes toward women, viewing them as inferior to men, relegating them to lesser or undesirable roles, and attributing gross stereotypes to them seem to be a common phenomena in nearly every society (Zastrow, 2004). Whether such attitudes and practices come from ancient hunting-gathering societies that differentiated roles for men and women (less physical freedom for women because of childbearing), physical characteristics between the sexes (greater physical strength of men than women), biological differences, or social learning are the subject of much debate. These beliefs and practices, however, have a long and continuing manifestation in religion.

Most religions like Christianity, Hinduism, Islam, and Judaism possess teachings, beliefs, and practices that relegate women to an inferior status. According to Christian religion, for example, it was said that woman was derived from man and man from God and thus woman was lesser than man (Genesis, Chapter 3; Zastrow, 2004). Some orthodox Jewish men offer daily thanks to God for not making them a woman (Zastrow, 2004). Even now, the Roman Catholic Church forbids women to become ministers or priests. In our society, God is often referred to by the male generic pronoun ("He").

Likewise, gender stereotypes and discrimination against women seem to be prevalent in interpersonal behaviors, institutional practices, and cultural values/beliefs (D. Sue, Sue, & Sue, 2010). For example, cultural scripts, the social and cultural beliefs and expectations that guide our behaviors and gender roles, can be explicit or implicit (Gagnon, 1990). "Stand by your man," "be ladylike," "nice girls don't initiate sex," and "don't be bitchy" are cultural scripts based upon beliefs and assumptions about appropriate female role behaviors and admonitions never to violate them. Nearly 40 years ago, one study found these stereotypes of women: *submissive, sensitive to slights, excitable, emotional, and conceited about appearance, dependent, less competitive, unaggressive, irrational, and unobjective* (Broverman & Broverman, 1970). The study revealed a double standard for mental health among males and females. Both men and women clinicians were asked to rate three categories of individuals on 122 antonymous (opposite) pairs of traits: healthy male, healthy female, and healthy adult. Descriptions of the healthy adult were the same as the healthy male, while the healthy female was described differently from both. In other words, to be a "healthy female" is to be an "unhealthy adult." Further, women are placed in a double bind as well. If "male characteristics" denote health and effectiveness in the workforce, it means that "healthy female traits" connote dysfunction and ineffectiveness in work situations. However, if women exhibit assertiveness at a work site (healthy male and healthy adult traits) she runs the risk of being perceived as an unhealthy female ("bitchy" or being "butch"). Even more disturbing is the finding that both male and female clinicians shared these perceptions!

More recent studies continue to confirm that gender stereotypes of men and women have changed little over time; men are expected to be logical, independent, aggressive, and fearless, while women are illogical, passive, fearful, affectionate, conforming, and concerned with domestic affairs (Bergin & Williams, 1991; Swim & Stangor, 1998). Women continue to be told to "stay in your place," and not to violate sex-role norms. Such sex-role stereotypes can (1) have a damaging effect upon task performance (women are not as good as men in math and science) despite having equal ability to men, (2) contribute to stereotype threat, and (3) provoke negative thoughts and feelings about the self (Cadinu, Maass, Rosabianca, & Kiesner, 2005).

Old-Fashioned Sexism: Patriarchy, Power, and Control

In nearly all societies, women have been considered lesser than men, encountered more social restrictions, and usually considered intellectually, emotionally, and psychologically inferior (Nelson, 2006; Zastrow, 2004). As a result, patriarchal policies, practices, and structures have granted men power over women, and provided men with a convenient justification for the subjugation of women. Sexism is any attitude or behavior of individuals, institutions, or societal norms based on the belief that men are naturally superior to women and should dominate them in all spheres of life: political, economic, and social.

Stereotyping and rigid gender-role beliefs serve as a source of control and power over women through *descriptive* and *prescriptive* means (Fiske, 1993). Descriptive female stereotypes are the false beliefs about women (emotional, illogical, sensitive, etc.) that are imposed by a dominant powerful group. These have the effect of indoctrinating the larger society about *how people in a group think, feel, and behave*. It also has the effect of potentially indoctrinating targets to these beliefs as well. For example, women may come to internalize and believe in these stereotypes. Prescriptive female stereotypes are believed to be more damaging and insidious than descriptive ones because they state *how women* should *think, feel, and behave* (Fiske & Stevens, 1993). They represent the ultimate form of control because they induce conformance to role behaviors and punish those who violate prescriptive roles. A female worker in a "hard hat" construction site may be punished by male colleagues because she is breaking from traditional role behaviors and engaging in activities meant for men. She may be teased, isolated, or become the victim of male pranks that assail her gender identity. Interestingly, it was found that prescriptive stereotypes and not descriptive stereotypes were predictive of sexism in males (Gill, 2004).

The history of the United States is filled with sexism or unequal treatment of women (Morales & Sheafor, 2004; Zastrow, 2004). They were confined to childrearing and home activities and not allowed to engage in outside employment, many laws openly discriminated against them, and it was not until 1920 that passage of the 19th Amendment to the Constitution gave women the right to vote. The women's movement was relatively dormant until World War II when out of necessity large numbers of women were employed outside the home, breaking one of the traditional gender restrictions of society. The restrictive place of women in society was further eroded during the 1960s when the Civil Rights movement increased equality consciousness and both racial and sexual discrimination came under attack.

Betty Friedan's book *The Feminine Mystique* (1963) gave renewed impetus to the women's movement and served as a rallying cry for gender-conscious women and men and the ultimate formation of the National Organization of Women (NOW) in 1966. This organization continues to be an influential force for women in our political system. Since that time, numerous federal and state statutes have passed that forbid sex discrimination, advocate for equal pay for equal work, bar using marital status or gender to determine credit worthiness, and extend affirmative action laws to include women (Zastrow, 2004).

In light of these massive changes, one could make a strong case that sexism has been successfully checked and that our attitudes are no longer biased. However, such a belief would be to ignore the many subtle and different manifestations of sexism. The Equal Rights Amendment (ERA) was proposed in 1972 (27th Amendment to the Constitution) and stated: "Equality of rights under the law shall not be denied or abridged by the United States or any state on account of sex." Yet, after 10 years of attempts to ratify the ERA, it failed to gain passage because it required ratification by three fourths of the states. Its failure to pass could be laid at the foundations of "modern sexism," which allowed opponents to claim they were against sex discrimination but concerned that such a well-intentioned act could actually foster greater disadvantage to women: fairness dictated granting maternity leaves to husbands, women would be equally liable for alimony, they could be drafted into the armed forces, and would lose preferential treatment in divorce proceedings.

While these arguments were bogus, they provided convenient rationalizations for not voting for the ERA.

Modern Sexism: Invisibility, Good Intentions, and Control

Just as the opponents of the ERA manifested many of the characteristics of modern sexism (invisibility, good intentions, but ultimately control of women), manifestations of sexism have evolved over time into a more subtle and insidious form (Swim, Aiken, Hall, & Hunter, 1995). Although not overt and intentional, these subtler forms of sexism nevertheless exert power over women and ultimately control their social, psychological, economic, and political opportunities in life (Swim & Cohen, 1997). Modern sexism is characterized by denial of personal bias and prejudice toward women, a general conscious belief in equality of the sexes, but unconscious attitudes that foster nonsupport for programs and legislation helpful to women. Modern sexism is likely to operate outside the level of conscious awareness through false belief systems that allow for discriminatory treatment: "Discrimination against women is a thing of the past." "Men and women now have an equal opportunity to succeed in society." "Women have no right to be angry as they have already advanced far in our society." "Women are no longer disadvantaged; indeed it is men who are being discriminated against." These beliefs serve to mask hostility toward equality for women.

A different but related form of modern sexism is *benevolent sexism* as opposed to *hostile sexism*; the former is composed of traditional stereotypes about women, yet they are viewed positively, while the latter evokes negative attitudes linked to beliefs about female inferiority (Glick & Fiske, 1996). Both share similar stereotypes of women, but benevolent sexists are motivated paternalistically to "protect the weaker sex," view them as objects of "romantic love," and admire them as "wives and mothers." Despite viewing women positively, it is based on an idealized stereotyped perception of the opposite sex and is equally controlling and harmful.

In Chapter 1, we used the example of a female subway rider who was jostled while trying to exit at her stop. A stranger saw her plight and without her permission physically interceded by placing his hand on the small of her back and escorting her out. The man no doubt thought he was being protective, helpful, and chivalrous, but the woman passenger felt uncomfortable receiving his help. He would be identified as a benevolent sexist, who conveyed a sex-role stereotype of women as the weaker sex, needing protection, and unable to fend on their own. His behavior and the hidden message contain the characteristics of a gender microaggression: unconscious sexism, good intentions, but ultimately power and control over the female passenger.

GENDER MICROAGGRESSIONS

In today's societal climate, it is not politically correct to hold overtly sexist attitudes or engage in obvious discriminatory actions toward women because it is at odds with beliefs of equality (Capodilupo et al., in press; Nadal, Rivera, & Corpus, in press). To be accused of being a sexist or of holding sex-role stereotypes toward women is to be considered unenlightened and a bigot. The strong social sanctions against sexism have changed its face and it has morphed into a more ambiguous, subtle, and invisible form. Like racial microaggressions, gender microaggressions may be manifested in three forms: microassaults, microinsults, and microinvalidations (Sue & Capodilupo, 2008).

Gender microassaults are most similar to individual manifestations of old-fashioned sexism: being called a sexist name, a man refusing to wash dishes because it is "woman's work," displaying nude pin-ups of women at places of employment, men making unwanted sexual advances toward women, sexual harassment, and forced sexual intercourse are examples of gender microassaults. There is usually recourse in dealing with overt forms of sexism because they are more easily recognized and condemned. Gender microassaults may be legally actionable; they may be considered forms of sexual harassment and of creating a hostile work climate or environment (Hinton, 2004; Rowe, 1990).

The more insidious and difficult types of gender microaggressions, such as microinsults and microinvalidations, are less obvious, subtle, and often not recognized by both perpetrator and target (Sue & Capodilupo, 2008). It is their invisibility that makes them so powerful and potentially lethal. Taxonomies of gender microaggressions were first proposed by Sue and Capodilupo (2008), and later researched and refined into their actual thematic manifestations (Capodilupo et al., in press; Nadal et al., in press). Several microaggressive themes have been identified through research and scholarly reviews: Sexual Objectification, Second-Class Citizenship, Use of Sexist Language, Assumptions of Inferiority, Denial of the Reality of Sexism, Traditional Gender Role Assumptions, Invisibility, Denial of Individual Sexism, and Sexist Jokes.

1. *Sexual Objectification*—The process of perceiving the female body as an object for the pleasure and psychological ownership of others, primarily

men; women are reduced to their physical appearance and/or sexuality (Fredrickson & Roberts, 1997; Buchanan, Fischer, Tokar, & Yoder, 2008). Pornography, for example, leaves little doubt of how it sexually objectifies women. Yet, sexual objectification by men through verbal, nonverbal, and environmental mediums can vary in their degree of consciousness and subtlety. Staring at a woman's breasts while talking to her, making catcalls or whistling, prolonged staring or leering, "checking out" another woman in your partner's presence, hanging pin-ups of nude women in an office, forcing unwanted sexual attention toward a woman, touching or rubbing up against a woman without her permission, making crude remarks about women's bodies, and telling sexual jokes are all examples of sexual objectification (Hill & Fischer, 2008). Women report that sexual objectification is a common and continuing reality in their day-to-day experience.

"Every day, when I come to work, I do my best to show I'm competent and hardworking. I want that promotion as well. But my male coworkers never seem to recognize that I do much more work than they do. Yet, when I wear my hair differently or wear a new dress or sweater . . . I get remarks . . . 'Oh, you look different, I like it . . . You really look sexy today, what's the occasion?' Or 'That dress really shows off your body well . . .' What gives them the right to comment on my body anyway? Is it so hard to say, 'You're doing a fine job . . . that last report was outstanding." Do they even notice? No, only my body and appearance matter to them. . . . What gets me is other women do the same thing, but usually in a negative way. 'Boy, that's a terrible outfit she has on. It makes her look frumpy.'"

The quote also points to another sexual objectification dilemma: self-objectification. The more women report being gazed at, encountering remarks about their appearance, garnering unwanted sexual attention, and experiencing sexual harassment, the more they also objectified themselves and other women as separate sexual beings (Hill & Fischer, 2008; Swim et al., 2001). Thus women, who are evaluated in an objectified culture regarding physical appearance, come to evaluate their own worthiness or self-esteem based upon appearance and physical attributes. Self-objectification has been found to be negatively related to mental health, happiness, and subjective well-being (Frederickson & Roberts, 1997).

2. *Second-Class Citizenship*—This category of gender microaggressions involves verbal, behavioral, or environmental communications indicating that women do not deserve the same opportunities, benefits, or privileges afforded to men (Capodilupo et al., in press; Sue & Capodilupo, 2008). When a group of women at a restaurant are seated at a table next to the kitchen door

despite the presence of other empty tables, when men are served first as customers, or when women are offered less desirable or less important tasks at a place of employment, these actions convey lesser treatment for an undeserving individual or group. The following quote indicates the second-class status accorded to female athletes (Capodilupo et al., in press):

"I guess the guys' teams would get you know, new uniforms every year . . . they would get new equipment, whereas the, umm . . . the girls teams really, we kept the same uniforms for like a good five years at a time, and our equipment wouldn't be as good, it would be broken."

3. **Use of Sexist Language**—Anthropologists were among the first to suggest the power of language in shaping our worldviews. The patriarchal nature of our society is reflected in the structure and content of language. Occupations, for example, often possess titles or names that suggest male or female occupancy: Chairman, policeman, repairman, mailman, doctor, airplane pilot, firefighter, and President of the United States evoke images of "men" in powerful and active positions, while nurse, secretary, teacher, day-care worker, receptionist, dental assistant, and clerical worker suggest images of women in less powerful and stereotyped supportive roles. Female doctors at hospitals often describe patients as mistaking them for nurses.

Use of the male generic pronoun ("he"), the word "mankind," or the phrase "May the best man win" to refer to both sexes is a practice that makes women invisible, restricts women's career/job choices, and communicates that they are lesser beings (Nelson, 2006). "We hold these truths to be self-evident, that all men are created equal" as written in the *Bill of Rights* is meant to ensure egalitarian relationships that ironically neglected over half the population of the United States (Sue, 2003). Language assumptions are so powerful because they are invisible, yet convey strong messages to women about their worth and roles in society (Swim, Mallett, & Stangor, 2001). Internalizing these messages can lead to lower feelings of self-worth and competency.

4. **Assumption of Inferiority**—While women may be perceived in this society as more skilled in interpersonal or social relationships, they are often considered inferior intellectually, temperamentally, and physically (Capodilupo et al., in press).

In 2005, then Harvard President Larry Summers (now director of President Obama's National Economic Council) suggested that innate differences between the sexes might help explain why relatively few women become professional scientists or engineers. His comments set off a furor with demands that he be fired. Women academicians were reported to have stormed out of the conference in disgust as Summers used "innate ability" as a possible explanation for sex differences in test scores. Ironically, Summers was lecturing to a room of the most accomplished women scholars in engineering and science in the nation.

If Summers truly believes that women are intellectually less capable, he is certainly not alone in that unspoken belief (Cadinu et al., 2005; Swim & Stangor, 1998). The belief that women are less talented in mathematics and logical thinking is a common, albeit less visible, thread that undergirds our educational system and influences career choices (Swim & Cohen, 1997; Swim, Hyers, Cohen, & Ferguson, 2001). Women are often perceived as too emotional to make logical decisions, as not possessing the intestinal fortitude to make tough decisions, and as having a difficult time being objective. School counselors often discourage female students from entering occupations in mathematics, sciences, or in fields that require leadership, influence, and command. Rather, they are counseled to accept supporting roles in fields that minimize decision-making or leadership positions. Female students often report that in class, boys are called on more frequently by the teacher, even when there are more girls in the classroom. They report feeling invisible, unimportant, and as knowing less than their male counterparts (Sue & Capodilupo, 2008).

Further, our patriarchal society emphasizes physical strength as a major index of power and control. Physical differences between the sexes are a reality; in general men are bigger, stronger, and run faster than women. Historically, men became hunters, while women were confined to roles as gatherers of nuts, fruits, and other food. Men became protectors, defenders, and skilled in playing active roles, while women were confined to roles such as childrearing, nursing, and the domestic tasks of cooking, washing, and serving. In our modern times, however, physical strength is often no longer important in determining the multiplicity of roles in our society. Indeed a case can be made that women are physically more resilient, are more resistant to illnesses, tolerate pain better, possess greater endurance except in short-term feats, and have a much longer life span than men. Yet, physical strength continues to play a large role in determining superiority and inferiority of the sexes.

5. *Restrictive Gender Roles*—Many microaggressions directed toward women relate specifically to the traditional roles they should play, and to admonitions not to break them. If they do so, they are likely to be viewed negatively, called names, or punished in one way or another. In one study (Capodilupo et al., in press), women reported that they received messages that they should be "soft and feminine," play care-giving roles, "not use

profanity or drinking," and be "domestic." In dating relationships, women were expected to allow "guys to make the decisions" and "not to undermine their authority." Getting an education for women is seen as less important than finding the right man and getting married. "Don't worry your pretty little head," "So, when are you going to get married?" and "Why do you want to take a job away from a man who needs it?" are examples of gender-role microaggressions that convey "A women's place is in the home."

Breaking gender roles can result in punitive and negative consequences. A man who has multiple sex partners is seen as a "stud." A woman who engages in such behavior is called promiscuous, "easy," a slut, or a whore. A man who takes command at the office and who shows flashes of anger may be perceived as assertive, competent, and "take charge." A woman who exhibits similar behavior is seen as "bitchy," "unladylike," "emotional," or angry and hostile (see Table 8.1). Punishment of those who break role prescriptions is captured in these statements by a female team leader who entered a primarily male worksite:

"It can be very lonely here. They hired me to manage a team of architects, but they don't like me telling them what to do. It's almost like they just wanted to fill a quota . . . 'You know, we have a woman in the office, you know and that's diversity.' My first week here was horrible. They resented me as the boss, insinuated I didn't know my place. They go out to lunch together and never invite me. I just stick to myself now."

6. *Denial of the Reality of Sexism*—These manifestations of microaggressions are the numerous messages sent to women that (1) sexism is a thing of the past, (2) women are actually now "advantaged" in our society, (3) those who complain about sexism are oversensitive, (4) women are externalizing their own shortcomings or unhappiness, and (5) trivialize sexist incidents. In other words, women's experiences of sexism are invalidated. Men and even many women may share a belief that sexism is a thing of the past and that it no longer represents a problem or obstacle to the career ambitions, for example, of women. The playing field is now considered level and competence will rise to the top.

In a faculty search in our department, for example, one male member of the search committee shared with me that women candidates were advantaged. He lamented that "Men don't stand a chance these days of being hired, because they are the wrong gender." Female employees tell stories of how their bosses would downplay their complaints of sexist behavior with a dismissive comment such as, "Don't be so oversensitive, it's just harmless fun."

Table 8.1   Contrasting Role Descriptions: Businessman and Businesswoman

- He's aggressive; she's pushy.
- He's good at details; she's picky.
- He loses his temper because he's so involved in the job; she's bitchy.
- When he's depressed (or hungover), everyone tiptoes past his office; she's moody so it must be her "time of the month."
- He follows through; she doesn't know when to quit.
- He's confident; she's conceited.
- He stands firm; she's hard.
- He has judgment; she's prejudiced.
- He's a man of the world; she's "been around."
- He drinks because of excessive job pressure; she's a lush.
- He isn't afraid to say what he thinks; she's mouthy.
- He excises authority diligently; she power-mad.
- He's close-mouthed; she's secretive.
- He's climbed the ladder to success; she slept her way to the top.

Source: Author unknown. Taken from Zastrow (2004, p. 450).

They are often admonished to not make a big deal about it and/or "ignore it or not to be oversensitive" (Capodilupo et al., in press). Often they told stories of how their complaints or observations were portrayed as personal short-comings and of their not taking personal responsibility for contributing to the situation (victim blame).

The denial of sexism flies in the face of reality. Both overt and subtle sexism are continuing realities found in sexual harassment, objectification, sexist humor, and many forms of discrimination (Klonoff & Landrine, 1995; Matteson & Moradi, 2005; Swim & Cohen, 1997). It was found that women of all ages reported frequent sexism in academics, social life, employment, and athletics. Ninety-nine percent of a female sample reported sexism at some time in their lives; 97% experienced it in the past year; and many reported high frequencies through their lives (Klonoff & Landrine, 1995).

7. *Denial of Individual Sexism*—Denial of individual sexism varies from deliberative to sincere levels. With respect to the former, men who hold traditional sex-role views of women and/or hold hostile and negative attitudes toward them may consciously and deliberately disguise their sexist thoughts or actions. Thus, they may consciously discriminate against a woman applying for a job but disguise the reason as "the male candidate was better qualified."

In our society, it is not politically correct or socially acceptable to discriminate against any one group. However, the majority of gender microaggressions directed at women are from men who sincerely believe they are not sexist, profess equality for women, and consciously abhor sex discrimination.

Most women who hear a man state "I'm not sexist, I have a wife and daughters, you know," "I don't see sex when I promote people," or "I treat everyone the same whether they are a man or a woman" may immediately become vigilant and "on guard." Experience has shown them that most men possess strong gender bias and the denial is either a "cover up" or "lack of self-awareness about their actions or attitudes." In situations where the topic of sexism or gender bias becomes salient, such men may become uncomfortable, anxious, or silent on the topic, for fear of appearing sexist. One of their greatest fears and apprehensions is that whatever they say or do in a social situation will appear sexist.

8. *Invisibility*—Women have often described the experience of "invisibility"—of being unseen, unworthy of recognition, unimportant, powerless, and overlooked. They are not seen by employers as candidates for promotion, ignored when they make contributions on a work team, and called on less frequently by both male and female teachers in the classroom. In his book *Invisible Man*, Ralph Ellison (1972) writes about his racial invisibility: "I am an invisible man. No, I am not a spook like those who haunted Edgar Allan Poe; nor am I one of your Hollywood-movie ectoplasms. I am a man of substance, of flesh and bone, fiber, and liquids—and I might even be said to possess a mind. I am invisible, understand, simply because people refuse to see me. Like the bodiless heads you see sometimes in circus sideshows, it is as though I have been surrounded by mirrors of hard, distorting glass. When they approach me they see only my surrounding, themselves, or figments of their imagination—indeed, everything and anything except me." (p. 3).

While referring to his invisibility as a Black man, the description given is similar to the experience of a multitude of marginalized groups in our society, such as women. The invisibility syndrome occurs when the talents, abilities, and character of women are not acknowledged or valued by others or by the larger society (Franklin, 1999). Gender microaggressions involve forgetting the names of female employees, but having no difficulty remembering male ones, serving men before women, or not recalling the ideas of a female coworker.

9. *Sexist Humor/Jokes*—It is difficult for any of us not to be exposed to sexist jokes or humor, told by friends and family, in cartoons or commercials, by stand-up comedians, and in TV programs/movies.

A very common joke describes how a male boss reacts to a female coworker when the work team is faced with a crisis. She asks: "How can I help?" He responds: "Just sit there and look pretty."

When some form of this joke is told, it generally evokes much laughter. Yet, the hidden message is filled with stereotypes, is demeaning, reinforces restrictions on the behavior of women, and is a clear "put-down." The stereotypes and messages are clear: women are bad problem solvers, useless, less capable, passive, and only valued by their appearance (objectification). If one looks at the joke even more closely, there appears to be a masked form of hostility directed toward women. Yet, we hear such jokes constantly in reference to "dumb blond jokes," "airhead women," and references to female anatomy. Sexist jokes seem to contain several characteristics: (1) they play out gender role stereotypes, (2) they make fun of or deride women, (3) they allow socially unacceptable hostility to be expressed toward women, (4) they culturally condition both men and women as to the beliefs and roles both sexes should play, and (5) they cause internalization of attitudes and beliefs by the target group. The fact that women may find sexist jokes equally humorous may indicate the latter, damaging process (Eckman & Friesen, 1982).

Studies on sexist jokes are revealing. In some studies, women reported increased feelings of anger, surprise, contempt, and hostility when exposed to hearing a number of sexist versus nonsexist jokes (LaFrance & Woodzicka, 1998). Men who found sexist jokes enjoyable and funny were most likely endorsed by those who were accepting of rape-myths, violence toward women, sexual aggression toward women as sexual objects, and as targets to be manipulated and controlled (Ryan & Kanjorski, 1998). In other words, sexist jokes are not harmless, but instead demean women and perpetuate stereotypes.

THE DETRIMENTAL IMPACT OF GENDER MICROAGGRESSIONS

A number of studies indicate that sexism and its various manifestations have detrimental effects on the standard of living for women; expose them to greater emotional and physical violence, sexual assaults, and sexual harassment; confine them to lesser roles in society; affect the quality of health care and education they receive; decrease their sense of self-worth; increase their psychological distress; and are associated with certain mental disorders (Lyness & Thompson, 2000; National Academies, 2006; Strickland, 1992; D. Sue, Sue, & Sue, 2010; U.S. Census Bureau, 2002). With the decrease of modern sexism and its overt manifestations, one would hope to see a major improvement in the lives of women. The fact that such inequities and negative consequences continue to exist suggests sexism must be continuing to operate.

One major speculation is that overt sexists are not the ones who contribute to inequities in employment, health care, and education, or to the detrimental psychological consequences experienced by women, but rather well-intentioned men, who believe in sexual equality and would never consciously or deliberately discriminate. As men, we have been culturally conditioned through a socio-political process that denigrates the importance of women, objectifies them, and views them as inferior beings. On the one hand, we may hold conscious beliefs of equality between the sexes, yet at another level also hold unconscious or hidden biases and negative attitudes toward women.

Impact on Standard of Living

Although single mothers constitute only 20% of all families, they make up nearly 50% of families living in poverty (U.S. Census Bureau, 2001); women are usually confined to the lowest status and paying positions, such as child-care workers, receptionists, cashiers, and secretaries, while men dominate higher-paying positions such as physicians, lawyers, judges, engineers, and dentists (U.S. Department of Labor, 2005); women earn less than three-quarters of the salaries of men (U.S. Census Bureau, 2002); they hold approximately 10% of elective offices in the United States; and there has never been a woman U.S. president; they hold only 14.8% of Fortune 500 board seats; they encounter the glass ceiling in places of employment and have difficulty being promoted even when otherwise qualified; and they comprise only 27% of corporate officers in Fortune 500 companies (Rubin, 2008). Even more discouraging when these statistics are seen from a trend perspective, progress in closing the pay gap, increasing the number of female officers in corporations, and increasing their representation in boards has stalled and even declined in the past few years (Rubin, 2008).

These statistics reveal that women face many barriers in career choices. Due to a primarily male-oriented work culture, women experience gender micro-aggressions from their bosses, coworkers, and even other women that affect the quality of their work experience, and ability to be hired, retained, and pro-moted (Sue, Lin, & Rivera, in press). In the workplace, gender microaggressions are manifested and impact women in the following ways (Lyness & Thompson, 2000; Piotrkowski, 1998):

- Women are made to feel like tokens and unqualified to fit senior man-agement levels. They experience social distancing from their male col-leagues and are often excluded from both formal and informal meetings. Women often describe their male coworkers as being uncomfortable in their presence.

- Men not only excluded female coworkers, but heightened cultural boundaries by emphasizing camaraderie with men while accentuating differences with women. This is most symbolized by the "old boy's network" and networking among men only, while excluding women.
- Women stated they had few mentors, were not effectively mentored when compared to men, and that male mentors often mistook their interactions as a sexual invitation.
- Women often described a hostile and invalidating work climate. Over 60% of women reported harassment at the workplace in the form of sexual innuendos, sexist jokes, unwanted sexual attention, and/or gender stereotypes.

Impact on Physical Health

The quality of life is oftentimes measured with respect to physical and mental health. The fact that women live longer than men and seem to have greater resilience to illnesses may be biologically determined, just as physical strength and speed are attributes of men. Little doubt exists, however, that there are gender differences in physical well-being, and illnesses as well. How much of these differences are related to sexism is difficult to determine. We often think about cardiovascular disease as a male problem, but it is the number-one cause of death among women (Misra, 2001). Deaths from lung and breast cancers for women are increasing, while general deaths for lung cancer for men have declined. Although it would be difficult to attribute the stress of sexism to increased cancer deaths (it appears that increased lung cancer is affected by increased cigarette smoking among women), some have observed that funding research in the areas of heart disease and cancer have been primarily conducted on men. Physicians also seem not to entertain these diseases in the forefront of diagnosis and treatment when they see female patients.

In Chapter 5 we described the relationship of microaggressive stress and its physiological and psychological correlates. It would not be far-fetched to entertain the notion that gender microaggressions represent stress to women. If it does, it would follow the same process of heightened physiological arousal, constant vigilance, and a mobilization of physical and psychological resources to deal with microaggressions. Coronary heart disease, hypertension, headaches, and even asthma are shown to be connected to stress, which decreases immunological functioning (D. Sue, Sue, & Sue, 2010). Women are more likely to suffer from migraine and tension headaches, and asthma (Hamelsky & Lipton, 2006;

National Center for Health Statistics, 2007). Studies suggest that women are more likely to be affected by stress in their roles as caregivers for children, partners, and parents (Stambor, 2006). For women, conflicts with societal standards, discrimination, cultural expectations, and exposure to gender microaggressions can significantly impact health.

Impact on Psychological Health

Scholars have concluded that women are consistently subjected to greater stressors than men (Morales & Sheafor, 2004; Spradlin & Parsons, 2008; National Academies, 2006):

- Women carry more of the domestic burden and more responsibility for social and interpersonal relationships and for childcare, despite holding full-time employment outside of the home.
- They must contend with low wages and low-skilled occupations.
- They must contend with frequent sexual harassment: 81% of girls in 8th to 11th grades report having been sexually harassed, as have 30% of undergraduates and 40% of graduate students.
- They are paid less than their male counterparts for similar jobs.
- They receive less recognition, approval, and encouragement in classrooms than do their male counterparts.
- They are more likely to live in poverty.
- They encounter greater discrimination and victimization.
- They face more barriers in their career choices.

Depression
It would be a denial of gender reality to say that women's sense of self-worth, sense of well-being, and mental health are unaffected by these daily and constant assaults, insults, and invalidations. Up to 7 million women suffer from depression, double the number of men (Kessler, 2003; Schwartzman & Glaus, 2000). While some argue that differences can be attributed to self-reporting (women are more inclined to seek treatment than men), gender bias in diagnosis toward depression, and biological differences associated with hormonal fluctuations, which may account for the higher incidence in women, it appears that a major explanation relates to sexism (Strickland, 1992). Gender role expectations diminish a sense of control in life, foster helplessness, impose self-subordination, and produce role conflicts that are oftentimes associated with depression.

Anxiety and Stress

Gender also plays an important role in anxiety disorders. Across all anxiety disorders, except for Obsessive-Compulsive Disorder, women suffer more than men (Nolen-Hoeksema, 2004). Again, the lack of power and status, and contending with chronic stressors that make life uncertain (poverty, lack of respect, sexual harassment, and limited career opportunities) may all contribute to a sense of anxiety, fear, apprehension, and dread. No wonder statistics suggest that women are also more likely to suffer from stress disorders, particularly Posttraumatic Stress Disorder (PTSD) (Galea et al., 2002; National Institute of Mental Health, 2007). By analyzing data from the National Violence Against Women Project, researchers concluded that the greater prevalence of stress disorders, especially PTSD, was strongly related to exposure (vicarious and direct) to more violent interpersonal situations (Cortina & Kubiak, 2006).

Body Image, Dissatisfaction, and Eating Disorders

Objectification theory posits that being raised in a sociocultural context that emphasizes women's appearance, specifically their bodies, socializes them to view themselves through an observer's perspective (Fredrickson & Roberts, 1997). Self-objectification is correlated with increased risk of anxiety, depression, sexual dysfunction, and eating disorders (Buchanan et al., 2008; Hill & Fischer, 2008). Body image and eating disorders are believed to arise from the constant preoccupation of our society with female attractiveness and sexuality. The APA Task Force on the Sexualization of Girls (2007) indicates that women are sexualized through television, music videos, lyrics, magazines, and advertising. Being bombarded with these messages, girls and women can become objectified and self-objectified (APA Task Force, 2007; Seitz, 2007; Thompson & Stice, 2004):

- Girls come to believe that their primary value comes from being attractive.
- They define themselves according to the bodily and beauty standards shown in the media.
- Their capacity for independent action and decision making is diminished through self-objectification.
- They develop an unattainable "thin-ideal" and operate from cultural scripts: *"Slender women are attractive"* and *"I am overweight."*
- Sixty percent of girls reported trying to change their appearance to resemble celebrities or actors.

The unrealistic standard of beauty for women is shown in the following facts. The average American woman is 5 feet, 4 inches tall, and weighs 162 pounds, but teenage girls describe their ideal body dimensions as 5 feet, 7 inches tall, 110 pounds and fitting a size 5 dress (Ogden, Fryar, Carroll, & Flegal, 2004). It is estimated that only 5% of women can attain the size required for fashion models (Irving, 2001).

Eating disorders are believed to be associated with dissatisfaction of body image and/or an attempt to achieve an unattainable physical beauty standard. Eating disorders are both life-threatening and likely to affect general health. Over 90% of diagnosed anorexia nervosa cases, whether the restricting or binge-eating/purging types, are suffered by females; over 90% of diagnosed cases of bulimia nervosa are female; and binge-eating disorders are 1.5 times more prevalent in females (American Psychiatric Association, 2000). Little doubt remains that body image, body dissatisfaction, and eating disorders are intimately related to one another.

The Way Forward

Overcoming Gender Microaggressions

It is clear that gender microaggressions can take a major toll on the quality of life of women in our society. Gender microaggressions in a broad sense are the overt and covert messages sent to women regarding their place in society and their identities. Gender microaggressions are reflections of a world view that defines a women's existence as lesser than that of a man, traps them with descriptive and prescriptive stereotypes, punishes them for breaking traditional sex roles, contributes to the climate of violence toward women, and objectifies and sexualizes them. To effectively overcome these injustices requires a three-pronged approach: individual intervention, institutional/organizational intervention, and societal intervention.

1. *Individual intervention*—Becoming aware of our own biases, prejudices, and stereotypes about women and their roles in society are major challenges to each and every one of us. Little doubt exists that we are all victims of a cultural conditioning process that has instilled biased attitudes, beliefs, and stereotypes about men and women, and socialized us

into what is considered appropriate gender roles. Some recommendations in working toward ending sexism are the following:

- An honest examination of beliefs, values, and attitudes toward women and gender roles is needed. Being open to challenging yourself and to challenges by others (without reacting defensively) are first steps.
- As a partner, question the role relationships you have with women and try to understand what it says about you and others.
- As a parent, raise your sons and daughters to respect the wishes of each gender. Try to expand their visions as to choice and the multiplicity of roles they can play in their personal and work lives.
- Be a role model in accepting and/or breaking traditional role constraints. Have others, especially children, see you engage in alternative gender behaviors, roles, and responsibilities. Your actions are a powerful means of communicating values, attitudes, and beliefs.
- Become an ally, activist, and member of community organizations/ groups that focus on eliminating oppression toward women.

2. *Organizational intervention*—As Chapter 11 thoroughly discusses, organizational or institutional change is required to combat sexism and sexual harassment and to break gender-role constraints. First and foremost, places of employment, education, and health care must take an active part in making sure that policies, practices, and structures of organizations allow for equal access and opportunity for all.

- Organizations must have a policy or vision statement that reaffirms their nondiscrimination policies in all facets of hiring, promotion, and retention of women employees.
- Leadership and management should not tolerate a hostile work environment toward women. They must play a proactive role in fostering a positive climate for women in organizations.
- The "old boys' network" must be transformed to include women as well as other racial groups. Competency should become the primary criteria for leadership roles.
- Education and training should be provided to employees regarding the manifestation of gender microaggressions, sexual harassment, and gender discrimination.
- Programs, policies, and practices should be carefully monitored to ensure they do not unfairly disadvantage women while advantaging men.
- Accountability for a bias-free environment is clearly defined for those in leadership positions.

(Continued)

3. *Societal/cultural intervention*—If we are all products of our cultural conditioning, then drastic societal change is required to overcome sexism—the individual and institutional expressions of the superiority of men over women. Our male-centered culture communicates these beliefs, attitudes, and behaviors through education, the mass media, institutions, and significant others.

- Social policy and legislation must be passed to rectify discriminatory practices and to foster and promote equal access and opportunity for women. As indicated in this chapter, one of the most disappointing outcomes of the Equal Rights Amendment was its failure to pass. All legal avenues must be utilized to strengthen or develop rules and regulations that open the gateway for women.
- In many respects, we are the products of a flawed culture and our focus has been primarily directed at remediation. All the suggestions given under individual, institutional, and societal changes imply an attempt to rectify a biased system. But were that our only goal, our work would be never-ending. Prevention offers the best solution to the problem. None of us were born into this world desiring to be "sexist." We took on prejudices and biases through a process of cultural conditioning. The question becomes one of how we create a culture that already values the contributions of all genders and which imbues within everyone bias-free worldviews. Education becomes one of the key channels to promote this social justice outlet. It is here in the pre-K–12 system of education that we can reach everyone. If our education was truly multicultural, we would go a long way in developing healthy children whose outlooks would be of positive gender roles and relationships. How we do that is a major challenge.

In closing, little doubt exists that sexism continues to harm girls and women in our society. The question is not whether these gender microaggressions are exaggerations or not, but "How can we as a society allow such injustices to continue against women, who are our mothers, wives, partners, lovers, daughters, and sisters?"

CHAPTER NINE

Sexual-Orientation Microaggressions and Heterosexism

The most effective way to keep a group out of any discourse is to keep them invisible. The struggle to be visible and validated is a common theme in contemporary lesbian, gay, bisexual, and transgender (LGBT) cultures. . . . Prior to the 1970s, anyone known to be homosexual or "LGB" was at great risk to lose his or her job, home, and family. Students were suspended and expelled from most colleges and universities for being known to be homosexual. The operative phrase here was "known to be," an early form of "Don't ask, don't tell." The price of being out to yourself was the deep closet. That closet took many forms: (a) the professional closet, with a healthy personal life, closed support network, and careful efforts to protect one another; (b) the painful closet of nearly complete secrecy and fear; or (c) the closet of internalized self-hatred or complete denial to self and others. (Douce, 2005, p. 59)

. . . I became aware of my sexual orientation only in my late teens. When I first experienced a same-sex attraction, I labeled it a "close friendship" and proceeded to deny my true self. My upbringing told me that being gay was wrong, "morally depraved." As an only son, I was expected to get married and have a son to perpetuate the family name. How could I disappoint my family? How could I allow myself to give in to "moral weakness"? . . . For several years, I struggled to maintain a heterosexual identity. I dated women but could never gain intimacy with them. Deep down, I knew "the unspeakable truth," that I was a gay man . . . Yet I had a deep-seated fear of how the process of coming out would impact relationships with my family. . . . After coming out, my worst fears initially came true. I lost the support of my parents and initially did not have contact with them. . . . Ultimately, the relationship settled into an uncomfortable silence about my life as a gay man. "Don't ask, don't tell" was the only way to maintain a connection with them. (O'Brien, 2005, pp. 97–98)

"Closeted," "hiding," "silence," "fear," "denial," "shame," "self-struggle," and "self-hate" seem to be a few of the words and concepts voiced from these two narratives of a lesbian woman and gay man. More than intellectual concepts, however, the voices are filled with the hurts, pains, fears, and real life consequences of being LGBT in a heterosexist society (Barret & Logan, 2002; Croteau, Lark, & Lance, 2005). The LGBT sexual-orientation reality is different from the sexual-orientation reality of heterosexuals (straights). It is often difficult for straights to understand the differences in experiential realities because of societal and personal aversions to recognizing LGBTs, the collusive silencing of their voices, and the fears of repercussions from "coming out" that keep them hidden from public view. The brief statements by Douce (2005) and O'Brien (2005) illustrate a few of these realities.

First, "hiding" and living in the closet represent times or situations in which an LGBT person chooses not to disclose his/her sexual orientation to others, often for fear of retaliation or loss of social support (Fukuyama, Miville, & Funderburk, 2005). One of O'Brien's greatest fears is the loss of parental support and/or the altering of his relationship with family members (being unable to speak on certain taboo topics). Other fears, as pointed out by Douce, involve being scorned, isolated, seen as depraved and sinful, losing a job, or not being promoted because of antigay attitudes, or even experiencing antigay harassment and hate crimes (Blank & Slipp, 1994). In our heterosexist society, there are powerful negative consequences to "coming out."

Second, struggling with sexual identity in a heterosexual society causes identity conflicts and confusion in LGBTs as they grow up with societal messages telling them that to be gay is to be deviant. Such messages can be quite overt or subtle/covert (Szymanski, 2009). If "normality" is equated with being straight, then experiencing same-sex attractions or bisexual attractions would be considered abnormal and even against the religious teachings of the church (Morrow & Beckstead, 2004). As LGBT boys and girls are constantly exposed to a heterosexual society, they are socialized into such beliefs, yet their burgeoning sexual-orientation identity increasingly fills them with thoughts and feelings that conflict with social norms of being and behaving. These "abhorrent" feelings of same-sex or bisexual attractions are denied, as the person struggles to maintain a false illusion to themselves and others that they are heterosexual. At some level, deep down, they begin to realize the conditioned "frightening" truth.

Third, Douce (2005) raises the issue of "self-hate," often referred to as internalized homophobia or internalized hate (Frost & Myer, 2009) or internalized oppression (Szymanski & Gupta, 2009). Perhaps the most inclusive term is "internalized oppression," which refers to the internalization and acceptance of negative societal attitudes, beliefs, and stereotypes directed toward a devalued or marginalized group by the LGBT individual. LGBTs, for example, may come to believe in their own inferiority, deviancy, and sinfulness. Their attitudes toward themselves may be self-loathing, fear of themselves, shame, and guilt for their existence, and a desire to deny their sexual-orientation identity.

> The first "person" to whom I came out was God. I was then 14 years old and was secretly in love with a male classmate. Around the same time, I first learned from a sermon in church that homosexuality was sinful. Subsequently, for a couple years, when I prayed at night, I asked God in tears to take back my life as soon as possible because He must have made a mistake in creating my "wrong existence." I felt ashamed, guilty, and was in pain to think of my gay orientation. Nevertheless, I could neither deny my feelings of love toward that classmate nor understand the intrinsic sinfulness of genuinely loving another person. (Chan, 2005, p. 47)

Last, there is a conspiracy of silence in our society to keep LGBTs and their issues invisible in our daily lives and in the broader society at large. Silence comes from the fears of "coming out," from the fact that LGBTs are not physically identifiable (unlike race or gender), from the discomfort of others in recognizing and addressing sexual-orientation issues, and from a society that deals with LGBTs through a formal and informal policy of "Don't ask, don't tell." Thus, invisibility makes it possible for many straights to state, "I don't personally know anyone who is gay, lesbian, or bisexual." They do, but simply do not know they do (Blank & Slipp, 1994). Later in this chapter, we present some social psychological reasons why invisibility plays such a powerful role in the sexual-orientation experience of LGBTs.

LGBT POPULATION IN THE UNITED STATES

It is extremely difficult to get an accurate count on the population of LGBTs in the United States because of societal sanctions against self-disclosure and definitional problems. With respect to the latter, it has been found that many people are not exclusively heterosexual or homosexual, and the incidence of early same-sex behavior among the general population is much higher than those who define themselves as gay, lesbian, or bisexual: overall, 6% of men and 11% of women admitted to oral and anal sex with members of the same sex (this does not include other forms of sexual activities such as kissing, caressing, etc.) (Mosher, Chandra, & Jones, 2005). The national survey of 18- to 44-year-olds revealed that 90% of men identified themselves as heterosexual, 2.3% as homosexual, 1.8% as bisexual, 3.9% something else, and 1.8% did not respond. With women, 90% identified as heterosexual, 1.3% as homosexual, 2.8% bisexual, 3.8% something else, and 1.8% did not answer. It appears that rates of identification among men and women were similar. However, some argue that the actual figure of homosexuals is around 10% (Hyde & DeLamater, 2000).

Like many marginalized groups in society, LGBTs tend to form their own communities and connections as a means to validate and support their group identities and as a buffer to a hostile and invalidating world. LGBTs are highest in the following cities: San Francisco (15.4%), Seattle (12.9%), Atlanta (12.8%), Minneapolis (12.5%), Boston (12.3%), Oakland (12.1%), Sacramento (9.8%), Portland, Oregon (8.8%), Denver (8.2%), and Long Beach (8.1%) (Williams Institute, 2006).

MENTAL DISORDER OR NORMAL ORIENTATION

Prior to 1973, homosexuality was considered a mental illness or a mental disorder (Douce, 2005). Even when the American Psychiatric Association voted to remove it in 1973, it created another new category, ego-dystonic homosexuality, in the third edition of the *Diagnostic and Statistical Manual of Mental Disorders* (DSM), for individuals with (1) "a lack of heterosexual arousal that interferes with heterosexual relationships" and (2) "a persistent distress from unwanted homosexual arousal." This category was later eliminated in the face of arguments that it is societal pressure and prejudice that causes the distress. Subsequently, the American Psychiatric Association has completely removed homosexuality as a mental disorder from the fourth edition of the DSM (DSM-IV-TR, APA, 2000), and other mental health organizations, including the American Psychological Association, no longer consider it a mental disorder.

However, simply removing it from a psychiatric classification has not convinced some that it is not a psychological disorder. Former majority leader of the Senate Trent Lott likened homosexuality to a disorder like alcoholism and kleptomania—conditions that should be treated (Mitchell, 1998), and religious leader Jerry Falwell stated that the September 11, 2001, terrorist attack that killed thousands was punishment by God for the growing influence of gay and lesbian groups. Unfortunately, beliefs that homosexuality is a pathological condition or a sin continue to distort the attitudes and beliefs of many. Unconscious biases and beliefs that equate LGBT psychosocial functioning to pathology are unconsciously shared by counselors and therapists alike (Mohr, Israel, & Sedlacek, 2001).

Given so much public and professional misunderstanding and misinformation about homosexuality, it seems important to answer one important question directly and firmly: Is homosexuality a mental disorder? The answer is *no!* First, heterosexuality should not be the sole standard by which other sexual behavior or affection is judged (Halderman, 2002). Second, research supports the conclusion that LGBT sexual orientation reflects a normal variant of sexual expression (D. Sue, Sue, & Sue, 2010). Third, homosexuality, in and of itself, is unrelated to psychological disturbance, and its higher correlations with mental disorders seem related to prejudice, discrimination, and minority stress (Berube, 1990; Gonsiorek, 1982). Discouragingly, however, it appears that, like the general public, many mental health professionals continue to view departure from heterosexual norms as repugnant or a sign of psychological disturbance.

FROM OVERT ANTI-GLBT SENTIMENTS TO INVISIBLE HETEROSEXISM

In 1998, Matthew Shepard, a gay University of Wyoming student, was tied to a fence and left for dead after being brutally tortured and beaten. Two 21-year-old men, high school drop-outs, had lured Shepard from a bar and targeted him because he was gay. During the trial, they were accused of being homophobic, filled with hate toward gays, and believing gays and lesbians were sick and did not deserve to live among the populace. The incident had a profound impact upon national and international hate crime laws, but more than anything else brought to the forefront the horrors of the extremes of hostile prejudice and anti-GLBT attitudes in our society.

Explicit and Overt Discrimination against LGBTs

Hate crimes and anti-GLBT harassment are lived realities for this group, and some believe that such incidents are on the rise. FBI statistics indicate that the incidence of hate crimes against LGBTs have increased over the recent years: 1,017 in 2005, 1,195 in 2006, and 1,265 in 2007 (Hansen-Weaver, 2009). In a University of California–Davis News and Information report (2007) the following statistics were found: (1) It was reported that nearly 40% of gay men and 12 to 13% of lesbians and bisexuals in the United States have been targets of violence or property crime because of their sexual orientation. (2) Across all groups (gays, lesbians, and bisexuals), violence included physical assaults, sexual assaults, thefts, and vandalism. (3) In addition, 49% reported incidents of verbal abuse, 23% reported threats of violence, 12.5% had objects thrown at them, and 11% reported housing and job discrimination. (d) Gay men reported experiencing higher numbers of incidences of harassment, violent crimes, and hate crimes than lesbians or bisexuals.

These facts are alarming because they give us a disturbing view of the constant threat of interpersonal, property, and verbal/nonverbal abuse and violence that LGBTs must experience in their daily lives. To be under constant threat to one's physical safety and psychological well-being is to live a life of perpetual fear, guardedness, and vigilance. These findings seem to fly in the face of a belief in the increasing tolerance of LGBTs in our society. Some speculate, however, that with increasing acceptance has come an increase in right-wing groups who have used the legislative route to reenergize anti-LGBT sentiments (Hansen-Weaver, 2009). The Defense of Marriage Act passed during the Clinton administration, anti-gay propositions 22 and 8 (defining marriage as only between a man and woman) in California, and other antigay legislation have allowed not only overt anti-GLBT prejudices to emerge, but also hidden and unconscious biases of the general population that portray LGBT people as immoral, sinful, and lesser beings. Such legislation is often based upon rationalizations that allow the population to act in a discriminatory manner while masking their conscious and unconscious biases.

Overt and open displays of anti-LGBT attitudes and discrimination can take many forms, such as antigay laws, threat of physical violence, verbal, nonverbal, and environmental harassment. Hate speech, negative portrayals or stereotypes, sodomy laws, gay panic defenses in assault or murder trials, adoption bans against same-sex couples, barring gays from serving in the military, and so on, are prime examples of overt, conscious, and deliberate LGBT discrimination. The overt and conscious manifestations of anti-LGBT acts, however, represent only the tip of the iceberg of heterosexism.

Invisible Heterosexism

Heterosexism may be defined as a sexual-orientation worldview that contains beliefs and attitudes that (a) all people are/or should be heterosexual, (b) it is more desirable to be heterosexual, and (c) it represents the norm of both gender identity and sexual attraction. By implication then, nonheterosexuals (LGBTs) do not exist or should become heterosexual, are undesirable, and are considered abnormal (Heterosexism, 2009; Safe Space, 2009). When this worldview is inculcated into individuals, institutions, and our society, it becomes a systemic and pervasive force that mistreats, denigrates, invalidates, insults, and oppresses LGBTs. Heterosexism can operate openly in a mean-spirited and deliberate manner, or can operate insidiously through invisibility, underrepresentation, erasure, lack of acknowledgment, the unspoken, and silence. The latter expressions of heterosexism constitute a major part of sexual-orientation microaggressions.

Heterosexism as a worldview contains many possible manifestations, such as homophobia and heterocentricism. The former term refers to the fear of homosexuality, fear of becoming gay, and a fear of homosexual contagion (Weinberg, 1972; Herek, 1984, 2004). The latter refers to an assumption that someone is heterosexual and/or the "privileging of heterosexual identities and relationships" (Hylton, 2005). While some have argued that heterocentricism is not a component of heterosexism, its active imposition on LGBTs constitutes a form of sexual prejudice. We prefer the term heterosexism to homophobia and heterocentricism because (1) many heterosexuals, despite their negative attitudes toward LGBTs, do not possess phobias of sexual minorities per se and (2) the harm rendered to LGBTs can come from assumptions of heterosexuality as well.

Visible heterosexism is more easily combated than its invisible manifestations. Invisible heterosexism is reflected in an unconscious worldview that is encoded into the individual's unconscious psyche, and our major social, cultural, and economic institutions. As a result, sexual-orientation prejudice, bias, and discriminatory behaviors operate in such a manner as to oppress sexual minorities, deny the humanity of our LGBT brothers and sisters, keep their existence hidden from public view, pathologize their sexual identities, contribute to psychological distress, and negatively impact mental health (Croteau, Lark, Lidderdale, & Chung, 2005; Frost & Meyer, 2009; Herek, Gillis, & Cogan, 2009; Rostosky, Riggle, Horne, & Miller, 2009).

SEXUAL-ORIENTATION MICROAGGRESSIONS

Sexual-orientation microaggressions are brief and commonplace daily verbal, behavioral, and environmental indignities, whether intentional or unintentional, that communicate hostile, derogatory, or negative LGBT slights and insults to the target group or person (Nadal, Rivera, & Corpus, in press; Sue & Capodilupo, 2008). As with previous chapters on racial and gender microaggressions, sexual-orientation microaggressions can span the continuum from being conscious and deliberate to unconscious and unintentional. Further, they also can be delivered as microassaults, microinsults, or microinvalidations. Sexual-orientation microassaults can occur via hate speech, terms of disparagement ("dyke" or "queer"), and telling heterosexist jokes; microinsults are embodied in "Don't ask, don't tell" policies; and microinvalidations might take the form of not inviting a gay or lesbian parent to "family" school days.

As indicated in earlier chapters, probably the most harmful forms of microaggressions are those that are outside the level of conscious awareness of perpetrators and, oftentimes, the targets as well. Sexual-orientation microaggressions hold their power because they are invisible, contain a hidden disparaging message to LGBTs, and when experienced by the target group, can result in extreme emotional distress and turmoil (Levitt et al., 2009; Szymanski, 2009; Szymanski & Gupta, 2009). Among sexual minorities, the process of self-stigma, self-hate, or internalized oppression is an additional powerful concern that strikes at the core of self-identity and self-esteem (Herek et al., 2009). A review of the research and scholarly literature on sexual-orientation microaggressions has identified a number of them: Oversexualization, Homophobia, Heterosexist Language/Terminology, Sinfulness, Assumption of Abnormality, Denial of Individual Heterosexism, and Endorsement of Heteronormative Culture/Behaviors (Arm, Horne, & Levitt, 2009; Blank & Slipp, 1994; Frost & Meyer, 2009; Levitt et al., 2009; Nadal, Rivera, & Corpus, in press; Sue & Capodilupo, 2008; Szymanski, 2009).

1. *Oversexualization*—When reference is made to gays, lesbians, or "homosexuals," many people immediately associate "sex" and "sexual activity" with this group. LGBTs are thought of as mere sexual beings rather than as complex people whose lives involve family, friends, careers, nonsexual relationships, hopes, and aspirations. These forms of microaggressions come out in any number of ways. From male heterosexual students: "Who wants to take a shower in the school gymnasium in front of a gay classmate?" "They should separate homosexuals in the men's locker room." From heterosexual neighbors: "I avoid physical contact with the lesbian couple next door in case they get the wrong idea." "Why do they have to flaunt their sexuality in public (holding hands)?" Perhaps one of the greatest concerns by some heterosexuals, especially parents, is a strong belief that lesbians and gays are sexually attracted to children, and are child molesters (Barrett & Logan, 2002). They avoid gays and make sure that their children are not exposed to them for fear that they will be molested sexually and/or be influenced and converted to a gay lifestyle.

The impact of viewing LGBTs in terms of their sexual lives is captured in the reactions described below:

> A lesbian programmer who is an open member of a gay and lesbian caucus group at work said, "Why am I defined only by my sexual orientation? All everyone sees is the sex thing." A gay accounts manager said, "There are no beds in the office. There are desks, chairs, and computers. But I feel that some people seem to define me solely by my sexual orientation and not by my professional capabilities." (Blank & Slipp, 1994, p. 144)

The oversexualization microaggression also seems to embolden some straights to steer conversations to sexual themes.

> I don't mind if someone expresses a genuine interest in my life, but what I strongly object to are prurient questions about my sexual practices or questions that try to educate me out of my "life-style." A few have actually said, "What do lesbians actually do together?" or "Do you think you'd feel differently toward men if you met a really nice, sensitive guy?" or "Don't you think you're upsetting your parents?" (Blank & Slipp, 1994, p. 144)

2. *Homophobia*—Homophobia is a term that has incorrectly been used to encompass the larger social meaning of prejudice and discrimination toward LGBTs. The correct usage and reference is more narrow, however, in that it was originally defined as fear (phobia) of homosexuals, often associated with the fear of being or becoming gay (Herek, 2004; Weinberg, 1972).

These apprehensions are often quite strong and are related to fears of contagion (becoming gay) or a fear of catching a disease from LGBTs. Beliefs that exposure to gays or gay lifestyles will unduly influence "normal people" to become gay, that children are being recruited or preyed upon by gays, or that heterosexuals will catch a deadly disease from them are part of homophobia. Gays, for example, are oftentimes blamed for the cause and spread of the deadly disease AIDS. While gay men suffer higher incidence, the cause is a virus; to believe that gays are consciously and willfully spreading the disease to others is the height of irrationality and ignorance.

Many verbal and nonverbal sexual-orientation microaggressions are related to this theme. Avoiding physical contact with LGBTs, washing one's hands immediately after shaking hands with a gay man, making sure that sons and daughters are restricted from going to a gay neighbor's home, and so forth communicate irrational apprehensions and anxieties toward LGBTs.

3. *Heterosexist Language/Terminology*—Heterosexist language can be quite obviously derogatory ("dyke," "queer," "butch," "queen," or "fag") or may manifest itself in more subtle everyday usage where the individuals using it are unaware of their demeaning message to the reference group. One of the most common terms in everyday usage among students in our schools is to refer to an action by others as "gay," signifying that it is "dumb" or "weird" behavior. Among straights, for example, evidence suggests that homophobic language is often not associated with sexual orientation (Thurlow, 2001), and that use of heterosexist language is not consciously related to strong biases toward LGBTs (Burn, 2000; Plummer, 2001). Yet, some suggest that use of heterosexist language has a negative impact upon self-identity and self-esteem of the targets, and that it reflects and reinforces a worldview of heterosexism among users and others who hear these comments (Burn et al., 2005; Nadal et al., in press; Sue & Capodilupo, 2008).

Terminology may also be heterosexist in its impact upon LGBTs. The terms "boyfriend," "girlfriend," "husband," and "wife" instead of "partner" or "spouse" are examples. "Marriage" that is defined as between a man and a woman has the impact of excluding LGBTs from equal rights and treating them as second-class citizens. A gay man who is told to "Bring your wife to the party" may feel invisible and invalidated. A lesbian who shares her night out on the town with friends who is asked "Did you go to a gay bar or a normal one?" is insulted by the unintentional equation of pathology with sexual orientation. An employer who unconsciously or consciously continues to refer to a female-to-male transgender individual as "she" negates the person's gender identity.

Heterosexist language not only shapes perception, but can communicate extremely different beliefs about a marginalized group. The terms "sexual orientation" and "sexual preference" are prime examples. Those who use the latter term believe that LGBTs have *freely chosen* their lifestyles, or choose to be, for example, homosexual. Those who use the term "sexual orientation" are more inclined to believe that there is a biological basis to sexual orientation, that it is a normative condition. There is much heated debate over whether one is biologically determined toward same-sex attraction or whether environmental upbringing/choice dictates the outcome (Nelson, 2006). Approximately half of the U.S. public believe that people choose to be homosexual (Whitely, 1990). Those who believe that homosexuality is controllable are more likely to blame LGBTs and to see them as having chosen a sinful life style (Sakalli, 2002). To many LGBTs the use of the phrase "sexual preference" represents a sexual-orientation microaggression because it communicates a message that LGBTs chose a deviant and sinful lifestyle, and that they could change if they really desired to.

4. *Sinfulness*—World religions differ in the degree of negativity and condemnation of homosexuals and homosexual sexual behaviors (Halderman, 2004; Tozer & Hayes, 2004). Some religions view same-sex orientation as intrinsically sinful, that such individuals are depraved and should be punished. Others are more lenient in that they do not view LGBs as evil sinners *as long as they do not act out their sexual desires.* To them, it is the sexual act that is the sin. Regardless of the explicitness in scriptures and traditions regarding same-sex attraction and acts, nearly all religions view homosexuality negatively, and teach that it represents a transgression against morality, the teachings of the church, and oftentimes toward God.

The impact of religiosity upon those who are strongly religious (both straights and LGBTs) has been explored in several studies. Researchers have identified two types of religiosity: intrinsically oriented and extrinsically oriented. Those with an intrinsic orientation "live" their religions, while those with an extrinsic orientation "use" their religions. People that are deeply religious in an intrinsic manner have been found to hold stronger prejudicial attitudes and are more likely to discriminate against LGBTs (Fisher, Derison, Polley, Cadman, & Johnston, 1994; Herek, 1987; Kirkpatrick, 1993). Anti-LGBT attitudes, however, are unrelated to extrinsic religious orientation (McFarland, 1989; Taylor, 2000). Because most religions are opposed to homosexuality, those who live their religions literally may be more likely to view it as a sin. Likewise, by viewing one's anti-LGBT position as morally right and an expression of God's will, these individuals may be more open about their negative sentiments toward homosexuality, actively condemn it as a sin, and engage in overt microassaults.

5. *Assumption of Abnormality*—One of the terms used to describe LGBTs is "sick." Despite removal from the DSM as a mental disorder, studies historically have focused on LGBTs from a "sick model" in attributing abnormal behaviors to internal attributes (Martin & Knox, 2000). Many in the general public continue to pathologize LGBTs and same-sex behavior by considering it a form of mental illness. In one survey, it was found that some mental health professionals believe that homosexuality, for example, represents a personality disorder or another form of mental disorder and not just a difference in lifestyle (Garnets, Hancock, Cochran, Goodchilds, & Peplau, 1998). The pathologizing of LGBTs is reflected in how some view and describe these individuals: When a woman describes her bisexuality, some refer to it as a "crisis of identity." When a young adolescent expresses concern about being gay, well-intentioned parents show fear and often reassure them by stating, "You're young yet, you'll grow out of it, and you'll have normal feelings soon. It's just a phase you are going through." Messages of abnormality continue to bombard LGBTs throughout their lives.

6. *Denial of Individual Heterosexism*—Like racism and sexism, many straights tend to deny any biases or prejudices that they may hold toward LGBTs. This may be done consciously/deliberately because of awareness of political correctness or sanctions against overt discrimination or in an unconscious/unintentional manner. We have repeatedly indicated that no one born and raised in this society is immune from inheriting the racial, gender, and sexual-orientation biases of this society. Being raised in a heterosexist society exposes one to beliefs and attitudes that may be detrimental to LGBTs and may manifest themselves in unconscious and unintentional ways. Yet, we are also raised to believe in equality, nondiscrimination, and a belief in our own moral goodness. Thus, while many straights hold conscious egalitarian views toward LGBTs and believe they are not prejudiced, they will deny holding heterosexist views or disclaim ever having discriminated when confronted by their biases: for example, statements like "I'm not homophobic, I have a gay friend," "It doesn't matter to me that you are gay," or becoming defensive when corrected about one's misuse of pronouns with a transgender person (Nadal et al., in press). When LGBTs hear such statements or responses, they sense a defensive denial by straights of their own prejudices. Instead of being reassured that the straight person is free of biases, it has the opposite effect

of making them suspect. Interestingly, such denials can be contradicted via nonverbal behaviors or a disruption of the straight person's speech pattern.

> Many people fumble when they even say the word lesbian or gay man. They just can't even get the words out of their mouths. . . . It would kill my boss to even say the words sexual orientation. It's like there's a horrible taboo about the topic. (Blank & Slipp, 1994, p. 142)

7. *Endorsement of Heteronormative Culture and Behaviors*—There is an old saying: "A fish in a lake does not realize that water is the necessary and normal medium that is required for its survival. It is only when it is caught and brought on land that the importance of water becomes crystal clear." While water nurtures and allows fish to survive and thrive in a lake or ocean, it may prove toxic to mammals that require a different medium for survival. Heteronormative culture and behaviors not only nourish, support, and validate a heterosexual lifestyle, but promote it as normative as well. It represents the "water" for straights, necessary for survival, but invisible to them. To gays and lesbians, however, heteronormative culture and behaviors may prove toxic to their existence and survival; it invalidates their existence and identity, oppresses, and dehumanizes, and it is highly visible to them.

In many respects, heteronormative culture and behaviors produce a climate of normality and abnormality that may lie as the root cause for heterosexism and the manifestation of most sexual-orientation microaggressions. There is an expectation that everyone is heterosexual, and everyone should behave in a manner consistent with the values, norms, and gender roles of our society. The invisibility syndrome is a part of the power of a heteronormative society (Greene, 2000). The standards and norms for behaviors are unintentionally imposed upon LGBTs. Always asking men about girlfriends and women about boyfriends, confining the definition of marriage to "between a man and a woman," having a family member tell an LGBT person "Please don't act so gay in public," and in human sexuality courses covering only topics related to sexual behavior among heterosexuals are all examples (Nadal et al., in press; Sue & Capodilupo, 2008).

Because heteronormative culture and behavior are often outside the level of conscious awareness of straights (invisible), they are likely to freely impose these standards on LGBTs with devastating consequences. It is interesting that LGBTs frequently use the words "invisible" and "closeted" to describe their status or everyday existence (Blank & Slipp, 1994; Greene, 2000). "Coming out" of the closet may have negative repercussions in their relationship with families, in employment, and many other situations (Zastrow, 2004). Thus, some describe how heteronormative pressures force LGBTs to collude in their invisibility:

> "I can sum up the work issue for gays and lesbians in two words: WE HIDE. . . . We are mostly in the closet—especially in the professions. . . . Although more gays and lesbians are coming out, most feel it is necessary to hide their sexual orientation—to be invisible—to avoid the risk of losing their jobs or of being harassed or rejected by fellow workers." (Blank & Slipp, 1994, p. 139)

THE DETRIMENTAL IMPACT OF SEXUAL-ORIENTATION MICROAGGRESSIONS

The quote above gives us a brief glimpse into the concerns and fears of LGBTs who are open about their sexual orientation, those who consider "coming out," and those who continue to remain in the closet. Bombarded daily in a heteronormative society with microaggressive messages that (1) view them as only sexual beings, (2) convey discomfort and fear of their presence and existence, (3) equate their lifestyles with sin and debauchery, and (4) perceive them and their actions as abnormal or pathological, little wonder that LGBTs are fearful that they will become victimized by these beliefs. These stressors directly assail their sexual-orientation identities, make them wary of coming out, and produce psychological distress. In a heterosexist society filled with sexual-orientation microaggressions, the detrimental impact on many LGBTs includes "hiding" or being closeted (Greene, 2000), internalized sexual stigma (Herek et al., 2009), identity conflicts (Barrett & Logan, 2002; Worthington & Reynolds, 2009), and psychological problems (Szymanski, 2009).

Hiding, Invisibility, and Being in the Closet

> "Hiding was exhausting. I always had to watch myself. I always had to make sure that I was not acting too butch, or dressing too much like a dyke. I always felt like I was trying to be someone who I wasn't, always trying to fit in where I knew I didn't fit. I really felt all alone, I thought I was the only person in the world who felt this way." (Mallon, 1998, p. 119)

Hiding, as the quote indicates, depletes one's energies because it requires constant vigilance, produces a constant fear of being found out, isolates the person, and makes for a lonely existence. Many LGBs pretend to be heterosexual in this society because of the many sanctions against homosexuality

(Carrubba, 2005; Fassinger, 1991). They fear losing friends and families, being socially ostracized, and physically assaulted (Morales & Sheafor, 2004). Because race and gender are visible physical traits that clearly convey the sociodemographic group to which a person belongs, hiding, in most cases, is not a possibility for an African American person or for a woman. Thus, hiding, physical invisibility, and being in the closet are not available to them as a means of dealing with discrimination and prejudice. Most LGBTs are in a completely different situation in that they are not visible minorities, and can keep their sexual orientation a secret if they so desire (Douce, 2005). On the surface, this might be viewed as an advantage, but there are many downsides to remaining in the closet as well.

First, hiding and being in the closet can occur through an identity struggle by LGBT youths who are experiencing identity conflicts between what and how they are suppose to act/feel (heterosexual) and their own burgeoning internal same-sex attractions (Barrett & Logan, 2002; Parker & Thompson, 1990). Many youths who experience feelings of differentness deny them because they are surrounded by messages that tell LGBs homosexuality is an abomination. Worse yet, these messages often come from their own parents. LGBT youths are left without anyone to share their concerns, fears, and apprehensions about their sexuality; their parents are heterosexual and assume their sons and daughters are likewise. In order to remain in the closet, they must sidetrack their sexual identity development, deny their own sexual orientation, and engage in self-deception (they are heterosexual). Such psychological maneuvers have major impact on the healthy development of LGBT youths, lead to feelings of isolation, confused identities, and psychological distress.

Second, silence and secrecy in LGBTs can occur in individuals who are consciously aware of their same-sex orientation but who are forced or choose not to disclose their sexual orientation for fear of negative consequences. In many respects, our society colludes with such a decision by enforcement of formal and informal "Don't ask, don't tell" policies (Douce, 2005). These policies represent microaggressions that communicate to LGBTs that there is something wrong with their sexual orientation and that coming out will result in major negative consequences: being discharged from the military, isolated at work, not being promoted, being fired, or disowned by your family (O'Brien, 2005). But what are the internal consequences to LGBTs who remain silent when they hear a homophobic comment, witness discriminatory sexual-orientation behaviors, and are placed in situations that require them to pretend to be heterosexual?

To be placed in situations that assail your sexual-orientation identity and forced to remain silent may do harm to one's sense of integrity. It may make an LGBT person constantly fearful that they will be "outed." It may make an LGBT person feel that they have sold out. It may make an LGBT person shameful and guilt-ridden that they did nothing. It may make the LGBT person feel like a spineless coward. These detrimental consequences can also result in suppressed or repressed rage and anger that finds only oneself as an outlet. Ultimately, sexual-orientation microaggressions assail not only the sexual identity of LGBTs, but also their personal integrity.

Internalized Sexual Stigma

Hiding one's sexual orientation and remaining in the closet can also be motivated by internalized sexual stigma, oftentimes labeled *internalized homophobia, internalized oppression, internalized heterosexism, self-hate, and internalized homonegativity* (Douce, 2005; Herek et al., 2009; Nadal et al., in press; Szymanski, Kashubeck-West, & Meyer, 2008). These terms are overlapping but describe a process and outcome whereby LGBTs experience individual, institutional, and cultural oppression in the form of heterosexist attitudes, beliefs, and feelings that become associated with their self-esteem system (Szymanski & Gupta, 2009). As a member of a devalued minority, the person internalizes these negative beliefs and attitudes about oneself and about members of their own group. Many scholars believe that internalized sexual minority stigma is the most insidious and harmful outcome of heterosexism for LGBTs (Meyer & Dean, 1998; Moradi, van den Berg, & Epting, 2009). It not only aborts the developmental process of LGBTs, but it results in extreme psychological distress for the person and group.

With respect to its internal consequences, internalized heterosexism is considered to have two manifestations: identity separation and identity denigration (Moradi, van den Berg, & Epting, 2009). The former refers to the separation of lesbian or gay identity from the self because of internalized prejudice. Fragmentation or compartmentalization of the self results in feelings of isolation, alienation, and a possible sense of existential unreality about one's identity. According to this view, the conflict is between a need to perceive oneself as a good, moral, and worthwhile person, contrasted against the belief that being gay or lesbian is immoral, indecent, and repugnant. Any situation that seems to merge these two disparate views of the self produces *feelings of threat*. Internal separation and distancing become the psychological maneuvers that allow the lesbian and gay person to maintain their sense of "goodness," although this is often experienced as inauthentic and false.

The second form is most closely associated with self-hate or self-loathing. While *threat* is related to separation, *guilt* is related to self-hate or self-denigration (Moradi et al., 2009). This second form means that a gay man at many levels is aware of the connection between the gay self as a part of one's being. Thus guilt represents recognition of self-denigration and the existence of undesirable attributes in the self. Both *threat and guilt* are constant and continuing experiences of internalized prejudice. It contributes to a constant state of inner emotional turmoil that ultimately takes it toll on subjective feelings of well-being.

Internalized heterosexism also affects how sexual minorities may believe, feel, and respond toward members of their own group. Internalized sexual stigma can become part of the person's value system through both conscious and unconscious acceptance and adoption of societal negative attitudes toward sexual minorities. In the former case, self-hate is directed internally, but its external manifestation results in sexual prejudice toward LGBTs. These individuals may actively campaign against laws, policies, and practices intended to provide equal protection for LGBTs, publicly condemn "homosexuality," and are more likely to be found among men, those who are strongly religious, and political conservatives (Herek et al., 2009).

Former Idaho U.S. Senator Larry Craig served 18 years in the Senate before being forced to resign in 2008. He was a known champion of anti-gay legislation, and actively campaigned and voted against gay rights. On August 27, 2007, a plainclothes police officer arrested Craig for lewd conduct and attempting to solicit gay sex in a public restroom. The incident made national headlines and detailed nonverbal signals used by gays in adjacent public restroom stalls to solicit sex. It also brought forth issues of hypocrisy, "outing," and the motivations or psychological dynamics of sexual prejudice toward one's own group. While Craig continues to maintain his innocence and claims to be heterosexual, considerable evidence suggests that he is gay.

Identity Development and Disruption

Human development from birth to death is filled with many challenges and does not occur in a smooth transition with respect to sexual-orientation identity formation. In addition to experiencing the normal developmental milestones of heterosexuals, LGBTs must cope with a heteronormative and heterosexist society that causes identity disruptions and conflicts: accepting or rejecting same-sex feelings, coming out or remaining hidden, dealing with societal denunciation and oppression, and developing and integrating a positive LGBT identity (Barrett & Logan, 2002; Hunter & Mallon, 2000). One particularly crucial period is that of adolescence, a period of exploration and experimentation regarding gender role and sexual identities. While most LGBTs are aware before puberty or adolescence that they experience feelings of differentness and same-sex feelings, they often remain unacknowledged (Hunter & Mallon, 2000). It is at the stage of adolescence, however, that physical growth and change, and emotional, cognitive, and sexual maturity most strongly pose a challenge to self-identity as a heterosexual or LGBT.

A major life stressor that confronts LGBT youths is the assumption that everyone is heterosexual and that same-sex feelings for adolescents are just "a passing phase." This microaggression is powerful because it prevents and/or negates the burgeoning development of a gay identity. It also has psychological consequences. The following was written by a gay student in his self-reflection journal about his childhood.

Imagine what it is like learning about sex, love, and sexuality in a heterosexual world from heterosexual friends and from heterosexual parents. Imagine what it is like when you express fears that you may be homosexual and your parents hide their anxieties by reassuring you it will "go away, that it's just a phase." Imagine the "terrible" secret you're forced to live with, how it takes over your life every moment of the day, makes it impossible to concentrate on homework, praying every day to god to make you straight. Imagine what it's like to pretend to be someone you're not, to live a lie, to deceive your parents and yourself. No, I don't think you can imagine it. You try, and I appreciate it, but only a gay person would know.

"Coming out" is a major choice point for LGBTs and can occur at any point in the lifespan. There are varying degrees of coming out which run from completely out of the closet to being out in safe situations only (gay friends and allies, but not casual acquaintances). To come out, however, is to acknowledge to oneself and others that one is gay or lesbian. Perhaps one of the most cited gay/lesbian identity development models is one posed by Cass (1979) in which six stages are posed. It describes the disruptive influences of heterosexism on identity development of gays and lesbians, and the eventual integration into a positive identity. Barrett and Logan (2002) capture the entire process in the following progression of quotes: (Awareness) "Am I gay?" to (Dissonance) "Oh no, I may be gay," to (Acceptance) "I'm probably gay," to (Identity Integration) "I'm gay and I'm okay."

1. *Identity Confusion*—This stage is characterized by being socialized and playing a heterosexual role, but experiencing same-sex feelings and a sense of "differentness." "Who am I?" expresses the confusion. Dissonance and inner turmoil caused by these urges may lead to feelings of shame, despair, and even suicidal ideation.

2. *Identity Comparison*—The person now begins to compare his or her own heterosexual messages/portrayals/self-deceptions to increasing realization of his or her gay/lesbian proclivities. For the first time the person increasingly entertains the notion that they may be gay. Four potential responses have been identified: (1) compartmentalizing one's life by portraying a heterosexual public persona from the private gay/lesbian life; (2) accept one's homo-sexual behavior but reject the notion of adopting a public homosexual identity; (3) accept self as gay/lesbian but refuse to engage in same-sex behaviors; and (4) reject both lifestyles and self-identities by seeking to change oneself (con-version therapy).

3. *Identity Tolerance*—The person may begin to accept their gay/lesbian iden-tity and progressively move away from the heterosexual world. Contact with LGBTs increases and the person may enter the gay community. Experiences with these initial contacts, however, have a major psychological effect. If the contacts are negative or undesirable, they may choose to once again inhibit same-sex feelings and behaviors. However, if the experiences are positive, it opens the door to a full adoption of gay/lesbian identity.

4. *Identity Acceptance*—At this stage, the person begins to have greater contact with the gay community, develops friendships with LGBTs, and tolerance moves to acceptance. The person selectively begins to disclose his or her sexual-orientation identity.

5. *Identity Pride*—The person is likely to experience increasingly positive feel-ings with a strong sense of identification with the gay community and to attain a sense of heightened sociopolitical awareness (internalized heterosexism is the result of oppression and prejudice). They may divide the world into two camps: heterosexuals who are blamed for their intolerance and discrimination and gays/lesbians who are credible, significant, and a positive force in society. They may become overtly political in their struggles against societal heterosexism.

6. *Identity Synthesis*—The "us" versus "them" mentality begins to disap-pear with the realization that many heterosexuals are understanding, credible,

trustworthy, and valuable allies in the struggle for equality. LGBTs begin to experience an increased sense of comfort with their sexual-orientation identity, and begin the process of synthesis and integration of individual identity, group identity, and universal identity.

It is important to note that sexual-orientation identity development models describe a process of movement from dealing with heterosexism to liberation. If we accept the Cass (1979) model as a description of desirable movement, it is important to realize that heterosexism is such a powerful force in our society that many LGBTs never make it out of the first stage, and that others may be stuck in earlier stages throughout their lives. The blame for the disruption or inability to develop a positive sexual-orientation identity, however, does not reside in being a gay or lesbian person, but rather can be attributed to a hostile and invalidating heterosexist culture.

Psychological Distress and Mental Disorders

Same-sex relationships are not signs of mental disorders (Sue & Sue, 2008). Studies show that "homosexuality" is unrelated to psychological disturbance or maladjustment, and that there are few adjustment differences between a gay/lesbian population and heterosexuals (Berube, 1990; Gonsiorek, 1982). However, considerable evidence exists that exposure to heterosexual prejudice and discrimination is related to elevated rates of Major Depression, Generalized Anxiety Disorder, and substance abuse among gays/lesbians (Szymanski, Kashubeck-West, & Meyer, 2008; Rienzo, Button, Sheu, & Li, 2006). Further, LGBTs are at higher risk for substance and alcohol related problems (Cochran, Keenan, Schober, & Mays, 2000; Kennedy, 2005), and internalized homophobia is found to be directly related to depressive symptoms (Frost & Meyer, 2009). LGBT youths report more substance use, high-risk sexual behaviors, suicidal thoughts or attempts, and personal safety issues (Blake, Ledsky, Lehman, & Goodenow, 2001; Rienzo et al., 2006). They are more likely to report social, emotional, and cognitive isolation, feelings of extreme sadness and loneliness, lack of authenticity, impaired social relationships, and constant feelings of threat and vigilance (Hunter & Mallon, 2000; Szymanski et al., 2008).

Understanding of how heterosexism creates a hostile and intimidating environment for LGBTs can be found in the following facts: compared with heterosexuals, LGBTs are more like to have been abused as children and adults, bullied in schools, and harassed in a multitude of environments

(Balsam, Rothblum, & Beauchaine, 2005), face the frustration of not being able to be marry in most states, are restricted from adopting children, face discrimination in housing and employment, and are often rejected by family and friends (Morales & Sheafor, 2004). Clearly, the negativity toward LGBTs diminishes self-esteem, depletes psychic energies, and affects a sense of well-being.

The Way Forward

Overcoming Heterosexism

Heterosexism is a rampant force in our society that has a detrimental impact upon LGBTs. Sexual-orientation microaggressions take many forms, but thematically contain overt and covert messages that include seeing LGBTs in a narrow sexual way, exposing them to homophobia, heterosexist language, religious concepts of sinfulness, to beliefs in their abnormality, and to invalidations of their attitudes, beliefs, and behaviors, which are central to healthy sexual identities. Bombarded from the moment of birth with heterosexist microaggressions, LGBTs find their identity development disrupted, which can result in internalized sexual stigma, self-hate, silence, and hiding (being in the closet), psychological distress, and decreased well-being. Research would be beneficial in understanding the unique experiences of oppression for LGBTs.

1. While LGBTs share many similar experiences with other marginalized groups (persons of color and women), their physical invisibility exposes them to a unique psychological dynamic not usually visited upon people of color or women (being in the closet vs. coming out). Being an invisible minority in the true physical sense (not just psychological) may possess different qualitative experiences of oppression. An African American who walks through a predominantly White neighborhood stands out like a sore thumb and the person is likely to be reported by residents or stopped by law enforcement officers. While an LGBT White person may go unnoticed while walking through a White neighborhood and thus not considered suspicious or undesirable, they may be prone to experiencing a different form of quandary. For example, when in the presence of classmates, coworkers, or neighbors, they may be subjected to overt heterosexist comments or jokes because of their physical invisibility and assumptions by others that

(Continued)

they are heterosexual. What impact does physical invisibility have on their experiences of sexual-orientation microaggressions?

2. Further, it is possible that of the three devalued groups discussed in this text, LGBTs may face more overt forms of prejudice and discrimination than women or people of color. No empirical support exists for this statement, but it is based upon individual observations of the explicitness, and the apparent comfort and freedom many of my straight brothers and sisters seem to have in making heterosexist comments and taking prejudicial actions against LGBTs in our society. If this is the case, microassaults (explicit, direct, and intentional) might be a more frequent experience than unintentional forms (microinsults and microinvalidations) for LGBTs.

3. The question is what can we personally do to deal with our own heterosexism, because the cultural changes that are called for are massive. However, there are things that can be done if we personally become committed to individual change.

- Keep yourself free of heterosexual assumptions by becoming aware of the ethnocentric heterosexist language and vocabulary in everyday use. Monitor your language and change it to be inclusive of LGBTs; this can go a long way to altering your own worldview. For example, language and words shape perceptions. Instead of using the phrase "sexual preference," say "sexual orientation." Instead of husband and wife, use the term *partners*. Become aware of other people's use of heterosexist language (e.g., "gay" used in a demeaning way). Being constantly vigilant of your own words and phrases and those of others is a powerful way to keep sexual identities in your awareness.
- Educate yourself. Develop partnerships and collaborative relationships and efforts with local and national LGBT organizations. Read their literature and make a strong effort to understand their hopes, fears, and concerns. Attend LGBT events, enroll in diversity workshops, and read literature for and by LGBTs.
- Become a valuable and powerful ally of the LGBT community. Become active in schools, employment committees, religious organizations, and neighborhood groups to educate others. Work against "don't ask, don't tell" policies, condemn "gay bashing," and support job protection for LGBTs, and antidiscrimination in housing, marriage, and so forth. Work on behalf of passing legislation that benefits LGBTs, and work against antigay legislations or efforts that would prove detrimental to

(Continued)

inclusion and equity. Let your pro-LGBT voice be heard during debates or important dialogues.

- Help educate others that homosexuality is not a mental disorder. When references or allusions are made to sexual orientation as pathological, challenge those innuendos or assumptions.

Microaggressions in Employment, Education, and Mental Health Practice

CHAPTER TEN

Microaggressive Impact in the Workplace and Employment

Thus far, our discussion of racial, gender, and sexual-orientation microaggressions has been to describe their etiology, manifestation, characteristics, and effects upon marginalized groups in America. We have repeatedly stressed that the power of microaggressions often lies in their invisibility to perpetrators and victims. Throughout the text we have given numerous examples of how microaggressions occur in interpersonal encounters, in the environment, under a variety of circumstances, and in many different situations. Microaggressions not only demean and harm targeted individuals and groups, but they also affect the quality of life of people of color, women, and LGBTs. In this chapter, we specifically trace the manifestations and potential harms that microaggressions cause in employment and the workplace.

MICROAGGRESSIONS IN THE WORKPLACE/EMPLOYMENT

It's not really the quid-pro-quo variety—"put-out-or-get-out" harassment—that's most prevalent.

It's sexual harassment in terms of creating a hostile and demeaning environment. I resent having my anatomy discussed in front of clients.

I'm furious at the men who toss condoms to each other in front of me and who have computer graphics of naked women.

When men make off-color remarks or tell bawdy jokes at meetings, I think it's meant to put me in my place. The comments about "how great your blouse shows your figure off" are meant to remind me and others of our sexual difference, which has always meant male dominance and female subservience.

It's not about flirtatiousness or even about sex. It's about humiliation of women and intimidation and resentment because we are moving into a formerly male world. The purpose is to undercut our professionalism and credibility. (Blank & Slipp, 1994, pp. 155–156)

These voices from five different women attest to the demeaning, insulting, and humiliating sexist work environment that they must endure in their daily transactions in many places of employment. Gender microaggressions (sexual objectification, sexist jokes, and assumptions of inferiority) in the above examples run the gamut from overt to subtle and intentional to unintentional, but they all have a negative impact on these female employees. As we have seen, psychological health, self-esteem, subjective well-being, and job performance suffer from the negative overt and covert messages directed toward women.

Workplace microaggressions are also experienced by people of color and LGBTs in many different forms. African American employees experience being tracked and "ghettoized" by being considered (assumption of inferior intelligence/skills) for only certain jobs and tasks in the workplace: support services, personnel, human resources, community relations, and "black products" departments instead of top decision-making positions. LGBTs tell stories of how "coming out" negatively impacted their hiring and promotional opportunities at work and subjected them to ridicule and violence (assumption of abnormality and sinfulness). There is little wonder that women, people of color, and LGBTs continue to be among the most underpaid, underemployed, and, for some, the most unemployed in the workforce. Microaggressions seem to play a pronounced role in creating disparities in employment, specifically in the recruitment, retention, and promotion of these three groups (Hinton, 2004; Rubin, 2008; Sue, Lin, & Rivera, 2009). With the diversification of the workforce, it seems imperative that we understand the relationship between microaggressions and their impact on diverse work groups in the workplace.

Diversification of the Workforce

The workforce of the United States is undergoing one of the most dramatic, sweeping changes of all time. Two of these can literally be described as the feminization of the workforce (Taylor & Kennedy, 2003) and the changing complexion of the workforce (Sue, Parham, & Santiago, 1998). These changes are especially significant for not only the world of work, but our society as well (Stevens, Plaut, & Sanches-Burks, 2008).

Feminization of the Workforce

Women now comprise 46.5% of the total U.S. labor force and they will reach 47% by the year 2016 (U.S. Department of Labor, 2009). The net increase in the labor force for women has progressively shown an upward trend: 38% in 1970; 42% in 1980; 45% in 1990; and over the next 10-year period from 2006 to 2016 will account for 49% of the growth (U.S. Department of Labor, 1992, 2009). The trend affects both single women and married women. Married women in 1950 accounted for less that 25% of the labor force; now, however, 58% of married women work. More complicated and stressful for women employees, however, is that 60% have preschoolers and 75% have school-age children. Two major issues arise with respect to women in the workforce.

First, women continue to occupy the lower rungs of the occupational ladder, to encounter the glass ceiling when promotions are considered, and to be paid much less than their male counterparts (U.S. Department of Labor, 2009). Some of the discrepancy may be due to how women are perceived through traditional gender-role microaggressions. Interestingly, the disparity in income and employment in lower paying and/or status occupations can be seen in the 10 most prevalent occupations for employed women in 2008:

- Secretaries and administrative assistants
- Registered nurses
- Elementary and middle school teachers
- Cashiers
- Retail salespersons
- Nursing, psychiatric, and home health aides
- First-line supervisors/managers of retail sales workers
- Waitresses
- Receptionists and information clerks
- Bookkeeping, accounting, and auditing clerks

Second, women continue to carry the major domestic and childcare responsibilities of the home and family life. For example, studies indicate that even when both partners have equivalent work demands, women continue to be more responsible for making childcare arrangements and for social interpersonal activities inside and outside of the home than their married or partnered men (Morales & Sheafor, 2004). Thus, it is not difficult to conclude that women are subjected to a greater number of stressors inside and outside of work than their male counterparts.

Changing Complexion of the Workforce

It is estimated that some time between the years 2030 and 2050, people of color will become a numerical majority in the United States (Sue & Sue, 2008). If we view the 10-year period from 1990 to 2000, figures indicate that the population increased 13% to over 281 million (U.S. Bureau of the Census, 2001). Interestingly, however, most of the population increase was in growth of visible racial/ethnic minority groups: 50% for Asian American/Pacific Islander, 58% for Latino/Hispanic, 16% for African American, and 15.5% for American Indian/Alaskan Native. This is in marked contrast to only 7.3% for Whites. Such demographic changes are due primarily to the recent immigration rates of documented immigrants, undocumented immigrants, and refugees, which are characterized as the largest in U.S. history. Further, the birthrates of people of color far surpass those of Whites as mothers of racial/ethnic minority groups have many more children per mother.

People of color, however, continue to be the most underemployed and unemployed when compared to their White counterparts (U.S. Department of Labor, 2005). The representation of people of color in higher levels of employment is much lower (except Asians) than Whites in management and professionally related occupations: 35.5% of Whites, 26% for African Americans, and 17% for Latinos. Although Asian Americans may be well represented in the higher echelons of management, evidence suggests that they must possess higher levels of education and training to attain a comparable position to their White colleagues (S. Sue, Sue, Zane, & Wong, 1985). In other words, the "super minority" syndrome must be achieved to obtain an equal occupational level as White employees. Like their female counterparts, many more employees of color are also more likely to be employed in service occupations: 23.9% African Americans, 23.8% Latinos, and 15.2% Whites.

Workplace Implications

Overall, these demographic shifts in society are reflected in the workforce where close to 75% of those now entering employment are racial/ethnic minorities and women (Sue & Sue, 2008). There are major economic implications of these changes. First, the majority of those that will be contributing to social security and pension plans will be women and employees of color. As the baby boomers retire (primarily White retirees), they will increasingly depend on their cow-orkers of color and women for economic stability in the retirement years. Yet if women and people of color continue to encounter the glass ceiling, be underpaid, underemployed, and unemployed, it bodes poorly for their future security.

Business and industry, educational institutions, and municipalities now recognize that their workforces must be drawn increasingly from a diverse labor pool and that sole dependence on White male workers is no longer a reality (Sue, 1991, 1994). The economic viability of businesses will depend on their ability to manage a diverse workforce effectively, allow for equal access and opportunity, and make appropriate multicultural organizational change (Stevens, Plaut, & Sanchez-Burks, 2008). In recognition of the changing com-position of the nation, there has been a movement by business and industry toward diversity training, the infusion of multicultural concepts into school curriculum, and many attempts to fight bigotry, bias, and discrimination in our social, economic, and political systems (Sue, Parham, et al., 1998).

Yet, marginalized groups continue to describe their work climates as hostile, invalidating, and insulting because of the many microaggressions that assail their race, gender, or sexual-orientation identities, deplete their psy-chic energies, restrict their work options, lower their work productivity, generate suppressed rage and anger, stereotype them as less worthy workers, and detrimentally impact their recruitment/hiring, retention, and promotion in organizations (Blank & Slipp, 1994; Deitch et al., 2003; Dovidio, Gaertner, Kawakami, & Hodson, 2002; Gore, 2000; Hinton, 2004; Purdie-Vaughns, Davis, Steele, & Ditlmann, 2008; Rowe, 1990; Sue, Lin, & Rivera, 2009).

Racial, gender, and sexual microaggressions are especially problematic because of their invisibility, difficulty in being proven (Deitch et al., 2003; Rowe, 1990), and because they are often minimized as trivial and innocuous (Sue, Capodilupo, et al., 2007). Discussions of racism and sexism in the work-place generally involve acts of discrimination that are considered unlawful or analyzed from a legal perspective (Coleman, 2004). Many places of employment that have instituted diversity training and/or passed policies that condemn overt discrimination and harassment in the workplace have concentrated efforts upon the obvious and overt bias-based acts of coworkers (sexist, racist, or homophobic jokes, epithets, inappropriate behaviors, unwanted sexual contact, and offensive displays—naked pictures of women, Confederate flags, nooses, etc.).

More difficult to control, however, are complaints by employees of color that they are "watched over" more carefully than their White coworkers (assumption of intellectual inferiority and/or criminality related to mistrust), that comments by women in team meetings are ignored (invisibility and assumption of inferiority), and that gay employees are often told by superiors that they should wear looser clothes and/or are told "We don't like they way you move" (oversexualization and endorsement of heteronormative culture/ behaviors). The messages behind these microaggressions are that people of color cannot be trusted or are less capable, and therefore require close monitoring, that contributions of women are less worthy than those of men, and that gays should conform to heterosexual roles. The unending parade of microaggressions creates a hostile and uninviting work environment for marginalized groups in our society. Rather than being able to focus on their work and productivity, they are left with having to attend to their own strong feelings of anger, rage, and frustration.

Psychological Implications of Workplace Microaggressions and Harassment

Being exposed to environments that contain racial, gender, and sexual-orientation microaggressions, as indicated earlier, has major psychological consequences. In her work with employees who experience chronic micro-assaults, microinsults, and microinvalidations, Root (2003) has identified ten clusters of the most common symptoms likely to emerge in marginalized employees. These clusters indicate that employees of color, women, and LGBTs are struggling against wounds to core aspects of their spirit, reputation, or personal integrity.

1. *Anxiety*—The employee experiences a dread of going to work, loses a sense of identity with his/her work or career, may experience physical problems (high blood pressure, migraine headaches), exacerbation of an existing medical condition, or periods of anxiety and even panic attacks.

2. *Paranoia*—The self-consciousness created by second-guessing of others, worry about the racial and gender attributions of others, fear of damage

to one's reputation from false beliefs and misinformation, and the close monitoring of their work make them guarded, suspicious, and mistrustful of the intents of others.

3. *Depression*—Depression is common in social or work withdrawal, isolation from coworkers, feelings of fatigue and exhaustion from even minor work tasks, and difficulty in getting out of bed to go to work. Work drains the emotional, psychological, and physical energies of the person.

4. *Sleep Difficulties*—While correlated with depression, this cluster of symptoms is generally likely to occur first. The person has difficulty falling asleep or staying asleep. Recurrent intrusive thoughts persist about work or anticipated future workdays, resulting in dissatisfaction with life and irritability.

5. *Lack of Confidence*—The worker begins to question their abilities, judgment, and decision making. Constantly being second-guessed, close and constant monitoring by superiors, and being treated as an inferior takes its toll on the worker. The person begins to doubt his or her own worth in the company.

6. *Worthlessness*—This feeling is related to a lack of confidence as the person now questions their value to coworkers, the company, and to themselves. The ultimate manifestation is a belief that one has nothing to offer and is truly replaceable.

7. *Intrusive Cognitions*—These are the constant and continuing thoughts that are replayed over and over in the mind of the person. They involve incidents at work that assail their integrity, and remind them of their ineptness and low value in the company. As mentioned earlier it may disrupt sleeping patterns and/or result in dreams or nightmares related to work.

8. *Helplessness*—This is most related to two facets of work. The person feels powerless to stop the microaggressions experienced in the workplace. Trying to confront the person may result in punitive consequences, especially from superiors. Quitting one's job may not be an option for economic reasons, thus causing the feeling of being trapped. Second, the constant mischaracterizations of one's abilities and/or person are filled with stereotypes.

9. *Loss of Drive*—The person's energy, spiritual and psychological, is sapped through chronic workplace microaggressions. The high ambition that characterized the person who has gone this far in the company is driven from the spirit and personal identity.

10. *False Positives*—Because of the constant and continuing feelings of harassment and put downs, the person begins to overgeneralize to coworkers or others all the negative experiences that they have had with others. Such an orientation has the unintended consequences of (1) further isolating oneself from others, (2) increasing mistrust—"everyone is out to get me," and (3) externalizing blame in a way that avoids personal responsibility for one's own actions.

Organizational Color-Blind Philosophy as a Microaggression

In their attempts to recognize, manage, cultivate, and utilize diversity as a positive rather than negative force, many organizations over the past several decades have attempted to (1) reduce bias and discrimination in the workplace, (2) allow for equal access and opportunities in hiring, retention, and promotion of all groups, and (3) develop a philosophy or vision statement that "treats everyone the same" (Sue & Sue, 1994; Stevens, Plaut, & Sanches-Burks, 2008; Purdie-Vaughns et al., 2008). It is suggested that one of the most dominant philosophical approaches to diversity in the workplace is the "color-blind approach" that attempts to emphasize commonalities rather than racial or gender differences (Plaut & Markus, 2007; Thomas & Plaut, 2008). Such a philosophy is grounded in the belief that "treating everyone the same regardless of race, gender, or sexual orientation" is consistent with the ideals of democracy (equality and meritocracy). Race, for example, is minimized or even seen as unrelated to individual accomplishments or merit, which should be the criteria used for hiring, retention, and promotion of *all* employees. Accompanying the color- and gender-blind approaches is an emphasis on similarities, shared goals, and an overall group identity.

Inherent in this philosophy, however, are less apparent assumptions or hidden messages that may serve as microaggressions to marginalized groups: (1) "differences are divisive so let's avoid them and emphasize our similarities," (2) women, employees of color, and LGBTs should assimilate and acculturate to the organizational culture, (3) leave your "cultural baggage" and racial, gender, and sexual-orientation identities at home, and (4) as an organization, we are not biased and do not discriminate because we treat everyone the same (Sue, 2008). Earlier, we indicated that research reveals that "color-blindness" and "denial of racism" for racial/ethnic minorities represent major racial microaggressions (Apfelbaum, Sommers, & Norton, 2008; Sue, 2005; Sue, Capodilupo, et al., 2007). From the perspective of employees of color, the color-blind approach, rather than including them, has the opposite effect of exclusion, makes them more suspicious and mistrustful of the organization and White coworkers, and may reveal hidden racial biases that are denied or covered up (Stevens et al., 2008).

In a revealing study of the effects of the color-blind philosophy on African American employees (Purdie-Vaughns et al., 2008), investigators addressed the question of how external cues in the environment (number of other minorities in the workplace and the organization's philosophy) may signal either safety or threat to marginalized groups. If individuals feel or believe their group identities are devalued in an organization, they may choose not to apply for the position, leave prematurely, or their job performance may suffer (Cadinu, Maass, Rosabianca, & Kiesner, 2005; Dovidio, 2001; Salvatore & Shelton, 2007; Sue, 1991). The study addressed only "institutional cues" rather than interpersonal ones. Color-blindness as an institutional cue or philosophy was manipulated in a fake company brochure that exposed African American professional prospective applicants to one of two conditions.

Color-Blind: While other consulting firms mistakenly focus on their staff's diversity, we train our diverse workforce to embrace their similarities. We feel that focusing on similarities creates a more unified, exciting, and collaborative work environment. Such an inclusive and accepting environment helps not only us but also our clients. And at CCG, if you're a team player, you'll have unlimited access to success. Your race, ethnicity, gender, and religion are immaterial as soon as you walk through our doors.

Value-Diversity: While other consulting firms mistakenly try to shape their staff into a single mold, we believe that embracing our diversity enriches our culture. Diversity fosters a more unified, exciting, and collaborative work environment. Such an inclusive and accepting environment helps not only us but also our clients. And at CCG, all individuals have unlimited access to success. As soon as you walk through our doors, you'll appreciate the strength that we derive from our diversity. (Purdie-Vaughns et al., 2008, pp. 618–619)

Contrary to the assumption of a color-blind approach that attempts to communicate inclusiveness, teamwork, trust, and fairness, emphasizing universal identities and minimizing differences, the philosophy had directly the opposite effect. African Americans expressed distrust of such an organization, indicated they would be uncomfortable working in such a company, felt a racial identity threat, and anticipated being treated more frequently in a biased manner. This study reveals that even in the absence of interpersonal microaggressions, the overall climate or philosophy of a company can serve as a powerful microaggresson. If we add an organization's overarching philosophy as a potent microaggression to the daily onslaught of interpersonal microaggressions for marginalized employees, the impact can be very detrimental. This can be seen at three levels of employment: recruitment, retention, and promotion (Sue & Sue, 1991, 1994). These three levels symbolically represent the "minority pipeline," where blockages in the form of overt or covert discrimination to employment and promotion make themselves felt.

Recruitment

While many companies are making a conscientious effort to recruit more employees of color, women, and LGBTs, they are often very unsuccessful, especially at high-status positions and occupations. "We can't find enough qualified Black candidates." "I would gladly hire a qualified woman engineer, if I could find one." "I have nothing against gays, but our employees just aren't ready for one."

These statements all represent various forms of microaggressions (denial of racism/sexism/heterosexism, assumptions of inferiority, homophobia, etc.) that may serve the same purpose: they help mask unconscious, biased decisions that justify not offering a job position to a minority applicant. In general, the assumption made by some White recruiters and interviewers is that minority candidates are less qualified than White ones or that the person is just not right for the position because he or she will not "fit in." Unconscious beliefs that Blacks are lacking in intelligence, women are poor in math/sciences, or that an "out of the closet" LGBT will cause discomfort and upheaval at the worksite enters into the evaluation of candidates.

These statements also relate to another important microaggression encountered by people of color, women, and LGBTs. The standards used to hire applicants are generally based upon White, male, and heterosexual criteria that determine "qualified." Good oral communication skills, for example, may equate to speaking without an accent. A Latino applicant who speaks with an accent, therefore, might be eliminated from consideration because of a mistaken belief that an accent equates to poor communication skills. Further, whether one speaks with an accent may be uncorrelated to successful job performance.

Environmental microaggressions can also serve to discourage prospective job applicants. As we have mentioned, when women candidates are being recruited and the company's reception area prominently displays framed pictures of an all-white male board of directors, and an all-male management team, the overall atmosphere is one of threat and devaluation to one's social group identity (environmental microaggression) (Purdie-Vaughns et al., 2008). When the company has low minority representation in the workforce, this constitutes a powerful statement that advancement opportunities are slim, and women are likely to see the company as unwelcoming.

Retention

Even when underrepresented groups make it into the workplace, companies may continue to have difficulty retaining them. Low retention rates may be the result when minority groups are constantly bombarded by organizational policies, practices, programs, and structures that make them feel unfairly treated (Sue, Lin, & Rivera, 2009). This is often compounded by interpersonal microaggressions, or what is referred to as "microinequities" or "the vast power of the small slight" (Hinton, 2004). While large, overt racial or gender gaffes and overt obvious acts of discrimination or prejudice may be addressed in the workplace by a quick remedy such as sensitivity training, how does one deal with microaggressions that involve speaking to a Black employee in a condescending tone of voice (second-class citizenship), not responding to a female coworker's ideas (invisibility), and indicating discomfort in the presence of an LGBT employee (homophobia)? Such microaggressions are equally disruptive and harmful, but more difficult to address. They are manifested in being ignored or not invited to lunches by coworkers, receiving little feedback or mentoring, closer supervision, the boss forgetting or mispronouncing your name, being assigned to lesser job tasks, and a continuing onslaught of other verbal microaggressions.

Within the workplace, microaggressions can occur in peer-to-peer or superior-to-subordinate relationships (Sue, Lin, & Rivera, 2009). These interactions, along with organizational policies and practices, constitute the organizational culture and climate.

Peer-to-Peer

Peer-to-peer microaggressions occur between individuals who occupy an equal status relationship in the organizational chart, but do not necessarily experience an equal amount of power and influence. The ability to define reality and to influence people in an organization generally resides with

White, heterosexual, male employees, even when they hold positions that are similar to those of employees of color, women, or LGBTs. Because the interactions are likely to be frequent and sometimes sustained, microaggressions may be difficult to avoid because of the amount of interaction required with coworkers. The bullying experienced by employees of color has been described as "subtle and often unconscious manifestations of racism in the form of incivility, neglect, humor, ostracism, inequitable treatment" that causes extreme distress and has a negative impact on work productivity (Fox & Stallworth, 2004). Not only do these microaggressions cause emotional turmoil, but they result in decreased job performance leading to detrimental conclusions by coworkers that their minority counterparts are less capable and competent.

Superior-to-Subordinate

Superior-to-subordinate relationships are especially difficult for employees of color, women, and LGBTs because the power discrepancy is great and obvious. Some support is found, for example, that relationships between minority employees and nonminority supervisors have a greater impact on stress levels than relationships between minority employees and their peers (Fox & Stallworth, 2004). When microaggressions are delivered by supervisors or superiors, minority employees describe lower life and job satisfaction, organizational commitment, morale, motivation, self-esteem, and work and family life satisfaction. The behaviors they describe involve isolation, withdrawing from work, lower work productivity, and working minimal hours despite tasks being incomplete. In other words, microaggressions from superiors have massive effects on the psyche and work productivity of the minority employee. Not only does the employee suffer, but the company is not utilizing the talents and potential contributions of the targeted person. Compounding the distress felt by employees of color, women, and LGBTs is the conflict described earlier of the catch-22 in responding: "Should I say something about the insult and slight that just occurred, or should I just suck it up? If I choose to confront my boss, what will the consequences be? Will I get a bad evaluation? Will I lose that promotion? Will I be fired?" Such microaggressive conflicts are emotionally painful and can lead to distancing, lesser commitment to the company, or even resignation.

Promotion

Racial, gender, and sexual-orientation microaggressions contribute to the perception held by many marginalized groups that promotion and advancement in organizations is limited (Sue, 1991). Microaggressions that involve ignoring or avoidance of culturally diverse groups in the workplace can place them at a disadvantage in networking, mentoring, and access to a flow of information important for advancing one's career. In one study conducted in six New England states, African American physicians were asked about their experiences of racial bias in their places of employment (Nunez-Smith et al., 2007). The microaggressions they noted included being infrequently invited to information networking events, social gatherings, and other informal group activities: "We won't get invited to the picnic or to the dinner parties . . . and that is where those jobs come up. . . . We're not in the corridors of power" (p. 47).

Oftentimes, the promotion or presence of minorities or women has the effect of lessening the importance of a position in the eyes of White male workers. Part of this problem is rooted in a belief that people or color and women are less capable and their consideration for, or presence in, a supervisory position means that it is less demanding and requires less skill. Support for this belief is also reflected in female-dominated professions (nursing and teaching), where occupational status is low, or by the fact that in occupations where women are increasing their presence significantly (counselors, psychologists, etc.), status and salaries may begin to decline. Statements such as "You're not ready yet" keep women in staff or service ghettos (the back room).

> You can be a star at the mid-management level, but that's it. . . . Men promote other men to the top corporate levels, even if they're mediocre. To have a woman at the top is to lessen the position in many men's eyes. I guess that's why only 3 percent of senior managers in Fortune 500 corporations are women. (Blank & Slipp, 1994, p. 159)

Perceptions of the capabilities and skills of underrepresented groups can often interact with performance appraisal systems that provide criteria or job descriptions for promotion. Some years back, a Fortune 500 company asked an external consultant to work with Asian American employees in their workforce. In a survey conducted by the company, large numbers of Asian American workers expressed dissatisfaction with their roles in the organization, believed that they were not promoted when qualified, and expressed a desire to leave the company in the near future (Sue, 2008). Although they constituted over 20% of the technical workforce, they were poorly represented in upper management positions. The company acknowledged this problem and was making a well-intentioned conscientious effort to rectify the situation. They asked the male consultant if he would be willing to conduct assertiveness and leadership training for the Asian American employees.

The consultant, himself an Asian American, was bothered by the company's definition of the problem and the possible hidden assumptions: The primary cause for underrepresentation in the higher echelons of the company was (1) Asian Americans make poor leaders and managers, and (2) are unassertive, passive, noncompetitive, and lack leadership skills. The employees would profit from training to achieve company-defined leadership criteria. While this was a possible explanation, the consultant was struck by how closely these descriptions followed societal stereotypes of Asians and Asian Americans: they are passive, inhibited, make poor leaders and managers, and are poor in relationships, but make good scientists and technicians (S. Sue, Sue, Zane, & Wong, 1985).

In working with top management, all those present repeatedly stressed how much they valued the contributions of Asian American employees, and that the company could not function effectively without their presence in the organization. They denied that there was bias in their selection of White coworkers over Asians who had the same seniority, but that "perhaps Asian Americans just don't make good leaders or top level business associates." To this the consultant posed an interesting question to the leadership team: If Asians and Asian Americans don't make good business leaders, how is it that businesses in Japan, Hong Kong, Taiwan, and China are so successful in competing on the worldwide stage?

Many organizations do not realize that "leadership effectiveness and behaviors" are culture-bound and may not be correlated with success. For example, among Asians and Asian Americans, leadership is defined as a person's ability to work behind the scenes, building group consensus and motivating fellow workers to increase productivity (Sue, 2008). This is in marked contrast to U.S. appraisal criteria of leadership: assertive, "take charge," highly visible, and competitive. In working with the company, the consultant used another approach to identify good potential managers. Members of the work team were asked to identify and rank in a private survey those coworkers most important in helping the team increase their productivity and who were most influential to the success of the task. Surprisingly, this method identified a number of Asian American names.

These findings allowed the consultant to work with the company in looking at their performance appraisal systems and the job descriptions (criteria) used for hiring, retention, and promotion of employees. It led the company to question whether the current criteria used to promote certain groups in the workplace (employees of color and women) were truly unbiased or the evaluations were culture-bound. There are several important implications to this particular work-related example.

First, while the criteria used to define leadership and managerial potential might be applicable to some groups (White males), it might be biased and inappropriate for others. Women, for example, who use a much more collaborative and relational approach to accomplishing goals as opposed to a competitive and task-oriented one may be overlooked as leadership material. Asian American employees who may "shun the spotlight" but be very effective in working behind the scenes are not visible to those in positions who determine promotion.

Second, it must be noted that performance appraisal systems serve gatekeeping functions that determine who is hired, retained, and promoted. If they, themselves, are culture-bound and biased toward employees of color, women, and LGBTs, disparities in employment will continue to exist. Programs, policies, and practices flow from performance appraisal systems; they are powerful organizational forces that determine who rises in an organization and who does not. Changing these biased policies and practices requires considerable work because a change in standards ultimately means that those groups who have benefited may no longer enjoy an advantage over others (Sue, 2008). Biased performance appraisal criteria have system-wide effects on the workplace. They perpetuate "glass walls" and "glass ceilings" that foster occupational segregation and restrict movement within a company, as well as maintain the status quo within an organization (Rowe, 1990).

ADDRESSING MICROAGGRESSIONS IN THE WORKPLACE

If racial, gender, and sexual-orientation microaggressions are so subtle and disguised, how do companies begin to address the detrimental effects of their workplace? What can business, industry, educational institutions, municipalities, health care agencies, and governmental agencies do to make the workplace more accepting and welcoming and ameliorate the harm of microaggressions? Several important changes and activities can be undertaken to enhance the valuing of underrepresented groups in work sites. Changes must occur at both the systemic and individual levels.

WORKPLACE/EMPLOYMENT: OVERCOMING SYSTEMIC BIASES AND MICROAGGRESSIONS

Studies on organizational culture, climate, and change suggest that work environments, through their philosophy, vision statements, and values, can directly affect the social identity contingencies of devalued groups in our society (Apfelbaum et al., 2008; Purdie-Vaughns et al., 2008; Thomas & Plaut, 2008). As indicated earlier, the effects of microaggressions are oftentimes felt not just interpersonally but through the environmental climate. Indeed, a strong case can be made that a company's policies, history, and tradition of how problems are defined and solved, and its values, inundate all sub-systems of an organization and are reflected in and influence the actions of workers.

Multicultural Philosophy versus Color Blindness

Color blindness (a race or gender neutral/free stance or perspective) in organizational philosophy serves to make many employees of color, women, and LGBTs feel more invalidated, oppressed, and unaccepted in the work-place, rather than increasing feelings of acceptance and inclusiveness. Color, gender, and sexual-orientation blindness serves to negate the racial, gender, and sexual identities of employees, ignores and invalidates their realities (Sue, Capodilupo, et al., 2007), prevents topics of race, gender, and sexual orientation from being freely and openly discussed (Young & Davis-Russell, 2002), suggests that everyone is the same, suggests that differences are bad and divisive (Thomas & Plaut, 2008), perpetuates the myth of meritocracy (Sue, 2005), allows White straight males to deny their unfair advantage and privilege (Bonilla-Silva, 2005), fosters complacency about inequities and unfairness in the workplace, and provides a convenient rationalization not to take responsible action against biases and systems of unfairness (Apfelbaum et al., 2008).

Organizations need to take a careful look at their corporate cultures and whether the underlying assumptions of equality and inclusiveness are based upon a mistaken notion of color, gender, and sexual-orientation blindness. While unintended, the "blindness" or "neutral" approach to differences can cause great harm to culturally diverse populations in the workforce. On the other hand, a multicultural philosophy that acknowledges differences, emphasizes the benefits of diversity, and recognizes/validates race, ethnicity, gender, sexual orientation, and religious affiliations of employees seems to make these groups feel valued, welcomed, and validated (Purdie-Vaughns et al., 2008). Moving an organization to a multicultural stance, however, is more than adjusting a statement in the company's vision statement or in a nondiscriminatory clause. Such changes are cosmetic and have no real impact on policies and practices. The meaning of being a multicultural organization must be carefully crafted, implemented, and monitored. One working definition proposed is the following:

> We define a multicultural organization as committed (action as well as words) to diverse representation throughout all levels, sensitive to maintaining an open, supportive, and responsive environment, working toward and purpose-fully including elements of diverse cultures in its ongoing operations, carefully monitoring organizational policies and practices to the goals of equal access and opportunity, and authentic in responding to changing policies and practices that block cultural diversity. (Sue & Constantine, 2005, p. 223)

This definition contains several important components that must be opera-tionalized to have meaning (Sue, 2008). First and foremost is the observation that marginalized groups continue to occupy the lower rungs of employment and that true multiculturalism and diversity must be at all levels. This leads to issues of underrepresentation and questions such as "What forces are preventing certain groups from being recruited, retained, and promoted?" and "What must be done organizationally to overcome these inequities?" Second, organizations must create and maintain an open and supportive environment, free of all microaggressions. The climate of an organization can either enhance or negate the work of employees. Third, the phrase "carefully monitoring organizational policies and practices" and "authentic in respond-ing to changing policies and practices" speaks to the long-term journey that organizations must take: Authenticity and commitment must be present, and change implies addressing those forces that block diversity.

Culture-Bound Performance Appraisal Systems: The Myth of Equal and Differential Treatments

Earlier in this chapter, an example was given about how performance appraisal systems unfairly discriminated against Asian American employees from being promoted to managerial or upper executive level positions. All organizations are composed of many interlocking subsystems (communica-tion channels, support services, human resources, chain of command, etc.) that are glued together by policies, practices, and structures. Rules governing the operation of these systems and how workers should behave often attain "Godfather"-like status (Sue, 1995). The most influential of the subsystems is the performance appraisal that serves a gate-keeping role because it contains the actual criteria and standards used to determine who is to be hired, where they will work, and what levels in the organization they will attain.

Rules and regulations are developed to normalize operating procedures, increase efficiency and clarity in roles and responsibilities, and ensure fair and equitable treatment of employees. Rather than achieving these goals, however, rules and regulations can foster economic and job segregation, decrease efficiency and effectiveness, and prevent certain groups from moving up in an organization. This occurs when criteria in performance appraisal systems are biased and when organizations espouse the principle of "equal treatment" in applying policies and practices. On the surface, this seems like a contradiction because when people are treated the same or equally, aren't we avoiding discrimination?

In fact, equal treatment can be discriminatory treatment and differential treatment is not necessarily preferential treatment. Equal treatment philosophies and practices have been a means for organizations to avoid charges of discrimination or bias. The complexity of this argument is exemplified in our Asian American managerial promotion example. Although the same criteria used in the job description were applied equally to all employees (White and Asian), it resulted in a differential outcome (Whites promoted over Asian Americans). Yet, those who made the decision are immunized from charges of discrimination because the same standard for promotion was used and no one was treated differently. This argument might have validity if it accurately predicted leadership qualities. But, for Asian American employees, ability to increase productivity and influence others was not correlated with the criteria used.

Organizations must begin to address the notion that "equal access and opportunity" may dictate differential policies and practices. A cultural audit of policies and practices (most strongly in performance appraisal systems) needs to be implemented if the organization hopes to become a multicultural one. Companies have always maintained that attracting the "best and brightest" employees in order to maintain a competitive advantage, retaining good employees, and not losing trained employees to better offers increases productivity in the workforce. Therefore, managing and minimizing diversity and providing everyone with equal opportunities are paramount to success in the marketplace (Gore, 2000). Employees of color, women, and LGBTs are not necessarily arguing for equal treatment. They are arguing for equal access and opportunities that may dictate differential treatment! Until organizations begin to understand these differences, large numbers of employees who do not fit the definition of the traditional worker (White, male, and heterosexual) will be prevented from maximizing their contributions to the company.

The Way Forward

Overcoming Individual Biases and Microaggressions

While organizations can do much in terms of developing multicultural philosophies to combat systemic microaggressions, reaching all employee groups is essential. To do this effectively, institutions can begin to institute initiatives, programs, and activities intended to (1) decrease the manifestation of microaggressions and harm to marginalized groups by allowing them to voice their concerns, forming coalitions that allow them to validate one another, and providing programs such as mentoring that allow them to understand and eventually enter the "corridors of power," and (2) educating the male, straight, and heterosexual workforce in the awareness, recognition, and impact of racial, gender, and sexual-orientation microaggressions. This last goal is an especially challenging one because it means workers must begin to acknowledge their hidden biases and become motivated to change their perceptions, thoughts, beliefs, and behaviors. Several suggestions are outlined below.

1. Hearing the voices of employees of color, women, and LGBTs in the workplace is essential for several different reasons. First, it validates the concerns and issues of these groups, who often are made to feel misunderstood, isolated, and devalued. Having focus groups or creating other minority employee organizations allows their voices to be heard by coworkers and/or management. These groups empower employees on issues of race, culture, gender, ethnicity, and sexual orientation. They may also immunize employees of color, for example, from racial microaggressions that invalidate their racial realities. Second, coalition-building and networking among employees of color, women, and LGBTs should be encouraged. Organizations must recognize that being a culturally different individual in a primarily monocultural situation can deplete energy, alienate, and discourage minority employees, and reduce their productivity. Clustering that allows for support and nourishment may lead to greater multicultural interactions in the long term. It provides a comfortable climate that allows them to relax, to be themselves, and to not be constantly vigilant. Third, organizations that create and foster such groups are seen by marginalized employees as sincere and accepting of their voices. It sends a strong message

(Continued)

to all employees about the importance that management gives to diversity and organizational inclusion. It works to the advantage of the organization because it also provides a rich source of information (work climate, policies and practices that do or don't work well, etc.).

2. As indicated earlier, superior–subordinate relationships, especially in the delivery of microaggressions, have a greater detrimental impact on marginalized groups than peer-to-peer relationships. Likewise, the elimination of microaggressive topics can also be seen as most effective if commitment comes from the very top levels. Diversity implementation is most effective when strong leadership is exerted on behalf of diversity and multiculturalism. Employees are most likely to watch the actions (not just words) of those in leadership positions. Thus, a CEO, provost, president, or director of a department who understands models and shows commitment to creating an open and bias-free work environment is most likely to effect workers in the company. Unfortunately, as indicated throughout this book, no one, whether a custodial worker, line worker, middle manager, or corporate CEO, is immune from inheriting the racial biases of society and free from expressing these through microaggressions. A positive role model at the leadership level also needs training and self-exploration.

3. We mentioned that organizations need a vision statement that frames multiculturalism and diversity into a meaningful operational definition. Words and statements may sound inspired, but not yet be completely implemented. To move toward creating an inclusive environment that truly values equal access and opportunity, organizations would be well advised to develop a multicultural and diversity action plan with clear objectives and timelines to address disparities in the company, to create a welcoming environment, and to institute inservice training. Many companies will form multicultural units or committees to discuss and explore racial and gender barriers, but not give these units the authority to institute change. Part of this is related to a lack of action plans with specific time frames for implementation of diversity goals.

4. Although well intentioned, many multicultural implementation committees or groups have little power or influence. Even with timelines and clear objectives, recommendations may go unheeded or remain unread. We have emphasized throughout that organizational change involves power. Organizations most successful in becoming inclusive advocate

(Continued)

the creation of a superordinate or oversight team/group that is empowered to assess, develop, and monitor the organization's development with respect to the goals of multiculturalism. Such groups have the power to operate rather independently and/or share an equal status relationship with other units in the organization. It must have the ability to influence, formulate, and implement multicultural initiatives, and report directly to the president or CEO.

5. If multicultural change is to occur in the organization, accountability must be built into the system. Certain divisions, departments, and individuals must be held responsible for achieving the goals of diversity and multiculturalism, for developing an inclusive and welcoming work environment, and for outcomes. For example, upper management in business or deans and chairs of institutions of higher education might be held responsible for recruiting, retaining, and promoting minorities and women within their own units. Professors might be held accountable for incorporating diversity into their curriculum; recognize the need for alternative teaching styles; and be unafraid to address topics likely to begin difficult dialogues in the classroom (race, gender, sexual orientation, etc.).

6. To successfully address systemic and individual microaggressions, organizations must develop a systematic and long-term commitment to educate the entire workforce concerning diversity issues, to address barriers that block multiculturalism, and to increase the sensitivity of employees at all levels to the manifestation and power of microaggressions. In-service multicultural training should be an intimate part of the organization's activities. In institutions of higher education, for example, training must include not only students, faculty, and staff, but should include the entire workforce up through administrators, to deans, the president of the university, and even the board of trustees. In business and industry, training is also important at all levels to the very top.

These suggestions are certainly not exhaustive. What is clearly evident, however, is how great the challenge is for our institutions and society. Racial, gender, and sexual-orientation microaggressions at present are played out in the many demeaning interpersonal interactions that occur in the workplace. Suggestion number 6 in the area of cultural diversity training will not be successful unless organizations view it as a long-term process and begin to realize that systemic change and individual change is needed. At the systems level, major resistance lies in the existing power structures of

(Continued)

organizations. At the individual level, resistance lies in employees' fears and apprehensions—in their inabilities to acknowledge their hidden biases and the meanings of them. Yet, to end the cycle of oppression for people of color, women, and LGBTs in the workplace means that we all must work together to overcome these resistances.

CHAPTER ELEVEN

Microaggressive Impact on Education and Teaching: Facilitating Difficult Dialogues on Race in the Classroom

I was teaching a sophomore class in urban education and lecturing on the "achievement gap" between Black and White students. Our topic for discussion dealt with analyzing a collection of brief biographical sketches of Black Americans who described how race impacted their lives and the special hardships they encountered in education. Usually students in my class are very talkative, but today the responses were tepid and brief. It felt like pulling teeth to get any type of response. I kept asking questions and making comments in an attempt to generate interest and to fill the long silences. Finally, one of the White female students stated that "I'm not sure this is a race issue, because as a woman, I've experienced low expectations from my teachers as well." Another White male student chimed in by asking "Isn't it a social class issue?" Another White female student immediately agreed, and went into a long monologue concerning how class issues are always neglected in discussions of social justice. She concluded by asking "Why is everything always about race?"

I could sense the energy in the classroom rise and felt eager to discuss these important issues when one of the few Black female students angrily confronted the White female with these words: "You have no idea what it's like to be Black! I don't care if you are poor or not, but you have White skin. Do you know what that means? Don't tell me that being Black isn't different from being White." A Latina student also added to the rejoinder by stating "You will never understand. Whites don't have to understand. Why are White people so scared to talk about race? Why do you always have to push it aside?" The two White female students seemed baffled and became obviously defensive. After an attempt to clarify their points, both White female students seemed to only inflame the dialogue. One of the female students began to cry, and the second student indignantly got up, stated she was not going to be insulted, and left the classroom.

As a White male professor, I felt paralyzed. This was truly "the classroom from hell." What had just happened? I was concerned about losing control of the classroom dynamics and immediately tried to calm the students down. I told them to respect one another, and to address these issues in a rational, calm, and objective manner. We could not let our emotions get the better of us. Because of the volatility of the situation, I suggested that we table the discussion and go on to another topic.

While I continued to lecture as if nothing had happened, I experienced a deep sense of failure and was concerned with the impact of this situation in our class. It was later substantiated when the student who broke out in tears dropped the course, and the one who left the room bitterly complained to the Dean, blaming me for handling the situation poorly. I was haunted by this classroom experience, did not understand what had happened, and felt at a loss of what to do. Nothing in my education had prepared me for handling this explosive difficult dialogue on race.

The above example is one that is reenacted frequently in classrooms throughout the United States, especially when topics revolve around those of race and racism. Studies reveal that many difficult dialogues on race are triggered by racial microaggressions not only in classroom settings, but in many public and private forums (Sue, Lin, Torino, Capodilupo, & Rivera, 2009; Sue, Rivera, Capodilupo, Lin , & Torino, 2009; Sue, Torino, Capodilupo, Rivera, & Lin, 2009; Young, 2004). Difficult racial dialogues are perceived quite differently between people of color and Whites. For students of color, race is an intimate part of their identities and avoiding topics related to it, dismissing it, negating it, or having it assailed create emotional reactions that may be brewed over in silence, or result in lashing out toward offenders (Young, 2004). For many White students, however, race is invisible—they seldom think about or investigate it, and they become defensive about their own privilege. Ultimately, this can lead to denial or minimization of race as an important aspect of life (Bolgatz, 2005). Let us briefly identify the issues illustrated in the example.

First, it is apparent that all three well-intentioned White students did not realize that they were delivering racial microaggressions toward students of color. In addressing how race influenced Blacks, the White students seemed to dilute its importance by refocusing the topic on gender and class issues. They did not realize that they were (1) assailing the racial identities of Black students, and (2) denying or invalidating their racial experiences and realities (Sue, Lin, et al., 2009) through their microaggressive comments. As you recall, both of these communications have been identified as forms of racial microaggressions. Further, by equating racial bias with gender/class biases, the legitimacy of racism and its detrimental impact on the lives of people of color is diminished, pushed aside, and considered unimportant. Again, as with all microaggressions, there is a difference between the legitimacy of the topics (importance of gender and class factors), and the hidden demeaning and invalidating messages that are sent. The White students were unaware that they might be delivering microaggressions.

Second, the invisibility of these interactional dynamics—what triggered the intense reaction of students of color (racial microaggressions)—is often outside the level of conscious awareness of the White students, and even the professor. When critical consciousness is missing and when the interpersonal dynamics are unclear, puzzlement and confusion reign supreme. The White students and professor are at a loss to understand what just happened, and what was responsible for the emotive reactions and statements of students of color. Thus, they are not in a position to respond in a helpful or enlightened manner. The White students are left with the feeling of being personally attacked and only vaguely sense that something they did or said offended students of color. But other than their own defensiveness, anxiety, and feeling hurt from the exchange, they have little understanding of their own roles in the difficult dialogue (Sue, Rivera, et al., 2009). The professor also realizes something is amiss (tentativeness in discussing racial topics, anxiety, heated exchanges, crying and leaving the room), but is at a loss to determine its meaning and how to respond appropriately (Sue, Torino, et al., 2009).

Third, difficult dialogues on race are seldom completed or resolved in such a way as to be a meaningful learning experience. Indeed, classroom interactions on topics of race, gender, and sexual orientation often deteriorate into monologues rather than develop into true dialogues (Sue & Constantine, 2007). There is no attempt to reach out to others, to hear their points of view, and to digest the meanings; instead, defensiveness, anger, and an attacking shouting match occur between participants (Young, 2003). Students seem more motivated to press their views (stating and restating their positions, and talking over each other) rather than attempting to listen to another's point of view. If sufficient emotional intensity is reached, students may leave the classroom, break down in tears (Accapadi, 2007), and not participate further in racial dialogues; the professor, on the other hand, may admonish students to respect one another, to control their emotions, or to "table the discussion." These avoidance maneuvers are intended to end the dialogue or *to place extreme restrictions on how to talk about race.*

Fourth, the unsuccessful outcome of difficult dialogues on race represents a major setback and failure in understanding and improving race relations. It can actually lead to a hardening of racially biased views on the part of White students (people of color are oversensitive and can't control their emotions), and it leaves the students of color pained, hurt, and invalidated, reinforcing beliefs that Whites cannot understand or be trusted. Further, by leaving the topic untouched and unresolved it will continue to represent the "elephant in the room" and negatively affect the learning environment by teaching students to avoid race topics. As a result, many students of color find the classroom situation oppressive and intolerable, reflecting the power and privilege of White students and professors to control the dialogue. While White students can avoid issues of race by leaving the situation or avoiding it, students of color have no such privilege. They must deal with race on a day-to-day basis; escape and leaving the situation are not options open to them.

Last, the White professor reflected upon how his training had never prepared him to facilitate these emotional interactions among students, or even between himself and his students. It is clear that the professor was baffled by the interaction and was unaware and unable to recognize racial microaggressions. While educators are often prepared to teach in classrooms by stressing knowledge acquisition and cognitive analysis, topics of race and racism are more than intellectual exercises because they involves taboos, and nested feelings of anxiety, fear, guilt, and anger. As we shall shortly see, facilitating difficult dialogues on race requires professors to (a) be aware of their own values, biases, and assumptions about human behavior, (b) understand the worldview of the culturally diverse students, and (c) possess a repertoire of teaching or facilitation strategies to aid students in self-reflection and learning.

MICROAGGRESSIONS IN EDUCATION

It is becoming increasingly clear that many inequities in education are due to lower expectations, stereotypes, and a hostile invalidating climate for people of color, women, and LGBTs (Bell, 2002; Cadinu, Maass, Rosabianca, & Kiesner, 2005; Sue, Rivera, et al., 2009). In the last chapter we analyzed how microaggressions operate systemically in worksites and their effects can be found in the hiring, retention, and promotion of employees. This is also true with respect to pre-K–12 schools, institutions of higher education, and professional graduate programs. The underrepresentation of women in science and engineering in elementary levels, secondary schools, and in professorial positions in colleges/universities may speak to possible discrimination. The low representation of minority faculty can also be the insidious operation of aversive forms of racism. Not only may such forces operate in an educational institution, affecting which teachers, staff, and administrators are hired, but a similar framework can be applied to students as well.

Microaggressions can affect the student body composition through recruitment (which students are selected), retention (which students drop out), and promotion (graduation rates) of students of color. If racial, gender, and sexual-orientation microaggressions present a hostile and invalidating learning climate, these groups are likely to suffer in any number of ways. Women, for example, have been found to experience stereotype threat because of gender microaggressions, may underperform in math and sciences despite having high abilities, and/or may become segregated in their career paths or vocational selections by well-intentioned educators (Bell, 2003; Gore, 2000; Morrison & Von Glinow, 1990). Such factors speak to educational inequities that are present systemically and may inundate the classroom environment.

Educational Disparities among Marginalized Groups

Despite parents of color encouraging their sons and daughters to develop educational and career goals, racism and poverty continue to create disparities, especially among African American, Latina/o, and American Indian students. The high school graduation rates for African Americans are significantly below those of Whites and even worse for those going to college (14.3% vs. 24.3%) (U.S. Census Bureau, 2005b); Latinas/os have fared poorly as approximately two of five aged 25 or older have not completed high school, and more than 25% have less than a ninth-grade education (U.S. Census Bureau, 2003); and Native Americans show an astounding pattern of dropping out beginning in the fourth grade, resulting in low rates of completing elementary and secondary schools and college (U.S. Census Bureau, 2006). Although Asian Americans are often perceived as a "successful minority" with higher educational levels, the statistics mask a bimodal distribution of this group; a large number of Asian subgroups have a large undereducated mass (U.S. Census Bureau, 2005a). Only 40% of Hmongs have completed high school and fewer than 14% of Tongans, Cambodians, Laotians, and Hmongs 25 years and older have a bachelor's degree.

Looking beyond these gross measures of academic achievement, it is undeniable that a large discrepancy exists between the academic performance of students of color and their White counterparts. American Indian children do well during the first four years of school, but by the end of fourth grade they begin to "drop out" and by the seventh grade significant decreases in academic performance are evident (Juntunen et al., 2001). Black students during middle and high school years evidence a separation of self-esteem from academic performance that results in loss of interest in schoolwork and resulting poor acquisition of knowledge and skills. Behavioral problems in schools, higher pregnancy rates among African American and Latina girls, and increasing alienation from school curriculum all contribute to poorer academic performance. Students of color are also many times more likely to be suspended from school and to receive harsher consequences than their White peers (Monroe, 2005).

For years, educators have attempted to understand the causes of "the achievement gap" in an attempt to close it. They have recognized that the in-ability to complete an education perpetuates the cycle of poverty, lack of job opportunities in the larger society, and detrimental psychological consequences associated with low self-esteem and subjective well-being (Sue & Sue, 2008). Appropriate intervention strategies can only arise, however, when the causes for school failure are identified. The causes of high drop-out rates and lower academic achievement among students of color are probably multidimensional and may vary from group to group. Explanations for the poorer academic performance of students of color, however, seem to fall into two camps: (1) causation resides internally, within the individual, group, or culture, and (2) causation resides externally in the system or the academic/classroom and societal environment.

Internal Causation—Individual Focus
We have already identified two major forms of microaggressions that seem to form a worldview with hidden assumptions and messages: (1) the myth

of meritocracy and (2) pathologizing cultural/communication styles of marginalized groups. Both take a person- or group-focused approach to explaining the poor academic performance of marginalized groups. The explanations can range from genetic speculations that biology determines intelligence and abilities (math/science capabilities are deficient in women) to factors associated with incompatible group characteristics and values. Educators and especially teachers often hold both conscious and unconscious stereotypes or preconceived notions that students of color are less capable and motivated, that parents are uninvolved in the educational welfare of their children, and/or that their cultural values are at odds with educational values (Sue & Sue, 2008).

School personnel, for example, often attribute the poor performance of African Americans to internal attributes or to their parents. One teacher stated: "The parents are the problem! They [African American children] have absolutely no social skills, such as not knowing how to walk, sit in a chair . . . it's cultural" (Harry, Klinger, & Hart, 2005, p. 105). With respect to Native American students, some have argued that Indian cultural values and beliefs are incompatible with those of the educational system, and that this is the culprit for their achievement gap. Likewise, many educators believe that much of the educational difficulties of Latinos are due primarily to their language, Spanish, which prevents them from acquiring the ability to speak "good standard English" (Hayes, 2006).

Although these explanations may contain some grain of truth, they all assume internal causation and have the unintended consequence of blaming the victim; the problem resides in the genes of the group, in their culture, or in their language. The genetic deficiency and inferiority models have been used to explain why African Americans, Mexican Americans, and Spanish Indian families perform poorly on intellectual tasks (Samuda, 1998). The culturally deficient model described marginalized groups in our society as deficient, disadvantaged, or deprived (Sue & Sue, 2008; Thomas & Sillen, 1972). Logically, the terms *deprived* or *deficient* suggest that people of color lack the advantages of middle-class culture (education, formal language, books, values, and traditions) to perform well in classes. While the cultural deprivation theories were proposed by well-intentioned White educators as a means of combating racist and sexist biological explanations, they only worsened our understanding by shifting the blame from genetics to a more acceptable one, culture.

At first glance, the phrase "culturally impoverished" appears more benign and less harmful. But explanations of cultural deprivation suffer from several problems. First, we can ask the question, how can any individual or group be culturally deprived or "lack a culture"? Such a phrase is contradictory because everyone inherits a culture and no one was born "culturally naked." Second, it causes conceptual and theoretical confusions that may adversely affect educational policy and practice. If African American family values and behaviors are at the root of the problem, then it opens the floodgates for us to infuse White Eurocentric notions into the family values of the Black community. Third, a hidden microaggressive assumption is that cultural deprivation is used synonymously with deviations from and superiority of White middle-class values. In essence, these models and explanations send the same message: People of color and many other marginalized groups lack the right culture! White Eurocentric norms, masculine norms, and heterosexist norms become the worldview that reflects racial, gender, and sexual-orientation microaggressions in the educational setting.

A society based upon the concept of "individualism"—that one's lot in life is based upon individual effort, abilities, and skills—is said to be oriented toward explaining behavior from a person-focused perspective. Three philosophical outlooks derive from an internal explanation of behavior or outcome: (1) stress is placed upon understanding individual motives, values, feelings, and goals; (2) causal attribution of success or failure is determined by the skills or inadequacies of the person; and (3) there is a strong belief in the relationship between abilities, effort, and success in education. Educational performance, educational attainment, and educational outcome of students of color, women, and LGBTs, for example, are the result of their own internal attributes. Success is explained as outstanding attributes, and failure is attributed to personal or group deficiencies.

External Causation—System Focus

While individual responsibility for achievement in school is an important factor in explaining academic performance, ignoring external forces (prejudice, discrimination, poverty, etc.) to explain academic disparities in education may result in blaming the victim. Many microaggressions originate from a myth of meritocracy ("any one can succeed in life if they work hard enough" and "the playing field is level"), and the failure to consider powerful external forces that affect outcome. Native American students report that educational curriculum, teaching and learning styles, and the classroom climate are unwelcoming, and ignore their cultural and social differences. They feel "pushed out" and mistrusted by teachers and liken the educational experience to forced compliance or being "civilized" (Deyhle & Swisher, 1999). Latina/o students, especially immigrants, must deal not only with racism, but acculturative stress, poverty, high unemployment, and culture-conflicts (Hovey, 2000). It is reported that this confluence of external factors not only saps the energies of Latina/o students for learning in the classroom, but predisposes them to higher rates of mental disorders such as depression and attempted suicide (Tortolero & Roberts, 2001). Dealing with family distress, discrimination in the school and community, and social isolation may result in increased gang activities as well (Baca & Koss-Chioino, 1997).

Likewise, gay and lesbian youths, especially those out of the closet, face discrimination and harassment in the schools at a high rate. They are more likely to have been involved in a fight that required medical attention (Russell, Franz, & Driscoll, 2001). Their tendency to be exposed to violence in schools is frighteningly high: a Massachusetts high school study revealed that LGB students are more likely to be confronted with a weapon in school (32.7 vs. 7.1%), and to avoid going to school because of safety concerns (25.1 vs. 5.1%). Furthermore, they were more likely to attempt suicide not because of their sexual orientation, but because their school, home, and social environments have proven hostile and invalidating (Russell & Joyner, 2001).

Given these brief examples, it is clear that systems forces can be powerful and influential in determining the academic outcome of students. A singular belief that people are "masters of their own fate" unfairly blames marginalized populations for their inability to achieve more in school or society. It fails to consider the operations of racism, sexism, and heterosexism in determining the outcome of school performance and achievement in other areas of life. Whether educators view the locus of responsibility as residing in the person or the system has major impact upon how they define a problem (achievement gap), the attributions made, and the strategies chosen to solve it. Poor academic performance of African Americans, for example, may be attributed to the group's inadequacies or shortcomings (person-focused), thus changing them (assimilation or acculturation) is seen as the solution. If, however, a system analysis is employed, racial discrimination and the lack of opportunities are identified as the culprits, and systemic intervention is recommended (Jones, 1997). Neither approach taken to the extreme tells the whole story. However, the values of individualism and autonomy undergird our beliefs in individual responsibility and self-reliance, making it difficult for many educators to see how their assumptions of equal access and opportunity may not apply to many devalued groups in our society. Systemic barriers to minority achievement can be found in the following culture-bound and culturally biased forces operating in schools at all levels.

How microaggressions make their appearance in the larger educational setting can be analyzed from a broader systemic level, as we have seen in Chapter 10. Racial, gender, and sexual-orientation microaggressions can be manifested in many areas:

- Faculty, administrators, staff, and students on an interactional level may unwittingly invalidate, insult, or assail the identities of people of color, women, and LGBTs.
- Microaggressions can make their appearance in the curriculum (culturally biased or culture-bound textbooks, lectures, teaching materials, etc.) that ignore or portray marginalized groups in unflattering ways.
- Low numerical minority representation among teachers and administrators may act as a symbolic cue signaling a threat to a group's social identity.
- The campus climate may be unwelcoming, not only through the actions of individuals (harassment, racist/sexist/heterosexist jokes, etc.), but also environmentally (foods served in cafeterias, music played at school events, what and how events are celebrated, how classrooms or buildings are decorated, etc.).
- Teaching and learning styles may clash with one another because of differences in how groups learn.
- The types of support services offered by the school may come from a primarily White European perspective that may be antagonistic to the life values and experiences of certain groups (student personnel services, counseling and guidance services, etc.).
- The programs, policies, and practices may be oppressive and unfair to many marginalized groups and serve to oppress rather than liberate.

MICROAGGRESSIONS AND DIFFICULT DIALOGUES ON RACE IN THE CLASSROOM

One of the most important educational forums in understanding how microaggressions affect learning is in the classroom, where students spend a large portion of their time. Some have made a distinction between schooling and education (Cokley, 2006; Shujaa, 2003), in which the former is the process and activities of going to and being in school while the latter is the by-product of the experience. To people of color, it is believed that schooling can either serve the interests of the group or betray it. These scholars have observed that the educational curriculum has become racialized (Sue, 2003) and that schooling can often be used as a tool to perpetuate and maintain the prevailing power arrangements and structures, whereas education is a means of transmitting eurocentric values, beliefs, customs, traditions, language, and arts/ crafts of the dominant society (Ford, Moore, & Whiting, 2006; Shujaa, 2003). The ultimate result is the (mis)education of students of color, in which education becomes a form of "domestication" (Cokley, 2006). These statements have considerable support when one realizes the many inaccuracies taught in our curriculum and imposed upon students of color as well as their White classmates: Columbus discovered America, the internment of Japanese Americans was necessary for national security, and the enslavement of Black people was justified because "living under unnatural conditions of freedom" made them prone to anxiety.

Earlier, we indicated that power is in a group's ability to define reality and that schooling/education is a major socialization portal (Sue, 2003). Through omission, fabrication, distortion, or selective emphasis, the history and contributions of White Western civilizations are reinforced and elevated to superior status and imposed upon all students. The result is perpetuation of myths and inaccuracies about persons of color. Microaggressions are reflections of a worldview of superiority-inferiority, normality-abnormality, and desirable-undesirable ways of thinking, feeling, and behaving. If we address the issue of race and racism, schooling and education may unintentionally reflect racial biases and oppress students of color while elevating the status of their White classmates and White teachers. When left unchallenged, they reinforce the attitudes, beliefs, and Eurocentric knowledge of Whites, while denigrating, demeaning, and invalidating those of students of color. When challenged, however, they can lead to difficult dialogues on race and represent a clash of racial realities. Many educators believe that classroom dialogues on race may represent a major tool in combating racism and helping to make racial microaggressions visible (Blum, 1998; Bolgatz, 2005; Sue & Constantine, 2007; Watt, 2007; Willow, 2008; Young, 2004; Young & Davis-Russell, 2002). We turn our attention now to analyzing the meaning and significance of difficult dialogues on race, but it is important to note that dialogues on gender and sexual orientation may share very similar manifestations and dynamics.

RACIAL DIALOGUES IN THE CLASSROOM

The increasing diversity in the United States is perhaps reflected most in our classrooms, where students of all colors represent a microcosm of race relations in our society. The increased interracial interactions often means greater opportunities for microaggressions to occur between students of color and their White classmates, between professors and their students, and in exposure to biased curricular topics and orientations. In a revealing study (Sue, Lin, et al., 2009), researchers found that these interactions often polarized students and teachers rather than contribute to mutual respect and understanding about race and race relations.

Many educators believe that effectively facilitating difficult dialogues on race in the classroom represents a golden opportunity to reduce and dispel prejudice and stereotypes, bridge ethnic divides, decrease mistrust and misunderstandings, increase empathy and compassion for others, and promote goodwill and understanding (President's Initiative on Race, 1998; Willow, 2008; Young, 2004). Unfortunately, racial dialogues in classrooms have frequently produced directly the opposite effect. They have resulted in disastrous consequences such as hardening of biases and prejudices; evoking strong feelings of anger, hostility, and rage; increasing misunderstanding; and blocking learning opportunities (Sue, Lin, et al., 2009; Sue, Rivera, et al., 2009). Yet, skillfully handled by enlightened teachers, difficult dialogues on race can prove to be an opportunity for growth, improved communication, and learning (Young, 2003; Sanchez-Hucles, & Jones, 2005).

Given the potential educational importance of being able to effectively facilitate difficult dialogues on race, the following questions may be imperative for educators to address: (1) What triggers (causes) a difficult dialogue on race? (2) Why is it so difficult for us to honestly dialogue about race, gender, and sexual orientation? (3) What makes a dialogue on race difficult? (4) Why do students and teachers alike become so guarded and uncomfortable when racial topics are raised in and outside of the classroom? (5) How can educators learn to become comfortable when addressing race issues, and what effective strategies can be used to facilitate a difficult dialogue?

Microaggressive Triggers to Difficult Racial Dialogues

Studies seem to suggest strongly that many difficult dialogues on race are caused by racial microaggressions that make their appearance in the classroom

(Solorzano et al., 2000; Sue, Lin, et al., 2009). In many cases they are delivered by White students and professors, either through a comment, tone of voice, nonverbals, insinuations, or the content of the course (curriculum). The microaggressions are found offensive by students of color, who may directly or indirectly confront perpetrators who attempt to avoid the topic and/or react defensively because they feel falsely accused of racism. While difficult racial dialogues can be triggered by other causes, it seems that racial microaggressions are the most common and prevalent instigator. Some of the most common racial microaggressions identified in the classroom are consistent with the thematic ones found in other formulations and studies in general (Sue, Capodilupo, et al., 2007; Sue, Capodilupo, Nadal, & Torino, 2008; Sue, Bucceri, Lin, Nadal, & Torino, 2007). Examples in classroom situations for four of them—"ascription of intelligence," "alien in one's own land," "denial of racial reality," and "assumption of criminality"—are given below. The following student quotes are taken from Sue, Lin, et al. (2009).

1. *Ascription of intelligence*—The following was reported by a Black student about a classroom incident where a fellow classmate asked her a question. She relates the following:

> "I started to explain, and the White girl said, 'Well, what she means is'—and she tried to talk for me. That I don't know what I'm talking about. I can't even articulate my own, my own idea. And I had to tell her, I can speak for myself, I can articulate my idea better than you can, you know? And only—I could not believe that she tried to speak for me." (p. 186).

The Black student was outraged and insulted because the White student assumed she was incapable of expressing her own ideas and wanted to do it for her.

2. *Alien in one's own land*—Although he did not show it, one Asian American male expressed controlled rage at another White female student because she assumed he could not speak or understand English well (perpetual foreigner association).

> "But she looked at me and spoke extra slow, like to explain what the professor had just said. And I was kind of like, okay. So when I spoke and I spoke in regular speech, she was kind of shocked . . . um, like wondering if I actually speak English."

3. *Denial of racial reality*—The following classroom incidents were reported to happen continually and would often trigger a difficult dialogue.

As in our opening case example, the student of color's racial reality is negated or invalidated:

> ". . . [They] keep rejecting whatever you say in class, it doesn't matter what you say, [they'd] disagree. They'll say [racial related matter] it's either irrelevant, it's not clear enough, um, I don't understand what you're saying, stuff like that . . ."

Many students reported how when bringing up topics of race or culture, they would be met with responses from White classmates like *"not everything is racial, you know"* or nonverbals (rolling of the eyeballs) that *"scream at you, here we go again."* Another informant states, *"When I share personal experiences of discrimination in class, they always want to find another reason for the behavior"* (p. 186).

4. *Assumption of criminality*—This was a common experience for African Americans students who witnessed White classmates not sitting next to them, or becoming extra vigilant with their personal belongings when they approached. They felt that White students communicated a fear of them, or that they might steal: *"They don't trust us, we're criminals, dope pushers and thieves"* (p. 186). Another Black student reported becoming angry at comments from White classmates after watching a counseling session with a Black client.

> "Some of the students started to comment automatically on . . . like, well, what if he gets violent? Like, it just was kind of like entertained by the professor, like, oh, well, you need to make sure where you sit is close to an exit, and you gotta do this and you gotta do that. But I thought to a larger picture as to like this man, he was older and he just was resistant, but he wasn't violent." (p. 186)

Impediments to Honest Racial Dialogues

If racial dialogues are often caused by microaggressions, it becomes important to understand why it is so difficult to clarify communications between the participants. As we indicated earlier, students of color find such communications offensive. Yet, it would be beneficial to understand how White students perceive, interpret, and react when difficult dialogues on race present themselves. Why do many White students find it so difficult to honestly dialogue on racial topics? What are the barriers that get in their way? What are they afraid of? Likewise, these questions can also be addressed to White teachers as well. Understanding the dynamics of racial dialogues can have many educational benefits: (1) it will aid educators to recognize and anticipate their appearance in classrooms and other settings; (2) recognition of the intense emotions of White students may allow educators a deeper understanding of affective resistances; and (3) knowledge and understanding of difficult dialogues on race may lead to the development of intervention strategies that prove successful and unsuccessful in overcoming resistances, thus making such experiences a learning opportunity for all students (Sue, Torino, et al., 2009).

In a series of studies exploring the perspective of both White students and White educators on why difficult dialogues on race are difficult, it was found that both students and teachers shared similar fears (Sue, Rivera, et al., 2009; Sue, Torino, et al., 2009). We first discuss difficult racial dialogues from the perspective of White students and then from that of White teachers.

White Students' Perspectives

It has been hypothesized that many Whites find dialogues on race difficult for four primary reasons: (1) fear of being perceived as racist, (2) fear of realizing one's racism, (3) fear of confronting White privilege, and (4) fear of taking actions to end racism (Sue & Constantine, 2007; Watt, 2007; Willow, 2008). While they may unintentionally deliver a microaggression during an interracial encounter, the challenge from the target group evokes anxiety and dread in Whites who attempt to deny the implications for their actions. Unwittingly, the form of the denial may result in additional microaggressions (denial of individual racism or denial of the racial reality of targets). In one study designed to investigate these conclusions, it was found that White students identified several reasons about why racial dialogues were difficult for them (Sue & Constantine, 2007; Sue, Rivera, et al., 2009).

Fear of Appearing Racist

One of the most dominant fears expressed by White students was that whatever they said or did in a racial dialogue might give people the mistaken impression that they were racist. The fear was quite overwhelming and hindered their abilities to participate in an honest and authentic manner, made them tentative in their responses, and more often than not they either remained silent or took a very passive approach to the topic. In classroom interactions they would refuse to participate or make only superficial observations. Some quotes from students illustrate their concerns and feelings: "... *if I talk about race, I'm going to reveal my racism,*" "... *fear of revealing my own biases,*" and "... *if I express any confusion or if I have any questions, they're sometimes construed as close-mindedness or an ignorance on my part."* . . . *"I wanted to say something, but I also felt very nervous. When I did finally speak, my thoughts weren't clear and I am sure difficult to follow"* (Sue, Rivera, et al., 2009). Ironically, rather than making themselves appear less biased, their behaviors were read by students of color as indicating attempts to conceal racist attitudes and beliefs. It has been conjectured that the fear of appearing racist is only a superficial level of defense by Whites because it really masks a deeper fear—fear of actually being racist (Sue & Constantine, 2007). This conclusion seems supported by another dominant concern of White students.

Denial of Whiteness and White Privilege

White students expressed resentment toward being blamed for racism and the association of Whiteness with privilege, power, and advantage. They appeared to react defensively to being called "White" and seemed aware of the negative associations with light skin color. Some even disavowed being White by claiming to identify with only an ethnic group: "I'm not White, I'm German." "I'm not White, I'm Irish Catholic." One White female student expressed her strong objections to such associations: *"White people this and White people that, because honestly, I don't really identify with—I definitely feel like I need to almost justify myself when those things come up . . . societal problems are out of my hands."* Defensiveness seemed central to their reactions.

White students had considerable difficulty entertaining the notion that their light skin color automatically advantaged them in this society and that darker skin color disadvantaged others. They would often ward off such suggestions with statements like, "Don't blame me, my parents didn't own slaves." "Don't blame me; I didn't take land from Native Americans." It was difficult for many White students to realize that despite not being the primary culprits in perpetrating these wrongs, they still benefited from the historical injustices and structural arrangements of their ancestors. The anger, resentment, denial, and guilt expressed by White students made them want to avoid conversations on race. Again, a deeper exploration of these resistances revealed an additional level of discomfort many had difficulty facing: If indeed they benefitted from White privilege, then two challenges confront them. First, they must now question the myth of meritocracy and the likelihood that their lot in life was attained not just through their own efforts, but by a biased system that favored them. Second, if one accepts the notion of "unfair advantage" due to White privilege, what implications does it have for one's life and what will Whites do about it?

Color Blindness

As we have indicated earlier, the issue of color blindness is a double-edged sword (Purdie-Vaughns, Davis, Steele, & Ditlmann, 2008; Thomas & Plant, 2008). In an attempt to appear unbiased, many Whites have adopted the stance that the color of one's skin is unimportant in American society. To see and acknowledge race or color is to potentially appear prejudiced and bigoted. Yet, many people of color find such a philosophy not only disingenuous, but an indicator of bias on the part of the person making such a claim. In classroom situations, White students may find topics on race difficult and uncomfortable because it may run counter to their beliefs that "we are all God's children," "we are all the same under the skin," and "we are all human beings or Americans." Professing color blindness has several perceived advantages for White students. First, it allows them not to acknowledge race and racial differences in classroom dialogues. Second, they can maintain the illusion that they are unbiased and do not discriminate against others. Third, if race is unimportant, then everyone has equal access and opportunity.

No Right to Dialogue on Race

Many students felt they had not experienced racism as students of color did, and thus had no right or credibility to talk about race matters. When asked about their reluctance to engage in racial conversations, many indicated that speaking to racism requires having been a victim. Others indicated they had limited contact with people of color, their knowledge was limited, and they felt uncomfortable speaking on such a topic. They indicated they did not possess a "valid voice" on the topic and were reluctant to participate: "... *if you haven't experienced racism, you know, as a victim, then you don't necessarily have a right to talk about race."* Again, this rationale seemed to be protective rather than real. It allows students to avoid exploring their own thoughts and reactions related to race issues, and to deceive themselves into believing that they play no role in the creation and maintenance of racism.

These four barriers to difficult dialogues on race were often accompanied by intense and extreme debilitating emotions that interfered with students' ability to attend, participate, and be open about their thoughts and feelings. An overwhelming number reported feeling **anxious and intimidated** about classroom conversations on race. They described fear and dread when racial topics were raised: *"I tried hard to say something thoughtful and it's hard for me to say, and my heart was pounding when I said it."* Another reaction was that of **helplessness.** This feeling very much related to an inability to understand or cope with feelings evoked from a classroom dialogue. A White student describes her reaction: *"And then it sort of turned into, you know, a lot of the Students of Color kind of venting their frustrations, which is, you know, completely understandable, but at the same time, I felt so helpless, like, I really don't know what to do right now."* These students were likely to acknowledge the existence of racial injustice, but felt at a loss of how to speak to it. Consistent with the fear of appearing racist, some students felt **misunderstood** when they made comments. When addressing the topic of "antisocial behavior and violence," one White student recalls listing risk factors and mentioned the Black community. She reports being confronted by Black students and unfairly accused of stereotyping. The incident was so upsetting that she failed to participate during the rest of the class.

White Teachers' Perspectives

Teachers and educators are in a unique position to help students understand racial issues, especially when such interactions arise in the classroom (Young, 2004). When difficult racial dialogues occur in the classroom, they are no longer purely abstract intellectual constructs, but their appearances are concrete and real for students and teachers alike (Bell, 2003). They represent a microcosm of race relation difficulties in our society. In the hands of a skilled facilitator, difficult dialogues on race can represent a potential learning opportunity for personal growth and understanding, improved communication, and racial harmony (Young & Davis-Russell, 2002). Because the majority of teachers in the United States are predominantly White, their roles are crucial in facilitating successful racial dialogues in the classroom. Unfortunately, studies seem to suggest that White educators are often (1) ill-prepared to recognize and understand the dynamics of racial microaggressions as causes to difficult dialogues, (2) confused as to what constitutes a difficult dialogue, and (3) at a loss of how to intervene when they occur (Sue, Torino, et al., 2009; Sue, Rivera, et al., 2009).

Teacher Fears

One of the greatest fears and concerns for teachers around race dialogues is loss of classroom control and the emotionally charged nature of the interactions. The loss of control is often related to the feeling of helplessness, inability to determine the nature of the conflict, and the lack of knowledge of how best to properly intervene (Sue, Torino, et al., 2009). These three are compounded by an acknowledgment by teachers about their own personal limitations and intense anxieties, similar to those expressed by White students (fear of appearing racist, fear of realizing their biases, and resistance to recognizing their own prejudices). In addition, they noted the following concerns.

1. *Inability to recognize racial microaggressions and uncertainty and confusion about the characteristics of a difficult dialogue.* When a difficult racial dialogue is occurring, many White teachers admit to being mystified and uncertain about the interactional dynamics. They know something is amiss, that tension has increased in the classroom, and that students of color and White students have taken a confrontational stance. They are at a loss to explain the dynamics and often misdiagnose the problem.

2. *Trouble understanding and dealing with intense student emotions and their own.* In many respects, White teachers overidentify with the feelings of White students because many of the emotions expressed are similar to the ones they experience. Fear, anxiety, anger, defensiveness, guilt, and helplessness can occur quickly and in a "garbled fashion" that interferes with understanding and teaching. The teacher may become overwhelmed and flooded with feelings that constrict their perceptions and ability to respond appropriately. The teacher may try to dilute, diminish, or "cut off the dialogue" for fear that it will turn into a physical fight among students.

3. *Fear of losing classroom control.* Teachers are expected to manage classroom interactions, to maintain a conducive learning environment, and to make sure proper respect exists among all students. Difficult dialogues on race can produce intense confrontations between students and result in intense hostility. Several teachers spoke about being paralyzed when students became so upset that they leave the room, or burst into tears.

4. *Deep sense of personal failure and inadequacies.* Avoidance by teachers of race topics is often motivated by past experiences of failure and personal questioning about one's teaching competencies. The sense of disappointment in themselves occurred because of their unsuccessful attempts to facilitate racial dialogues.

5. *Feelings of incompetence and lack of knowledge and skills to effectively intervene.* A very common admission from teachers was that of not possessing the experience, knowledge, or teaching strategies to facilitate a difficult dialogue on race. In coping with race topics, they admitted to ignoring it in class, making sure it was discussed only on a cognitive level, or playing a passive role in class and "letting students take over."

Disturbingly, these overall findings indicate that White educators are no more immune to having difficulties with racial dialogues than their White students. In one study, it was found that even the most experienced teachers were ill-prepared to productively and successfully facilitate racial discussions and interactions (Sue, Torino, et al., 2009). It is important to note that both students of color and White students were unanimous in attributing a successful or failed facilitation to the cultural awareness, knowledge, and skills of the teacher (Sue, Lin, et al., 2009; Sue, Rivera, et al., 2009).

The Way Forward

What Must Educators Do to Become Effective Facilitators of Difficult Dialogues on Race?: Overcoming Microaggressions

If the above conclusions are correct, then it bodes ill for race education in the United States unless educators seriously explore their own biases and prejudices, confront their own fears and apprehensions, and actively develop the awareness, knowledge, and skills to successfully facilitate difficult racial dialogues. A number of personal/professional developmental issues and strategies have been identified as potentially helpful (Bell, 2003; Bolgatz, 2005; Sue, Lin, et al., 2009; Sue, Rivera, et al., 2009; Sue, Torino, et al., 2009; Watt, 2007; Willow, 2008; Winter, 1977; Young, 2004).

1. Possess a Working Definition and Understanding of Racial Microaggressions and Difficult Dialogues

When critical consciousness and awareness of race issues, racial microaggressions, and racial dialogues are absent, it leads to disorientation, confusion, and bafflement that prevent problem definition and intervention. Thus it is imperative that educators possess a working definition and enlightened understanding of the cases, manifestation, and dynamics of racial microaggressions and difficult dialogues on race. As we have already spent considerable time on the former, I briefly supply one on the latter. Note, however, that the following definition of difficult dialogues is complex and must be understood in terms of lived reality to have true meaning.

> Broadly defined, difficult dialogues on race represent potentially threatening conversations or interactions between members of different racial or ethnic

(Continued)

groups when they (a) involve an unequal status relationship of power and privilege, (b) highlight major differences in worldviews, personalities, and perspectives, (c) are challenged publicly, (d) are found to be offensive to others, (e) may reveal biases and prejudices, and (f) trigger intense emotional responses (Sue & Constantine, 2007; Young, 2003). Any individual or group engaged in a difficult dialogue may feel at risk for potentially disclosing intimate thoughts, beliefs or feelings related to the topic of race. (Sue, Lin, et al., 2009, p. 184)

2. Understanding Self as a Racial/Cultural Being by Making the "Invisible, Visible"

Being an effective facilitator cannot occur unless the person is aware of her or his own values, biases, and assumptions about human behavior. Questions that he or she must constantly work on exploring include: What does it mean to be White, Black/African American, Asian American/Pacific Islander, Latino/Hispanic American, or Native American?

3. Intellectually Acknowledge One's Own Cultural Conditioning and Biases

On an intellectual/cognitive level, teachers must be able to acknowledge and accept the fact that they are products of the cultural conditioning of this society and, as such, they have inherited the biases, fears, and stereotypes of their ancestors.

This honest acknowledgment does several things: (1) it frees the teacher from the constant guardedness and vigilance exercised in denying their own racism, sexism, and other biases; (2) the teacher can use it to model truthfulness, openness, and honesty to students on conversations about race and racism; (3) it can communicate courage in making the teacher vulnerable by taking a risk to share with students their own biases, limitations, and attempts to deal with racism; and (4) it may encourage other students to approach the topic with honesty, because their own teacher is equally "flawed."

4. Emotional Comfort in Dealing with Race and Racism

On an emotional level, it is to the advantage of teachers if they are comfortable in discussing issues of race and racism, and/or being open, honest, and vulnerable to exploring their own biases and those of students. If students sense teachers are uncomfortable, it will only add fuel to their own discomfort and defenses. Attaining comfort means practice outside of the classroom, lived experience in interacting with people or groups

(Continued)

different from the teacher. It requires experience in dialoguing with people who differ from the teacher in terms of race, culture, and ethnicity. It ultimately means the teacher must be proactive in placing himself or herself in "uncomfortable" and new situations.

5. Understanding and Making Sense of One's Own Emotions

Because very few teachers can have experiences with all groups who differ from them in worldviews, they will always feel discomfort and confusion when different diversity/multicultural issues arise. These feelings are natural and should not be avoided; rather making sense of them is important. Being able to monitor them and infer meaning to feelings and emotional reactions and those of students are important in facilitating dialogues. It has been found that emotive responses often serve as "emotional roadblocks" to having a successful difficult dialogue. Feelings have diagnostic significance. For example, these feelings often have hidden meanings:

- I FEEL GUILTY. "I could be doing more."
- I FEEL ANGRY. "I don't like to feel I'm wrong."
- I FEEL DEFENSIVE. "Why blame me, I do enough already!"
- I FEEL TURNED OFF. "I have other priorities in life."
- I FEEL HELPLESS. "The problem is too big . . . what can I do?"
- I FEEL AFRAID. "I'm going to lose something" or "I don't know what will happen."

Unless a teacher gets beyond his or her own feeling level or that of students, blockages in learning will occur. If a teacher experiences these feelings, it helps to acknowledge them even when they do not make immediate sense. Teaching and encouraging students to do so as well will lessen their detrimental impact.

6. Control the Process and Not the Content

When a heated dialogue occurs on race, the duel between students is nearly always at the content level. When referring to dreams, Freud took the stance that the manifest content (conscious level) is not the "real" or latent content of the unconscious. Some common statements when racism is discussed, expressed by both White students and students of color, are:

- "So what, we women are oppressed too!"
- "My family didn't own slaves. I had nothing to do with the incarceration of Japanese Americans or the taking away of lands from Native Americans."

(Continued)

- "Excuse me, sir, but prejudice and oppression were and are part of every society in the world ad infinitum, not just the United States."
- "We Italians (Irish; Polish; Koreans) experienced severe discrimination when we arrived here. Did my family harp on the prejudice? We excelled despite the prejudice. Why? Because the basic founding principles of this country made it possible!"
- "I resent you calling me White. You are equally guilty of stereotyping. We are all human beings and we are all unique."

These emotive reactions are defensive maneuvers used to avoid feelings of guilt and blame. Unmask the difficult dialogue by (1) acknowledging the accuracy of statements (when appropriate), (2) intervening in the process rather than the content, (3) helping students see the difference between intention and impact, and (4) moving to the feeling tone level of the communication.

While these statements are to the greatest extent "true," they can hinder a successful dialogue by covering up the real dialogue. By agreeing with the statement, it no longer becomes the distraction and allows the facilitator to focus on the real issues, feelings, and conflicts in worldview. Avoid being "sucked into the dialogue" by taking sides in the debate of content. Rather intervene in the process by directing students to examine their own reactions and feelings. Encourage them to explore how their feelings may be saying something about them.

The blame game creates monologues. Help students differentiate between their intention and the impact. When a White female student says "So what, we women are oppressed as well!" Help them distinguish between intention and impact. Refocus the dialogue to feelings. "I wonder if you can tell me how and what you are feeling." Teacher: "John (Black student) has just agreed with you that women are an oppressed group. Does that make you feel better? (Usually the student says "no".) "No, I wonder why not?" (Try to help the student to explore why the feelings are still there. If there is continued difficulty, enlist speculation from the whole class. The last option is that you, the teacher, make the observation or interpretation.)

7. Do Not Be Passive or Allow the Dialogue to Be Brewed Over in Silence

When a difficult dialogue occurs and an impasse seems to have been reached, do not allow it to be brewed over in silence. The facilitator has

(Continued)

three options: (1) tell the class that you want the group to take it up at the next meeting, after everyone has had time to process their thoughts and feelings; (2) personally intervene by using interpersonal recall, microtraining, or any number of relationship models that attempt to have students listen, observe, and reflect or paraphrase back to one another; or (3) enlist the aid of the class members. This latter technique is very useful because it actively involves other members of the class by asking: "What do you see happening between John and Mary?"

8. Express Your Appreciation to the Participating Students

It is important to recognize, validate, and express appreciation to students for their courage, openness, and willingness to risk participating in a difficult dialogue. This strategy should be employed throughout the class.

- "Mary, I know this has been a very emotional experience for you, but I value your courage in sharing with the group your personal thoughts and feelings. I hope I can be equally brave when topics of sexism or homophobia are brought up in this class."
- "As a class, we have just experienced a difficult dialogue. I admire you all for not 'running away' but facing it squarely. I hope you all will continue to feel free about bringing up these topics. Real courage is being honest and risking offending others when the situation is not safe. Today, that is what I saw happen with several of you and for that, the class should be grateful."

These suggestions for dealing with racial microaggressions in the classroom and for successful facilitation of difficult dialogues on race may be equally applicable to conversations on gender, sexual orientation, and other difficult topics. Education holds one of the primary keys to combating and overcoming the harm delivered to people of color, women, LGBTs, and other marginalized groups. Unfortunately, few teachers or educators are sufficiently trained in antiracism, antisexism, and antiheterosexism strategies. If our society is to become truly inclusive and allow for equal access and opportunity, then our educational systems must reflect a multicultural philosophy and stance that is operationalized into the policies and practices of schools, the curriculum, teaching/learning styles, and in the teachers who educate our children.

CHAPTER TWELVE

Microaggressive Impact on Mental Health Practice

Years ago, while fulfilling my fieldwork hours as a social casework intern, I had the unfortunate experience of working with a Black client at the agency. I must admit that I have worked with very few African American clients and wanted to treat Peter like everyone else, a fellow human being. I pride myself on being fair and openminded, so I saw my first encounter with a Black client a test of my ability to establish rapport with someone of a different race. Even though I'm a White male, I tried not to let his being Black get in the way of our sessions.

At the onset, Peter came across as guarded, mistrustful, and frustrated when talking about his reasons for coming. While his intake form listed depression as the problem, he seemed more concerned about nonclinical matters. He spoke about his inability to find a job, about the need to obtain help with job-hunting skills, and about advice in how best to write his résumé. He was quite demanding in asking for advice and information. It was almost as if Peter wanted everything handed to him on a silver platter without putting any work into our sessions. Not only did he appear reluctant to take responsibility to change his own life, but also I felt he needed to go elsewhere for help. After all, this was a social service agency and not an employment agency. Further, I was a clinician, not a job specialist! Confronting him about his avoidance of responsibility would probably prove counterproductive, so I chose to use my best clinical skills and focus on his feelings. I reflected his feelings, paraphrased his thoughts, and summarized his dilemmas. Despite my best efforts, I sensed an increase in the tension level, and he seemed antagonistic toward me.

After several attempts by Peter to obtain direct advice from me, I stated, "My role is to help you make decisions on your own." It was clear that this angered Peter. Getting up in a very menacing manner, he stood over me and angrily shouted, "Forget it, man! I don't have time to play your silly games." For one brief moment, I felt in danger of being physically assaulted before he stormed out of the office.

This incident occurred several years ago, and I must admit that I was left with a very unfavorable impression of Blacks. I see myself as basically a good person who truly wants to help others less fortunate than myself. I know it sounds racist, but Peter's behavior only reinforces my belief that Black men have trouble controlling their anger, like to take the easy way out, and find it difficult to be open and trusting of others. If I am wrong in this belief, I hope this workshop [multicultural counseling/therapy] will help me better understand the Black personality. (Sue, 2006, pp. 43–44).

All helping professionals, whether they are in mental health, social service, health care, or employment, rely heavily upon the establishment of a working relationship between the help giver and the help seeker (Horvath & Symonds, 1991; Sue & Sue, 2008). The establishment of rapport is paramount to good therapy. In the helping professions, this is referred to as the "therapeutic working alliance," and most professionals agree that a successful outcome is related to the quality, nature, and strength of the therapeutic relationship (Constantine, 2007; Grencavage & Norcross, 1990; Kazdin, Marciano, & Whitley, 2005; Liu & Pope-Davis, 2005). On a dynamic level, counseling and psychotherapy may be defined as a process of interpersonal interaction, communication, and influence between helping professionals and their clients. For effective counseling to occur, several conditions must be a part of the process: (1) communication must be clear, accurate, and appropriate, and (2) the helping professional must establish credibility in the eyes of the client (Sue & Sue, 2008). When microaggressions are unknowingly and inappropriately delivered by the helping professional, communication clarity and credibility suffer with the possibility of creating a rupture or impasse in the helping relationship (Liu & Pope-Davis, 2005).

For example, a multitude of possible racial microaggressions are present in the vignette. The caseworker (1) defines Peter's race (being Black) as problematic, (2) professes a desire to be color blind, (3) ascribes to a racial stereotype that Black people are dangerous and potentially violent, (4) pathologizes the client's communication style, (5) operates from a belief in individual autonomy and effort, (6) engages in dysfunctional helping/patronization, and (7) denies any individual bias or racism. All of these beliefs or assumptions, if acted upon by the caseworker, might constitute various forms of racial microaggressions that would impede the therapeutic relationship. Let's use the above case study to illustrate how microaggressions impact clients, the counseling process, establishment of rapport, and the working alliance.

Racial Microaggression Number One: Blackness Is the Problem—Blame the Victim

It is quite obvious that the social work intern is sincere in his desire to help the client. Yet, his worldview reflects a dichotomy between recognizing the race of the client (African American) and attempting to avoid acknowledging it. The caseworker seems to believe the client's race is the problem rather than his unconscious perception of "blackness." His statement that he tried not to let Peter's "being Black get in the way" of the session is a typical statement often made by Whites who unconsciously subscribe to a belief that to be different is to be bad, deviant, pathological, abnormal, or "the problem." This assumption assumes that the locus of the problem resides internally with Peter's racial heritage, and stereotypes that are attributed to it. Often we hear people talk about minorities as "problem people": the "Black problem," the "Asian problem," the "Gay problem," the "immigrant problem," or the "person of color problem." In reality, color is not the problem. It is society's perception of color that more accurately represents the problem. In other words, the locus of the problem (racism, sexism, and homophobia) resides not in marginalized groups, but in the society at large.

Adding to the "blame the victim" mentality is the clash between the equating of mental health with individualism, individual responsibility, and autonomy (Sue & Sue, 2008). Because people are seen as being responsible for their own actions and predicaments, clients are expected to "make decisions on their own" and to "be primarily responsible for their fate in life." The traditional clinical role is to encourage self-exploration so that clients can act on their own behalf. The individual-centered approach tends to view problems as residing within the person. If something goes wrong, it is the client's fault. Faulty diagnosis is clearly seen in the caseworker's words: Peter's wanting things handed to him on a "silver platter," his "avoidance of responsibility," and his "wanting to take the easy way out" are symbolic of social stereotypes that Blacks are lazy and unmotivated. In previous chapters we pointed out how many difficulties encountered by minority clients reside externally to them and that they should not be faulted for the obstacles they encounter. To do so is to engage in victim blaming.

Racial Microaggression Number Two: Color Blindness

Very much related to seeing race as problematic is the myth of color blindness: If color is the problem, let's "pretend not to see it." Studies suggest this is nearly impossible to do because race and gender, for example, are the most readily and automatically identifiable and categorized features in the human encounter (Apfelbaum, Sommers, & Norton, 2008; Banaji, 2001; Dovidio, 2001; Dovidio, Gaertner, Kawakami, & Hodson, 2002). Thus, it is difficult to overlook the fact that a client is Black, Asian American, Hispanic, and so forth. To claim color blindness strains the helping professional's honesty and challenges his/her credibility. There are many other downsides to a color-blind approach as well.

First, helping professionals may actually be obscuring their understandings of who their clients really are and prevent therapists from relating to minority life experiences. Issues of prejudice and discrimination are thus ignored in the life experiences of marginalized groups. Efforts to "treat everyone the same" mean pretending not to see or respond to differences in client history, experience, and group-specific qualities. Second, overlooking one's group membership not only minimizes and negates racial, gender, and sexual-orientation differences, but it attacks the social group identities of individuals, and serves to allow Whites, in this case, to avoid guilt associated with White privilege (Bowser & Hunt, 1996; Neville, Lilly, Duran, Lee, & Browne, 2000; Wildman & Davis, 2002). Third, recent research suggests that a color-blind approach in therapy is often associated with increased levels of unconscious racism, lower empathic understanding of client concerns, increased nonverbal signs of anxieties on racial topics, lower levels of cultural competence, and increased tendency to attribute fault to the client (Constantine, 2007; Burkard & Knox, 2004; Spanierman, Poteat, Wang, & Oh, 2008; Utsey, Gernat, & Hammar, 2005).

Racial Microaggression Number Three: Ascription of Dangerousness (Criminality)

The ascription of dangerousness/criminality and the pathologizing of cultural communication styles have been identified as two common racial microaggressions directed toward Black Americans (Sue, Capodilupo, et al., 2007;

Sue, Capodilupo, Nadal, & Torino, 2008). The caseworker who describes Peter as "menacing" and states that he was in fear of being assaulted paints the picture of the hostile, angry, and violent Black male—a common image of African Americans shared by many Whites in society (Jones, 1997; Ridley, 2005). In a major possible misdiagnosis, the intern concludes that Blacks have difficulty controlling their anger and trusting others, and are unmotivated. It is highly possible that the emotional outburst by Peter might be due to real frustration and anger brought on by the caseworker's inability to relate to Peter's pressing situation. Or the fear of the client may be due to a more passionate cultural communication style evident in many African Americans. Black styles of communication have been found to be high-keyed, animated, heated, interpersonal, and confrontational (Kochman, 1994). Much affect, emotions, and feelings are generated relative to conversation conventions of White Americans which are detached, unemotional, objective, and non-challenging. Among many Black Americans, passion indicates honesty and sincerity, while objective and unemotional communications indicate "fronting" (insincerity or concealing one's true feelings) (Kochman, 1981, 1994; Sue & Sue, 2008). These contrasting communication styles can cause the intern to misinterpret the meaning of Peter's actions, especially if a stereotype of "Black dangerousness" exists.

Racial Microaggression Number Four: Culturally Insensitive and Antagonistic Treatment

Culturally insensitive treatment has been identified as a microaggressive theme directed toward Black Americans (Constantine, 2007). The imposition of antagonistic therapy due to an ethnocentric definition of appropriate help-giving can be forced upon clients of color, resulting in unneeded and inappropriate services (Constantine, 2007; Constantine & Sue, 2007). From the perspective of Western psychology, standards of practice and codes of ethics in psychotherapeutic practice stress what has been called therapeutic taboos: (1) helping professionals do not give advice and suggestions, and (2) clinicians should avoid disclosing their thoughts and feelings because they may unduly influence clients and arrest individual development (Sue & Sue, 2008). There is great fear that becoming too involved with clients emotionally may result in loss of objectivity and blur the boundaries of the helping relationship (Pope & Vasquez, 2005). In contrast to the Western European view, however, Parham (1997) states that a fundamental African principle is that human essence is realized only in moral relations to others (collectivity instead of individuality): "Consequently, application of an African-centered worldview will cause one to question the need for objectivity absent emotions, the need for distance rather than connectedness, and the need for dichotomous relationships rather than multiple roles" (p. 110).

The caseworker's avoidance of giving advice and suggestions, perceiving his role as a facilitator of self-exploration, and separating himself from Peter might be viewed as inappropriate and a barrier to establishing a therapeutic alliance. In other words, the African American perspective views the helping relationship as bound together emotionally and spiritually. The European American style of objectivity encourages separation that may be interpreted by Peter as uninvolved, uncaring, insincere, and dishonest—that is, "playing silly games" (Paniagua, 1998).

Racial Microaggression Number Five: Denial of Individual Racism or Racial Biases

The belief that one is free of biases and somehow immune from inheriting the racial, gender, and sexual-orientation prejudices of society has been challenged in many studies, scholarly analyses, and in guidelines and standards developed by professional organizations (American Counseling Association, 1999; American Psychological Association, 2003; Biernat, 2003; Broverman & Broverman, 1970; Dovidio & Gaertner, 1991, 1993, 2000; Greene, 2000; Pope & Vasquez, 2005; Swim, Mallet, & Stangor, 2004). Earlier, we indicated how microaggressive communications operate on two different levels, from the explicit statement "I'm not a racist, I have many Black friends" to the metacommunication (hidden), "I am immune to racism, so don't blame me."

It is obvious the caseworker experiences himself as a good, moral, and fair-minded human being who consciously wants to help an African American client. At the beginning of the case narrative, he anticipates that working with Peter will be a test of his unbiased nature. The intern ends by hoping that the workshop training will "help me better understand the Black personality." Like most counselors, he views prejudice, discrimination, racism, and sexism as overt and intentional acts of unfairness and violence; however, unintentional and covert forms of bias may be the greater enemy in the therapeutic sessions because they are unseen and more pervasive:

> Unintentional behavior is perhaps the most insidious form of racism. Unintentional racists are unaware of the harmful consequences of their behavior. They may be

well-intentioned, and on the surface, their behavior may appear to be responsible. Because individuals, groups, or institutions that engage in unintentional racism do not wish to do harm, it is difficult to get them to see themselves as racists. They are more likely to deny their racism. . . . The major challenge facing counselors is to overcome unintentional racism and provide more equitable service delivery. (Ridley, 1995, p. 38)

In one telling example in the helping professions, it was found that traditional cultural competency training increased the awareness, knowledge, and skills of trainees to work with people of color, but it left untouched implicit attitudes and biases (Boysen & Vogel, 2008). The social work intern may sincerely believe in his unbiased nature, but may still hold powerful prejudices that make their appearance in the therapeutic encounter. There is a common saying that many Black Americans use to describe the attitude of their White brothers and sisters: "Say one thing, but mean another." Behind that statement is a belief that Whites are deceptive, conceal their prejudices, and likely to justify their biases through rationalizations. Thus, in a counseling situation, clients of color are likely to approach the White helping professional with considerable hesitation and mistrust. When White helping professionals are unaware of their biased actions, they only reinforce the beliefs of the clients and create a rupture that may be irreparable in the therapeutic relationship.

Conclusion

In conclusion, these five racial microaggressions represent a few that may interact in multiple and complex ways to create ruptures and impasses in the counseling/therapy relationship. If racial microaggressions occur in everyday life, they also occur frequently in nearly all helping relationships. Three major barriers to effective therapy seem operative in this particular case: (1) therapy sessions are likely to represent a microcosm of race relations in our larger society, (2) mental health professionals often inherit the biases of their forebears, and (3) the clinical process represents a European American definition of normality and abnormality that clashes with the worldviews and life experiences of diverse groups. A helping professional's ability to establish rapport and a working relationship is seriously undermined when his or her attitudes, beliefs, and behaviors fill the therapeutic hour with racial microaggressions. Table 12.1 summarizes common counseling/therapy microaggressions identified as often occurring in the therapeutic relationship and directed toward clients of color, women, and LGBTs.

Table 12.1   Examples of Racial, Gender, and Sexual-Orientation Microaggressions in Therapeutic Practice

THEMES	MICROAGGRESSION	MESSAGE
Alien in One's Own Land When Asian Americans and Latino Americans are assumed to be foreign-born	A White client does not want to work with an Asian American therapist because she "will not understand my problem."	You are not American.
	A White therapist tells an American-born Latino client that he or she should seek a Spanish-speaking therapist.	
Ascription of Intelligence Assigning a degree of intelligence to a person of color or woman based on their race or gender	A school counselor reacts with surprise when an Asian American student has trouble on the math portion of a standardized test.	All Asians are smart and good at math.
	A career counselor asks a Black or Latino student "Do you think you're ready for college?"	It is unusual for people of color to succeed.
	A school counselor reacts with surprise that a female student scored high on a math portion of a standardized test.	It is unusual for women to be smart and good in math.
Color Blindness Statements that indicate that a White person does not want to acknowledge race	A therapist says "I think you are being too paranoid. We should emphasize similarities, not people's differences" when a client of color attempts to discuss her feelings about being the only person of color at her job and feeling alienated and dismissed by her coworkers.	Race and culture are not important variables that affect people's lives.
	A client of color expresses concern in discussing racial issues with her therapist. Her therapist replies, "When I see you, I don't see color."	Your racial experiences are not valid.

(Continued)

Table 12.1 *(Continued)*

THEMES	MICROAGGRESSION	MESSAGE
Criminality/Assumption of Criminal Status A person of color is presumed to be dangerous, criminal, or deviant, based solely on their race	When a Black client states that she was accused of stealing from work, the therapist encourages the client to explore how she might have contributed to her employer's mistrust of her.	You are a criminal.
	A therapist takes great care to ask all substance-abuse questions in an intake with a Native American client, and is disbelieving of the client's nonexistent history with substances.	You are deviant.
Use of Sexist/Heterosexist Language Terms that exclude or degrade women and LGB groups	During the intake session, a female client discloses that she has been in her current relationship for one year. The therapist asks how long the client has known her boyfriend.	Heterosexuality is the norm.
	When an adult female client explains she is feeling isolated at work, her male therapist asks, "Aren't there any girls you can gossip with there?"	Application of language that applies to adolescent females to adult females; your problems are trivial.
Denial of Individual Racism/ Sexism/Heterosexism A statement made when a member of the power group renounces their biases	A client of color asks his or her therapist about how race affects their working relationship. The therapist replies, "Race does not affect the way I treat you."	Your racial and/or ethnic experience is not important.
	A client of color expresses hesitancy in discussing racial issues with his White female therapist. She replies "I understand. As a woman, I face discrimination, also."	Your racial oppression is no different from my gender oppression.

(Continued)

Table 12.1 *(Continued)*

THEMES	MICROAGGRESSION	MESSAGE
	A therapist's nonverbal behavior conveys discomfort when a bisexual male client is describing a recent sexual experience with a man. When he asks her about it, she insists she has "no negative feelings toward gay people" and says it is important to keep the conversation on him.	I am incapable of homonegativity, yet I am unwilling to explore this.
Myth of Meritocracy Statements that assert that race or gender does not play a role in succeeding in career advancement or education	A school counselor tells a Black student that "if you work hard, you can succeed like everyone else."	People of color/ women are lazy and/or incompetent and need to work harder. If you don't succeed, you have only yourself to blame (blaming the victim).
	A female client visits a career counselor to share her concerns that a male coworker was chosen for a managerial position over her, despite the fact that she is better qualified and has been with the company longer. The counselor responds that "he must have been better suited for some of the job requirements."	
Pathologizing Cultural Values/Communication Styles The notion that the values and communication styles of the dominant/White culture are ideal	A Black client is loud, emotional, and confrontational in a counseling session. The therapist diagnoses her with Borderline Personality Disorder.	Assimilate to dominant culture.
	A client of Asian or Native American descent has trouble maintaining eye contact with his therapist. The therapist diagnoses him with a Social Anxiety Disorder.	

(Continued)

Table 12.1   *(Continued)*

THEMES	MICROAGGRESSION	MESSAGE
	Advising a client, "Do you really think your problem stems from racism?	Leave your cultural baggage outside.
Second-Class Citizen Occurs when a member of the power group is given preferential treatment over a target group member	A male client calls and requests a session time that is currently taken by a female client. The therapist grants the male client the appointment without calling the female client to see if she can change times.	Males are more valued than women.
	Clients of color are not welcomed or acknowledged by receptionists.	White clients are more valued than clients of color.
Culturally Insensitive/ Antagonistic Treatment Occurs when ethnocentric definitions of counseling/ therapy are imposed on clients	A therapist refuses to play other roles but the traditional one of self-exploration.	There is only one way to be cured: the White, Western European way.
Traditional Gender Role Prejudicing and Stereotyping Occurs when expectations of traditional roles or stereotypes are conveyed	A therapist continually asks the middle-aged female client about dating and "putting herself out there," despite the fact that the client has not expressed interest in exploring this area.	Women should be married, and dating should be an important topic/part of your life.
	A gay male client has been with his partner for 5 years. His therapist continually probes his desires to meet other men and be unfaithful.	Gay men are promiscuous. Gay men cannot have monogamous relationships.
	A therapist raises her eyebrows when a female client mentions that she has had a one-night stand.	Women should not be sexually adventurous.
Sexual Objectification Occurs when women are treated like objects at men's disposal	A male therapist puts his hands on a female client's back as she walks out of the session.	Your body is not yours.
	A male therapist is looking at his female client's breasts while she is talking.	Your body/appearance is for men's enjoyment and pleasure.

(Continued)

Table 12.1   *(Continued)*

THEMES	MICROAGGRESSION	MESSAGE
Assumption of Abnormality Occurs when it is implied that there is something wrong with being LGBT	When discussing her bisexuality, the therapist continues to imply that there is a "crisis of identity."	Bisexuality represents confusion about sexual orientation.
	The therapist of a 20-year-old lesbian inadvertently refers to her sexuality as a "phase."	Your sexuality is something that is not stable.

Source: Adapted from Sue, Capodilupo, et al., 2007 and Sue & Capodilupo, 2008.

Given that clients of color are frequently the victims of microaggressions from helping professionals, clients of color may become suspicious of their motives, believe they are untrustworthy, feel oppressed rather than liberated, become alienated, and fail to continue in the sessions. When the emotional climate is negative, and when little trust or understanding exists between social worker and client, the clinical process can be both ineffective and destructive.

SOCIOPOLITICAL FACTORS IN THE HELPING PROFESSIONAL'S CREDIBILITY

It is certainly ironic when many people who seek therapy because of problems in their lives are further damaged by microaggressions delivered by well-intentioned helping professionals. Worse yet, they are never provided the help they need if they prematurely terminate their sessions, or if they are provided with inappropriate and antagonistic therapy.

It is important to note, however, that while we will continue to discuss the therapeutic relationship, what occurs between therapists and clients is no different from relationships between physicians and patients, police and citizens, teachers and students, sales clerks and customers, employers and employees, coworkers, neighbors, and family members. Racial, gender, and sexual-orientation microaggressions can prevent the development of trust in the formation of a burgeoning relationship, or seriously alter, impair, or end an existing one. For the helping professional, it is important to recognize how sociopolitical factors play a significant role in the manifestation of microaggressions.

Historical Dimensions Affecting Trust–Mistrust

In previous chapters, we build a strong case that the sociopolitical history of race relations in the United States has been the history of racism (Sue, 2003). In the mental health field, that history is equally unenviable. A common theme throughout the psychiatric and psychological scientific literature is one of equating minorities with pathology (Jones, 1997; Samuda, 1998). Sue and Sue (2008) summarize the groundbreaking work of Thomas and Sillen (1972) and cite numerous examples of false beliefs couched as scientific facts: (1) mental health for Blacks was contentment with subservience, (2) anxiety was the result of Blacks living under "unnatural" conditions of freedom, (3) influential medical journals portrayed Blacks as inferior to Whites in anatomical development and neurological functioning, (4) the brains of Blacks were smaller and less developed than Whites, (5) they were less prone to mental illness because their "minds were simple," (6) dreams of Blacks were more juvenile and less complex than Whites, and (7) "normal" Blacks were "happy-go-lucky" and content to be taken care of by Whites. Such beliefs were present throughout history and are reflected, albeit in more sophisticated and disguised forms, to this present day.

- de Gobineau's (1915) "Essay on the Inequality of Human Races" and Darwin's (1859) *The Origin of Species by Means of Natural Selection* supported the notion of the inferiority of "lower races." Galton (1869) stated explicitly that African "negroes" were "half-witted men" who made "childish, stupid and simpleton like mistakes."
- Terman (1916), creator of the famed and influential Binet tests of intelligence, concluded that Blacks, Mexican Americans, and Spanish Indians were "uneducable."
- The first President of the American Psychological Association, Dr. G. Stanley Hall, believed that human groups existed at different stages of biological evolution and placed Africans, Indians, and Chinese much lower than Whites; they were "adolescent races" in incomplete development (Thomas & Sillen, 1972). The fact that Hall was a renowned psychologist and often referred to as the "father of child study" did not prevent him from inheriting the racial biases of the society.
- Shockley (1972) believed that the accumulation of weak or low intelligence genes in Blacks would seriously lower overall intelligence of the general population and that they either should not be allowed to bear children or be sterilized.

- Publication of *The Bell Curve* by Hernstein and Murray in 1994 set off a firestorm of controversy concerning recommendations that allocation of funds to Head Start and Affirmative Action did little good because intelligence was inherited. Instead, such funds should go to White Americans who could profit from increased enrichment.

While many of these beliefs are now recognized as falsehoods and stereotypes on a cognitive and rational level, a number of surveys continue to reveal that many White Americans continue to hold such beliefs in varying forms. Frighteningly, approximately 20% of Whites expressed public beliefs that Blacks are innately inferior in thinking ability and that they have thicker craniums (Plous & Williams, 1995). It is disturbing to think about how many Whites privately hold such beliefs and how many well-intentioned people may be unaware that they hold them.

UNDERUTILIZATION OF MENTAL HEALTH SERVICES AND PREMATURE TERMINATION

Given the historical and continuing embeddedness of bias and prejudice that reside in most helping professionals, we can ask the question, "How do experiences of microaggressions with their accompanying feelings of invalidation, insult, denigration, and disrespect impact clients of color, or those contemplating seeking help?" In a series of groundbreaking studies on the utilization of mental health services by American Indians, Asian Americans, Blacks, and Hispanics, it was found that (1) all four groups of color underutilized traditional mental health services and (2) they terminated after only one contact with the therapist at a rate of over 50% in comparison to a 30% rate for White clients (S. Sue, Allen, & Conaway, 1975; S. Sue et al., 1974; S. Sue & McKinney, 1975). While there are variations and differences in other studies (public vs. private services, types of problems presented, etc.), these findings are supported by more recent ones as well (Barnes, 1994; Burkard & Knox, 2004; Kearney, Draper, & Baron, 2005; S. Sue, Fujino, Hu, Takeuchi, & Zane, 1991).

Underutilization

A number of reasons have been proposed for why people of color are less likely to utilize mental health services. First, people of color may perceive mental health providers as lacking in understanding of their lifestyles and experiences and unable to relate to them (Sue & Sue, 2008). This perception is reinforced because most mental health providers are White (environmental microaggression). The lack of providers of color may send a loud microaggressive message to the minority community that they are not welcome, or that the help they seek will not be appropriate to them (Burkard & Knox, 2004). Second, the services provided may be perceived as antagonistic or incompatible to their cultural perceptions of helping. The reliance on a one-to-one in the office "talk therapy" aimed at insight may not be valued by people of color who desire concrete advice and information (Parham, 1999). Third, potential stigma may also diminish service utilization. Among Asian Americans, for example, psychological problems may be viewed as weaknesses bringing shame and disgrace not only to the client but his/her family as well (Kearney, Draper, & Baron, 2005). Fourth, culturally appropriate forms of "healing" or reliance on indigenous community resources may be the preferred choice of persons of color (Leong, Wagner, & Tata, 1995). In this respect, people of color may prefer seeking support, advice, and suggestions from community agencies such as their churches or indigenous, informal healing networks.

Last, it is possible, but improbable, that people of color are "mentally healthier" and do not require as many mental health services as their counterparts. While all the other reasons just cited contain validity, this last one is not supported by indirect data. Although the manifestation of psychological disorders is culturally determined, their rates appear similar across all groups (Sue & Sue, 2008). If true, people of color are likely to seek help from traditional European American sources only when more culturally appropriate means have failed to give them relief. Thus, we might conjecture that those who seek mental health services would be more likely to be severely disturbed than their White counterparts. In other words, clients of color are more likely to be in greater distress and evidence greater pathology. Indeed, in a nationwide sample of 1,166 clients of African American, Asian American, White, and Latino students across 40 university counseling centers, it was found that clients of color had higher levels of distress than Whites before and after their sessions: Asian Americans, followed by Latinos, African Americans, and then Whites (Kearney et al., 2005).

Premature Termination
While stigma plays an important role in keeping certain groups of color from utilizing mental health services, beliefs that services are irrelevant to their needs and operate from a biased White Western European perspective constitute a major racial microaggression that discourages traditional mental health

utilization (Burkard & Knox, 2004). Likewise, racial microaggressions may also explain why clients of color frequently fail to return for appointments (Sue, Capodilupo, et al., 2007). Most research indicates that Whites attend many more therapy sessions than clients of color, who often fail to return (premature termination) even when scheduled and in distress (Barnes, 1994; Kearney et al., 2005; S. Sue, Fujino, Hu, Takeuchi, & Zane, 1991). Sue and Sue (2008) have argued that the generic characteristics of counseling (culture-bound values, class-bound values, and linguistic factors) might be antagonistic to the life values and experiences of clients of color; they are made to feel uncomfortable and oppressed in sessions with therapists who impose their standards of normality and abnormality on culturally diverse clients, and communicate to them how they *should* think, feel, and act.

Not only do these Western approaches to mental health cause problems for clients of color, but the well-intentioned helping professional may communicate these restrictive qualities via racial microaggressions. Our opening case example illustrates a complex interplay of racial microaggressions that damage and rupture the helping relationship. Counseling and psychotherapy depend on the establishment of a deeply personal relationship between the therapist and client. Therapy is an intimate personal journey that relies on a trusting relationship and the credibility of the helper. Counselors are trained to listen, to communicate understanding, to be empathic, to be objective, to value the client's integrity, to uphold the best interests of the client, and to use their skills and expertise to aid clients in solving their problems (Grencavage & Norcross, 1990). More importantly, the best predictor of a successful outcome in counseling is *the client's perception of an accepting and positive relationship* (Horvath & Symonds, 1991). How clients of color perceive counselors and helping relationships is more important than how counselors perceive helpers. Racial microaggressions destroy or seriously impair the establishment of rapport and a working relationship. A failed therapeutic relationship may result in inability to share intimate fears and concerns, lead to a premature termination, or lead to a failure to return for a future session.

CULTURAL MISTRUST IN MULTICULTURAL COUNSELING RELATIONSHIPS

What therapists do and say in sessions can either enhance or diminish their credibility. When a therapist appears inattentive, seems to lack empathy or understanding, or makes/engages in offensive microaggressions, clients of color may become guarded, vigilant, and not trust the relationship sufficiently to disclose personal information. A relationship distance between Whites and people of color has been identified as due to aversive racism and cultural mistrust (Dovidio et al., 2002; Crocker, Major, & Steele, 1998; Ridley, 2005). A large proportion of White Americans report never having an intimate relationship with someone from another race and may be disinclined to do so because of unconscious bias (Cheatham, 1994; Sue & Sue, 2008). On the other hand, people of color may have difficulty trusting Whites in light of the history of discrimination and continuing experiences of oppression (Jones, 1997; Ridley, 2005; Sue & Sue, 2008). Clients of color, therefore, are likely to approach a therapy session with considerable guardedness and mistrust of the White helping professional.

The term "cultural mistrust" refers to a suspicion of the intent and motives of Whites, their rules and regulations, and their institutions (Terrell & Terrell, 1984; Whaley, 2001). The assumption is that White Americans have inherited a worldview of superiority, are likely to treat people of color as inferior, to be biased against them, and to act in ways that are detrimental to psychological well-being and life decisions (Constantine, 2007). Thus, the guardedness exhibited by people of color toward White Americans may be based upon reality rather than pathological perceptions (Ridley, 2005). During the Third World and the Civil Rights movements, for example, many people of color openly questioned the well-intentioned motives of Whites. Rather than seeing their mistrust of Whites as "paranoia" or pathology, many Black helping professionals stressed that it was a healthy psychological mechanism. Cultural mistrust on the part of Blacks toward Whites has been described as a functional survival mechanism used to combat racism and to prevent being deceived (Grier & Cobbs, 1971).

Heightened Perceptual Wisdom

Because of their experiences with racism, sexism, and heterosexism, many marginalized groups have developed a heightened perceptual wisdom (Sue, 2003) that allows them to more accurately discern the truth as it relates to oppressors (Hanna, Talley, & Guindon, 2000). This power of perception is all important for those most disempowered because it allows them to not be easily fooled, to read between the lines, and to intuitively ascertain the true attitudes, motives, and meanings of biased contradictory messages of oppressors. Thus, people of color may become hypervigilant toward Whites; women become hypervigilant toward men; and LGBTs become hypervigilant toward straights. The vigilance allows marginalized groups to develop an intuitive understanding of the actions, thoughts, and unstated motives of well-intentioned Whites, men, and heterosexuals.

Nonverbal Communications

Heightened perceptual wisdom has been associated with the ability to accurately read nonverbal communications (Hanna et al., 2000). People of color and women have been found to be better "readers" of nonverbal cues than White men (Jenkins, 1982; Pearson, 1985; Weber, 1985). Part of this deals with the need of those with least power in interpersonal relationships to understand those who have the power to influence or determine their lives. Blacks also have a saying that speaks to the importance of nonverbal communications: *"If you really want to know where Mr. White is coming from, don't listen to what he says, but how he says it."* Behind this statement is the belief that nonverbals are least under conscious control and more likely to reveal the true motives of the speaker or actor (DePaulo, 1992; Kochman, 1981; Singelis, 1994). Clues to conscious deception and unconscious biases are believed to be revealed in nonverbal communications. Nonverbal cues include proxemics (use of personal and interpersonal distance), kinesics (body movements—facial expression, posture, gestures, and eye contact), and paralanguage (vocal cues—pauses, loudness of voice, hesitations, silences, inflection, rate of speech, etc.). In a study of interracial interactions, for example, it was found that while claiming to be unbiased and comfortable in discussing race topics, White counselor trainees' speech patterns revealed anxiety, stammering, constriction, and tangential speech. In other words, the unconscious messages contradicted the conscious ones. When racial, gender, or sexual-orientation microaggressions are delivered, people of color, women, and LGBTs are likely to read the contextualized meanings of the communication, to use nonverbal cues to discern the truth, and to evaluate the credibility of the communicator on the basis of the hidden message imparted. While a microaggression may be invisible to the perpetrator, it is quite clear to the target person or group.

COUNSELOR/THERAPIST CREDIBILITY

In the therapeutic context, helping professionals who are perceived as credible are more likely to exert greater social influence over their client's attitudes, beliefs, and behaviors than those who are perceived as less credible (Strong, 1968). Social psychological studies on interpersonal influence suggest that credibility can be broken down into two components: expertness and trustworthiness (Heesacker, Conner, & Pritchard, 1995; Heppner & Frazier, 1992; Strong & Schmidt, 1970). Expertness is an *ability* dimension while trustworthiness is a *motivational* component. The former refers to how informed, capable, intelligent, and skilled counselors appear, while the latter refers to the motivational validity of helpers. Both summate to determine credibility, but they may also work somewhat independently of one another. Helping professionals may possess high expertness-high trustworthiness; low expertness-low trustworthiness; high expertness-low trustworthiness; and high trustworthiness-low expertness. In the area of cultural mistrust, it would seem that the trustworthiness dimension would be central in determining credibility.

Expertness

In general, this dimension of credibility involves how much knowledge, skills, experiences, and training therapists possess to communicate to clients that they are experts and qualified to help. Expertness is generally a function of reputation, evidence of specialized training, and culturally appropriate therapeutic actions during sessions. Having worked in communities of color, attended special workshops on multicultural therapy, and having clients of color attest to their expertise may enhance expertness for White therapists who work with minority populations. Having advanced degrees or certificates from prestigious institutions, however, does not necessarily enhance expertness. Rather, cultural mistrust may simply predispose clients of color to perceive these credentials as indicative of ethnocentric training; it may actually have the opposite effect of reducing credibility. For many clients of color, expertness is most likely determined through behavioral-expertise, the ability to evidence culturally appropriate diagnosis, and using strategies and interventions consistent with the cultural values and lifestyles of culturally diverse populations. Again, what counselors say or do, how problems or issues are defined and conceptualized, and their awareness, knowledge, and skills related to the specific population are paramount in determining expertness.

Trustworthiness

It is possible for helping professionals to be high in expertness and low in trustworthiness. In my years of work in the field, I have concluded that trustworthiness in multicultural counseling is perhaps the most important dimension of credibility. A therapist with good cognitive knowledge of minority groups, but who is not trusted, will ultimately possess low credibility. A therapist with low knowledge of minority groups but who is trustworthy will often be forgiven for their lack of knowledge or expertise. Of course, both expertness and trustworthiness are important, but it is possible for helpers to possess expertise, yet not be able to establish a therapeutic alliance because they are not trusted. Trustworthiness encompasses factors such as sincerity, authenticity, honesty, and a perceived lack of motivation for personal gain. Clients of color often enter therapy with these questions related to trustworthiness: *"Is the helping professional sincere in his or her desire to help me?" "Will they be honest in owning up to their prejudices and biases when working with me?" "Will it interfere with our ability to establish a working relationship?" "Will the therapist be open with me rather than become defensive when race issues/topics are raised?"* Finally, a question in the mind of many clients of color is *"What makes this White helping professional any different from my White teacher, White counselor, White neighbor, or White employer, who professed a desire to help, but wound up stereotyping, disrespecting, and denigrating my racial/cultural heritage and identity?"*

All of these questions entertained by clients of color and other marginalized groups are generally tests of "trustworthiness." In the therapeutic session, culturally diverse clients are likely to engage in actions or make statements in the form of subtle and overt challenges that are tests aimed at trustworthiness or expertness. Depending how one responds to these challenges in the therapeutic session will either enhance or negate credibility. When microaggressions come from the speech or actions of the helping professional, trustworthiness is severely diminished. The following excerpt adapted by Sue (2006, pp. 60–61) from Pedersen's triad training model (1981) illustrates a test of trustworthiness:

BLACK FEMALE CLIENT: *Students in my drama class expect me to laugh when they do "steppin' fetchin'" routines and tell Black jokes. . . . I'm wondering whether you've ever laughed at any of those jokes.*

WHITE MALE SOCIAL WORKER: [long pause] *Yes, I'm sure I have. Have you ever laughed at any White jokes?*

BLACK CLIENT: *What's a White joke?*

SOCIAL WORKER: *I don't know* [laughs nervously, strained look on face, constricted tone of voice]. *I suppose one making fun of Whites. Look, I'm Irish. Have you ever laughed at Irish jokes?*

BLACK CLIENT: *People tell me many jokes, but I don't laugh at racial jokes. I feel we're all minorities and should respect each other.*

Asking the question about whether the social worker has ever laughed at a Black joke is a direct test of honesty and sincerity (trustworthiness). As almost everyone has laughed at racist jokes, to answer "no" would appear a deliberate lie or by denying or refusing to answer would appear to be concealing the truth. There are many layers to the challenge being presented to the social worker. On the surface one can make a case that the Black client is trying to find out whether the therapist has laughed at racist jokes, and at a deeper level, some might argue it is an attempt to find out whether the person is a racist. In actuality, the client, rightly or wrongly, already knows the answer and assumes all Whites have racial biases. The true test here is one of trustworthiness: "How honest and open are you about your racism, are you aware of it, and will it interfere with our ability to work together?" While the social worker seems to have answered truthfully, he also conveys considerable discomfort with the question (nonverbally) and defends himself by attempting to get the Black client to admit to also being equally guilty (laughing at White jokes). In this case, trustworthiness suffers because the social worker appears more motivated to preserve his own self-image and esteem by making the client appear equally biased.

The Way Forward

Implications and Directions in Mental Health Practice: Overcoming Microaggressions

Prior to our discussion of implications for mental health practice, it is important to note that racial, gender, and sexual-orientation micro-aggressions occur in almost all human encounters and interactions. I have purposely used the clinical realm to illustrate how microaggressions make their appearance in the counselor-client interaction, provoke mistrust toward majority group members from marginalized groups, impair the quality and nature of relationships, and prevent target individuals or groups from receiving needed services. The nature of intergroup and interpersonal relations along racial, gender, and sexual-orientation lines is played out in all types of relationships and encounters (counselor–client, teacher–student, employer–employee, doctor–patient, neighbor–neighbor, and among family members, coworkers, and students), and in nearly every setting (mental health agencies, hospitals, businesses, industries, other places of employment, classrooms, communities, municipalities, etc.). Thus, many of the suggestions given below for mental health practitioners

(Continued)

about dealing with microaggressions are equally applicable to interpersonal interactions of nearly all forms.

One of the greatest challenges facing mental health practitioners is how to become culturally competent in delivering relevant services to people of color, women, LGBTs, and other marginalized groups such as those with disabilities, religious minorities, and immigrants/refugees. Traditional training such as taking courses, workshops, and reading the professional literature on diverse groups in our society may be helpful, but it seems to have minimal effect on implicit biases (Boysen & Vogel, 2008). In other words, multicultural training may help in acquiring expertise (knowledge and skills), but if it does not tap into and change unconscious and unintentional biases, trustworthiness will not be established. Researchers, practitioners, and professional organizations in mental health have come up with guiding principles and suggestions that may best overcome aversive forms of racism, sexism, and heterosexism that are manifested in microaggressions (American Counseling Association, 1999; American Psychological Association, 2003; CCPTP, ACCTA, SCP, 2009; Hughes, 2005; Johnson & Longerbeam, 2007; Sue, 2003; Sue, Arredondo, & McDavis, 1992).

1. The development of a vision statement (as also discussed in Chapter 10) can guide areas of education and training and mental health practice and is a necessity in framing the values/goals/objectives of mental health practice. The Council of Counseling Psychology Training Programs, the Association of Counseling Center Training Agencies, and the Society of Counseling Psychology have been among the first to create a "Counseling Psychology Model Training Values Statement Addressing Diversity" (CCPTP, ACCTA, & SCP, 2009). This model statement on the values associated with diversity can serve as a valuable guide for the helping professions in general (Winterowd, Adams, Miville, & Mintz, 2009). It explicitly states that (1) respect for values different from one's own is a central value of counseling; (2) the field exists within multicultural communities (race, gender, sexual orientation, class, religious affiliations, ages, physical abilities, and so forth) and openness to learning about others is a necessary attribute of helping; (3) self-examination and openness about one's biases and prejudices is a continuing and ongoing journey; (4) providing equal access and opportunity—that is, social justice—is a central component of helping; and (5) there is an ethical obligation to educate each other *on the existence and effects of racism, sexism, ageism, heterosexism, religious intolerance, and other forms of invidious prejudice"* (p. 643).

(Continued)

Perhaps the most powerful sentence that has direct relevance for racial, gender, and sexual-orientation microaggressions is the following: *"Evidence of bias, stereotyped thinking, and prejudicial beliefs and attitudes will not go unchallenged, even when such behavior is rationalized as being a function of ignorance, joking, cultural differences, or substance abuse. When these actions result in physical or psychological abuse, harassment, intimidation, substandard psychological services or research, or violence against persons or property, members of the training community will intervene appropriately"* (p. 643). As microaggressions are reflections of biased worldviews, oftentimes invisible to the perpetrator, rationalized away as an innocent remark due to some other benign excuse, and represent violence directed toward socially devalued groups in clinical or training environments, they MUST be challenged by fellow professionals. To ignore or excuse them is to perpetuate injustice and oppression.

2. Since the early 1980s, the terms multicultural or cultural competence in the helping professions have become a central feature that guides mental health practice, education and training, and research in psychological service delivery (APA, 2003; Sue, Arredondo, & McDavis, 1992; Sue, Bernier et al., 1982). Sue and Torino (2005) give the following definition:

> Cultural competence is the ability to engage in actions or create conditions that maximize the optimal development of client and client systems. Multicultural counseling competence is defined as the counselor's acquisition of awareness, knowledge, and skills needed to function effectively in a pluralistic democratic society (ability to communicate, interact, negotiate, and intervene on behalf of clients from diverse backgrounds), and on a organizational/societal level, advocating effectively to develop new theories, practices, policies, and organizational structures that are more responsive to all groups. (p. 8)

Four objectives can be distilled from the definition that have relevance to combating microaggressions: making the "invisible" visible, establishing expertise and trust, and providing appropriate services to diverse populations.

- The old adage "physician [or therapist], heal thyself" before healing others is all-important in having helping professionals become aware of their own values, biases, and assumptions about human behavior. What stereotypes, perceptions, and beliefs are held about marginalized groups that may hinder the ability to form a helpful and effective

(Continued)

counseling/therapy relationship? What are the worldviews brought to the clinical encounter by therapists that may prove detrimental to people of color, women, or LGBTs? Without such an awareness and understanding, therapists may continue in their oppressive ways and continue to deliver microaggressions. When this happens, therapists may become guilty of cultural oppression, imposing values on marginalized clients.

- Acquiring knowledge and understanding of the worldviews of diverse groups and clients are all important in providing culturally relevant services. It is important to understand the racial, gender, and sexual-orientation realities of people of color, women, and LGBTs. As we have consistently indicated, Whites are generally disadvantaged in understanding the personal and systemic experiences of oppressed groups in our society, the everyday traumas they experience from both overt and covert discrimination. Without this understanding and awareness, they are likely to continue invalidating, denigrating, and insulting socially devalued groups unintentionally. The result is that they become part of the problem rather than the solution.

- Helping professionals must begin the process of developing culturally appropriate and effective intervention strategies in working with clients different from them. As we have emphasized, credibility is established not only through trustworthiness, but by providing evidence of cultural proficiency in practice (expertness). We have not dealt with issues of culturally appropriate helping, but they often are in direct violation of therapeutic taboos derived from ethnocentric standards of practice and codes of ethics. Yet it is important to note that therapeutic actions considered unhelpful and unethical from a Western perspective may be considered qualities of helping for different cultural groups.

- As we saw from Chapter 10, microaggressions and oppression can come from institutional structures, policies, practices, and regulations. Increasing the professional's understanding of organizational dynamics and development, how to effectively intervene in the system, and being able to recognize how system forces affect the life experiences of marginalized groups will prove helpful in treatment strategies. Helping professionals must develop skills that involve interventions aimed at organizational structures, policies, practices, and regulations within institutions, if they are to become culturally competent.

(Continued)

3. Vision statements on the values of diversity, definitions of cultural competence, and personal goals and objectives of self-exploration and awareness for mental health professionals are not only admirable, lofty, and inspirational, but the question still remains: How can these be achieved on a personal level? As indicated, while reading texts and attending classes, conferences, and workshops on multicultural or diversity issues are helpful and important, it is simply not enough. Being aware of one's racial/cultural, gender, and sexual-orientation identities and those who differ from you is more than an intellectual exercise. In many respects, it requires experiential reality. Thus, the following recommendations may prove helpful (APA, 2000; Sue, 2003).

- *Principle One—Learn about People of Color, Women, and LGBTs from Sources within the Group.* This suggestion strikes at the core of ethnocentric notions by encouraging us to check out the validity of our assumptions and understanding from sources that come from groups other than ourselves. Acquiring information or being exposed to minority-run businesses, radio and TV stations, or poetry and writings from minority authors allows one to understand the thoughts, hopes, fears, and aspirations of the people from their perspective rather than from the perspective of the majority society.

- *Principle Two—Learn from Healthy and Strong People of the Group.* Therapists, like most people, often obtain information about other groups through mass media, educational texts (written from the perspective of the dominant culture), and what relatives, friends, and neighbors say. The beliefs and images they have, however, are often stereotypes or unflattering portrayals of the various marginalized groups in our society. Blacks are portrayed as criminals on TV, women's place is in the home, and LGBTs are pathologized. Further, as therapists, we are often exposed to a very small segment of the population that suffers from emotional distress, so it is easy to associate negative features to specific populations. We seldom view strong and health minority people in action. We must counterbalance these biased perceptions: frequent minority-owned businesses, invite minority colleagues and coworkers to your home for dinner or a holiday, and attend churches, synagogues, temples, and other places of worship to learn about different faiths and to meet church leaders.

- *Principle Three—Learn from Experiential Reality.* The factual understanding of diverse groups must be supplemented by experiences with people you hope to understand. Sometimes it is helpful to identify a

(Continued)

cultural guide who is willing to help you understand their group, someone willing to introduce you to new experiences and who can aid you in processing thoughts, feelings, and behaviors. Being in new situations is uncomfortable and often awakens fears and apprehensions that can block your experiential development. This leads us to the importance of the next principle.

- *Principle Four—Learn from Constant Vigilance of Biases and Fears.* This is probably a most difficult thing to do. As we saw in our analysis on difficult dialogues on race, when biases and fears come to the surface, the strong powerful emotions of anxiety, guilt, and defensiveness often act as emotional roadblocks that hinder monitoring and exploring biases. Yet, to overcome this immediate reaction, to entertain the possibility of harboring prejudices or making/behaving in a biased fashion, and to continue open communication with someone who might have been offended is to start the difficult journal of being honest with oneself. Engaging and being open to exploring one's own biases with a minority friend, for example, results in positive changes for you and your friend.

- *Principle Five—Learn by Being Committed to Personal Action Against Racism, Sexism, and Heterosexism.* This principle is very much related to Counseling Psychology Model Training Values Statement Addressing Diversity which makes it clear that in the face of prejudicial actions that harass and intimidate, helping professionals have a moral and ethical responsibility to intervene appropriately. Racist remarks, jokes, or biased actions are challenged even if embarrassing and frightening. It means noticing the possibility of direct action against discrimination and prejudice in everyday life, not just in a clinical setting. It means taking action in one's family, employment, and community to correct injustices.

The suggestions given above, and many others in previous chapters, have the major goal of providing equal access and opportunity for all groups in our society. Microaggressions are reflections of a worldview that harms, restricts, hinders, and oppresses various marginalized groups in this nation.

As such, they reveal unpleasant truths about us that are painful and uncomfortable. Microaggressions are manifestations of systems of unfairness in our nation because they do psychological harm to marginalized groups through a process of denigration and invalidation; they create disparities in education, employment, and health care; and they contradict the stated values of a democratic nation. As such, our nation must actively address these abuses not only on a personal level, but through systemic action.

References

Abelson, R. P., Dasgupta, N., Park, J., & Banaji, M. R. (1998). Perceptions of the collective other. *Personality and Social Psychology Review, 2*, 243–250.

Aboud, F. E. (1988). *Children and prejudice*. Cambridge, MA: Basil Blackwell.

Accapadi, M. M. (2007). When White women cry: How White women's tears oppress women of color. *College Student Affairs Journal, 26*, 208–215.

Adorno, T. W., Frenkel-Brunswik, E., Levinson, D. J., & Sanford, R. N. (1950). *The authoritarian personality*. New York: Harper.

Alcantara, C., & Gone, J. P. (2008). Suicide in Native American communities. In F. T. L. Leong & M. M. Leach (Eds.), *Suicide among racial and ethnic minority groups* (pp. 173–199). New York: Routledge.

Allport, G. (1954). *The nature of prejudice*. New York: Doubleday.

American Counseling Association. (1999). *Racism: Healing its effects*. Alexandria, VA: Author.

American Psychiatric Association. (2000). *Diagnostic and statistical manual of mental disorders* (4th edition, text rev.). Washington, DC: Author.

American Psychological Association. (2000.) *Racism and psychology*. Washington, DC: Author.

American Psychological Association. (2003). Guidelines on multicultural education, training, research, practice, and organizational change for psychologists. *American Psychologist, 58*, 377–402.

American Psychological Association. (2007). *Report of the task force on the sexualization of girls*. Retrieved May 26, 2009, from www.apa.or/pe/wpo/sexualization.html.

Apfelbaum, E. P., Sommers, S. R., & Norton, M. I. (2008). Seeing race and seeming racist: Evaluating strategic colorblindness in social interaction. *Journal of Personality and Social Psychology, 95*, 918–932.

Arm, J. R., Horne, S. G., & Levitt, H. M. (2009). Negotiating connection to GLBT experience: Family members' experiences of anti-GLBT movements and policies. *Journal of Counseling Psychology, 56,* 82–96.

Armstead, C. A., Lawler, K. A., Gorden, G., Cross, J., & Gibbons, J. (1989). Relationship of racial stressors to blood pressure responses and anger expression in Black college students. *Health Psychology, 8,* 541–556.

Astin, M. C., Ogland-Hand, S. M., Foy, D. W., & Coleman, E. M. (1995). Posttraumatic Stress Disorder and childhood abuse in battered women: Comparisons with maritally distressed women. *Journal of Consulting and Clinical Psychology, 63,* 308–313.

Astor, C. (1997). Gallup poll: Progress in Black/White relations, but race is still an issue. *U.S. Society & Values.* Retrieved February 16, 2007, from http://usinfo.state.gov/journals/itsv/0897/ijse/gallup.htm.

Babbington, C. (2008). Poll shows gap between blacks and whites over racial discrimination. Retrieved March 15, 2009, from http://news.yahoo.com/page/election-2008-political-pulse-race-in-america.

Baca, L. M., & Koss-Chioino, J. D. (1997). Development of a culturally responsive group counseling model for Mexican American adolescents. *Journal of Multicultural Counseling and Development, 25,* 130–141.

Baker, J. G., & Fishbein, H. D. (1998). The development of prejudice towards gay and lesbian adolescents. *Journal of Homosexuality, 36,* 89–100.

Balsam, K. F., Rothblum, E. D., & Beauchaine, T. P. (2005). Victimization over the life span: A comparison of lesbian, gay, bisexual, and heterosexual siblings. *Journal of Consulting and Clinical Psychology, 73,* 477–487.

Banaji, M. R. (2001). Implicit attitudes can be measured. In H. L. Roediger, III, J. S. Nairne, I. Neath, & A. Surprenant (Eds.), *The nature of remembering: Essays in honor of Robert G. Crowder* (pp. 117–150). Washington, DC: American Psychological Association.

Banaji, M. R., Hardin, C., & Rothman, A. J. (1993). Implicit stereotyping in person judgment. *Journal of Personality and Social Psychology, 65,* 272–281.

Banaji, M. R., & Greenwald, A. G. (1995). Implicit gender stereotyping in judgments of fame. *Journal of Personality and Social Psychology, 68,* 181–198.

Banks, J. A. (2004). Multicultural education: Historical development, dimensions, and practice. In J. A. Banks & C. A. M. Banks (Eds.), *Handbook of research on multicultural education* (2nd ed., pp. 3–29). San Francisco: Jossey Bass.

Barnes, M. (1994). Clinical treatment issues regarding Black African Americans. In J. L. Ronch, W. Van Ornum, & N. C. Stilwell (Eds.), *The counseling sourcebook: A practical reference on contemporary issues* (pp. 157–164). New York: Crossroad.

Baron, A. S., & Banaji, M. R. (2006). The development of implicit attitudes. *Psychological Science, 17,* 53–58.

Barret, B., & Logan, C. (2002). *Counseling gay men and lesbians.* Pacific Grove, CA: Brooks Cole.

Barry, D. T., & Grillo, C. M. (2003). Cultural self-esteem and demographic correlates of perception of personal and group discrimination among East Asian immigrants. *American Journal of Orthopsychiatry, 73,* 223–229.

Bell, L. A. (2002). Sincere fictions: The pedagogical challenges of preparing white teachers for multicultural classrooms. *Equity and Excellence in Education, 35,* 236–244.

Bell, L. A. (2003). Telling tales: What stories can teach us about racism. *Race Ethnicity and Education, 6,* 3–28.

Benokraitis, N. V. (1997). *Subtle sexism: Current practice and prospects for change.* Thousand Oaks, CA: Sage.

Bergin, D. J., & Williams, J. E. (1991). Sex stereotypes in the United States revisited: 1972–1988. *Sex Roles, 24,* 413–423.

Berube, A. (1990). *Coming out under fire: The history of gay men and women in World War II.* New York: Free Press.

Biernat, M. (2003). Toward a broader view of social stereotyping. *American Psychologist, 58,* 1019–1027.

Blair, I. V., Judd, C. M., & Chapleau, K. M. (2004). The influence of afrocentric facial features in criminal sentencing. *Psychological Science, 15,* 674–679.

Blake, S. M., Ledsky, R., Lehman, T., & Goodenow, C. (2001). Preventing sexual risk behaviors among gay, lesbian, and bisexual adolescents: The benefits of gay-sensitive HIV instruction in schools. *American Journal of Publish Health, 91,* 940–946.

Blank, R., & Slipp, S. (1994). *Voices of diversity.* New York: AMACON.

Blum, L. (1998). Can we talk? Interracial dialogue in the classroom. *Change, 30*(6), 26–37.

Bolgatz, J. (2005). *Talking race in the classroom.* New York: Educators College Press.

Bonilla-Silva, E. (2006). *Racism without racists: Color-blind racism and the persistence of racial inequality in the United States.* Lanham, MD: Rowman & Littlefield.

Bowser, B. P., & Hunt, R. G. (Eds.). (1981). *Impacts of racism on White Americans.* Beverly Hills, CA: Sage.

Bowser, B. P., & Hunt, R. G. (Eds.). (1996). *Impacts of racism on White Americans* (2nd ed.). Beverly Hills, CA: Sage.

Boyd-Franklin, N. (2003). *Black families in therapy.* New York: Guilford Press.

Boysen, G. A., & Vogel, D. L. (2008). The relationship between level of training, implicit bias, and multicultural competency among counselor trainees. *Training and Education in Professional Psychology, 2,* 103–110.

Broman, C. L., Mavaddat, R., & Hsu, S. Y. (2000). The experience and consequences of perceived racial discrimination: A study of African Americans. *Journal of Black Psychology, 26,* 165–180.

Brondolo, E., Beatty, D. L., Cubbin, C., Pencille, M., Saegert, S., Wellington, R., et al. (2009). Sociodemographic variations in self-reported racism in a community sample of Blacks and Latino(a)s. *Journal of Applied Social Psychology, 39,* 407–429.

Brondolo, E., Brady, N., Thompson, S., Tobin, J. N., Cassells, A., Sweeney, M., et al. (2008). Perceived racism and negative affect: Analysis of trait and state measures of affect in a community sample. *Journal of Social and Clinical Psychology, 27,* 150–173.

Brondolo, E., Kelly, K. P., Coakley, V., Gordon, T., Thompson, S., Levy, E., et al. (2005). The perceived ethnic discrimination questionnaire: Development and preliminary validations of a community version. *Journal of Applied Social Psychology, 35,* 335–365.

Brondolo, E., Rieppi, R., Kelly, K. P., & Gerin, K. W. (2003). Perceived racism and blood pressure: A review of the literature and conceptual and methodological critique. *Annals of Behavioral Medicine, 25,* 55–65.

Broverman, I. K., & Broverman, D. (1970). Sex role stereotypes and clinical judgments of mental health. *Journal of Consulting and Clinical Psychology, 34,* 1–7.

Brown, G. W., & Harris, T. O. (1989). Depression. In G. W. Brown & T. O. Harris (Eds.), *Life events and illness* (pp. 49–93). New York: Guilford Press.

Buchanan, T. S., Fischer, A. R., Tokar, D. M., & Yoder, J. D. (2008). Testing a culture-specific extension of objectification theory regarding African American women's body image. *The Counseling Psychologist, 16,* 697–718.

Burkard, A. W., & Knox, S. (2004). Effect of therapist color-blindness on empathy and attributions in cross-cultural counseling. *Journal of Counseling Psychology, 51,* 387–397.

Burn, S. M. (2000). Heterosexuals' use of "fag" and "queer" to deride one another: A contributor to heterosexism and stigma. *Journal of Homosexuality, 40,* 1–11.

Burn, S. M., Kadlec, K., & Rexer, R. (2005). Effects of subtle heterosexism on gays, lesbians, and bisexuals. *Journal of Homosexuality, 40,* 23–38.

Buser, J. K. (2009). Treatment-seeking disparity between African Americans and Whites: Attitudes toward treatment, coping resources, and racism. *Journal of Multicultural Counseling and Development, 37,* 94–104.

Butler, D., & Geis, F. L. (1990). Nonverbal affect responses to male and female leaders: Implications for leadership evaluations. *Journal of Personality and Social Psychology, 58,* 48–59.

Cadinu, M., Maass, A., Rosabianca, A., & Kiesner, J. (2005). Why do women under-perform under stereotype threat? Evidence for the role of negative thinking. *Psychological Science, 16,* 572–578.

Capodilupo, C. M., Nadal, K. L., Corman, L., Hamit, S., Lyons, O., & Weinberg, A. (in press). The manifestation of gender microaggressions. In D. W. Sue (Ed.), *Microaggressions and marginalized groups in society: Race, gender, sexual orientation, class, international and religious manifestations.* Hoboken, NJ: John Wiley & Sons.

Carrubba, M. D. (2005). Invisibility, alienation, and misperceptions. In J. M. Croteau, J. S. Lark, M. A. Lidderdale, & Y. Barry Chung (Eds.), *Deconstructing heterosexism in the counseling professions* (pp. 41–45). Thousand Oaks, CA: Sage.

Carter, R. T. (2007). Racism and psychological and emotional injury: Recognizing and assessing race-based traumatic stress. *The Counseling Psychologist, 35,* 13–105.

Casas, J. M., Vasquez, M. J. T., & de Esparza, C. A. (2002). Counseling the Latina/o. In Pedersen, P. B., Draguns, J. G., Lonner, W. J., & Trimble, J. E. (Eds.), *Counseling across cultures* (pp. 133–159). Thousand Oaks, CA: Sage.

Cass, V. C. (1979). Homosexual identity formation: A theoretical model. *Journal of Homosexuality, 4,* 219–235.

Chakraborty, A., & McKenzie, K. (2002). Does racial discrimination cause mental illness? *British Journal of Psychiatry, 180*(6), 475–477.

Chan, K.-M. (2005). Transforming heterosexism. In J. M. Croteau, J. S. Lark, M. A. Lidderdale, & Y. Barry Chung (Eds.), *Deconstructing heterosexism in the counseling profession* (pp. 47–52). Thousand Oaks, CA: Sage.

Cheatham, H. E. (1994). Multicultural training: Re-examination, operationalization and integration response. *Counseling Psychologist, 22,* 290–295.

Children Now (1998). *A different world: Children's perceptions of race and class in the media.* www.childrennow.org, New York.

Chung, R., & Okazaki, S. (1991). Counseling Americans of Southeast Asian descent: The impact of the refugee experience. In C. C. Lee & B. L. Richardson (Eds.), *Multicultural issues in counseling: New approaches to diversity* (pp. 107–126). Alexandria, VA: American Counseling Association.

Clark, R. (2000). Perceptions of inter-ethnic group racism predict increased blood pressure responses to a laboratory challenge in college women. *Annals of Behavioral Medicine, 22,* 214–222.

Clark, R. (2006). Perceived racism and vascular reactivity in Black college women: Moderating effects of seeking social support. *Health Psychology, 25,* 20–25.

Clark, R., Anderson, N. B., Clark, V. R., & Williams, D. R. (1999). Racism as a stressor for African Americans. *American Psychologist, 54,* 805–816.

Cochran, S. D., Keenan, C., Schober, C., & Mays, V. M. (2000). Estimates of alcohol use and clinical treatment needs among homosexually active men and women in the U.S. population. *Journal of Consulting and Clinical Psychology, 68,* 1062–1071.

Cohen, S., Frank, E., Doyle, W. J., Skoner, D. P., Rabin, B. S., & Gwalmey, J. M. (1998). Types of stressors that increase susceptibility in the common cold in health adults. *Health Psychology, 17,* 214–223.

Cokley, K. (2006). The impact of racialized schools and racist (mis)education on African American students' academic identity. In M. G. Constantine & D. W. Sue (Eds.), *Addressing racism* (pp. 127–144). Hoboken, NJ: John Wiley & Sons.

Coleman, M. G. (2004). Racial discrimination in the workplace: Does market structure make a difference? *Industrial Relations, 43,* 660–689.

Conley, T. D., Calhoun, C., Evett, S. R., & Devine, P. G. (2001). Mistakes that heterosexual people make when trying to appear non-prejudiced: The view from LGB people. *Journal of Homosexuality, 42,* 21–43.

Constantine, M. G. (2007). Racial microaggressions against African American clients in cross-racial counseling relationships. *Journal of Counseling Psychology, 54.*

Constantine, M. G., & Sue, D. W. (2007). Perceptions of racial microaggressions among Black supervisees in cross-racial dyads. *Journal of Counseling Psychology, 54,* 142–153.

Contrada, R. J., Ashmore, R. D., Gary, M. L., Coups, E., Egeth, J. D., Sewell, A., et al. (2001). Measures of ethnicity-related stress: Psychometric properties, ethnic group differences, and associations with well-being. *Journal of Applied Social Psychology, 31,* 1775–1820.

Cortes, C. E. (2004). Knowledge construction and popular culture: The media as multicultural educator. In J. A. Banks & C. A. M. Banks (Eds.), *Handbook of research on multicultural education* (2nd ed., pp. 211–227). San Francisco: Jossey Bass.

Cortina, I. M., & Kubiak, S. P. (2006). Gender and posttraumatic stress: Sexual violence as an explanation for women's increased risk. *Journal of Abnormal Psychology, 115,* 753–759.

Council of Counseling Psychology Training Programs, Association of Counseling Center Training Agencies, and Society of Counseling Psychology. (2009). Counseling psychology model training values statement addressing diversity. *The Counseling Psychologist, 37,* 641–643.

Crandall, C. S., Preisler, J. J., & Aussprung, J. (1992). Measuring life event stress in the lives of college students: The Undergraduate Stress Questionnaire (USQ). *Journal of Behavioral Medicine, 15,* 627–662.

Crocker, J., & Major, B. (1989). Social stigma and self-esteem: The self-protective properties of stigma. *Psychological Review, 96,* 608–630.

Crocker, J., Major, B., & Steele, C. (1998). Social stigma. In D. Gilbert, S. T. Fiske, & G. Lindzey (Eds.), *The handbook of social psychology* (pp. 504–553). New York: McGraw-Hill.

Croteau, J. M., Lark, J. S., & Lance, T. S. (2005). Our stories will be told. In J. M. Croteau, J. S. Lark, M. A. Lidderdale, & Y. Barry Chung (Eds.), *Deconstructing heterosexism in the counseling professions* (pp. 1–15). Thousand Oaks, CA: Sage.

Croteau, J. M., Lark, J. S., Lidderdale, M. A., & Chung, B. Y. (Eds.). (2005). *Deconstructing heterosexism in the counseling professions.* Thousand Oaks, CA: Sage.

Darwin, C. (1859). *On the origin of species by natural selection.* London: Murray.

Davis, M. C., Mathews, K. A., Meilahn, E. N., & Kiss, J. E. (1995). Are job characteristics related to fibrinogen levels in middle-aged women? *Health Psychology, 14,* 310–318.

De La Fuente, R. (1990). The mental health consequences of the 1985 earthquakes in Mexico. *International Journal of Mental Health, 19,* 21–29.

de Gobineau, A. (1915). *The inequality of human races.* New York: Putnam.

Deitch, E. A., Barsky, A., Butz, R. M., Chan, S., Brief, A., & Bradley, J. C. (2003). Subtle yet significant: The existence and impact of everyday racial discrimination in the workplace. *Human Relations, 56*(11), 1299–1324.

DePaulo, B. M. (1992). Nonverbal behavior and self-presentation. *Psychological Bulletin, 111,* 203–243.

DeVos, T., & Banaji, M. R. (2005). American = White? *Journal of Personality and Social Psychology, 88,* 447–466.

Deyhle, D., & Swisher, K. (1999). Research in American Indian and Alaska Native Education: From assimilation to self-determination. *Review of Research in Education, 22,* 113–194.

Douce, L. A. (2005). Coming out on the wave of feminism, coming of age on the ocean of multiculturalism. In J. M. Croteau, J. S. Lark, M. A. Lidderdale, & Y. Barry Chung (Eds.), *Deconstructing heterosexism in the counseling professions* (pp. 59–64). Thousand Oaks, CA: Sage.

Dovidio, J. F. (2001). On the nature of contemporary prejudice: The third wave. *Journal of Social Issues, 57,* 829–849.

Dovidio, J. F., & Gaertner, S. L. (1991). Changes in the expression of racial prejudice. In H. Knopke, J. Norrell, & R. Rogers (Eds.), *Opening doors: An appraisal of race relations in contemporary America* (pp. 201–241). Tuscaloosa: University of Alabama Press.

Dovidio, J. F., & Gaertner, S. L. (1993). Stereotypes and evaluative intergroup bias. In D. M. Mackie & D. L. Hamilton (Eds.), *Affect, cognition, and stereotyping: Interactive processes in group perception* (pp. 167–194). New York: Academic Press.

Dovidio, J. F., & Gaertner, S. L. (1996). Affirmative action, unintentional racial biases, and intergroup relations. *Journal of Social Issues, 52,* 51–75.

Dovidio, J. F., & Gaertner, S. L. (2000). Aversive racism and selective decisions: 1989–1999. *Psychological Science, 11,* 315–319.

Dovidio, J. F., Gaertner, S. L., Kawakami, K., & Hodson, G. (2002). Why can't we all just get along? Interpersonal biases and interracial distrust. *Cultural Diversity and Ethnic Minority Psychology, 8,* 88–102.

Dovidio, J. F., Kawakami, K., Smoak, N., & Gaertner, S. L. (2009). Implicit measures of attitudes. In R. Petty, R. Fazio, & P. Brinol (Eds.), *Implicit measures* (pp. 165–192). New York: Psychology Press.

Dunton, B., & Fazio, R. (1997). An individual difference measure of motivation to control prejudiced reactions. *Personality and Social Psychology Bulletin, 23,* 316–326.

Duran, E. (2006). *Healing the soul wound.* New York: Teachers College Press.

Eckman, P., & Friesen, W. V. (1982). Felt, false, and miserable smile. *Journal of Nonverbal Behavior, 6,* 238–258.

Eidelson, R. J., & Eidelson, J. I. (2003). Dangerous ideas: Five beliefs that propel groups toward conflict. *American Psychologist, 58,* 182–192.

Ellison, R. (1972). *Invisible man.* New York: Vintage Books.

Ensel, W. M., & Lin, N. (1991). The life stress paradigm and psychological distress. *Journal of Health and Social Behavior, 32,* 321–341.

Fang, C. Y., & Myers, H. F. (2001). The effects of racial stressors and hostility on cardiovascular reactivity in African American and Caucasian men. *Health Psychology, 20,* 64–70.

Fassinger, R. E. (1991). The hidden minority: Issues and challenges in working with lesbian women and gay men. *The Counseling Psychologist, 19,* 157–176.

Feagin, J. R. (2001). *Racist America: Roots, current realities, and future reparations.* New York: Routledge.

Feagin, J. R. (2006). Systemic racism: *A theory of oppression.* New York: Routledge.

Feagin, J. R., & Feagin, C. B. (1996). *Racial and ethnic relations* (5th ed.). Upper Saddle River, NJ: Prentice-Hall.

Feagin, J. R., & McKinney, K. D. (2003). *The many costs of racism.* New York: Rowman & Littlefield.

Feagin, J. R., & Sykes, M. P. (1994). *Living with racism.* Boston: Beacon.

Finch, B. K., Kolody, B., & Vega, W. A. (2000). Perceived discrimination and depression among Mexican-origin adults in California. *Journal of Health and Social Behavior, 41,* 295–313.

Fisher, R. D., Derison, D., Polley, C. F., Cadman, J., & Johnston, D. (1994). Religiousness, religious orientation, and attitudes towards gays and lesbians. *Journal of Applied Social Psychology, 24,* 614–630.

Fiske, S. T. (1993). Controlling other people: The impact of power on stereotyping. *American Psychologist, 48,* 621–628.

Fiske, S. T., & Stevens, S. L. E. (1993). What's so special about sex? Gender stereotyping and discrimination. In S. Oskamp (Ed.), *Gender issues in contemporary society* (pp. 173–196). Newbury Park, CA: Sage.

Flack, J. M., Amaro, H., Jenkins, W., Kunitz, S., Levy, J., Mixon, M., et al. (1995). Panel I: Epidemiology of mental health. *Health Psychology, 14,* 592–600.

Ford, D. Y., Moore, J. L., & Whiting, G. W. (2006). Eliminating deficit orientations. In M. G. Constantine & D. W. Sue (Eds.), *Addressing racism* (pp. 173–193). Hoboken, NJ: John Wiley & Sons.

Fox, S., & Stallworth, L. E. (2004). Paper presentation from SIOP Conference 2004. *Bullying, racism, and power: An investigation of racial/ethnic bullying in the U.S. workplace.* Chicago: Society of Industrial and Organizational Psychology.

Franklin, A. J. (1999). Invisibility syndrome and racial identity development in psychotherapy and counseling African American men. *The Counseling Psychologist, 27,* 761–793.

Franklin, A. J. (2004). From brotherhood to manhood: *How Black men rescue their relationships and dreams from the invisibility syndrome.* Hoboken, NJ: John Wiley & Sons.

Franklin, A. J., & Franklin-Boyd, N. (2000). Invisibility syndrome: A clinical model of the effects of racism on African-American males. *American Journal of Orthopsychiatry, 70,* 33–41.

Fredrickson, B. L., & Roberts, T. (1997). Objectification theory: Toward understanding women's lived experiences and mental health risks. *Psychology of Women Quarterly, 21,* 173–206.

Freire, P. (1970). *Pedagogy of the oppressed.* New York: Continuum.

Friedan, B. (1963). *The feminine mystique.* New York: W. W. Norton Publishers.

Fritsch, J. (February 26, 2000). The Diallo Verdict: The overview; 4 officers in Diallo shooting are acquitted of all charges. *New York Times.* Retrieved March 15, 2009, from http://query.nytimes.com/gst/fullpage.html?res=9C01E7D61639F935A15751C0A9669C8B63.

Frost, D. M., & Meyer, H. H. (2009). Internalized homophobia and relationship quality among lesbians, gay men, and bisexuals. *Journal of Counseling Psychology, 56,* 97–109.

Fukuyama, M. A., Miville, M. L., & Funderburk, J. R. (2005). In J. M. Croteau, J. S. Lark, M. A. Lidderdale, & Y. Barry Chung (Eds.), *Deconstructing heterosexism in the counseling professions* (pp. 137–157). Thousand Oaks, CA: Sage.

Gaertner, S. L., & Dovidio, J. F. (1986). The aversive form of racism. In J. F. Dovidio & S. L. Gaertner (Eds.), *Prejudice, discrimination, and racism* (pp. 61–89). San Diego, CA: Academic Press.

Gaertner, S. L., & Dovidio, J. F. (2005). Understanding and addressing contemporary racism: From aversive racism to the common ingroup identity model. *Journal of Social Issues, 61*(3), 615–639.

Gagnon, J. H. (1990). The explicit and implicit use of the scripting perspective in sex research. *Annual Review of Sex Research, 1,* 1–43.

Galea, S., Ahern, J., Resnick, H., Kilpatrick, D., Bucuvalas, M., Gold, J., et al. (2002). Psychological sequelae of the September 11 terrorist attacks in New York City. *New England Journal of Medicine, 346,* 982–987.

Galton, R. (1869). *Hereditary genius: An inquiry into its laws and consequences.* London: Macmillan.

Garnets, L., Hancock, K. A., Cochran, S. D., Goodchilds, J., & Peplau, L. A. (1998). Issues in psychotherapy with lesbians and gay men: A survey of psychologists. In D. R. Atkinson & G. Hackett (Eds.), *Counseling diverse populations* (pp. 297–316). Boston: McGraw-Hill.

Gill, M. J. (2004). When information does not deter stereotyping: Prescriptive stereotyping can foster bias under conditions that deter descriptive stereotyping. *Journal of Experimental Social Psychology, 40,* 619–632.

Glick, P., & Fiske, S. T. (1996). The antivalent sexism inventory: Differentiating hostile and benevolent sexism. *Journal of Personality and Social Psychology, 70,* 491–512.

Gloria, A. M., Hird, J. S., & Tao, K. W. (2008). Self-reported multicultural supervision competence of White predoctoral intern supervisors. *Training and Education in Professional Psychology, 2,* 129–136.

Goldberg, D. (2006). The aetiology of depression. *Psychological Medicine, 36,* 1341–1347.

Gonsiorek, J. C. (1982). Results of psychological testing on homosexual populations. *American Behavioral Scientist, 25,* 94–106.

Goodman, D. J. (1995). Difficult dialogues: Enhancing discussions about diversity. *College Teaching, 43,* 47–52.

Goodman, D. J. (2001). *Promoting diversity and social justice: Educating people from privileged groups.* Thousand Oaks, CA: Sage.

Gore, S. (2000). The Lesbian and Gay workplace. In B. Greene, & G. L. Croom, (Eds.), *Education, research, and practice in lesbian, gay, bisexual, and transgendered psychology* (pp. 282–302). Thousand Oaks, CA: Sage.

Greene, B. (2000). Beyond heterosexism and across the cultural divide. In B. Greene & G. L. Croom (Eds.), *Education, research, and practice in lesbian, gay, bisexual, and transgendered psychology* (pp. 1–45). Thousand Oaks, CA: Sage.

Greenwald, A. G., McGhee, D. E., & Schwartz, J. L. K. (1998). Measuring individual differences in implicit cognition: The Implicit Association Test. *Journal of Personality and Social Psychology, 74,* 1464–1480.

Grencavage, L. M., & Norcross, J. C. (1990). Where are the commonalities among the therapeutic common factors? *Professional Psychology: Research and Practice, 21,* 372–378.

Grier, W., & Cobbs, P. (1971). *Black rage.* New York: Basic Books.

Guthrie, R. V. (1998). *Even the rat was White* (2nd ed.). New York: Harper & Row.

Halderman, D. C. (2002). Gay rights, patient rights: The implications of sexual orientation conversion therapy. *Professional Psychology: Research and Practice, 33,* 260–264.

Halderman, D. C. (2004). When sexual and religious orientation collide. *The Counseling Psychologist, 32,* 691–715.

Hamelsky, S. W., & Lipton, R. B. (2006). Psychiatric comorbidity of migraine. *Headache, 46,* 1327–1333.

Hamilton, C. J., & Mahalik, J. R. (2009). Minority stress, masculinity, and social norms predicting gay men's health risk behaviors. *Journal of Counseling Psychology, 56,* 132–141.

Hammen, C. (2006). Stress generation in depression: Reflections on origins, research, and future directions. *Journal of Clinical Psychology, 62,* 1065–1082.

Hanna, F. J., Talley, W. B., & Guindon, M. H. (2000). The power of perception: Toward a model of cultural oppression and liberation. *Journal of Counseling and Development, 78,* 430–446.

Hansen-Weaver, J. (2009). *Behind the wave of anti-gay hate crimes.* Socialistworker.org. Retrieved May 29, 2009, from http://socialistworker.org/2009/01/19/anti-gay-hate-crimes May 29.

Harrell, J. P. (2000). A multidimensional conceptualization of racism-related stress: Implications for the well-being of people of color. *American Journal of Orthopsychiatry, 70,* 42–57.

Harrell, J. P., Hall, S., & Taliaferro, J. (2003). Physiological responses to racism and discrimination: An assessment of the evidence. *American Journal of Public Health, 93,* 243–248.

Harris Poll (1994). *Minority mistrust and perceptions.* National Conference of Christians and Jews.

Harry, B., Klingner, J. K., & Hart, J. (2005). African American families under fire: Ethnographic views of family strengths. *Remedial and Special Education, 26,* 101–112.

Hayes, D. (2006). ACE report cites enrollment gains, retention problems. *Diverse Issues in Higher Education, 23,* 21.

Heesacker, M., Conner, K., & Pritchard, S. (1995). Individual counseling and psychotherapy: Allocations from the social psychology of attitude change. *The Counseling Psychologist, 23,* 611–632.

Helms, J. E. (1990). *Black and White racial identity: Theory, research, and practice.* New York: Greenwood Press.

Helms, J. E. (1992). *A race is a nice thing to have: A guide to being a White person or understanding the White persons in your life.* Topeka, KS: Content Communications.

Helms, J. E. (1995). An update of Helms's White and people of color racial identity models. In J. G. Ponterotto, J. M. Casas, L. A. Suzuki, & C. M. Alexander (Eds.), *Handbook of multicultural counseling* (pp. 181–191). Thousand Oaks, CA: Sage.

Helms, J. E., & Cook, D. (1999). *Using race and culture in counseling and psychotherapy: Theory and process.* Needham Heights, MA: Allyn & Bacon.

Helms, J. E., Jernigan, M., & Mascher, J. (2005). The meaning of race in psychology and how to change it: A methodological perspective. *The Counseling Psychologist, 60,* 27–36.

Henry, W., Cobb-Roberts, D., Dorn, S., Exum, H. A., Keller, H., & Shircliffe, B. (2007). When the dialogue becomes too difficult: A case study of resistance and backlash. *College Student Affairs Journal, 26,* 160–168.

Heppner, P. P., Cook, S. W., Wright, D. M., & Johnson, C. (1995). Progress in resolving problems: A problem-focused style of coping. *Journal of Counseling Psychology, 42,* 279–293.

Heppner, P. P., & Frazier, P. A. (1992). Social psychological processes in psychotherapy: Extrapolating basic research to counseling psychology. *Handbook of Counseling Psychology.* Oxford, England: John Wiley & Sons.

Herek, G. M. (1984). Assessing heterosexuals' attitudes toward lesbians and gay men: A review of the empirical research with the ATLG scale. In B. Greene & G. M. Herek (Eds.), *Contemporary perspectives in lesbian and gay issues in psychology* (pp. 206–228). Newbury Park, CA: Sage.

Herek, G. M. (1987). Religious orientation and prejudices: A comparison of racial and sexual attitudes. *Personality and Social Psychology Bulletin, 13,* 34–44.

Herek, G. M. (Ed.). (1998). *Stigma and sexual orientation: Understanding prejudice against lesbians, gay men, and bisexuals.* Thousand Oaks, CA: Sage.

Herek, G. M. (2004). Beyond "homophobia": Thinking about sexual prejudice and stigma in the twenty-first century. *Sexuality Research & Social Policy, 1,* 6–24.

Herek, G. M., Gillis, J. R., & Cogan, J. C. (2009). Internalized stigma among sexual minority adults: Insights from a social psychological perspective. *Journal of Counseling Psychology, 56,* 32–43.

Hernstein, R., & Murray, C. (1994). *The bell curve: Intelligence and class structure in American life.* New York: Free Press.

Heterosexism. (2009). *Fact and information sheet about: Heterosexism.* Retrieved May 28, 2009, from www.jmu.edu/safezone/wmlibrary/heterosexism.

Hill, M. S., & Fischer, A. R. (2008). Lesbian and heterosexual women's experiences with sexual- and self-objectification. *The Counseling Psychologist, 36,* 745–776.

Hinton, E. L. (March/April 2004). Microinequities: When small slights lead to huge problems in the workplace. *Diversity Inc.*

Hire Diversity (2001, April 25). *Survey reveals American attitudes towards Asian Americans.* Obtained April 21, 2009, from www.hirediversity.com/news/2001/4/25survey_reveals_american_attitudes-towards.

Hirschfield, L. A. (2001). On a folk theory of society: Children, evolution, and mental representations of social groups. *Personality and Social Psychology Review, 5,* 107–117.

Ho, D. D., Neumann, A. U., Perelson, A. S., Chen, W., Leonard, J. M., & Markowitz, M. (1995). Rapid turnover of plasma virions and CD4 lymphocytes in HIV-1 infection. *Nature, 373,* 123–126.

Holmes, T. H., & Rahe, R. H. (1967). The social readjustment rating scale. *Journal of Psychosomatic Research, 11,* 213–218.

Holmes, T. S., & Holmes, T. H. (1970). Short-term intrusion into the life style routine. *Journal of Psychosomatic Research, 14,* 121–132.

Horvath, A. O., & Symonds, B. D. (1991). Relationship between working alliance and outcome in psychotherapy: A meta-analysis. *Journal of Counseling Psychology, 38,* 139–149.

Hovey, J. D. (2000). Acculturative stress, depression, and suicidal ideation in Mexican immigrants. *Cultural Diversity and Ethnic Minority Psychology, 6,* 134–151.

Hughes, S. A. (2005). *What we still don't know about teaching race: How to talk about it in the classroom.* Lewiston, NY: The Edwin Mellen Press.

Hunter, J., & Mallon, G. P. (2000). Lesbian, gay and bisexual adolescent development. In B. Greene & G. L. Croom (Eds.), *Education, research, and practice in lesbian, gay, bisexual, and transgendered psychology* (pp. 226–243). Thousand Oaks, CA: Sage.

Hwang, W., & Goto, S. (2008). The impact of perceived racial discrimination on the mental health of Asian American and Latino college students. *Cultural Diversity and Ethnic Minority Psychology, 74,* 326–335.

Hyde, J. S., & DeLamater, J. D. (2000). *Understanding human sexuality.* Boston: McGraw-Hill.

Hylton, M. E. (2005). Heteronormativity and the experiences of lesbian and bisexual women as social work students. *Journal of Social Work Education 41,* 67–82.

Igartua, J. J., Gill, K., & Montoro, R. (2003). Internalized homophobia: A factor in depression, anxiety, and suicide in the gay and lesbian population. *Canadian Journal of Community Mental Health, 22,* 15–30.

Inman, A. G., & Yeh, C. J. (2007). Asian American stress and coping. In F. T. L. Leong, A. Inman, A. Ebreo, L. H. Yang, L. Kinoshita, & M. Fu (Eds.), *Handbook of Asian American Psychology* (pp. 323–339). Thousand Oaks, CA: Sage.

Inzlicht, M., & Good, C. (2006). How environments threaten academic performance, self-knowledge, and sense of belonging. In S. Levin & C. van Laar (Eds.), *Stigma and group inequality: Social psychological approaches* (pp. 129–150). Mahwah, NJ: Erlbaum.

Irving, I. M. (2001). Media exposure and disordered eating: Introduction to the special section. *Journal of Social and Clinical Psychology, 20,* 259–263.

Ito, T. A., & Urland, G. R. (2003). Race and gender on the brain: Electrocortical measures of attention to the race and gender of multiply catgorizable individuals. *Journal of Personality and Social Psychology, 85,* 616–625.

Jackson, J. S., Brown, K. T., & Kirby, D. C. (1998). International perspectives on prejudice and racism. In J. L. Eberhardt & S. T. Fiske (Eds.), *Confronting racism* (pp. 101–135). Thousand Oaks, CA: Sage.

Jackson, J. S., Brown, T. N., Williams, D. R., Torres, M., Sellers, S. L., & Brown, K. (1992). *Racism and the physical and mental health status of African Americans: A thirteen year national panel study.* Ann Arbor: University of Michigan Institute for Social Research.

James, K., Lovato, C., & Khoo, G. (1994). Social identity correlates of minority workers' health. *The Academy of Management Journal, 37,* 383–396.

Jemeno-Ingrum, D., Berdahl, J. L., & Lucero-Wagoner, B. (2009). Stereotypes of Latinos and Whites: Do they guide evaluations in diverse work groups? *Cultural Diversity and Ethnic Minority Psychology, 15,* 158–164.

Jenkins, A. H. (1982). *The psychology of the Afro-American.* New York: Pergamon.

Jensen, R. (2002). White privilege shapes the U.S. In P. S. Rothenberg (Ed.), *White privilege* (pp. 103–106). New York: Worth.

Johnson, D. R., & Longerbeam, S. D. (2007). Implications for the privileged identity: Exploration model in student affairs theory and practice. *College Student Affairs Journal, 26,* 216–221.

Johnson, K. W., Anderson, N. B., Bastida, E., Kramer, B. J., Williams, D., & Wong, M. (1995). Macrosocial and environmental influences on minority health. *Health Psychology, 14,* 601–612.

Johnson, S. (1988). Unconscious racism and the criminal law. *Cornell Law Review, 73,* 1016–1037.

Jones, D. R., Harrell, J. P., Morris-Prather, C. E., Thomas, J., & Omowale, N. (1996). Affective and physiological responses to racism: The roles of Afrocentrism and mode of presentation. *Ethnicity and Disease, 6,* 109–122.

Jones, J. M. (1997). *Prejudice and racism* (2nd ed.). Washington, DC: McGraw-Hill.

Juntunen, C. L., Barraclough, D. J., Broneck, C. L., Seibel, G. A., Winrow, S. A., & Morin, P. M. (2001). American Indian perspectives on the career journey. *Journal of Counseling psychology, 48,* 274–285.

Karlsen, S., & Nazroo, J. Y. (2002). Relations between racial discrimination, social class, and health among ethnic minority groups. *American Journal of Public health, 92,* 624–631.

Kawakami, K., Dunn, E., Karmali, F., & Dovidio, J. F. (2009). Mispredicting affective and behavioral responses to racism. *Science, 323,* 276–278.

Katz, J. H. (1985). The sociopolitical nature of counseling. *The Counseling Psychologist, 13,* 615–624.

Kazdin, A. E., Marciano, P. L., & Whitley, M. K. (2005). The therapeutic alliance in cognitive-behavioral treatment of children referred for opposition, aggressive, and antisocial behavior. *Journal of Consulting and Clinical Psychology, 73,* 726–730.

Kearney, L. K., Draper, M., & Baron, A. (2005). Counseling utilization by ethnic minority college students. *Cultural Diversity and Ethnic Minority Psychology, 11,* 272–285.

Keltner, D., & Robinson, R. J. (1996). Extremism, power, and imagined basis of social conflict. *Current directions in psychological science, 5,* 101–105.

Keltner, N. G., & Dowben, J. S. (2007). Psychobiological substrates of Posttraumatic Stress Disorder: Part I. *Perspectives in Psychiatric Care, 43,* 97–101.

Kennedy, A. (2005, April). Rainbow recovery: Counseling GLBT substance abusers. *Counseling Today,* 29–30.

Kessler, R. C. (2003). Epidemiology of women and depression. *Journal of Affective Disorders, 74,* 5–13.

Kiecolt-Glazer, J. K., & Glaser, R. (1995). Psychoneuroimmunology and health consequences: Data and shared mechanisms. *Psychosomatic Medicine, 57,* 269–274.

Kiecolt-Glazer, J. K., Glaser, R., Cacioppo, J. T., MacCallum, R. C., et al. (1997). Marital conflict in older adults: Endocrinological and immunological correlates. *Psychosomatic Medicine, 59,* 339–349.

Kiecolt-Glazer, J. K., Glaser, R., Shuttleworth, E. C., Dyer, C. S., Ogrocki P., & Speicher, C. E. (1987). Chronic stress and immunity in family caregivers of Alzheimer's disease victims. *Psychosomatic Medicine, 49,* 523–535.

Kim, J. G. S. (2002). Racial perceptions and psychological well being in Asian and Hispanic Americans. *Dissertation Abstracts International, 63*(2–B), 1033B.

King, K. R. (2005). Why is discrimination stressful? The mediating role of cognitive appraisal. *Cultural Diversity and Ethnic Minority Psychology, 11,* 202–212.

Kirkpatrick, L. A. (1993). Fundamentalism, Christian orthodoxy, and intrinsic religious orientation as predictors of discriminatory attitudes. *Journal for the Scientific Study of Religion, 32,* 256–268.

Kiselica, M. (1998). Preparing Anglos for the challenges and joys of multiculturalism. *The Counseling Psychologist, 26,* 5–21.

Kivel, P. (1996). *Uprooting racism: How white people can work for racial justice*. Philadelphia, PA: New Society Publishers.

Klonoff, E. A., & Landrine, H. (1995). The schedule of sexist events: A measure of lifetime and recent sexist discrimination in women's lives. *Psychology of Women Quarterly, 19*, 439–472.

Kochman, T. (1981). *Black and White styles in conflict*. Chicago: University of Chicago Press.

Kochman, T. (1994). Black and White cultural styles in pluralistic perspective. In G. R. Weaver (Ed.), *Culture, communication, and conflict: Readings in intercultural relations* (pp. 293–308). Needham Heights, MA: Ginn Press.

Krupin, S. (2000, July 25). Prejudice, schools key concerns of Hispanics. *Seattle PostIntelligencer*, A7.

Kumanyika, S. K. (1993). Special issues regarding obesity in minority populations. *Annuals of International Medicine, 119*, 650–654.

LaFrance, M., & Woodzicka, J. A. (1998). No laughing matter: Women's verbal and nonverbal reactions to sexist humor. In J. K. Swim & C. Stangor (Eds.), *Prejudice: The target's perspective* (pp. 62–80). New York: Academic Press.

Landrine, H., & Klonoff, E. A. (1996). The schedule of racist events: A measure of racial discrimination and a study of its negative physical and mental health consequences. *The Journal of Black Psychology, 22*, 144–168.

Lara, M. E., Klein, D. N., & Kasch, K. L. (2000). Psychosocial predictors of the short-term course and outcome of major depression: A longitudinal study of a nonclinical sample with recent-onset episodes. *Journal of Abnormal Psychology, 109*, 644–650.

Lazarus, R. S. (1966). *Psychological stress and the coping process*. New York: McGraw-Hill.

Lazarus, R. S., & Folkman, S. (1984). *Stress, appraisal, and coping*. New York: Springer.

Lee, R. M. (2003). Do ethnic identity and other-group orientation protect against discrimination for Asian Americans? *Journal of Counseling Psychology, 50*, 36–44.

Lee, W. H. (2001). *My country versus me*. New York: Hyperion.

Leland, J. (2008, October 7). In "Sweetie" and "Dear," a hurt for the elderly. *New York Times*. Retrieved from www.nytimes.com/2008/10/07/us/07aging.html?=todayspaper&pagewanted=print.

Leong, R. T. L., Wagner, N. S., & Tata, S. P. (1995). Racial and ethnic variations in help seeking attitudes. In J. G. Ponterotto, J. M. Casa, L. A. Suzuki, & C. M. Alexander (Eds.), *Handbook of multicultural counseling* (pp. 415–438). Thousand Oaks, CA: Sage.

Levenstein, C., Prantera, C., Varvo, V., Scribano, M. L., Berto, E., Luzi, C., & Andreoli, A. (1993). Development of the perceived stress questionnaire: A new tool for psychosomatic research. *Journal of Psychosomatic Research, 37*, 19–32.

Levitt, H. M., Ovrebo, E., Anderson-Cleveland, M. B., Leone, C., Jeong, J. Y., Arm, J. R., et al. (2009). Balancing dangers: GLBT experience in a time of anti-GLBT legislations. *Journal of Counseling Psychology, 56*, 67–81.

Liang, C. T. H., Alvarez, A. N., Juang, L. P., & Liang, M. X. (2007). The role of coping in the relationship between perceived racism and racism-related stress for Asian Americans: Gender differences. *Journal of Counseling Psychology, 54*, 132–141.

Liang, C. T. H., & Fassinger, R. E. (2008). The role of collective self-esteem for Asian Americans experiencing racism-related stress: A test of moderator and mediator hypotheses. *Cultural Diversity and Ethnic Minority Psychology, 14*, 19–28.

Liang, C. T. H., Li, L. C., & Kim, B. S. K. (2004). The Asian American Racism-Related Stress Inventory: Development, factor analysis, reliability, and validity. *Journal of Counseling Psychology, 51*, 103–114.

Liu, W. M., & Pope-Davis, D. B. (2005). The working alliance, therapy ruptures and impasses, and counseling competence: Implications for counselor training and education. In Robert T. Carter (Ed.), *Handbook of racial-cultural psychology and counseling* (pp. 148–167). Hoboken, NJ: John Wiley & Sons.

Locke, D. C. (1994). Fatigue: An essay, Ashville (N.C.). *African American News*, October 1994, 30.

Lopez, J. D. (2005). Race-related stress and sociocultural orientation among Latino students during their transition into a predominantly White, highly selective institution. *Journal of Hispanic Higher Education, 4*, 354–365.

Lott, B., Aquith, K., & Doyon, T. (2001). Relationship of ethnicity and age to women's responses to personal experiences of sexist discrimination in the United States. *The Journal of Social Psychology, 141*, 309–315.

Luoma, J. B., Pearson, M. A., & Pearson, J. L. (2002). Suicide and marital risk in the United States, 1991–1996: Is widowhood a risk factor? *American Journal of Public Health, 92*, 1518–1582.

Lyness, K. S., & Thompson, D. E. (2000). Climbing the corporate ladder: Do female and male executives follow the same route? *Journal of Applied Psychology, 85*, 86–101.

Mallon, G. P. (1998). Gay, lesbian, and bisexual childhood and adolescent development: An ecological perspective. In G. Appleby & J. Anastas (Eds.), *Not just a passing phase: Social work with gay, lesbian, and bisexual persons*. New York: Columbia University Press.

Martin, J. I., & Knox, J. (2000). Methodological and ethical issues in research on lesbians and gay men. *Social Work Research, 24*, 51–59.

Matteson, A. V., & Moradi, B. (2005). Examining the structure of the Schedule of Sexist Events: Replication and extension. *Psychology of Women Quarterly, 29*, 47–57.

Matthee, I. (1997, Sept. 9). Anti-Asian hate crimes on rise in U.S. but state sees decline in such offenses. *Seattle Post-Intelligencer*, A3.

McConahay, J. B. (1986). Modern racism, ambivalence, and the modern racism scale. In J. F. Dovidio & S. L. Gaertner (Eds.), *Prejudice, discrimination, and racism* (pp. 91–126). Orlando, FL: Academic Press.

McCord, C., & Freeman, H. P. (1990). Excess mortality in Harlem. *New England Journal of Medicine, 322*, 173–177.

McFarland, S. G. (1989). Religious orientations and the targets of discrimination. *The Journal for the Scientific Study of Religions, 28,* 324–336.

McGonagle, K. A., & Kessler, R. C. (1990). Chronic stress, acute stress, and depressive symptoms. *American Journal of Community Psychology, 18,* 681–706.

McIntosh, P. (2002). White privilege: Unpacking the invisible knapsack. In P. S. Rothenberg (Ed.), *White privilege* (pp. 97–101). New York: Worth.

Merritt, M. M., Bennett, G. G., Jr., Williams, R. B., Edwards, C. l., & Sollers, J. J., III. (2006). Perceived racism and cardiovascular reactivity and recovery to personally relevant stress. *Health Psychology, 25,* 364–369.

Meyer, I. H. (1995). Minority stress and mental health in gay men. *Journal of Health and social Behavior, 3,* 38–56.

Meyer, I. H. (2003). Prejudice as stress: Conceptual and measurement problems. *American Journal of Public Health, 93,* 262–265.

Meyer, I. H., & Dean, L. (1998). Internalized homophobia, intimacy and sexual behavior among gay and bisexual men. In G. M. Herek (Ed.), *Stigma and sexual orientation: Understanding prejudice against lesbians, gay men, and bisexuals* (pp. 160–186). Thousand Oaks, CA: Sage.

Meyer, I. H., Schwartz, S., & Frost, D. M. (2008). Social patterning of stress and coping: Does disadvantaged social status confer excess exposure and fewer coping resources? *Social Science and Medicine, 67,* 368–379.

Miller, G. E., Chen, E., & Zhou, E. S. (2007). If it goes up, must it come down? Chronic stress and the hypothalamic-pituitary-adrenocortical axis in humans. *Psychological Bulletin, 133,* 25–45.

Miller, J., & Garran, A. M. (2008). *Racism in the United States.* Belmont, CA: Brooks Cole.

Mio, J. S., Nagata, D. K., Tsai, A. H., & Tewari, N. (2007). Racism against Asian/Pacific Island Americans. In F. T. L. Leong, A. Inman, A. Ebreo, L. H. Yang, L. Kinoshita, & M. Fu (Eds.), pp. 341–361. Thousand Oaks, CA: Sage.

Misra, D. (2001). *Women's health data book: A profile of women's health in the United States.* Washington, DC: Jacobs Institute of Women's Health and the Henry J. Kaiser Family Foundation.

Mitchell, A. (1998, June 17). Controversy over Lott's view of homosexuality. *New York Times,* p. 24.

Mohr, J. J., Israel, T., & Sedlacek, W. E. (2001). Counselors' attitudes regarding bisexuality as predictors of counselors' clinical responses: An analogue study of a female bisexual client. *Journal of Counseling Psychology, 48,* 212–222.

Monroe, C. R. (2005). Why are "bad boys" always Black? Causes of disproportionality in school discipline and recommendations for change. *The Clearing House, 79,* 45–50.

Moradi, B., & Risco, C. (2006). Perceived discrimination experiences and mental health of Latina/o American persons. *Journal of Counseling Psychology, 53,* 411–421.

Moradi, B., van den Berg, J. J., & Epting, F. R. (2009). Threat and guilt aspects of internalized antilesbian and gay prejudice: An application of personal construct theory. *Journal of Counseling Psychology, 56,* 119–131.

Morales, A. T., & Sheafor, B. W. (2004). *Social work.* Boston: Pearson.

Morrison, A. M., & Von Glinow, M. A. (1990). Women and minorities in management. *American Psychologist, 45,* 200–208.

Morrison, M. A., & Morrison, T. G. (2002). Development and validation of a scale measuring prejudice toward gay men and lesbian women. *Journal of Homosexuality, 43,* 15–37.

Morrissey, M. (1997, October). The invisible minority: Counseling Asian Americans. *Counseling Today, 1,* 21–22.

Morrow, S. L., & Beckstead, A. L. (2004). Conversion therapies for same-sex attracted clients in religion conflict: Context, predisposing factors, experiences and implications for therapy. *The Counseling Psychologist, 32,* 641–650.

Mosher, W. D., Chandra, A., & Jones, J. (2005, September 15). Sexual behavior and selected health measures: Men and women 15–44 years of age, United States, 2002. *Advance Data from Vital and Health Statistics,* No. 362. Hyattsville, MD: National Center for Health Statistics.

Nadal, K. L. (in press). Gender microaggressions and women: Implications for therapy. In M. Paludi (Ed.), *Feminism and women's rights worldwide.* Westport, CT: Praeger Publishers.

Nadal, K. L., Rivera, D. P., & Corpus, M. J. H. (in press). Sexual orientation and transgender microaggressions in everyday life: Experiences of lesbians, gays, bisexuals, and transgender individuals. In D. W. Sue (Ed.). *Microaggressions and marginalized groups in society: Race, gender, sexual orientation, class and religious manifestations.* Hoboken, NJ: John Wiley & Sons.

National Academy of Sciences, National Academy of Engineering, & Institute of Medicine. (2006). *Beyond bias and barriers: Fulfilling the potential of women in academic science, and engineering.* Washington, DC: National Academies Press.

National Center for Health Statistics. (1996). *Health, United States, 1995.* Hyattsville, MD: Public Health Service.

National Center for Health Statistics. (2007). Asthma prevalence, health care use and mortality: United States, 2003–2005. Retrieved October 8, 2007, from www.cdc.gov/nchs/producs/pubs/pubd/hestats/asthma03-05.htm.

National Institute of Mental Health. (2007). *Anxiety disorders.* Retrieved February 19, 2008, from www.nimh.nih.gov/publica/NIMHanxiety.pdf.

National Survey of Latinos. (2002). *National Survey of Latinos: Summary of findings. Washington, DC: Pew Hispanic Center and Menlo Park, CA: Henry J. Kaiser Family Foundation.* Retrieved April 29, 2009 from http://www.kff.org/kaiserpolls/upload/2002-National-Survey-Of-Latinos-Summary-of Findings.pdf.

Nelson, T. D. (2006). *The psychology of prejudice.* Boston: Pearson Publishers.

Neville, H. A., Lilly, R. L., Duran, G., Lee, R., & Browne, L. (2000). Construction and initial validation of the Color Blind Racial Attitudes Scale (COBRAS). *Journal of Counseling Psychology, 47*, 59–70.

Noh, S., & Kaspar, V. (2003). Perceived discrimination and depression: Moderating effects of coping, acculturation, and ethnic support. *American Journal of Public Health, 93*, 232–238.

Nolen–Hoeksema, S. (2004). Gender differences in depression. In T. F. Oltmanns & R. F. Emery (Eds.), *Current directions in abnormal psychology* (pp. 49–55). Upper Saddle River, NJ: Prentice-Hall.

Nunez-Smith, M., Currey, L. A., Bigby, J., Berg, D., Krumholz, H. M., & Bradley, E. H. (2007). Impact of race on the professional lives of physicians of African descent. *Annals of Internal Medicine, 146*, 45–51.

O'Brien, J. M., (2005). Sexual orientation, shame and silence. In J. M. Croteau, J. S. Lark, M. A. Lidderdale, & Y. Barry Chung (Eds.), *Deconstructing heterosexism in the counseling profession.* (pp. 97–102). Thousand Oaks, CA: Sage.

Office of Ethnic Minority Affairs. (2006). Hurricane Katrina: A multicultural disaster. *Communique.* Washington, DC: American Psychological Association.

Ogden, C. I., Fryar, C. D., Carroll, M. D., & Flegal, K. M. (2004). *Mean body weight, height, and body mass index. United States 1960–2002: Advance data from vital and health statistics (no. 347).* Hyattsville, MD: National Center for Health Statistics.

Paniagua, F. A. (1998). *Assessing and treating culturally diverse clients.* Thousand Oaks, CA: Sage.

Parham, T. A. (1997). An African-centered view of dual relationships. In B. Herlihy & G. Corey (Eds.), *Boundary issues in counseling* (pp. 109–112). Alexandria, VA: American Counseling Association.

Parker, S., & Thompson, T. (1990). Gay and bisexual men: Developing a healthy identity. In D. Moor & F. Leafgren (Eds.), *Men in conflict* (pp. 113–121). Alexandria, VA: American Counseling Association.

Pearson, J. C. (1985). *Gender and communication.* Dubuque, IA: W. C. Brown.

Pettigrew, T. F. (1981) The mental health impact. In B. P. Bowser & R. G. Hunt (Eds.), *Impacts of racism on White Americans* (pp. 97–118). Thousand Oaks, CA: Sage.

Pew Research Center. (2007). *Blacks see growing values gap between poor and middle class.* Washington, DC: Author.

Pierce, C. (1988). Stress in the workplace. In A. F. Concer-Edwards & J. Spurlock (Eds.), *Black families in crisis: The middle class* (pp. 27–34). New York: Brunner/Mazel.

Pierce, C. M. (1978). Entitlement dysfunctions. *Australian and New Zealand Journal of Psychiatry, 12*(4), 215–219.

Pierce, C. (1995). Stress analogs of racism and sexism: Terrorism, torture, and disaster. In C. Willie, P. Rieker, B. Kramer, & B. Brown (Eds.), *Mental heath, racism, and sexism* (pp. 277–293). Pittsburgh: University of Pittsburgh Press.

Pierce, C., Carew, J., Pierce-Gonzalez, D., & Willis, D. (1978). An experiment in racism: TV commercials. In C. Pierce (Ed.), *Television and education* (pp. 62–88). Beverly Hills, CA: Sage.

Pike, J. L., Smith, T. L., Hauger, R. I., et al. (1997). Chronic life stress alters sympathetic, neuroendocrine, and immune responsibility to an acute psychological stressor in humans. *Psychosomatic Medicine, 59*, 447–457.

Pinterits, E. J., Poteat, P. V., & Spanierman, L. B. (2009). The White privilege attitudes scale: Development and initial validation. *Journal of Counseling Psychology, 56*, 417–429.

Piotrkowski, C. S. (1998). Gender harassment, job satisfaction, and distress among employed White and minority women. *Journal of Occupational Health psychology, 3*, 33–43.

Plant, E. A., & Devine, P. G. (1998). Internal and external motivation to respond without prejudice. *Journal of Personality and Social Psychology, 75*, 811–832.

Plant, E. A., & Peruche, B. M. (2005). The consequences of race for police officers' responses to criminal suspects. *Psychological Science, 16*, 180–183.

Plous, S., & Williams, T. (1995). Racial stereotypes from the days of American slavery: A continuing legacy. *Journal of Applied Social Psychology, 25*, 795–817.

Plummer, D. C. (2001). The quest for modern manhood: Masculine stereotypes, peer culture and the social significance of homophobia. *Journal of Adolescence, 24*, 15–23.

Ponterotto, J. G., Utsey, S. O., & Pedersen, P. B. (2006). *Preventing prejudice*. Thousand Oaks, CA: Sage.

Pope, K. S., & Vasquez, M. J. T. (2005). *How to survive and thrive as a therapist*. Washington, DC: American Psychological Association.

President's Initiative on Race. (1998). *One American in the twenty-first century*. Washington, DC: U.S. Government Printing Office.

Purdie-Vaughns, V., Davis, P. G., Steele, C. M., & Ditlmann, R. (2008). Social identity contingencies: How diversity cues signal threat or safety for African Americans in mainstream institutions. *Journal of Personality and Social Psychology, 94*, 615–630.

Quina, K. (Ed.), (2003). *Teaching gender and multicultural awareness* (pp. 360–437). Washington, DC: APA.

Rahe, R. H. (1994). The more things change… . *Psychosomatic Medicine, 56*, 306–307.

Rahe, R. H., & Arthur, R. J. (1978). Life change and illness studies: Past history and future directions. *Journal of Human Stress, 4*, 3–15.

Reid, L. D., & Radhakrishnan, P. (2003). Race matters: The relations between race and general campus climate. *Cultural Diversity and Ethnic Minority Psychology, 9*, 263–275.

Ricker, P. P., & Bird, C. E. (2005). Rethinking gender differences in health: Why we need to integrate social and biological perspectives. *Journal of Gerontology, 60*, 540–547.

Ridley, C. R. (1995). *Overcoming unintentional racism in counseling and therapy* (1st ed.). Thousand Oaks, CA: Sage.

Ridley, C. R. (2005). *Overcoming unintentional racism in counseling and therapy* (2nd ed.). Thousand Oaks, CA: Sage.

Rienzo, B. A., Button, J. W., Sheu, J.-J., & Li, Y. (2006). The politics of sexual orientation issues in Americans schools. *Journal of School Health, 76,* 93–97.

Rivera, D. P., Forquer, E. E., & Rangel, R. (in press). Microaggressions and the life experience of Latina/o Americans. In D. W. Sue (Ed.), *Microaggressions and marginalized groups in society: Race, gender, sexual orientation, class, international and religious manifestations.* Hoboken, NJ: John Wiley & Sons.

Root, M. P. P. (2003). Racial and ethnic origins of harassment in the workplace. In D. B. Pope Davis, H. L. K. Coleman, W. M. Liu, & R. L. Toporek (Eds.), *Handbook of multicultural competencies in counseling and psychology* (pp. 478–492). Thousand Oaks, CA: Sage.

Rostosky, S. S., Riggle, E. D. B., Horne, S. G., & Miller, A. D. (2009). Marriage amendments and psychological distress in Lesbian, Gay, and Bisexual (LGB) adults. *Journal of Counseling Psychology, 56,* 56–66.

Rowe, D. C. (2005). Under the skin: On the impartial treatment of genetic and environmental hypotheses of racial differences. *American Psychologist,* 60–70.

Rowe, M. P. (1990). Barriers to equality: The power of subtle discrimination to maintain unequal opportunity. *Employee Responsibilities and Rights Journal, 3,* 153–163.

Rubin, H. (April 2008). *Sexism.* Retrieved May 14, 2009, from http://www.portfolio.com/executives/features/2008/03/17/Sexism-in-the-Workplace?.

Russell, S. T., Franz, B. T., & Driscoll, A. K. (2001). Same-sex romantic attraction and experience of violence in adolescence. *American Journal of Public Health, 91,* 903–906.

Russell, S. T., & Joyner, K. (2001). Suicide attempts more likely among adolescents with same-sex sexual orientation. *American Journal of Public Health, 91,* 1276–1281.

Russell, S. T., & Lee, F. C. H. (2004). Practitioners' perspectives on effective practices for Hispanic teenage pregnancy prevention. *Perspectives on sexual and reproductive health, 36,* 142–149.

Safe Space (2009). *Heterosexism.* Retrieved May 28, 2009, from http://studentorgs.utexas.edu/urha/safespace/what is/heterosexism/.

Sakalli, N. (2002). Application of the attribution-value model of prejudice to homosexuality. *Journal of Social Psychology, 142,* 264–271.

Salvatore, J., & Shelton, J. N. (2007). Cognitive costs of exposure to racial prejudice. *Psychological Science, 18,* 810–815.

Samuda, R. J. (1998). *Psychological testing of American minorities.* Thousand Oaks, CA: Sage.

Sanchez-Hucles, J., & Jones, N. (2005). Breaking the silence around race in training, practice, and research. *Counseling Psychologist, 33,* 547–558.

Sandhu, D. S. (1997). Psychocultural profiles of Asian and Pacific Islander Americans: Implications for counseling and psychotherapy. *Journal of Multicultural Counseling and Development, 25,* 7–22.

Satcher, J., & Leggett, M. (2007). Homonegativity among professional school counselors: An exploratory study. *Professional School Counselor, 11,*

Schacht, T. (2008). A broader view of racial microaggression in psychotherapy. *American Psychologist, 63,* 273.

Schujaa, M. (2005). Education and schooling: You can have one without the other. In A. Mazama (Ed.), *The Afrocentric paradigm* (pp. 245–264). Trenton, NJ: Africa World Press.

Schwartzman, J. B., & Glaus, K. D. (2000). Depression and coronary heart disease in women: Implications for clinical practice and research. *Professional Psychology: Research and Practice, 31,* 48–57.

Scott, M. J., & Stradling, S. G. (1994). Posttraumatic Stress Disorder without the trauma. *British Journal of Clinical Psychology, 33,* 71–74.

Sears, D. O. (1988). Symbolic racism. In P. A. Katz & D. A. Taylor (Eds.), *Eliminating racism: Profiles in controversy* (pp. 53–84). New York: Plenum.

Segerstrom, S. C., & Miller, G. E. (2004). Psychological stress and the human immune system: A meta-analytic study of 30 years of inquiry. *Psychological Bulletin, 30,* 601–630.

Seitz, V. (2007). The impact of media spokeswoman on teen girls' body image: An empirical assessment. *Business Review, 7,* 228–236.

Sellers, R. M., & Shelton, J. N. (2003). The role of racial identity in perceived racial discrimination. *Journal of Personality and Social Psychology, 84,* 1070–1092.

Selye, H. (1956). *The stress of life.* New York: McGraw–Hill.

Selye, H. (1982). Stress: Eustress, distress, and human perspectives. In S. B. Day (Ed.), *Life Stress* (pp. 3–13). New York: Van Nostrand Reinhold.

Shockley, W. (1972). Determination of human intelligence. *Journal of Criminal Law and Criminology, 7,* 530–543.

Shujaa, M. (2003). Education and schooling: You can have one without the other. In A. Mazama (Ed.), *The Afrocentric paradigm* (pp. 245–264). Trenton, NJ: Africa World Press.

Sinclair, S. L. (2006). Object lessons: A theoretical and empirical study of objectified body consciousness in women. *Journal of Mental Health Counseling, 28,* 48–68.

Singelis, T. (1994). Nonverbal communication in intercultural interactions. In R. W. Brislin & T. Yoshida (Eds.), *Improving intercultural interactions* (pp. 268–294). Thousand Oaks, CA: Sage.

Slavin, L. A., Rainer, K. I., McCreary, M. L., & Gowda, K. K. (1991). Toward a multicultural model of the stress process. *Journal of Counseling and Development, 70,* 156–163.

Sleeter, C. E., & Bernal, D. D. (2004). Critical pedagogy, critical race theory, and antiracist education. In J. A. Banks (Ed.), *Handbook of research on multicultural education* (2nd ed., pp. 240–258). San Francisco: Jossey Bass.

Smedley, A., & Smedley, B. D. (2005). Race as biology is fiction, racism as a social problem is real. *American Psychologist, 60,* 16–26.

Smith, N. G., & Ingram, K. M. (2004). Workplace heterosexism and adjustment among lesbian, gay, and bisexual individuals: The role of unsupportive social interactions. *Journal of Counseling Psychology, 51,* 57–67.

Solórzano, D., Ceja, M., & Yosso, T. (2000). Critical race theory, racial microaggressions, and campus racial climate: The experiences of African American college students. *The Journal of Negro Education, 69*(1/2), 60–73.

Spangenberg, J. J., & Pieterse, C. (1995). Stressful life events and psychological status in Black South African women. *Journal of Social Psychology, 135,* 439–445.

Spanierman, L. B., & Heppner, M. J. (2004). Psychosocial costs of racism to Whites scale (PCRW): Development and initial validation. *Journal of Counseling Psychology, 51,* 249–262.

Spanierman, L. B., Oh, E., Poteat, V. P., Hunt, A. R., McClair, V. L., Beer, A. M., et al. (2008). White University students' responses to societal racism. *The Counseling Psychologist, 36,* 839–870.

Spanierman, L. B., Poteat, V. P., Beer, A. M., & Armstrong, P. I. (2006). Psychosocial costs of racism to Whites: Exploring patterns through cluster analysis. *Journal of Counseling Psychology, 53,* 434–441.

Spanierman, L. B., Poteat, V. P., Wang, Y. F., & Oh, E. (2008). Psychosocial costs of racism to White counselors: Predicting various dimensions of multicultural counseling competence. *Journal of Counseling Psychology, 55,* 75–88.

Spanierman, L. B., Todd, N. R., & Anderson, C. J. (2009). Psychosocial costs of racism to Whites: Understanding patterns among university students. *Journal of Counseling Psychology, 56,* 239–252.

Spradlin, I. K., & Parsons, R. D. (2008). *Diversity matters.* Belmont, CA: Thompson Wadsworth.

Stambor, Z. (2006). Stressed-out nation. *Monitor in Psychology, 37,* 28–29.

Steele, C. M. (1997). A threat in the air: How stereotypes shape intellectual identity and performance. *American Psychologist, 52*(6), 613–629.

Steele, C. M. (2003). Race and the schooling of Black Americans. In S. Plous (Ed.), *Understanding prejudice and discrimination* (pp. 98–107). New York: McGraw-Hill.

Steele, C. M., Spencer, S. J., & Aronson, J. (2002). Contending with group image: The psychology of stereotype and social identity threat. In M. Zanna (Ed.), *Advances in experimental social psychology* (Vol. 23, pp. 379–440). New York: Academic Press.

Steele, M. S., & McGarvey, S. T. (1997). Anger expression, age, and blood pressure in modernizing Samoan adults. *Psychosomatic Medicine, 59,* 632–637.

Steinem, G. (2008, January 10). Women are never front-runners. *New York Times.*

Stevens, F. G., Plaut, V. C., & Sanches-Burks, J. (2008). Unlocking the benefits of diversity. *The Journal of Applied Behavioral Science, 44,* 116–133.

Stir-Fry Productions (1994). *The color of fear.* Video. Berkeley, CA: Author.

Stolberg, S. G. (2009, July 15). Sotomayor leaves passion behind. *The New York Times.*

Strickland, B. R. (1992). Women and depression. *Current Directions in Psychological Science, 1,* 132–135.

Strong, S. R. (1969). Counseling: An interpersonal influence process. *Journal of Counseling Psychology, 15,* 215–224.

Strong, S. R., & Schmidt, L. D. (1970). Expertness and influence in counseling. *Journal of Counseling Psychology, 15,* 31–35.

Sue, D., Sue, D. W., & Sue, S. (2010). *Understanding abnormal behavior* (9th ed.). Boston, MA: Wadsworth.

Sue, D. W. (1991). A model for cultural diversity training. *Journal of Counseling and Development, 70,* 99–105.

Sue, D. W. (1994). U.S. Business and the challenge of cultural diversity. *The Diversity Factor, Winter,* 24–28.

Sue, D. W. (1995). Multicultural organizational development. In J. G. Ponterotto, J. M. Casas, L. A. Suzuki, & C. M. Alexander (Eds.), *Handbook of multicultural counseling* (pp. 474–492). Thousand Oaks, CA: Sage.

Sue, D. W. (2003). *Overcoming our racism: The journey to liberation.* San Francisco: Jossey-Bass.

Sue, D. W. (2004). Whiteness and ethnocentric monoculturalism: Making the "invisible" visible. *American Psychologist, 59,* 759–769.

Sue, D. W. (2005). Racism and the conspiracy of silence. *The Counseling Psychologist, 33* (1), 100–114.

Sue, D. W. (2006a). The invisible whiteness of being: Whiteness, White supremacy, White privilege, and racism. In M. C. Constantine & D. W. Sue (Eds.), *Addressing racism* (pp. 15–30). Hoboken, NJ: John Wiley & Sons.

Sue, D. W. (2006b). *Multicultural social work practice.* Hoboken, NJ: John Wiley & Sons.

Sue, D. W. (2008a). Hate crimes are illegal, but racial microaggressions are not! *Communique,* August, 5–10.

Sue, D. W. (2008b). Multicultural organizational consultation: A social justice perspective. *Consulting Psychology Journal: Practice and Research, 60,* 157–169.

Sue, D. W., Arredondo, P., & McDavis, R. J. (1992). Multicultural competencies/standards: A call to the profession. *Journal of Counseling and Development, 70*(4), 477–486.

Sue, D. W., Bernier, J. B., Duran, M., Feinberg, L., Pedersen, P., Smith, E., et al. (1982). Position paper: Cross-cultural counseling competencies. *Counseling Psychologist, 10,* 45–52.

Sue, D. W., Bucceri, J., Lin, A. I., Nadal, K. L., & Torino, G. C. (2007). Racial microaggressions and the Asian American experience. *Cultural Diversity and Ethnic Minority Psychology, 13,* 72–81.

Sue, D. W., & Capodilupo, C. M. (2008). Racial, gender, and sexual orientation microaggressions: Implications for counseling and psychotherapy. In D. W. Sue &

D. Sue (Eds.), *Counseling the culturally diverse: Theory and practice*. Hoboken, NJ: John Wiley & Sons.

Sue, D. W., Capodilupo, C. M., & Holder, A. (2008). Racial microaggressions in the life experience of Black Americans. *Professional Psychology: Research and Practice, 39,* 329–336.

Sue, D. W., Capodilupo, C. M., Nadal, K. L., & Torino, G. C. (2008). Racial microaggressions and the power to define reality. *American Psychologist, 63,* 277–279.

Sue, D. W., Capodilupo, C. M., Torino, G. C., Bucceri, J. M., Holder, A. M. B., Nadal, K. L., et al. (2007). Racial microaggressions in everyday life: Implications for clinical practice. *American Psychologist, 62,* 271–286.

Sue, D. W., & Constantine, M. G. (2007). Racial microaggressions as instigators to difficult dialogues on race: Implications for student affairs educators and students. *Journal of Student College Personnel, 26,* 136–143.

Sue, D. W., Lin, A. I., & Rivera, D. P. (2009). Racial microaggressions in the workplace: Manifestation and impact. In J. Chin (Ed.), *Diversity in mind and in action* (pp.157-172). Westport, CT: Praeger Press.

Sue, D. W., Lin, A. I., Torino, G. C., Capodilupo, C. M., & Rivera, D. P. (2009). Racial microaggressions and difficult dialogues in the classroom. *Cultural Diversity and Ethnic Minority Psychology, 15,* 183–190.

Sue, D. W., Nadal, K. L., Capodilupo, C. M., Lin, A. I., Torino, G. C., & Rivera, D. P. (2008). Racial microaggressions against Black Americans: Implications for counseling. *Journal of Counseling and Development, 86,* 330–338.

Sue, D. W., Parham, T. A., & Santiago, G. B. (1998). The changing face of work in the United States: Implications for individual, institutional and societal survival. *Cultural Diversity and Mental Health, 4,* 153–164.

Sue, D. W., Rivera, D. P., Capodilupo, C. M., Lin, A. I., & Torino, G. C. (2009). Racial dialogues and White trainee fears: Implications for education and training. *Cultural Diversity and Ethnic Minority Psychology.*

Sue, D. W., & Sue, D. (2008). *Counseling the culturally diverse: Theory and practice* (4th ed.). New York: John Wiley & Sons.

Sue, D. W., & Torino, G. C. (2005). Racial-cultural competence: Awareness, knowledge, and skills. In R. T. Carter (Ed.), *Handbook of racial-cultural psychology and counseling,* (Vol. 2, pp. 3–18.). Hoboken, NJ: John Wiley & Sons.

Sue, D. W., Torino, G. C., Capodilupo, C. M., Rivera, D. P., & Lin, A. I. (2009). How White faculty perceive and react to difficult dialogues on race: Implications for education and training. *The Counseling Psychologist.*

Sue, S., Allen, D., & Conaway, L. (1975). The responsiveness and equality of mental health care to Chicanos and Native Americans. *American Journal of Community Psychology, 45,* 111–118.

Sue, S., Fujino, D. C., Hu, L., Takeuchi, D. T., & Zane, N. W. S. (1991). Community mental health services for ethnic minority groups: A test of the cultural responsiveness hypothesis. *Journal of Consulting and Clinical Psychology, 59,* 533–540.

Sue, S., McKinney, H., Allen, D., & Hall, J. (1974). Delivery of community health services to Black and White clients. *Journal of Consulting and Clinical Psychology, 42,* 794–801.

Sue, S., Sue, D. W., Zane, N., & Wong, H. Z. (1985). Where are the Asian American leaders and top executives? *P/AAMHRC Review, 4,* 13–15.

Swim, J. K., Aikin, K. J., Hall, W. S., & Hunter, B. A. (1995). Sexism and racism: Old-fashioned and modern prejudices. *Journal of Personality and Social Psychology, 68,* 199–214.

Swim, J. K., & Cohen, L. L. (1997). Overt, covert, and subtle sexism. *Psychology of Women Quarterly, 21,* 103–118.

Swim, J. K., Hyers, L. L., Cohen, L. L., & Ferguson, M. J. (2001). Everyday sexism: Evidence for its incidence, nature, and psychological impact from three daily diary studies. *Journal of Social issues, 57,* 31–53.

Swim, J. K., Mallett, R., & Stangor, C. (2004). Understanding subtle sexism: Detection and use of sexist language. *Sex Roles, 51,* 117–128.

Swim, J. K., & Stangor, C. (1998). *Prejudice: The target's perspective.* San Diego, CA: Academic Press.

Szymanski, D. M. (2009). Examining potential moderators of the link between hetero-sexist events and gay and bisexual men's psychological distress. *Journal of Counseling Psychology 56,* 142–151.

Szymanski, D. M., & Gupta, A. (2009). Examining the relationship between multiple internalized oppressions and African American lesbian, gay, bisexual, and questioning person' self-esteem and psychological distress. *Journal of Counseling Psychology, 56,* 110–118.

Szymanski, D. M., Kashubeck-West, S., & Meyer, J. (2008). Internalized heterosexism. *The Counseling Psychologist, 36,* 510–524.

Tatum, B. (2002). Breaking the silence. In P. S. Rothenberg (Ed.), *White privilege* (pp. 115–120). New York: Worth.

Taylor, S., & Kennedy, R. (2003). Feminist framework. In J. Anderson & R. W. Carter (Eds.), *Diversity perspectives for social work practice* (pp. 171–197). Boston: Allyn & Bacon.

Taylor, T. S. (2000). Is God good for you, good for your neighbor? The influence of religious orientation on demoralization and attitudes towards lesbians and gay men. *Dissertation Abstracts International Section A: Humanities and Social Sciences, 60* (12A), 4472.

Terman, L. M. (1916). *The measurement of intelligence.* Boston: Houghton Mifflin.

Terrell, F., & Terrell, S. (1984). Race of counselor, client sex, cultural mistrust level, and premature termination from counseling among Black clients. *Journal of Counseling Psychology, 31,* 371–375.

Thomas, A., & Sillen, S. (1972). *Racism and psychiatry.* New York: Brunner/Mazel.

Thomas, K. M., & Plaut, V. C. (2008). The many faces of diversity resistance in the workplace. In K. M. Thomas (Ed.), *Diversity resistance in organizations* (pp. 1–22). New York: Lawrence Erlbaum Associates.

Thomas, K. R. (2008). Macrononsense in multiculturalism. *American Psychologist, 63,* 274–275.

Thompson, C. E., & Neville, H. A. (1999). Racism, mental health, and mental health practice. *The Counseling Psychologist, 27(2),* 155–223.

Thompson, J. K., & Stice, E. (2004). Thin-ideal internalization: Mounting evidence for a new risk factor for body image disturbance and eating pathology. In T. F. Oltmanns & R. E. Emery (Eds.), *Current directions in abnormal psychology* (pp. 97–101). Upper Saddle River, NJ: Prentice Hall.

Thurlow, C. (2001). Naming the "outsider within": Homophobia, pejoratives, and the verbal abuse of lesbian, gay, and bisexual high school pupils. *Journal of Adolescence, 24,* 25–38.

Tortolero, S. R., & Roberts, R. E. (2001). Differences in nonfatal suicide behavior among Mexican and European American middle school children. *Suicide and Life-Threatening Behavior, 31,* 214–223.

Tozer, E. E., & Hayes, J. A. (2004). Why do individuals seek conversion therapy? *The Counseling Psychologist, 32,* 716–740.

Trimble, J. E., & Thurman, P. J. (2002). Ethnocultural considerations and strategies for providing counseling services to Native American Indians. In P. B. Pedersen, J. G. Draguns, W. J. Lonner, & J. E. Trimble (Eds.), *Counseling across cultures* (pp. 53–91). Thousand Oaks, CA: Sage.

Underwood, A. (2005, October 3). The good heart. *Newsweek,* 49–55.

University of California–Davis News and Information. (June 28, 2007). *Anti-gay hate crimes widespread.* Retrieved May 29, 2009, from http://www.news.ucdavis.edu/search/printable_news.lasso?id=8224&table=news.

U.S. Bureau of Census Statistics. (2007). Retrieved April 29, 2009, from http://www.census.gov/population/www/projections/2008projections.html

U.S. Bureau of the Census. (2001). *Population profile of the United States.* Washington, DC: U.S. Government Printing Office.

U.S. Bureau of the Census. (2002). *Poverty in the United States.* Washington, DC: U.S. Government Printing Office.

U.S. Census Bureau. (2003). *The Hispanic population in the United States: March 2002.* Washington, DC: U.S. Government Printing Office.

U.S. Census Bureau. (2005a). *We the people: Asian Pacific Islanders in the United States.* Washington, DC: U.S. Government Printing Office.

U.S. Census Bureau. (2005b). *We the people: Blacks in the United States.* Washington, DC: U.S. Government Printing Office.

U.S. Census Bureau. (2006). *We the people: American Indians and Alaska Natives in the United States.* Washington, DC: U.S. Government Printing Office.

U.S. Department of Health and Human Services. (2001). *Mental health: Culture, race, and ethnicity—A supplement to* Mental health: A report of the surgeon general. Rockville,

MD: U.S. Department of Health and Human Services, Substance Abuse and Mental Health Service Administration, Center for Mental Health Services.

U.S. Department of Labor. (1992). *Women workers outlook to 2005*. Washington, DC: Author.

U.S. Department of Labor. (2005). *20 leading occupations of employed women*. Rockville, MD: Author.

U.S. Department of Labor. (2009). *Quick stats on women workers, 2008*. Retrieved June 11, 2009, from www.dol.gov/wb/stats/main.htm.

Utsey, S. O., Chae, M. H., Brown, C. F., & Kelly, F. (2002). Effect of ethnic group membership on ethnic identity, race-related stress, and quality of life. *Cultural Diversity and Ethnic Minority Psychology, 8*, 224–233.

Utsey, S. O., Gernat, C. A., & Hammar, L. (2005). Examining White counselor trainees' reactions to racial issues in counseling and supervision dyads. *The Counseling Psychologist, 33*, 449–478.

Utsey, S. O., Giesbrecht, N., Hook, J., & Stanard, P. M. (2008). Cultural, sociofamilial, and psychological resources that inhibit psychological distress in African Americans exposed to stressful life events and race-related stress. *Journal of Counseling Psychology, 55*, 49–62.

Utsey, S. O., & Hook, J. N. (2007). Heart rate variability as a physiological moderator of the relationship between race-related stress and psychological distress in African Americans. *Journal of Counseling Psychology, 13*, 250–253.

Utsey, S. O., & Ponterotto, J. G. (1996). Development and validation of the Index of Race-Related Stress (IRRS). *Journal of Counseling Psychology, 43*, 490–502.

Valentiner, D. P., Foa, E. B., Riggs, D. S., & Gershuny, B. S. (1996). Coping strategies and Posttraumatic Stress Disorder in female victims of sexual and nonsexual assault. *Journal of Abnormal Psychology, 105*, 455–458.

Vanman, E. J., Saltz, J. L., Nathan, L. R., & Warren, J. A. (2004). Racial discrimination by low-prejudiced whites. *Psychological Science, 15*, 711–719.

Vega, W., & Rumbaut, R. G. (1991). Ethnic minorities and mental health. *Annual Review of Sociology, 17*, 351–383.

Wang, V. O., & Sue, S. (2005). In the eye of the storm: Race and genomics in research and practice. *American Psychologist, 60*, 37–45.

Watt, S. K. (2007). Difficult dialogues and social justice: Uses of the privileged identity exploration (PIE) model in student affairs practice. *The College Student Affairs Journal, 26*, 114–125.

Weber, S. N. (1985). The need to be: The socio-cultural significance of Black language. In L. A. Samovar & R. E. Porter (Eds.), *Intercultural communication: A reader* (pp. 232–242). Belmont, CA: Wadsworth.

Wei, M., Ku, T-Y., Russell, D. W., Mallinckrodt, B., & Liao, K. Y-H. (2008). Moderating effects of three coping strategies and self-esteem on perceived discrimination and depressive symptoms: A minority stress model for Asian international students. *Journal of Counseling Psychology, 55,* 451–561.

Weinberg, G. (1972). *Society and the healthy homosexual.* New York: St. Martin's Press.

Welsing, R. C. (1991). *The Isis papers: The keys to the colors.* Chicago: Third World Press.

Whaley, A. L. (2001). Cultural mistrust: An important psychological construct for diagnosis and treatment of Blacks. *Professional Psychology: Research & Practice, 32,* 555–562.

Whitely, B. E. (1990). The relationship of heterosexuals' attributions for the causes of homosexuality to attitudes towards lesbians and gay men. *Personality and Social Psychology Bulletin, 16,* 369–377.

Wikipedia. (2009). Chief Illiniwek. Retrieved March 13, 2009, from http://en.wikipedia.org/wiki/Chief_Illiniwek.

Wilding, T. (1984). Is stress making you sick? *American Health, 6,* 2–5.

Wildman, S. M., & Davis, A. D. (2002). Making systems of privilege visible. In P. S. Rothenberg (Ed.), *White privilege* (pp. 89–95). New York: Worth.

Williams Institute. (2006). Cities with highest percentage of gays, lesbians, bisexuals. Retrieved December 8, 2006, from http://www.law.ucla.edu/williamsinstitute/press/.

Williams, D. R., & Collins, C. (1995). U.S. socioeconomic and racial differences in health: Patterns and explanations. *Annual Review of Sociology, 21,* 349–386.

Williams, D. R., Lavizzo-Mourey, R., & Warren, R. C. (1994). The concept of race and health status in America. *Public Health Reports, 109,* 26–41.

Williams, D. R., Neighbors, H. W., & Jackson, J. S. (2003). Racial/ethnic discrimination and health: Findings from community studies. *American Journal of Public Health, 93*(2), 200–208.

Williams, D. R., Yu, Y., & Jackson, J. S. (1997). Racial differences in physical and mental health. *Journal of Health Psychology, 2*(3), 335–351.

Willow, R. A. (2008). Lived experience of interracial dialogue on race: Proclivity to participate. *Journal of Multicultural Counseling and Development, 36,* 40–51.

Winter, S. (1977). Rooting out racism. *Issues in Radical Therapy, 17,* 24–30.

Winterowd, C. L., Adams, E. M., Miville, M. L., & Mintz, L. B. (2009). Operationalizing, instilling, and assessing counseling psychology training values related to diversity in academic programs. *The Counseling Psychologist, 37,* 676–704.

Wong, F., & Halgin, R. (2006). The "Model Minority," bane or blessing for Asian Americans? *Journal of Multicultural Counseling and Development, 34,* 38–49.

Worthington, R. L., & Reynolds, A. L. (2009). Within-group differences in sexual orientation and identity. *Journal of Counseling Psychology, 56,* 44–55.

Yoo, H. C., & Lee, R. M. (2008). Does ethnic identity buffer or exacerbate the effects of frequent racial discrimination on situational well-being of Asian Americans? *Journal of Counseling Psychology, 55,* 63–74.

Young, G. (2004). Dealing with difficult classroom dialogues. In P. Bronstein & K. Quina, (Eds.), *Teaching gender and multicultural awareness* (pp. 360–437). Washington, DC: APA.

Young, G., & Davis-Russell, E. (2002). The vicissitudes of cultural competence: Dealing with difficult classroom dialogue. In E. Davis-Russell (Ed.), *The California School of Professional Psychology handbook of multicultural education, research, intervention, and training* (pp. 37–53). San Francisco: Jossey-Bass.

Zane, N., & Song, A. (2007). Interpersonal effectiveness among Asian Americans: Issues of leadership, career advancement and social competence. In F. T. L. Leong, A. Inman, A. Ebreo, L. H. Yang, L. Kinoshita, & M. Fu (Eds.), *Handbook of Asian American Psychology* (pp. 283–301). Thousand Oaks, CA: Sage.

Zastrow, C. (2004). *Social work and social welfare.* Belmont, CA: Brooks/Cole.

Author Index

Subject Index

321